THE PRINCE OF SILICON VALLEY

Frank Quattrone and
the Dot-Com Bubble

Randall Smith

THE PRINCE OF SILICON VALLEY

St. Martin's Press New York

www.stmartins.com

Book design by Elina D. Nudelman

Library of Congress Cataloging-in-Publication Data

Smith, Randall, 1950–
    The Prince of Silicon Valley : Frank Quattrone and the dot-com bubble / Randall Smith.—1st ed.
        p. cm.
    ISBN 978-0-312-55560-3
  1. Quattrone, Frank Peter, 1955—United States—Biography.   2. Investment bankers—United
States.   3. Investment banking—Corrupt practices—United States.   I. Title.
    HG2463.Q38S654 2009
    332.66092—dc22
    [B]

                                                                                    2009024042

First Edition: November 2009

10   9   8   7   6   5   4   3   2   1

FOR TINA

CONTENTS

ACKNOWLEDGMENTS

THIS BOOK might not exist had Susan Pulliam, a colleague of mine at *The Wall Street Journal*, not asked for my help in mid-2000 on what turned out to be a pair of stories about possible abuses in the allocation of hot initial public stock offerings during the Bubble. It wasn't until December of that year that we wrote our first stories on the subject. By then the allocations were being investigated by securities regulators and a federal grand jury. And it was Frank Quattrone's alleged effort to obstruct that probe, which didn't come to light until January 2003, that resulted in the criminal trials that underpin this book. So, thanks to Susan foremost among the many editors and reporters at the *Journal* whom I owe for help on this project.

Also at the *Journal*, my former colleague Rebecca Buckman, then the *WSJ*'s online brokerage reporter, played what turned out to be a significant role by relaying an offer from the Quattrone group in mid-1999 to cooperate on a profile of Quattrone at the peak of his power in the middle of the tech-stock boom. My profile of Quattrone, which ran on September 24, 1999, gave me context helpful in understanding his business and style. Anita Raghavan, who herself had chronicled Quattrone's moves from Morgan Stanley to Deutsche Bank in 1996 and to CSFB in 1998, contributed her memories of those reporting experiences—some of which had occurred when I was her editor from 1996 to 1998. At Quattrone's trials, the *WSJ*'s Kara Scannell and David Glovin of Bloomberg news service provided valuable help. And, in San Francisco, the *WSJ*'s Kara Swisher introduced me to several tech-company executives who knew Quattrone.

Thanks also to Dan Hertzberg, a former senior *Journal* editor who gave permission for a leave of absence so I could attempt this project, and Michael Siconolfi, who edited most of the Quattrone coverage in the *Journal* and wrote the first and best stories on research and IPO abuses in the *Journal* in the 1990s. Former Money and Investing editor Dave Kansas kindly allowed me to work on this in my *WSJ* office. My M&I colleagues and cubicle mates Susanne Craig and Kate Kelly provided moral support. My former *WSJ* colleague Roger Lowenstein was kind enough to let me draw from an unpublished draft of his book, *Origins of the Crash*, which included his own reporting on Quattrone and some of his team members. Two other M&I editors, Ken Brown and Rick Brooks, allowed me to take a few vacation weeks at the height of the Wall Street meltdown in fall 2008 so I could complete some revisions.

Then *WSJ* library keepers Lottie Lindberg and Elizabeth Yeh, as well as Rich Peterson of Thomson Financial and Natalie Cogan of Dealogic, patiently answered many requests for information about people, past articles, and Wall Street data. Former *WSJ* photo editor Darrell Perry also provided invaluable assistance in assembling graphic art for the photo section.

Many other denizens of Wall Street past and present and the white-collar bar helped me by sitting for much-appreciated interviews either in person or by telephone, many on the condition they not be identified. Although I can't thank them publicly I hope they understand my gratitude.

Thanks to my first book editor, Leah Spiro, for believing in this project from the very beginning, and for her many wise suggestions in the course of getting it ready for publication. Thanks to my agent Joelle delBourgo for her help, and for interesting my second editor, Phil Revzin at St. Martin's, in the project. Phil, himself a former colleague of mine at the *WSJ*, provided key guidance to shape the finished work.

My late father, Leigh, a veteran public relations executive who enjoyed working with reporters, and my stepmother, Miraed, stoked my journalistic and literary ambitions. Thanks also go to my wife, Tina, and our boys, Will and Jack, for supporting my hopes with enthusiasm and love. None of us had any idea that what began as an eight-month project would take five years to complete.

A NOTE ON SOURCING

This book relies on several types of sources, some of which may be clearly identified while others may not.

Much of the material is based on public records. Foremost among those are transcripts of Quattrone's two criminal trials, the related prosecution and defense exhibits, and my own observation of the two trials while covering them as a reporter for *The Wall Street Journal*. My coverage of the regulatory probes he was accused of obstructing, as well as later probes of his firm, also provided a wealth of raw material. Eventually I also obtained transcripts of many interviews done by regulators for those probes.

The book also draws from the voluminous press coverage of Quattrone's career. Throughout his rise to the top of the Wall Street food chain, Quattrone was often accessible to reporters and received generally favorable coverage in which he was regularly quoted. At Credit Suisse First Boston during his heyday between 1998 and 2001, he had his own public-relations team, unlike other bankers there.

While Quattrone's accessibility was curtailed after the start of post-Bubble investigations of him and his firm starting in mid-2000, he continued to communicate to the press through his personal lawyer, Ken Hausman, and a public-relations aide, Elizabeth Burr. They usually spoke on background on the condition that they not be quoted or identified.

After he was charged with criminal obstruction of justice in April 2003, Quattrone continued to maintain communication with the press via a Washington-based "crisis" public-relations specialist, Bob Chlopak. Chlopak and his assistant Elizabeth Cholis attended both trials and generally conveyed Quattrone's point of view to the press, including me.

This book also relies on several books that provided accounts of key episodes in Quattrone's career. They include *Wall Street Meat* by Andy Kessler, *Going Public: MIPS Computer and the Entrepreneurial Dream*, by Michael S. Malone, *Netscape Time: The Making of the Billion-Dollar Start-Up That Took on Microsoft*, by Jim Clark with Owen Edwards, and *The Internet Bubble*, by Anthony B. Perkins and Michael C. Perkins. Some material was also drawn from a draft of *The Origins of the Crash* by Roger Lowenstein, which contained anecdotes about Quattrone and his team cut from the published version.

Finally, the book also draws from interviews with scores of people who came into contact with Quattrone and his team. They included school classmates, business colleagues, competitors, clients, investors, regulators and lawyers. While some of those interviewed agreed to be quoted, many spoke on the condition that material they provided wouldn't be attributed to them.

Where conversations are portrayed between two or more people, based on an account by one person, I have usually chosen to render the words in italics, to indicate that they are a close approximation of what was said, but may not be the exact words. If there is good reason to think those exact words were spoken, I put them in quotes.

Frank Quattrone, the subject of this book, didn't cooperate, and asked his friends and business associates not to help either. Although it was Quattrone's own staffers who solicited the profile I wrote of him in September 1999, I can understand his logic in not cooperating here because the sequence of events portrayed was adverse to him. His legal team advised Quattrone's colleagues that my reporting about Quattrone—from the first investigations in December 2000 through the guilty verdict in May 2004—"has been unfair."

In asking Quattrone's friends not to cooperate, Quattrone lawyer Hausman said my coverage of Quattrone in the *Journal* had been unfair, and derided the project by putting the word "research" into quotes. Quattrone himself endorsed

Hausman's e-mail messages. This of course made it more difficult to obtain firsthand information about some of the events portrayed in the book.

In a conversation with me in June 2004, one of Quattrone's advisers said he was hoping the book wouldn't be published. "Unless you buy into our thesis" that Quattrone had been unjustly accused, "it isn't going to help us" to cooperate, he explained. While Quattrone didn't blame all his regulatory woes solely on the *Journal's* coverage, one of his advisers compared the *Journal's* role to that of the shooting of the Archduke Ferdinand at the start of World War I.

Certainly some *Journal* articles did have some influence in spotlighting Quattrone and thus making him a higher-profile target for regulators. But of course the articles reflected Quattrone's own actions and those of his group members, together with his stature as the foremost banker of his era.

Two of the articles were written by me and a *Journal* colleague, Susan Pulliam, and appeared on the *Journal's* front page. The first, in May 2001, profiled Quattrone after three of his brokers were suspended for demanding extra commissions for hot IPOs. The article noted that Quattrone enjoyed unusual autonomy in a "fief" at CSFB, and had earned about $100 million a year—an estimate that turned out to be low by $20 million. The second appeared in September 2002 and offered details of the "Friends of Frank" program under which Quattrone's brokers steered hot IPOs to banking clients who could give his group more business. Many similar details of the "Friends of Frank" program appeared in the charges brought by the SEC against Credit Suisse Group seven months later.

The third article, by myself, Susan Pulliam, and Charles Gasparino, revealed in late January 2003 the existence of the Quattrone-endorsed e-mail entitled "time to clean up those files." It was read by the federal prosecutors who used the e-mail as the basis of obstruction charges against the banker three months later.

INTRODUCTION

THE TECH-STOCK bubble of 1998–2000 and its aftermath seems almost quaint by now, compared with the scale of economic destruction wrought by the credit-markets bubble and meltdown that began unraveling in 2007, which brought the wreckage of some of the best-known names on Wall Street and a punishing jolt to the economy.

The more recent market carnage saw the demise of Bear Stearns Cos., the bankruptcy of Lehman Brothers Holdings Inc., the forced sale in a single weekend of Merrill Lynch & Co., and the living deaths of insurance giant American International Group Inc. and Citigroup Inc., a financial colossus assembled to great fanfare a decade earlier. Both AIG and Citi became virtual wards of the state, kept alive by multiple government life-supports.

One big difference between the most recent market debacle and its predecessor was the impact on leading financial institutions. The damage wrought by the tech-stock bubble was more widely dispersed, especially among individuals like the online traders who loaded up on Internet stocks and then saw their prices plummet by 80 percent to 90 percent or more.

After the tech-stock bubble popped, the Dow Jones Industrial Average fell by about 36 percent between early 2000 and late 2002, the Nasdaq stock market by about 80 percent. Yet in that same period not a single major Wall Street securities firm suffered a quarterly loss, because they didn't have many technology or telecommunications stocks on their balance sheets.

The latest credit bubble, by comparison, hurt the big securities firms and banks as much or more as the individuals who lost their homes when their mortgage terms reset, or whose retirement savings lost a third or more in value, or who lost their jobs when the economy felt the impact in 2008.

The top executives of Merrill, Lehman, AIG, and Citi loaded up their firms' balance sheets with assets linked to risky mortgages because they appeared to be generating profits, fattening payrolls and bonuses all across Wall Street. Because the assets were financed with borrowed money at a ratio of 20 to 1 or more, it didn't take long for the losses to eat through their capital base and cost those firms' CEOs their jobs or their firms.

What the two bubbles had in common was overpriced assets. In the mortgage bubble, it was securities linked to so-called subprime loans made to the least-credit-worthy borrowers, secured by homes purchased at often overinflated prices. In the tech-stock bubble, it was Internet and telecom stocks that soared on overoptimistic, futuristic visions of the degree to which commerce would migrate to the Internet. Migrate it did, but not to the degree that would have been needed to support the scores of Internet startups that came out of the woodwork to cash in on the boom.

In between the two periods, the pendulum of regulation swung first against Wall Street, then moved back in its favor. Because the tech-stock bubble had hurt so many individuals, regulators led by New York Attorney General Eliot Spitzer scrambled to find villains or scapegoats for the damage done. The big-name firms were soon besieged by regulators and lawyers for aggrieved investors, who charged that they acted to rig some of the market movements through biased research, or to abet the phony accounting of some big companies that later collapsed, such as Enron Corporation and WorldCom Inc.

The investigation and criminal trials of Frank Quattrone took place at the height of this regulatory crackdown. Charges of fraudulent research ended the careers of two top Wall Street analysts. Questions about Enron's bookkeeping brought down an entire accounting firm. And bankers from Merrill Lynch who were convicted of helping Enron pad its earnings even briefly served jail time before their convictions were overturned.

As for Quattrone, the reversal of his criminal conviction in 2006 on obstruction-of-justice charges and the quick follow-on withdrawal of civil charges against him by securities regulators coincided with a pushback against what Wall Street viewed as regulatory overkill.

In the period between Quattrone's conviction in 2004 and his court victory in 2006, as the credit bubble gathered steam and the stock market rebounded, Wall Street executives argued that overly aggressive regulation could drive securities business offshore where regulation was lighter. In London, they noted approvingly, regulation was "principles-based" instead of "rules-based." The translation was that major firms and their officials were rarely disciplined.

This backlash put U.S. regulators led by the Securities and Exchange Commission and the National Association of Securities Dealers on the defensive. The number of enforcement actions against Wall Street declined. Techniques multiplied for banks and securities firms to keep risky assets off their balance sheets. Risk-taking to drive profits, by putting more and more assets on the books financed by debt, also mushroomed. By the time regulators finally voiced concerns in late 2006 and early 2007, it was too late.

THE BANKER

BOOK
ONE

BUBBLES

THE APPROACH of New Year's Eve 1999 carried a millennial mixture of giddy euphoria and lurking fear beyond the simple turning of the calendar page from 1999 to 2000. The year 1999 had brought a stock market boom, with the Dow Jones Industrial Average surging 25 percent, its fifth consecutive year of double-digit gains, breaking 10,000 for the first time in March, having entered the decade of the 1990s around the 3,000 level.

Leading the boom were stocks of companies that benefited from usage of the Internet, a technology still in relative infancy yet promising to transform nearly all industries—from media to car sales. Already in 1999, the stock market value of online stock brokerage Charles Schwab Corporation, leader of the discount-commission Web sites where a new breed of day traders went to buy Internet stocks, had topped that of old-economy broker Merrill Lynch & Company. In June of that year, Merrill had even waved a white flag, dropping its stated opposition to this sort of brokerless "do-it-yourself" investing by offering a new online trading capability of its own.

Everywhere other old-economy companies were rolling out their own Internet strategies too. Old-media colossus Time Warner Inc., rich with incumbency holdings of magazines, movies, and cable TV, would attempt to get ahead of the trend in January 2000 by merging with Internet challenger America Online Inc., itself the hottest big stock of the 1990s. General Electric, with its industrial strength in turbines and power plants, would produce an Internet plan. Companies that even just announced Internet strategies would see their stocks surge; when venerable high-end auction house Sotheby's Holdings Inc. did so on January 19, 1999, its stock rose 25 percent that day. The promised surge in Internet commerce was seen especially likely to benefit telecommunications companies such as Global Crossing Ltd., which would carry this burgeoning Internet traffic. Their stocks were also soaring.

The Internet-led stock market boom accompanied growth in the real economy as well. In the fourth quarter of 1999, the U.S. economy was growing at a 7.3 percent clip, the fastest since 1984 and a level that wouldn't be exceeded for nearly four years. Capital gains fueled by the market boom, and the real economic growth, had swollen government tax receipts enough—when coupled with modest tax increases enacted early in the Clinton administration—to produce a balanced federal budget, a feat that hadn't been achieved in forty years and which wouldn't come close to recurring in the eight-year Bush administration.

Adding wind to the back of the technology boom was the element of fear. In this case, the fear was that there might be a worldwide series of computer-system crashes based on something called the Y2K bug. Y2K, short for the year 2000, threatened computer systems—the theory was—if they misread "00" for 1900 instead of 2000. Prodded by Congress, the Clinton administration had established a Y2K task force, which eventually estimated that private industry and governments had spent more than $100 billion on tackling the Y2K bug threat.

So real was the Y2K threat perceived to be hanging over December 31, 1999, that some Wall Street bankers took out thousands in cash from their checking accounts in case cash machines broke down. Merrill Lynch booked hundreds of hotel rooms for executives who had to work through the New Year's weekend, and Schwab banned vacations from December 27 through January 15. And on the national TV news that New Year's Eve, no less a personage than Michael Armstrong, the chief executive of telecom cable giant AT&T, who chaired a federal advisory council on network reliability, appeared to reassure viewers that he didn't expect any widespread disruption in the phone systems.

Armstrong was cochair with Michael Powell, the chairman of the Federal Communications Commission, of an obscurely named interoperability and reliability council—tasked by the federal government with minimizing Y2K disruptions. Among its concerns, he recalled in a 2008 interview, was that entire networks might "go dark," or consumers might even get screwed-up bills.

Armstrong believed that fear and uncertainty themselves could "create problems that weren't really there." And so he took to the airwaves on live network TV from AT&T's network operations center in Bedminster, New Jersey, to reassure the public that all was well. His goal was to send "a message of confidence that the systems would be performing . . . a show of confidence that the CEO is there hands-on."

O

That same month of December 1999, in a Wall Street deal that would years later be cited and investigated as an epicenter of sorts of the excesses of the technology stock fever, a computer software company called VA Linux Systems

Inc. went public. VA Linux marketed "open-source" software, which was created by users and available free by download from the Internet and thought to pose a challenge to the standard programs embedded in most desktop computers by Microsoft Corporation.

So strong was the investor frenzy for open-source software stocks that the initial public offering of VA Linux on December 9 set a record for the biggest first-day gain of any IPO before or since. From its IPO price of $30 a share, VA Linux soared 697.5 percent to close at $239.25. The previous record holder, TheGlobe.com, an online "community" provider, had risen 605 percent on its first day of trading in November 1998. David Menlow, president of IPOfinancial network.com, told *The News & Observer (Raleigh, North Carolina)* that the run-up was an "emotional feeding frenzy" based on earlier first-day gains of 400 percent or more for other Linux-related stocks. One of the first to go public, Red Hat Inc., whose stock had more than tripled on its first day of trading in August 1999, had risen more than twentyfold by December.[1] The $9.5 billion first-day stock market value of VA Linux, *The Wall Street Journal* noted, was more than half that of Apple Computer Inc.[2]

The next month, the Wall Street firm that led the VA Linux IPO, Credit Suisse First Boston, issued a release crowing that the VA Linux deal and fifty-two others like it in 1999 had helped make it the leader in technology investment banking. "We are thrilled to have achieved our goal of #1 market share in by far the most active year the technology industry has seen to date," the announcement said.

The leader of the First Boston technology banking group was a forty-four-year old banker with a twinkle in his eye and a mischievous grin who often chose off-beat sweaters over pinstriped suits. His name was Frank Quattrone. With an unruly brown mustache and hair parted down the middle, Quattrone ran the operation from a second-floor corner office in a low-rise brick building near Stanford University in Palo Alto, California, the center of Silicon Valley, south of San Francisco, where so many technology start-ups were hatched. He lived just four miles away in Los Altos Hills, on a spectacular rise overlooking the Valley. It was all far from the vaulted marble lobby of CSFB headquarters in New York.

The technology stocks he specialized in had led the market to what one venture capitalist, John Doerr, famously described as "the largest legal creation of wealth in history." In March 1995, the market value of technology stocks was $510 billion, or about one tenth of the entire U.S. market, according to Wilshire Associates. Five years later, at the top in March 2000, the value of tech stocks had soared more than tenfold, to $6 trillion, or 35 percent of the market. (Three years later the value had shrunk back to $1.5 trillion.)

The sizzling sector lifted the entire market to new records in a phenomenon that gripped the nation. A member of the Ramones rock group had written a song about Maria Bartiromo, the CNBC-TV newscaster who stood on the floor of the New York Stock Exchange giving stock market updates each morning. And singer Barbra Streisand took to calling technology companies just before they went public in search of hot stock allocations.

In many ways Quattrone's was the type of Horatio Alger story common on Wall Street. The son of a garment union official from the poor side of Philadelphia, he had earned a scholarship to that city's best high school and college, joining Morgan Stanley, one of the top Wall Street firms, after graduating summa cum laude, and then attending Stanford's business school. Bucking Morgan Stanley's at times stodgy ways, he had blazed his own maverick career path by forging close ties with technology entrepreneurs and investors in the heart of Silicon Valley, at the dawn of the revolution in personal computers that would eventually give birth to the explosion of Internet activity.

At Morgan Stanley, Quattrone had participated in the IPOs of computer networking company Cisco Systems Inc. and Internet browser Netscape Communications Corporation. Bolting from the firm where he had learned the business, in 1996 Quattrone had taken charge of a small band of followers at a time that coincided with the Internet boom and consequent stock market bubble. First at Deutsche Bank AG and then at Credit Suisse First Boston, he had shown that if he could share control of the analysts and brokers who followed technology stocks and served their executives, he could offer a unique integrated service that gave him an edge over more traditional firms that had more entrenched controls and bureaucracies.

At Deutsche Bank his team had led the IPO of the Internet bookseller Amazon.com. And at First Boston, which he joined in mid-1998, he had a juggernaut that led Wall Street in the number of high-tech IPOs. On Tuesday March 14, 2000—at the very peak of that bubble—he had sent an e-mail updating members of his technology banking group on his ultimately successful efforts to sweeten the group's contract at Credit Suisse First Boston. He said, "guys, we are on the verge of global domination in this business and I appreciate all of the hard work and sacrifice on your parts that have made it possible." The same e-mail projected his group's banking revenues, which topped $600 million in 1999, would exceed $1 billion in 2000.[3]

O

But Quattrone also became an archetype of another classically American story: the rise and fall of a gifted individual who gains wealth and power but then is tripped up by the same drive that propels him to the top. The self-confidence and win-at-all costs mentality that underpins his success eventually blinds him to the risks of his tactics—and of the backlash his very success may provoke.

In this case, just as Quattrone was propelled to the pinnacle of the Wall Street banking world by the force of the Internet stock bubble, his career was wrenched away from him by the bursting of that same bubble, and by the backlash it engendered from investors and politicians and regulators acting on their behalf. Although the criminal obstruction-of-justice charges eventually leveled against him by federal prosecutors seemed trivial to some, they were brought against the backdrop of a crackdown by a broad coalition of regulators against practices that, they charged, helped pump up the bubble and greased the palms of insiders at the expense of average investors.

The time span of regulatory pursuit of Quattrone, his firm, and the brokers who worked in his group eventually rivaled or exceeded the length of his reign as the bubble's top banker. The reign lasted, by one measure, for the five years between the IPO of Netscape in mid-1995 and the start of the market's descent in mid-2000. The regulatory pursuit of Credit Suisse First Boston and Quattrone lasted more than six years, from May 2000—with the receipt of an anonymous letter alleging improprieties in how CSFB allocated IPOs—until August 2006, when prosecutors agreed to drop criminal charges against Quattrone.

His criminal trials—which had featured the disclosure that he had been paid $120 million for a single year's work in 2000—provided a coda to the regulatory pursuit of a wide array of executives from Wall Street to telecom, cable TV, and energy after the stock market bust brought the collapse of high-profile companies such as Enron and WorldCom. The Quattrone trials—which closely followed the filing of civil charges that he and his group had misused hot stock offerings during the bubble to win banking business, and that his firm had issued fraudulent research to hype stocks during the market mania—were a harsh comedown from the zenith of his Icarus-like career.

Though the charges against Quattrone personally were dropped in 2006, his firm had fired three brokers who worked with his group in June 2001 for cutting off accounts that wouldn't pay higher commissions to keep getting hot initial public offerings. And his firm in April 2003 had agreed to pay $200 million to settle charges by the Securities and Exchange Commission, working in concert with other regulators, that its analysts had issued fraudulent or exaggerated research and its brokers engaged in the "spinning" of hot IPOs to corporate executives. Although Quattrone wasn't party to the settlement and Credit Suisse didn't admit any wrongdoing, the SEC charges focused on actions by Quattrone's group members and mentioned Quattrone by name two dozen times.[4]

○

When he testified to securities industry regulators probing the alleged IPO misconduct in September 2002, Quattrone had explained that after working for a year as an investment-banking generalist in the San Francisco office of his former firm, Morgan Stanley, in 1982 he had begun specializing in technology stocks. To win assignments selling stock or arranging mergers, he told the investigators—with four lawyers present representing him and his firm—he had concentrated on getting to know the leading venture capitalists who themselves specialized in finding companies with the best futures. Getting close to them, he said, meant he and his team would know when their companies needed more capital, or were ready to go public.

The venture capital business of Silicon Valley had grown up after World War II, as recounted in the book *Creative Capital: Georges Doriot and the Birth of Venture Capital* by Spencer Ante. Indeed, Doerr's firm, Kleiner Perkins Caufield & Byers in Menlo Park, was one of its founding pioneers. Thomas Perkins had been a computer-division marketing manager at Hewlett-Packard, the protean Silicon Valley start-up launched in David Packard's garage, now a museum in Palo Alto, in 1939. Eugene Kleiner had worked in sales at another bellwether Valley technology company, Fairchild Semiconductor, after a stint at the Shockley Semiconductor Laboratory division of Beckman Instruments in Mountain View, California.[5] The head of sales at Fairchild, launched in 1958, was Donald Valentine, who went on to form his own venture capital colossus, Sequoia Capital, in 1972.

In 1958, with the backing of Fairchild's founder, Sherman Fairchild, the first prominent West Coast venture firm Draper, Gaither & Anderson was founded, cementing its stature a decade later with its backing of Intel Corporation along with the firm of East Coast VC pioneer Arthur Rock. Intel became the leading microprocessor company, whose chips powered the desktop computers that became ubiquitous in the 1980s. It was in 1971 that computer journalist Don Hoefler christened the area "Silicon Valley," and that decade saw a proliferation of VC firms, powered in part by a federal law requiring corporations to back up their pension promises with dedicated investments. That law was passed in 1974, more than a decade after the bankruptcy of Studebaker Company had left many of its workers without promised pensions.

It was an East Coast venture firm, American Research and Development, which in 1957 helped launch one of the most successful computer companies of the 1960s, Digital Equipment Corporation, a mini-computer maker that challenged the monopolylike dominance of mainframe goliath International Business Machines Corporation (IBM).

In the 1970s, some of the high-tech action moved down the food chain to video games and primitive small computers. In 1976, Valentine's Sequoia led a group of venture investors who backed Atari, the creator of the Pong video game, before it was sold to Warner Communications. One of Atari's game designers, Steve Jobs, raised $517,500 in 1978 from a group led by Rock and

Sequoia for a desktop computer company he envisioned that was named Apple. When Apple went public in December 1980, Rock's own $57,000 investment became worth $2.2 million. As Jobs made the rounds before the IPO, Quattrone heard him speak at Stanford's business school, and became determined to find "the next Apple."

Such bankers historically attempted to mediate between the companies seeking capital to grow and investors seeking higher long-term returns. In pricing the new stock issues, they worked to strike a balance each side would regard as fair, and avoid the perception that they are favoring one side or the other.

Before Quattrone, the biggest Wall Street firms, such as Morgan Stanley, Goldman Sachs, or Merrill Lynch, had viewed technology as merely one of many different industry sectors, and hadn't thrown a disproportionate share of their resources toward such companies. Some "boutique" firms did specialize in technology, but they didn't have the same firepower of hundred-member sales forces to sell stock. And so, when they brought big new issues to the market they would sometimes enlist the help of a bigger "bulge-bracket" Wall Street player. For the Apple IPO, a San Francisco growth-stock boutique named Hambrecht & Quist joined forces with Morgan Stanley.

Quattrone had left Morgan Stanley in 1996, he said later, because the firm wouldn't give him the resources he believed he needed to develop his own business. When he joined Credit Suisse in 1998, he had arranged a hybrid reporting structure that gave him access to a big firm sales force that could sell his stock deals—but with more freedom to determine his own group's head count, with research analysts and brokers reporting jointly to executives in his own organization and to other executives in New York. He often said he wanted "a boutique in a bulge-bracket firm."

But the structure, which gave Quattrone team members the power to hire and fire and set bonuses for the analysts and brokers, reduced the power and control of the New York executives. Testifying in March 2003 in the post-bubble investigations, one of them, Credit Suisse research chief Al Jackson of New York, said that when he visited California and tried to engage the Quattrone group analysts, who nominally reported jointly to him, they eventually ignored him. "I felt like, you know, a third wheel," he said. The Quattrone organization hired and fired and set their pay, and even had the power to approve their reports, he said. "I was just wasting my time."[6]

The head of the Credit Suisse brokerage force, Andrew Benjamin, voiced similar thoughts about the influence Quattrone wielded over the technology private-client services brokers. Even though Quattrone had moved up "to the top of the ladder" quickly at Credit Suisse based on the revenues he was bringing in, Benjamin said he was "a very control-oriented person. He basically wanted to control everything." While Benjamin acknowledged that "it's not an unusual personality for someone in that, you know, in that position," but Quattrone oversaw people "right down to, I guess my point is, controlling right down to three PCS brokers, it was, you know, kind of weird, right? . . . You would think he would have more important things to deal with," Benjamin said. "This was completely penny-ante relative to the things he was doing. . . . I think he did that with everything. I think if you were his gardener, he would probably treat you the same way."[7]

○

On March 18, 2008, a small technology-focused financial services firm opened for business with the oddly spelled name Qatalyst Group. The announcement of the new merchant bank featured endorsements from some of the best-known names in the technology world, including top executives at Google, Facebook, and Intuit.

The spelling of Qatalyst with a Q appeared to be an allusion to its cofounder and chief executive, Frank Quattrone. Some of Quattrone's clients and supporters wanted to show they had remained loyal to him throughout his legal ordeal. "The launch of Qatalyst is an important development for the technology industry," Google's chief executive, Eric Schmidt, said in the Qatalyst announcement.[8]

"His name cleared and his four years of legal battles behind him, Frank P. Quattrone is back in business in Silicon Valley" began the article about Qatalyst in the *San Francisco Chronicle.*[9] And Quattrone soon showed he was indeed back in the business.

A few weeks later, Google, the Internet search-engine company whose initial public offering had been led by Quattrone's old firm, now called Credit Suisse Group, during Quattrone's second criminal trial in April 2004, hired Qatalyst for advice. The issue was what to do about a bid by software giant Microsoft to acquire Internet destination Yahoo Inc., potentially forming a stronger Google rival.

Unfortunately, Quattrone's return to the banking business occurred just a few months before an epic collapse of the next bubble. The debt-bubble meltdown sank the entire stock market in late 2008, becalming the market for initial public offerings of any kind. The carnage left the technology sector stagnant at best, barely a footnote to the wider devastation. But by June 2009, he was back in the news, advising a storage technology company, Data Domain, on a $1.5 billion takeover bid.[10]

○

This is the story of the Bubble banker's rise, fall, and return.

SOUTH PHILLY

THROUGHOUT HIS CAREER, Frank Quattrone brandished his scrappy, humble beginnings in South Philadelphia as a badge of honor. "Somebody told me the other day that you grew up in south philly, as I did," he said in a July 2000 e-mail to Tom Meredith, a money manager. Quattrone added that he was "from 9th and shunk, stella maris parish, st. joe's prep."[1]

Many of the bankers at prestigious firms such as Goldman Sachs Group Inc. or Morgan Stanley, he told colleagues, couldn't survive if they didn't have their firms' blue-chip brand names behind them. He could beat them, he said, by outhustling and outdelivering them. When Mark Veverka, a reporter for *Barron's* magazine, asked him in late 2000 what kept him going after all he had accomplished, he replied that he still wanted "to fuck Morgan Stanley."[2]

More lightheartedly, he mocked his ethnic background as well. When high-tech consultant Richard Shaffer first made a date to meet up with him in the mid-1980s at a student hangout near Stanford University in Palo Alto, California, called The Duck, Quattrone told Shaffer he would be able to recognize him easily. "I look like everybody's idea of an Italian waiter," he explained.[3]

Depending on who was describing him, Quattrone looked like actor Kevin Kline, or Cheech Marin circa *Up in Smoke*, or Ernie Kovacs, the pioneer TV comedian, or even one of the Super Mario Brothers. His mustache and working-class appearance constantly confounded colleagues. "He looked like a car thief," said one, "but when he started talking, he turned into Cary Grant."

O

Frank Peter Quattrone was born on October 14, 1955, the grandson of a woman who immigrated to the United States in the early 1900s and ran a corner luncheonette. She had a display proudly showing her membership in patriotic organizations such as the Sons and Daughters of Italy.[4]

His mother, Rose, was a sewing machine operator who quit work at his birth.

And his father, Frank, was a presser in a tailor shop who became a union official. Together with his younger sister, Mary Ann, they lived in a narrow two-story row house at 2538 South Darien Street on a block packed with twenty brownstones on each side.

Three blocks south of their home, Quattrone's grade school, Stella Maris, which is attached to the local Catholic church of the same name, is located just across the highway from the two main local football and baseball stadiums, a constant hulking presence. In those days, recalls Monsignor James Connelly, 98 percent of the parishioners were Italian American.[5]

Frank and his best friend, Rosario "Rusty" Lamberto, who lived on the next block, would often—having finished their homework right after school—play baseball in the street, then repair to Rusty's house for iced tea.[6] At the same time, Frank distinguished himself in the classroom at Stella Maris. When his cousin Josephine Hirsch tested him in the first grade, his scores indicated that he read at fifth-grade level—and he continued to read four grades higher throughout his time there.[7]

His academic ability helped him win a scholarship to St. Joseph's Prep, a boys' high school in north central Philadelphia, about ten blocks north of City Hall, whose academic excellence drew an ethnic mix of Italian, Irish, and African American teenagers along with Main-Line WASPs. Such was the pride of students and faculty in the school that they called it "The Prep." And some say it was at this Jesuit school that Frank acquired the tendency to parse, or draw ultrafine distinctions, that persisted in his business career.

In Latin class at St. Joe's, Frank got a 105 on his first test by a teacher, Father William "Pop" Ryan, known for failing the whole class on his first exam. Ryan, who was also Quattrone's homeroom teacher that freshman year, called his star pupil "Big Four"—a literal translation of what "quattrone" means in Italian.[8] Francis Rabuck, who shared a locker with Quattrone in their freshman year, said Frank was "aggressive" and "confident," and always had "a South Philly swagger about him" that derived from his less privileged background. "He had a boisterous laugh, and always enjoyed a good joke or a good prank. There's always a lot of tension in high school and he was the type of person who could give it and take it."[9] By sophomore year he was already showing the wispy beginnings of the mustache that would become his trademark.

Even then, Quattrone displayed a competitive urge to shape events around him. Mike Ciocca, who attended both high school and college with Quattrone, recalled that on St. Patrick's Day, a day of celebration for the Irish and not the Italians, Frank tried to persuade his buddies *not* to wear green. When he noticed Ciocca using a green towel in the shower one March 17, he gave him a hard time about it—"What's with the green towel?"[10]

"We were an average family living from paycheck to paycheck," his mother

Rose recalled in a letter to the judge who would sentence Frank to eighteen months in prison. "We could not afford any extras so, when the children were old enough, they worked during the summer to earn money. During high school, Frank worked in a tailor shop as a bundle boy, as a life guard, and in maintenance at a swim club."[11]

Frank liked jazz, played the saxophone, and enjoyed the first album by the jazz-rock group Chicago. Sometimes, before classes, Ciocca recalled, boys would draw the logos of their favorite sports team or consumer brand on the blackboard before class began. One classmate drew the GM Mark of Excellence. But Frank had mastered the more convoluted Chicago logo.[12]

Quattrone made one unsuccessful run for political office during his junior year at St. Joe's. He was the candidate for vice president on a slate whose label was "the partnership for growth," according to classmate Roger Kashlak, who later taught international management at Loyola College in Maryland and ran as the treasurer candidate on the same slate. The ticket was geographically diverse to the extent that Kashlak was from north Philadelphia.[13]

St. Joe students typically chose a program of either classical languages, featuring Latin and Greek, or science. Frank chose the classics, inspired by his faculty mentor, Harry Bender, who called Frank's work there "an example of the Jesuit ethic, to strive to do more and strive to do better. Frank was a terrific guy—competitive as hell, disciplined, organized, focused."[14]

Dr. Bender still has his notes from a senior year presentation Frank gave on Homer's *Odyssey*, which he read in the original Greek. The idea for the presentation grew out of a conversation they had had while on a class trip to Greece and Italy—which Dr. Bender had helped Frank pay for—together with an in-class discussion.[15]

"We were translating the scene in Book 9 of the *Odyssey* where the civilized, passionate family man confronts the huge unmovable lawless giant Cyclops," Dr. Bender wrote to Frank's judge. "Odysseus loses several of his men but in the end survives, rescuing his crew from what seemed like unavoidable death and disaster."[16]

Even though the dangerous situation had been created by the "irresponsibility of his men, who went into the cave of the Cyclops and wolfed down the cheese and milk and bread," Dr. Bender said that despite the danger, Odysseus didn't lose sight of his goal of getting his men home safely, despite his great fear of the man-eating Cyclops.[17]

Frank's next stop after graduating from St. Joe's was less than twenty blocks to the southwest in downtown Philadelphia at the Wharton School of the University of Pennsylvania. For the first two years, Frank lived on campus, in a dormitory with several roommates. His tuition and room charges were paid by a full Mayoral and Senatorial scholarship, his mother Rose recalled. But he took out a loan and worked part-time to pay for food and other expenses. One of his jobs was to streamline the budget at the Philadelphia Quartermaster Depot, since renamed the Defense Supply Center Philadelphia.[18]

During his sophomore year he was reintroduced to a young woman, Denise Foderaro—who was also from South Philadelphia, and had attended a Catholic school, St. Maria Goretti High—by her close friend and classmate from grade school and high school, Marlene Markel.[19] (Marlene and Denise had once won a Halloween costume contest by dressing up as monsters, one of them as Medusa, the Greek gorgon who turned her viewers into stone.) At the time Denise was a freshman at Penn, and she would go on to study rehabilitative nursing at a school called SAMP, short for the School of Allied Medical Professions.

One of their first dates occurred at the wedding of one of Frank's high school friends, James Keeley.[20] For another date, Denise later told Frank's colleagues, she asked Frank if he would like to attend a Phillies baseball game with her. "After he cheerfully accepted, she explained that they would actually be attending as volunteers, taking disabled patients to and from the stadium and even emptying the occasional 'leg bag.' Frank happily agreed, and the rest is family history," said the colleague, Lindsey Cronk, a former events coordinator in Quattrone's banking group.[21]

But Quattrone did his share of carousing as a college student as well. Armand Della Porta Jr., a Philadelphia lawyer who played tennis and learned Greek with Quattrone at St. Joe's, recalled being knocked awake by a case of beer Quattrone was wielding at 4:00 A.M. in Della Porta's student quarters at Georgetown University in Washington, D.C. Quattrone, who was near the end of a road trip, had breakfast with Della Porta, then drove back to Philadelphia.[22]

Ciocca remembers one evening in their college years that showed both the Quattrone family's straitened circumstances and Frank's winning personal style.

Another classmate, Joseph Garzone, had season tickets to Philadelphia Flyers hockey games. "Frank and I were big Flyers fans," Ciocca said, and Garzone's family also belonged to the Blue Line club at the Spectrum arena where the Flyers played. "Joe picked me up at my house," then they went to pick up Frank and went inside to meet his mom.

Ciocca said he knew the Prep was a melting pot, with "the well-to-do from the Main Line as well as inner-city kids." Ciocca was a resident of the Kensington area of Philadelphia whose family members were also Italian immigrants, and whose father was a stonemason who never made more than twenty-five thousand dollars a year; he said, "I never considered myself poor until I saw people from the Main Line."

But, as they entered Frank's house, Ciocca noticed that "the rugs were worn out so much that they were worn through almost to the floor. They had such huge gaping holes and had obviously been worn out for a while that I realized Frank's family might be worse off than mine."

When they got to the Spectrum, they went to the Blue Line club, where they were able to watch the game on closed-circuit TV. It was a big game, a 1976 play-off contest against the Boston Bruins, on a night when a substitute goalie kept the Flyers close enough to win. As the evening neared an end, Quattrone suggested to Ciocca, "Let's go give Mrs. Garzone a nice big kiss for letting us in"—which indeed made an impression on their friend's mom. "He just knew the proper things to do, how to make friends," Ciocca said.[23]

In his junior and senior college years, Frank lived off campus, in an apartment with three or more bedrooms above Koch's Deli. There was more street crime in those days, and the location several blocks from campus was four blocks past Fortieth Street, which one of his classmates considered the outer limit of safety.

Still, "visiting their apartment was always a wonderful event," recalls Kevin Vaughan, a Penn classmate who was the president of the Student Activities Council that year, and who went on to work in government and politics. "There was lots of Italian cooking, lasagna, and Frank would pull out the guitar." Even in those days, Quattrone liked a song that later became his trade mark, "Rocky Raccoon," from the Beatles' *White Album*, as well as songs by Cat Stevens and Harry Chapin.[24]

The class of 1977, Vaughan contends, was the first that didn't have to fear the draft and service in Vietnam, and thus missed out on any form of serious campus protest. So they had a wistful nostalgia for the idealistic music of that era. They had been in grade school when the Beatles first landed in the United States in 1964, and they had even missed out on the height of campus protest, Woodstock and the *White Album* itself in 1968 and 1969.

And so they also pursued their own peacetime brand of campus activism. Vaughan and Rob Adler, one of Quattrone's roommates at Koch's, as well as Denise Foderaro, were members of the Student Activities Council together. Adler also worked with Frank on the Penn Consumers Board, which with a handful of student volunteers provided a guide to off-campus housing that included landlord ratings. The group also offered help in landlord-tenant and consumer-merchant disputes. One of the group's other members recalls that Frank organized the agency's files and work structure so that all of its members had more clearly defined jobs.

Frank's relationship with Denise, however, may have influenced an even more intense bout of campus protest during his senior year, which would bring him center stage at a rally in which the president of the university, Martin Myerson, was hung in effigy.

The issue was Denise's school at Penn, the School of Allied Medical Professions. Faced with a Myerson-backed move to phase it out, partly because of the slim chance it could gain the level of research excellence as some of the other Penn units, the students demonstrated in November 1976. The 1977 yearbook has a picture of a long-haired Quattrone reading a speech that he held in his left hand while carrying a sign in his right hand that read: "MYERSON: If <u>research</u> is your <u>priority</u>, Why Don't <u>You</u> Have A P.H.D.?"[25]

The message was barbed but punchy and compelling—a harbinger of the kind of salesmanship he would wield on Wall Street.

It was in this melting pot of Philadelphia that Quattrone acquired the chip on his shoulder. He had a tendency to dramatize himself in a grandiose way, a view of himself as a hero of mythic proportions. And he had above all the story line of how the hero lifted himself out of humble beginnings and, via brains and hard work, outclassed the competition.

MORGAN STANLEY

FRANK QUATTRONE was one of three members of his 1977 graduating class at Penn to accept an offer to work at Morgan Stanley, then a private partnership and one of Wall Street's most prestigious and blue-blooded securities firms. It traced its origins to the pre-1929 era as part of J.P. Morgan & Co. Its chief executives had names that reeked of old money, such as Parker Gilbert or Robert Baldwin. But though the firm tried to evoke a patrician aura—with yellowed prints of sailing ships in its reception areas—its ranks were also studded with relative newcomers, like Quattrone, from more diverse backgrounds. His starting pay was $12,500.[1]

It was in his first two years, working as a junior analyst at Morgan Stanley, whose headquarters in those days was in the Exxon building on West Fiftieth Street and Sixth Avenue at Rockefeller Center, that Quattrone forged the relationship that was probably the most important in shaping his career.

Carter McClelland, a Californian who grew up in Los Angeles, had an unusual background for an investment banker. McClelland was 3/16 Cherokee Indian, and his mother's family had migrated to California from Oklahoma in the Dustbowl era. The son of an X-ray machine sales and service manager, he attended public high school in Glendale, California, just north of Los Angeles, and majored in aeronautical engineering at Stanford.

While people on Wall Street joke about mathematically skilled traders being "rocket scientists," McClelland actually had worked for NASA's Jet Propulsion Laboratory in Pasadena for a year, designing computers to do ground-based testing of unmanned satellites. But his focus shifted to Wall Street when, as a student at Stanford's business school, he took a course on money and capital markets.

The affable, bespectacled McClelland always seemed to have a twinkle in his eye. The bon vivant soon acquired a taste for New York sophistication, eventually occupying a luxury apartment in the swanky San Remo, one of Manhattan's most stylish co-op buildings.

The Morgan Stanley analyst program, like many on Wall Street, generally offered recent college graduates a grunt's eye view of work in the securities business, which is at its broadest aimed at helping companies, governments, and individuals manage their financial affairs.

In the 1970s, an Arab embargo had sent oil prices skyrocketing, touching off an epic bull market in the prices of all commodities, including gold, and fueling near runaway inflation. It had also touched off a boom in oil exploration and development, and made oil companies such as Exxon and Mobil the kings of the Fortune 500.

On Wall Street, all that translated into a bonanza of financing work for energy companies. Quattrone was assigned to work for McClelland in the project finance and leasing group, including one financing tankers used by Standard Oil of Ohio.

Donald Kendall, another Morgan Stanley banker who supervised Frank, remembers that they would enjoy "video games at Times Square, movies and many a late-night meal."[2]

The work itself was otherwise unremarkable in the context of Quattrone's later career. But when the two-year analyst apprentice program neared an end, McClelland pushed Quattrone to consider Stanford's business school. Although some analysts stay on with the firm or move elsewhere in the securities business, many return for more specialized training in M.B.A. programs. And Frank's choice of Stanford was the turning point in his career.

When Frank left Philadelphia to attend Stanford, Richard Brust, a Chicago lawyer and journalist, recalled that they took a roundabout cross-country road trip that extended up to the Trans-Canada highway and camping in Banff, riding out a rainstorm in a tent, and a series of "honky-tonk hotels." Brust also noted how much Frank talked about Denise, who had to remain on the East Coast to complete a service requirement for her education, and "how deeply in love he was."[3]

At the bachelor party before their South Philadelphia wedding mass in August 1980, one attendee recalls, a group of about eight of them drank Moscow mules and ginger beer at a bar near the university before deciding to make their next stop a strip bar. But Quattrone actually seemed relieved that the raucous mood was broken when one of the members of his party lost a contact lens, and the houselights had to be brought up while a search was conducted. At Stanford, the Quattrones would attend monthly potluck dinners with a group of other married couples.

One of the highlights of Quattrone's days at Stanford was the visit by Steven Jobs, in the fall of 1980, to a class taught by Stanford professor Jack McDonald. Jobs wore jeans, had longish hair, and wasn't much older than the students. He displayed a copy of the prospectus for his Apple Computer Company, the desktop computer maker that was being taken public by Wall Street underwriters led by Morgan Stanley. Jobs told the class that he had sold his Volkswagon bus to launch Apple, and that personal computers were going to change the world.[4] The class assignment was to price the IPO.

Morgan Stanley had landed a lead role in the $101 million Apple IPO based partly on the relationship between William Hambrecht, whose firm had underwritten both Apple and the hot new biotech IPO Genentech Inc., and Richard Fisher, who then ran the capital-markets division at Morgan Stanley. Hambrecht and Fisher had been classmates at Princeton, class of 1957, and Hambrecht believed that having a name-brand East Coast firm would lend credibility to such risky start-ups.[5]

If Quattrone had his humble background to rise above, the middle-class Fisher, who also came from Philadelphia, had a different obstacle to overcome. Fisher contracted polio at the age of eight and walked on crutches much of his life. His father sold cigarettes to drugstores in the 1920s and 1930s, and later sold caulking to shipbuilders for Minnesota Mining. Fisher attended the Quaker Penn Charter high school and Princeton on scholarships.

Fisher personified the traditional values and standards Morgan Stanley stood for. He was considered the best listener on Wall Street. A connoisseur of modern art and classical music, his judgment was superb. The firm valued getting the best ideas from senior and junior bankers alike; Fisher would hear out all sides of a debate, then decide. Morgan Stanley's role in comanaging the Apple offering was a signal that it was committed to the market for emerging growth companies. In bygone days, Morgan Stanley would seldom have stooped to comanage an offering with another firm, Hambrecht recalls.[6]

Quattrone's time at Stanford formed the roots of his tech evangelism. He wasn't alone in that. One of his classmates, Steve Ballmer, dropped out to rejoin a friend from his undergraduate days at Harvard, William Gates, who was just starting up a company that became Microsoft.

When his Stanford graduation rolled around in the spring of 1981, Frank wanted to rejoin Morgan Stanley—but only on his own terms. Although it was standard operating procedure at the firm for newly minted M.B.A.s to start back at headquarters in New York City, Frank wanted to remain in Silicon Valley. One reason he gave was that Denise had made a two-year job commitment there that she couldn't break, to create a cardiac rehabilitation program at a San Jose hospital.[7]

"During those 'sell-dinners,' in which hiring firms take out recruits and their wives, Denise was a formidable presence and very much interested in how these recruiters balanced their family obligations," recalled Terry C. Vance, a Stanford classmate, in a letter to the judge. "Less well known is that after Frank was hired by Morgan Stanley he refused a 'mandatory' transfer back to New

York because Denise had established her own career as a medical specialist locally. When Morgan Stanley acted as if no junior associate would seriously jeopardize his career over a spouse's job at a fraction of his own compensation, Frank quietly bought a house in the Bay area and not so quietly began to interview with local firms. Morgan Stanley backed down."[8]

By the time he graduated, Frank's father was ill with terminal cancer, and Frank pushed him around in a wheelchair from celebration event to celebration event—so much so, Vance said, "one would have thought that Frank's father was being honored, not Frank, because Frank brought his Dad to every event."[9]

One of the Morgan Stanley bankers involved in hiring Frank at that point recalled that he was obviously "a hard worker, aggressive, charming, with a lot of personality." But, he added, "I've often thought it was a terrible mistake on our part and his part" for Quattrone not to return to headquarters. As a result, he said, Quattrone missed out on "getting the culture—what Morgan Stanley is all about, building relationships with peers and senior people," that might have imbued him with more team spirit. That culture called for individual bankers to make sacrifices for the good of the entire enterprise. Quattrone's disregard for that ethos became an important factor in his ultimate decision to leave in 1996.

THE PRINCE OF SILICON VALLEY

4

WHEN he rejoined Morgan Stanley in 1981, Quattrone's pay was $35,000 a year.[1] At the time, Morgan Stanley's San Francisco office at 101 California Street in the financial district was considered a real outpost. The breezy, easy-going McClelland moved out to the San Francisco office in 1983, and the pair quickly became an effective team.

At first, some of the deals were almost laughably small. But they showed Quattrone's eagerness to roll up his sleeves and deliver the services of a prestigious New York firm at the nitty-gritty level. He connected with the technology entrepreneurs who were bursting forth from Silicon Valley in the early days of the desktop computer revolution.

One of their first deals together in the fall of 1983 was the sale of just $10 million in venture capital financing for Bridge Communications Inc., an early player in networking—helping computers talk to each other via what were then called local-area networks. It was Quattrone who had spotted Bridge, run by the management team of Bill Carrico, an alumnus of Fairchild Semiconductor, and his girlfriend, Judy Estrin, a couple who later married (and divorced).

The vast majority of start-up companies backed by venture capital financing don't survive. That's the nature of the venture business—a crapshoot in which the home runs may earn their backers 20 or 100 times their investment, but where as many as nine out of ten investments may be complete washouts. The venture business thus has a pioneering spirit that must necessarily be tolerant of failure.

The 1983 Bridge venture fund-raising, and Bridge itself, was successful enough that Bridge was ready to go public by the spring of 1985, in an IPO of $24 million that looks tiny by today's standards. Two years later Bridge merged with 3Com Corporation, with merger advice from Morgan Stanley. The Bridge financings became the basis for a Stanford case study, which Quattrone helped write, on how to value a company.[2]

In another of their early deals together, Morgan Stanley was hired to raise money for Synapse Computer Corporation, which specialized in fault-tolerant computers. An outside lawyer for Synapse, Allen Morgan, recalled that Mc-Clelland was late for an organizational meeting for the deal, leaving a room full of twenty people cooling their heels. Among them were two members of the Synapse management team, chief financial officer Stan Meresman and chief executive Mark Leslie.

"We waited and waited, and finally Carter showed up," Morgan recalled. "This was back in the days when we all wore suits. And Carter walks in, and he's dressed in loafers and slacks, a blazer and an open-collared shirt. And he dispensed some typical senior-partner holy water on the meeting for about five minutes" and then left abruptly. His brief appearance created a little awkwardness, Morgan noted.

Where is Carter going? one of the Synapse executives asked Quattrone.

Quattrone made a lighthearted remark about McClelland having an appointment outside the office. A few people chuckled indulgently.

But then the Synapse chief executive spoke up: *Seriously, Frank, what is Carter's involvement in this deal going to be?*

Some people in the room were obviously thinking "fly-by appearance," Morgan recalls. But the question put Quattrone on the spot, and Morgan could tell that his mind was racing.

Quattrone leaned back in his chair. *Carter's involvement is really going to be more at the policy level*, he replied.

"It was a very smooth way of deflecting a pointed question with an answer that was truthful but very sophisticated," Morgan recalls admiringly. "Was it Omaha Beach? No. But it was a pressure situation, and Frank very quickly became an important guy at Morgan Stanley."[3]

○

Morgan Stanley shot to the top of the rankings among Wall Street firms in technology underwriting. Morgan, which ranked number seven in 1980, ranked number one from 1981 to 1984, according to Thomson Financial, which tracks securities transactions. Many of the companies going public then were tied to the personal-computing boom. Morgan Stanley led IPOs for disk-drive maker Quantum Corporation, engineering workstation maker Apollo Computer Inc., and networking company 3Com.

Quattrone's vision in those days was to take the Morgan Stanley franchise, which traditionally emphasized how many of the Fortune 50 companies were clients, to the world of much smaller, emerging technology companies. "These companies are going public at $100 million," he told McClelland. "But they'll be one billion dollars when they grow up."[4]

The connection with Meresman, the Synapse Computer CFO, showed how the burgeoning Quattrone technology network would pay off.

While Synapse closed its doors in 1985, Meresman went on to become the chief financial officer at a company that would become a "reference transaction," cited for its quality, for Quattrone. The company was Silicon Graphics Inc., which had been formed by a group of former Stanford engineers led by Jim Clark, and whose three-dimensional computer renderings were in big demand for Hollywood special effects. Years later Quattrone praised Clark's ability to woo money managers: "He could convince investors—most of whom didn't know why you needed 2D technology—why you needed 3D technology."[5]

Morgan Stanley eventually advised Silicon Graphics on a dozen transactions, starting with a $22 million IPO in 1986.[6] Clark himself would go on to cofound Netscape Communications Corporation, whose Morgan Stanley–led IPO in 1995 signaled the dawn of the dot-com era.

Not only did Silicon Graphics itself generate business for Quattrone, so did its alumni as they went to other companies. For example, Mike Ramsay, who ran the Silicon Graphics workstation business, worked with Quattrone on an outside computer maker's investment in SGI. He left Silicon Graphics in 1997 to cofound TiVo Inc., the TV viewing service, and when TiVo chose an underwriter for its IPO in 1999, Ramsey helped Quattrone get the business.

Quattrone's relationship with technology consultant Richard Shaffer shows his easygoing yet thorough style in foraging for business. A former *Wall Street Journal* reporter, Shaffer had left the paper in 1984 to start a newsletter, and he also organized industry conferences and other meetings. Once a year he would publish a list of the companies that were likeliest to go public. When he and Quattrone met for lunch or drinks, they would swap ideas about hot companies.[7]

"It was a two-way street. It was like being a reporter on the police beat. You give a little bit, you get a little bit," Shaffer recalls. "I would tell Frank the companies I thought were interesting, and the ones I knew were looking for bankers." And Quattrone would pass along names to Shaffer. Quattrone also appeared at conferences sponsored by Shaffer's Technologic Partners. "Frank was very focused on visibility," Shaffer says.

One of the hallmarks of Frank's investment banking style became client entertainment. It is a Wall Street staple, and all securities firms do it. But Quattrone took it to a higher level, using river rafting, golf, and skiing to bond with clients. "Become friends with clients," Quattrone would tell his group. "People hate disappointing their friends."[8]

As early as 1983, Quattrone and his wife shared a ski cabin in Lake Tahoe with partners from several venture capital firms, including the Mayfield Fund and Merrill, Pickard, Anderson & Eyre.[9] He saw the VCs, who sat on companies' boards, as the inside track to winning business. "There are twenty VCs who are funding these companies," he told McClelland. If we get to know them, he added, we'll get to do the financings.[10]

If client entertainment was a Wall Street staple, battles to win new business also had their own folkways. A series of competing presentations by rival investment banks for a particular deal is called a "bake-off." The tea-party term nicely equates the cutthroat battle for tens of millions of dollars in fees with the fluttering of 1950s housewives.

Around the end of 1985, Microsoft, the personal-computer software leader, held a bake-off to choose a Wall Street firm to lead its initial public offering. It was a landmark event. Microsoft itself would become one of the best technology investments ever. And it signaled the advent of the technology stock boom that Quattrone would ride throughout the 1980s and 1990s. But the way the Microsoft bake-off was won and lost would also have a profound influence on the conduct of Wall Street research, pushing the bankers and research analysts closer together in ways that wouldn't be widely questioned for more than fifteen years.

Microsoft had signaled to the Morgan Stanley bankers that they were in the "pole position" to win. At the bake-off, the Morgan Stanley team was led by Dick Fisher, then the firm's president, along with McClelland and another banker. Also present were software research analyst James Mendelson and another research executive.

But Mendelson, who generally followed companies that sold software for the giant mainframe computers that then dominated the business computing market, candidly told the Microsoft representatives, in an offhand comment, that he had doubts about their business. *Gee*, he said, *I'm not sure there's much of a future for PC software.*

The comment knocked the wind out of Morgan Stanley's bankers. "It was a horrible moment," McClelland later recalled.[11] Afterward, Microsoft chose Morgan's downtown rival Goldman Sachs, whose own analyst, Rick Sherlund, was more enthusiastic. In a call explaining the decision, Microsoft told the Morgan Stanley bankers: *Look, you don't have an analyst that's going to be supportive.* The win put Goldman on the map in Silicon Valley.

In the context of the times, the Mendelson comment wasn't as off base as it might now seem, noted Alec Ellison, a young tech banker at Morgan Stanley in the 1980s, who in spring 2009 was cohead of investment banking at Jefferies & Co. An earlier tech bubble in 1982–83 had burst, and the stock of Apple, the personal-computer bellwether, had fallen by about 75 percent. A successor to the hit Lotus spreadsheet program 1-2-3 had flopped, and "there were serious doubts about the PC software business model," Ellison said. It wasn't until Intel introduced the new higher-powered 386 chip in 1986 that the business began to recover.[12]

Quattrone and other bankers later found ways to engineer around Mendelson-type problems, according to Andy Kessler, a former Morgan Stanley analyst who worked with Quattrone. For the technology IPOs he was pitching, analysts would be involved in advance. In the middle of the bake-off pitch, the analyst would "position the company in a way that had been agreed to [among members of the technology banking team] ahead of time," Kessler later wrote. Not only did this head off any Mendelson-like surprises, it showed executives of the company going public that they could expect research from "a ranked analyst" at Morgan Stanley, Kessler said.[13]

Because so many of the technology deals were so small, much of the financing work in Silicon Valley was left to smaller, "boutique" investment banks. They included Hambrecht & Quist (H&Q), which had underwritten Genentech and Apple; Baltimore-based Alex. Brown & Sons; Robertson Stephens; and Montgomery Securities, the last of which became known for a lavish investor conference.

The boutiques could move faster, deliver more personalized attention, and enjoy more freedom than bankers operating within big firms. In the early 1980s, Quattrone explained a decade later, "some of the visionary venture capitalists, who wanted to 'legitimize' the technology IPO market, started talking to firms like Morgan Stanley."[14] Bigger firms like Morgan Stanley and Goldman had better reputations, bigger sales and trading operations, and a broader array of services globally.

Quattrone told McClelland that their challenge was to create something within Morgan Stanley that would contain the elements of a much smaller firm like H&Q. The unit, Quattrone argued, should combine bankers with dedicated research analysts, capital-markets staffers, and institutional sales people who could all be marshaled to sell an IPO by "presenting a united front in the marketplace." At new-business pitches, Quattrone would tout his technology group at Morgan Stanley as a "boutique in a bulge bracket firm."

It was the dawn of a new era. The same week Microsoft went public, in March 1986, two other companies that achieved lasting success also launched IPOs. Oracle Corporation, the enterprise software company, was led by Alex. Brown and Merrill Lynch. And Sun Microsystems Inc., a network computing company, was led by Robertson Stephens and Alex. Brown.

Silicon Graphics was one of eight technology IPOs Morgan Stanley led in 1986, a boom year for new tech issues. Another was Cypress Semiconductor Corporation, whose outspoken chief executive, T. J. Rodgers, would become one of Quattrone's staunchest defenders after the technology stock bubble burst beginning in 2000.

Quattrone played a role in hiring analyst Andy Kessler away from Paine Webber. Kessler had just made runner-up in a high-profile industry survey, the *Institutional Investor* All Star team, in the electronics category.[15] Around late

1988, Kessler flew to San Francisco to meet Quattrone, then the head of West Coast technology banking. Quattrone asked him how soon he could start; he said he had some deals for Kessler to work on.

Kessler told Rod Berens, Morgan Stanley's head of research, that he didn't want to be a "whore to banking," meaning an analyst who was so heavily influenced by bankers, and pressured to say good things about investment-banking clients, that he lost credibility and respect among the institutional investors who were supposed to be his primary audience. "Don't worry," said Berens. "That doesn't happen at Morgan Stanley."

After a week in New York, Kessler visited Quattrone in California, and the two drove around to visit companies. "I decided to call him Frankie. He was a local boy done good out of Philadelphia," Kessler wrote in his book. "He was also the worst dresser on Wall Street. He had a bushy mustache, a $3 Casio watch, [cheap looking ties], and there was always some rip or tear in his suits. He was also smarter than shit. Within five minutes he could tell whether a company was going to be a franchise player five years down the road. It was uncanny how right he was."

Quattrone and Kessler, along with junior banker Steve Strandberg, first visited the chief executive of a custom-chip company in Milpitas, California. Kessler said he didn't think much of the company, and Quattrone told him he generally agreed. Then they stopped in San Jose to meet Bernard Vonderschmitt, a top executive of Xilinx Inc., which made programmable gate arrays. Kessler was about to give Quattrone his opinion of this second company when Quattrone cut him off. "We are already set to file the deal when the cycle turns," Quattrone said. "I just wanted Bernie to meet you and agree that you were a good enough analyst to follow his company."

Aa Kessler recalled it, "that popped my balloon. A week on the job and . . . I was already a piece of Wall Street meat."[16]

MINISCRIBE

MORE THAN a decade after the fraud charges, the case of Miniscribe Corporation remains a benchmark for white-collar defense attorneys trying to minimize the seriousness of their client's conduct. *What my client did isn't fraud*, they will argue in meetings with regulators. *Fraud is shipping bricks. This is a long way from shipping bricks.*

In November 1983, Morgan Stanley led a $23 million initial public offering for Miniscribe of Longmont, Colorado, one of dozens of disk-drive makers going public as personal computers proliferated. Before the IPO, McClelland, Quattrone, and another Morgan banker had all participated in the "due diligence" work on the company, Quattrone later testified.[1] That is, when investment bankers sell stocks, they are supposed to spot-check the accuracy of facts supplied to them by the companies.

Miniscribe, like many rivals, ran into trouble quickly. Its largest customer, IBM, first cut its orders, and then decided to make its own drives.[2] After the CEO resigned and the stock price plummeted, Hambrecht & Quist mounted a rescue effort in mid-1985 led by turnaround expert Q. T. Wiles.

Wiles had saved so many companies for H&Q that he had become its chairman. In the Miniscribe rescue, Wiles came in to lead new management, H&Q had led a $20 million investment, and Bill Hambrecht and another H&Q executive also went on the Miniscribe board.[3]

At first, the Wiles treatment seemed to work. The stock price soared. Sales tripled. In May 1987, Miniscribe raised $97.7 million in high-risk, below-investment-grade "junk" bonds, convertible into Miniscribe stock, led by Hambrecht and Morgan Stanley. Again Quattrone's group at Morgan Stanley did their due diligence.

After disk-drive sales started slipping in mid-1988, Wiles resigned abruptly in early 1989, and Miniscribe directors retained Harvey Pitt, the former general counsel at the Securities and Exchange Commission, to investigate. On

September 12, 1989, Pitt reported that senior management had apparently "perpetrated a massive fraud."[4]

The Pitt probe found Wiles had pressured staffers to engage in the fraud, by overstating profits and inventory values. But his most sensational finding was that $3.7 million of false inventory value was generated "by packaging bricks as finished products and shipping them to distributors at the end of the year, so that these items would be in transit during the fiscal 1987 physical inventory."

Shipping bricks—a cruder form of fraud could scarcely be imagined.

In December 1989, a money manager in Galveston, Texas, Harris L. "Shrub" Kempner, whose U.S. National Bank had incurred heavy losses on $18 million of the Miniscribe junk bonds, filed suit in Galveston state court. The lawsuit, filed by high-profile tort lawyer Joseph Jamail, said the investors had been defrauded by Wiles, Hambrecht, Miniscribe's outside auditors, and Morgan Stanley, and asked for $51 million in damages and $500 million in punitive damages.

On New Year's Day 1990, Miniscribe landed in Denver bankruptcy court. In 1991, the Securities and Exchange Commission charged sixteen former Miniscribe executives, led by Wiles, with insider trading and cooking the books.[5] Ten of them had made more than $3.5 million by selling Miniscribe stock at inflated prices, the agency said.

O

The investor lawsuit put Frank Quattrone on the spot. He had been the Morgan Stanley banker with primary responsibility for the Miniscribe bond sale.[6]

The bond offering had occurred after a few previous attempts were halted. At first, Morgan Stanley concluded it was too soon. Another offering was halted after receipt of a whistle-blower letter from an employee alleging improper accounting. The actual bond sale had gone forward only after those allegations were investigated.

Quattrone believed that halting the deal when such issues arose showed the firm had done the required due diligence.

On Tuesday evening, April 2, 1991, Quattrone flew from California to Houston with one of Morgan's outside attorneys, Robert F. Wise of Davis Polk & Wardwell. Wise had helped the banker prepare to give pretrial testimony.

Beyond the importance of its outcome to his immediate future, the Miniscribe case would have more lasting significance for Quattrone. It was still on his mind a decade later in December 2000, when he typed out an e-mail that got him charged with obstruction of justice.

O

At 9:30 A.M. on April 3, 1991, Quattrone appeared for the pretrial deposition at the offices of Jamail & Kolius.

Jamail, then one of the Forbes 400 richest Americans, was a feared Wall Street giant killer. He had risen to national fame in the Texaco-Pennzoil case, winning a $10.5 billion judgment in 1987 that forced Texaco into bankruptcy court. Texaco had outbid Pennzoil for Getty Oil after Getty had reached a handshake "agreement in principle" to sell at a lower price to Pennzoil.

In a trial over Pennozil's claim that Texaco had illegally interfered with the Getty-Pennzoil pact, Jamail had scored heavily in his questioning of prominent takeover lawyer Martin Lipton, who testified wearing a double-breasted jacket and a bright red handkerchief, by painting him as a slick New Yorker before the Texas jurors.[7]

On this day four years later, much of Quattrone's questioning was handled by Jamail's associate, Frank Staggs Jr. The investors' lawyers had been "surprised" at how few documents Morgan Stanley had turned over, considering that the bankers had done due diligence on Miniscribe several times, Staggs recalls.[8]

While it was just a deposition, the pretrial warm-up quickly showed Quattrone's ability to dance away from tough questions. His glib salesman's skill and keen intelligence were more than a match for his adversaries.

Staggs asked whether documents from the due diligence Morgan Stanley had conducted for the 1983 Miniscribe IPO were still in existence, and if they had been reviewed for the 1987 bond offering. Quattrone said he didn't remember.[9]

"It's generally our practice," Quattrone said, "once an offering is completed, if we had taken things like notes as part of our due diligence process, to dispose of the notes prior to or subsequent to the offering once they no longer have any relevance."

"Dispose of meaning destroy?" Staggs asked.

"Dispose of meaning dispose," Quattrone answered.

Quattrone continued, "Our practice is generally to dispose of due diligence notes once they no longer become relevant, which is shortly after an offering." Later in the session, he compared the procedure to discarding "a grocery shopping list once you've bought the groceries."

When Jamail took up the questioning, Quattrone easily parried his questions, too. "You destroyed some stuff, didn't you?" Jamail asked.

"We probably discarded some stuff," Quattrone said.

"Well, discard, destroy. Is there a difference?" Jamail said.

"Yes, there is," said Wise.

"Yes," said Quattrone.

O

The jury trial to consider the Miniscribe bond investors' claims began in October 1991 in state court in Galveston. It took the investor plaintiffs about two and a half months, until just before Christmas, to put on their case. Each witness was examined for days by Jamail.

The defense witnesses appeared in the order in which they had been named, with Morgan Stanley last up. Morgan Stanley's defense was that the investment bank had done what it was supposed to do, and there wasn't any evidence its employees were complicit. Quattrone, who appeared on January 27, 1992, testified that he had gone about his due diligence in the usual way.

When it came time for Jamail to cross examine Quattrone, the Morgan Stanley team believed the outcome for their firm hung on how well the thirty-six-year-old banker could hold up, and whether the jury would find him credible. Jamail's questioning took the better part of the afternoon.

When Jamail asked Quattrone for the notes he had made during the due diligence, Quattrone said, "I have some of them right here."[10] When Jamail asked whether he had brought all of them, Quattrone replied adroitly: "I brought the ones the lawyers gave me that were exhibits." When Jamail asked him about the rest, Quattrone said, "I think they have all been produced."

At this point, Jamail shifted gears and took a rougher tone. "Mr. Quattrone, the facts are you destroyed some of them, didn't you?"

"No, that's not true."

"You said so on your deposition," Jamail said.

"I did not," Quattrone said.

"What did you say?"

"Well, why don't you read back the deposition?" Quattrone shot back at the Texan.

Jamail then reviewed questions and answers from the deposition transcript, in which Quattrone had described the firm's practice of discarding or disposing of notes taken during due diligence that have outlived their usefulness after a transaction.

"So," Jamail asked, resuming his trial questions, "you have discarded some of your notes?"

Quattrone ducked giving a yes-or-no answer, replying, "I did not say." He explained, "I said it's generally our policy that the notes are discarded. I did not say we discarded any in this particular case."

Jamail came back at him. "But sir, I don't want to quibble with you, but you said this is some of the stuff you had."

"I did not say that," Quattrone replied. "You just read what I said."

"Well, sir, you don't need to be—" Jamail began.

"I don't like it when you are putting words in my mouth," Quattrone said. "We are talking about a general policy here." Far from being put on the defensive, Quattrone had seized the initiative and put Jamail himself back on his heels.

"We were talking about Miniscribe due diligence," Jamail said.

Quattrone pressed his advantage. "It says there it's our practice that after a transaction, it's the general policy of ours if there are any notes that were taken that have outlived their usefulness, we discard or dispose of them," he said, again with a slightly patronizing tone. "It's quite obvious we did not discard or dispose of all of our notes in this thing, and we have produced everything that we had to."

"You don't know whether everything has been produced or whether something has been destroyed?" Jamail said.

"I told you that we had everything in our files and turned everything in our files over to you," Quattrone said, "and I could not give you assurances that everything in our files was everything that had ever been produced."

O

When Quattrone stepped down, it seemed to the Morgan Stanley team as if he had more than held his own. Jamail, the tort titan, hadn't dented Quattrone's composure or his account.

A week later that impression was reinforced: The verdict came out as a massive victory for Morgan Stanley. On February 4, 1992, by a 10–2 vote, the jury ordered some of the defendants to pay $29 million in actual damages and a harsh $530 million in punitive damages.

For Hambrecht, the outcome was a disaster. The firm was ordered to pay $45 million in damages. Bill Hambrecht personally owed $35 million. Wiles himself fared even worse. He was ordered to pay $250 million in punitive damages. Coopers & Lybrand, Miniscribe's auditor, was ordered to pay $200 million.

At the same time, Morgan Stanley and one other venture capital investor were let completely off the hook—zero damages. Inside Morgan Stanley, the outcome was viewed as a stunning win for the young banker, Frank Quattrone.

When Wise, Morgan Stanley's outside lawyer, phoned Morgan Stanley lawyers in New York to brief them on the outcome, he said, *It felt like being the only person left standing after a bomb had gone off.*

Within a week, Hambrecht and the other defendants settled the case, for undisclosed sums. Wiles himself was convicted in July 1994 of criminal insider trading and securities fraud in Denver federal court. Jurors found him guilty of issuing false statements about Miniscribe's finances and illegally profiting by $1.7 million on stock sales. Wiles was sentenced to three years in prison that December at the age of seventy-five, and served two years starting in April 1997.

O

Beyond setting a benchmark of sorts for white-collar crime, the Miniscribe case provided some unusual humorous mementos. Wise and Staggs both received commemorative bricks.

But some former colleagues said later that the trial's outcome had planted the seeds of overconfidence in Quattrone. The case also drove home the importance of keeping fewer documents, the kinds of files that could prove difficult to explain in court. One of the plaintiffs' lawyers, Galveston lawyer Andrew Mytelka, recalled in mid-2004, "The problem with the case against Morgan Stanley was that we didn't have any documents," Mytelka said. "They basically got rid of everything."[11]

AN EARLY BRUSH WITH THE SEC

6

QUATTRONE lived in a nondescript one-story ranch-style house in a middle-class neighborhood in San Carlos, California—midway between San Francisco, where Morgan Stanley's office was, and Palo Alto, a leafy suburb home to both Stanford University and many venture capital firms. Eventually Quattrone moved the Morgan Stanley technology group to Menlo Park, a town next door to Palo Alto.

At the time, Quattrone's neighborhood was unexceptional, and his career seemed undistinguished as well. The pace of technology deals slowed after the stock market crash of October 1987. In 1988, Quattrone lost the on-scene presence of his friend and rabbi when Carter McClelland left the San Francisco office to return to New York, though Quattrone continued to report to him.

Despite Quattrone's high profile in Silicon Valley, the technology banking effort was sometimes derided within Morgan Stanley as the "dinky deals department." On Wall Street, the big action was elsewhere. During the 1980s, the financial landscape was dominated by hostile takeover battles, ever-larger leveraged buyouts, and junk bond issues, all offering enormous fees. In the epic $25 billion leveraged buyout of RJR Nabisco Inc. in 1989, for example, Morgan Stanley was one of four firms that earned advisory fees of $25 million each.

By comparison, in those days, a home run–size deal for the tech group was the $198 million merger, announced in July 1987, between 3Com and Bridge Communications. "And that was an absolute landmark transaction," one group member recalls. The fee for Morgan Stanley was just $1.5 million.

Back at Morgan Stanley headquarters on Sixth Avenue in Manhattan, Joe Fogg, head of investment banking at the height of the takeover craze, scanned a list of his bankers and their fee production. Appraising Quattrone's production, he cracked, "I've got guys whose *fees* are bigger than the *companies* he covers." As a measure of his frustration: Once when Fogg gave him his year-end bonus check, Quattrone literally threw it on the floor and walked out. (Somehow, by the time Fogg returned the next day, the check was gone, and it was cashed.)

"Everyone in New York thought Frank was this crazy, Lone Ranger type, spending all this time doing fifteen-million-dollar IPOs for these small companies," one of his colleagues, George Boutros, recalled later, as the bubble was ending.[1]

Well, not everyone. In 1989, Quattrone persuaded a second-year analyst not to attend business school after two years at the firm, the standard Morgan Stanley career path. Instead, the analyst transferred to California to work full-time with Quattrone. His name was William John Barrett Brady III.

In some ways, Brady was everything Quattrone wasn't. He was born on the right side of the tracks, on the Main Line of Philadelphia, not in South Philly like Frank. His father was a judge. And he was a thoroughgoing preppy, graduating from the Hill School and Princeton, where he was a member of the elite Ivy club and played varsity hockey.

Brady looked older than he really was. And so he became Quattrone's deputy, bag carrier, and all-around execution guy. Pleasant and dogged, Brady had a way of bonding with clients. And he was junior enough that Quattrone could commandeer him completely.

○

A deal that heralded the start of the 1990s technology boom would also put Quattrone's aggressive salesmanship on display, to the firm's mild embarrassment.

On May 2, 1989, a six-member team of Morgan Stanley executives, bankers, and a research analyst trooped out to Sunnyvale, California, for a bake-off pitch to lead the IPO of MIPS Computer Systems Inc. The team was led by no less than Morgan Stanley president Richard Fisher, and also included McClelland, Quattrone, junior banker Steve Strandberg, and research analyst Carol Muratore.[2]

A one-hundred-page pitch book , bound in a blue binder with gold lettering, the firm's colors, proposed a sale of 5 million shares at a price of $15 to $20 per share. A MIPS offering in January 1990, it said, could make MIPS "the First Deal of the 1990s." The last page said, "MIPS: The IPO of the 1990s . . . We Want Your Business!"

On his flight back to the East Coast from the pitch, Fisher sat next to MIPS chief executive Robert Miller—a seating assignment Quattrone personally arranged.[3] The two hit it off, and Fisher even asked Miller to join him on the board of the Urban Institute. Miller accepted.

Miller, a fifteen-year veteran of IBM, was press friendly and highly promotional. And the MIPS IPO wound up testing the SEC's limits in enforcing its rules against pre-IPO hype, known as "gun jumping." The SEC had rules mandating a so-called quiet period once an IPO had been announced and its plans filed with the SEC. The rules limited how much a company and its executives could appear in the press promoting their business prospects—to limit trading at frothy levels.

In Washington, as they reviewed the preliminary MIPS offering statement, SEC officials noticed a steady drumbeat of favorable articles about MIPS in *The Wall Street Journal* and *BusinessWeek*.

The SEC was worried that "the deal was getting overheated," and threatened a delay, said Bob Latta, MIPS's outside counsel at Wilson, Sonsini, Goodrich & Rosati, whose partner Larry Sonsini was the leading legal guru of tech IPOs. But Miller, the MIPS chief executive, became furious about the possibility of any delay, thinking it could risk the whole deal.[4]

On Sunday December 3, 1989, Miller rode the Concorde from New York to London to meet big investors. A week later, a *New York Times* columnist wrote an article hailing the advent of "a hot High-Technology Offering." The article contained upbeat comments from several analysts. As a result, their firms were all kicked out of the group of underwriters by the SEC—as a signal that the Wall Street firms involved should refrain from hyping the deal.[5]

Next came a *USA Today* article, which appeared on December 13 and was headlined MIPS: FROM UGLY DUCKLING TO SWAN. MIPS and its lawyers had unsuccessfully asked the reporter to delay the article; instead, Sonsini persuaded Howard Morin, an assistant director of the SEC's corporate-finance division, to give the MIPS IPO a week to "cool off" afterward.

So on December 20, the bankers at Morgan Stanley settled on a price for the deal of $17.50 a share, and the legal team prepared to address a last batch of questions from the SEC examiner, David Thelander, a junior attorney just two years out of Vermont Law School. But at the end of the day, an irritated-sounding Morin called.

In San Francisco, Morin's voice crackled over the speaker phone in the crowded printer's office, where the final prospectus was about to go to press.[6] "The reason why I'm involved in this telephone call," Morin said, "is that there was an article in the December 11 issue of *Corporate Finance Weekly*, that there was an article dealing with the MIPS IPO." Morgan Stanley banker Steve Strandberg "turned white," Bob Latta later recalled.

Dave Ludvigson, the MIPS chief financial officer, looked around, thinking, "All right, who screwed up?" The answer quickly became apparent: Quattrone had spoken to the *Corporate Finance Weekly* reporter. He said later he thought he wouldn't be quoted.

Morin, who had a thick, Mason-Dixon Beltway drawl, then proceeded to read the entire article, word-for-word, pausing each time there was a puffy quote from Quattrone. Each time he did he mispronounced Quattrone's name, sometimes as "Quatron" but occasionally rendering it as "Quotron"—a then commonly used stock-quote terminal.

The tone of the article throughout was raw, unfiltered hype, much of it attributed directly to Quattrone. Morin read: "'It's the new platform for the computer industry. The company is perceived in the industry as a winner because its revenues come not only from the sale of its products, but also from licensing arrangements for its technology with the leading computer and semi-conductor companies around the world, *he said.*'" Finishing his recital, Morin repeated Quattrone's name and then spelled it out: ". . . mutual courting process, according to Quotron. Or Quatron. I'm not sure how you say it. Q-U-A-T-T-R-O-N-E."

Incensed by the drumbeat of hype, the SEC's Thelander actually had recommended to Morin that Morgan Stanley be kicked off the deal, too. But Morin, a twenty-five-year agency veteran, didn't think that was necessary. Dumping Morgan Stanley, the lead underwriter, could have torpedoed the IPO.

At the time, Quattrone himself was actually in Philadelphia, visiting his wife's family. Reaching Morin by phone, Sonsini persuaded him to allow the underwriters to include the deal's price and a corrective disclosure for the Quattrone article as a final amendment to the prospectus the next day.

The disclosure was contained in a section labeled "Customer contract announcements and other publicity." Quoting nine sentences from the *Corporate Finance Week* article attributed to Quattrone, the filing said investors shouldn't rely on the comments by the unnamed "representative of Morgan Stanley & Co.," which could be "misleading."[7]

Although he had pushed the envelope, Quattrone again had dodged a bullet. Like some other MIPS executives and Wall Street analysts, he had participated in hyping the deal, aggressively skirting the SEC rules. The cops at the SEC had pulled him over for speeding but savvy lawyers got him and the firm off with a warning.

TECH TAKES OFF

7

AS THE 1990S BEGAN, the technology banking business began picking up.

The first deal out of the chute in February 1990 would prove to be one of Quattrone's most enduring calling cards. Cisco Systems sold a new type of router, a device to connect computer networks. Quattrone noticed in reviewing Cisco's financials that the San Jose–based company's sales were growing by 60 percent a year. He asked Cisco chief executive John Morgridge, a fellow Stanford M.B.A., "Where will you get the sales people to support your growth?"

Morgridge replied in a distinctive Wisconsin twang, "Well, to date, we haven't found the *need* to have a sales force because people are ordering these things like hotcakes over the *Internet*." The offhand remark illuminated for Quattrone—who had thought of the Internet as a government-sponsored network used mainly by scientists—the commercial possibilities of the net.[1] Morgridge had gone on one of Morgan Stanley's rafting trips with Quattrone.

The importance of the Cisco deal grew over time. At one point during the dot-com bubble, Cisco briefly became the U.S. company with the largest stock market capitalization. But Cisco's 1990 IPO raised only $50.4 million. Cisco's strongest tie to Morgan Stanley became veteran communications equipment analyst George Kelly, who had worked at AT&T and IBM before Wall Street.

Indeed, the tenor of the home office's low regard for Quattrone and his "dinky deals" could be seen in another deal a few months after Cisco.

Andy Kessler, the semiconductor analyst who had joined Morgan Stanley in New York in 1989, worked on the IPO of Xilinx, a programmable chip company, starting in March 1990 along with Strandberg, the junior banker on the MIPS IPO. An IPO, or most any other financing commitment, must get approval in most securities firms from a group called the commitment committee. The group provides a second opinion, or jaundiced eye, to make sure the banker on the business hasn't lost perspective or overlooked some basic reason to be careful. Quattrone asked Kessler to lobby the commitment committee members for him to approve Xilinx.

When he approached one committee member, Robert Metzler, and asked to go through the report, Kessler recalled in his book, the executive shot him an "annoyed" look.

"Is it alive?" the busy Metzler asked.

"What do you mean?" Kessler asked.

"Look, I can't be bothered with these piss shit little deals. I've got bigger things to worry about. If you say they have a pulse, if you say they're okay, I'm in. Now get out of my office."[2]

Why so grumpy? The deal's size was a minuscule $25 million.

Quattrone asked Kessler, who covered electronics and companies like Intel, the big semiconductor company, to follow personal-computer hardware and software stocks. "Morgan Stanley was sort of management by fire," Kessler recalled. "The only carrot was the year-end bonus, but the other 364 days were filled with lots of sticks, i.e. people beating up on you to do more for them." Because research generates no revenue, "people who do generate revenue constantly bug you. Frank Quattrone bugged me, just about every day. That was okay, up to a point. I wanted to do more banking deals because I figured that was how I was going to get paid."[3]

In the middle of the year, Carol Muratore, the research analyst who had covered MIPS when it went public, left the firm, leaving MIPS without an analyst as its lead underwriter. "The analyst we met before the deal had the story down," recalled MIPS chief executive officer Bob Miller. After she quit, he said, "Morgan never backfilled her."[4]

With the stock under pressure only a few months after the IPO, Quattrone blamed Morgan Stanley's research department for the gap in coverage.[5] Then Quattrone prodded another analyst, Rick Ruvkun, to take over the responsibility of keeping investors posted on how MIPS was doing.[6]

In a landmark article two years later on the influence of investment banking on research analysts at Morgan Stanley, *Wall Street Journal* reporter Michael Siconolfi wrote in July 1992 that Quattrone had "prodded Mr. Ruvkun to put out a positive report, people familiar with the firm say. When Mr. Ruvkun eventually wrote the report, however, he recommended a 'hold'—not the 'buy' that research analysts say Mr. Quattrone sought, angering investment bankers, people familiar with Morgan say."

In the same article, Quattrone denied pressuring Ruvkun to make favorable comments, saying he was only concerned about the temporary lack of coverage. "We had brought MIPS public only six months before and suddenly we weren't covering it anymore," Quattrone said. "As a sponsor of a new security, we have a commitment to provide ongoing research coverage. Sure, I pushed for re-sumed coverage, but that's the extent of it."

The *Journal* article noted that Morgan officials "concede that investment bankers occasionally have put pressure on the firm's research analysts to influ-ence their views on stocks." But it said they chalked up past conflicts to man-agement lapses, and Fisher told Siconolfi that the firm managed such tension "as well as anyone."

As the pace of technology IPOs picked up, there were six at Morgan Stanley in 1990, compared to just two apiece in 1988 and 1989. In December 1990, Quattrone was elected a managing director. At Morgan Stanley, this was akin to making partner at a law firm. Around the same time, he became cohead of the firm's global technology group.

In 1991, Quattrone asked Kessler to help him find another analyst to follow Microsoft, Lotus Development Corporation (another top software company), Compaq Computer Corporation, and Apple. Not long afterward, Kessler no-ticed the firm's head of research walking down the hall with a woman he rec-ognized vaguely. They stopped at the empty office next to his. "This will be yours," the research chief told the woman. The following Monday the new-comer poked her head in Kessler's office and introduced herself. "Hi, I'm Mary Meeker," she said.[7]

Meeker, a graduate of DePauw University in Indiana, had spent two years at Merrill Lynch before getting an M.B.A. from Cornell in 1986. After three years at Salomon Brothers, she had gone to work as an associate to another analyst, Michele Preston, at a smaller Boston-based firm, Cowen & Co., when Quattrone and Morgan Stanley were setting off in search of a replacement for Muratore.

Quattrone had asked around among technology-oriented investors he knew, such as Roger McNamee of T. Rowe Price, Peter Anastos of Alliance Capital Management, and Jay Hoag at Chancellor Capital Management, and they had given Meeker good reviews. He had met Meeker once before in San Jose, after a Richard Shaffer technology conference, giving her a ride in his BMW back to her hotel.

Just before she made her decision in April 1991, Meeker found herself on a red-eye flight from California back to New York with Quattrone's colleague Bill Brady. They spent some time chatting as they walked around the plane. After landing, they shared a cab into Manhattan. While they were riding through Central Park in the fog on the way to Brady's hotel on Fifth Avenue, he pulled out a spare Morgan Stanley pitch book extolling the technology group.

Meeker was sold.

THE DREAM HOUSE

8

IN THE SPRING of 1988, the Quattrones began planning what they called their "dream house."[1] Later that year, they paid $610,000 to buy a 1.25 acre lot in Los Altos Hills.[2] The lot was located a few miles south of the Stanford campus, on a ridge that offered a spectacular view overlooking both Palo Alto and San Francisco Bay some eight miles away. Los Altos was Spanish for "the heights," and the location seemed to carry symbolic significance. As Quattrone rose in stature in Silicon Valley and on Wall Street, he would overlook the valley from on high.

But the construction project, begun with such high hopes, would cast a pall over his life and career. It offered a glimpse of the dark side of his scrappy nature. As charming as he could be to clients, he could also be harsh and bullying to those paid to serve him.

In 1990, the Quattrones told architect David Terpening that, in light of their Italian heritage, they wanted a Mediterranean design.[3] The entryway would have an inlaid marble starburst.[4] In November 1990, the Quattrones signed an agreement with a prominent local home builder, Gary Lencioni. The contract called for Lencioni to build the four-bedroom, sixty-six-hundred-square-foot house, complete with elevator, pool, and eight hundred-foot cabana, for a guaranteed maximum price of $1.5 million.[5]

Lencioni was known as a "builder to the stars," having built a home for San Francisco 49ers football star Jerry Rice and having another in progress for San Francisco Giants owner Bob Lurie.

The Quattrone home was originally due to be completed in a year, by September 1991. But as the year progressed, many seemingly routine problems arose; Denise, keeping tabs on the project, authorized ninety-two different changes, all documented in writing. The projected completion date slipped to Christmas 1991.[6]

Amid the changes and confusion, an error occurred that caused the project to disintegrate into chaos and recriminations. As the Quattrones later laid it out in a series of written complaints, this is their view of what happened:

The painters mistakenly primed all the window frames with white paint, when they were supposed to have been stained to show their natural wood finish, the Quattrones later charged. The Quattrones said they had paid a premium for high-grade windows.[7]

Although Frank was concerned that permanent damage had occurred, Lencioni assured him that the white paint could be stripped off and the finish would be "good as new."[8] But when the windows and doors were stripped and stained, many were scratched and the frames damaged.[9] When this was discovered, Lencioni informed the Quattrones that their move-in date would have to be postponed again, to mid-February 1992.[10]

Lencioni then told the Quattrones that he had decided to replace each glass pane, but not the wood frames and sashes, for all the windows and doors in the house. The cost, it appeared, could be paid for with proceeds of an insurance claim filed with the painter's insurer. The Quattrones wanted all the windows and doors replaced. Instead, Lencioni's "attempt to replace the scratched panes resulted in a hodgepodge of poorly glazed windows with different color panes," the Quattrones said later.[11]

After considerable research during their initial planning, the Quattrones had chosen Kolbe & Kolbe Woodworks premium windows and doors.[12] They contacted a local Kolbe representative, Katie Nickerson. Touring the new home in March 1992, Nickerson informed Denise that many of the windows and doors were not in fact from Kolbe & Kolbe.[13]

At this point, the Quattrones hired a consultant, John Page, who was also an attorney, to help them investigate other possible problems.[14] Page found other defects, including cracks in the Italian marble and tile floors. Exterior paint was peeling. Stucco was defective. The foundation was leaking. Steel welds were defective, the welder uncertified. The wood cabinets hadn't been fastened to the walls as specified. Water mains to both the house and cabana, which were supposed to be copper pipe, were plastic instead.[15]

The move in was postponed until April 30, 1992. The day before, architect Terpening gave Lencioni an extensive "punch list" of defects to be repaired, and asked for a written response within five days, including a bar chart schedule showing the time frame for each action item. On May 11, Lencioni responded, asking for another fourteen days to review the punch list and consult his subcontractors. On July 19, the Quattrones demanded a refund on $730,000 they had paid to Lencioni.[16]

On July 27, 1992, Frank and Denise faxed an angry, nine-page letter to Lencioni. "We are extremely disappointed and frustrated by your **non-response** to our Punch List and our repeated requests that you acknowledge the problems with our house and commit to fix them," it began. "We are very, very tired of your excuses, misrepresentations and lame explanations." Listing the problems Page had found, they asked Lencioni: "Would you really like this litany of events to be part of the public record in an arbitration or court proceeding?"[17]

Demanding a promise to correct all the issues they had raised, they issued a warning to Lencioni: "You may have underestimated our resolve in this matter, but let us make perfectly clear that we intend to pursue our satisfaction to the full extent of the law."

The letter also displayed pique that the Quattrones didn't get the services of the agreed-on job supervisor "because of the greater size and perceived prestige of your project for Bob Lurie, owner of the San Francisco Giants." The Quattrones also accused Lencioni of "contract-padding," and demanded "a full accounting" of Lencioni's expenses.

They sent a copy of the letter to Terpening and their family lawyer, Ken Hausman. A partner at a law firm in downtown San Francisco, Hausman was every bit as feisty and pugnacious as Quattrone. Tall, with thick dark hair and prominent front teeth, Hausman was nicknamed Bucky Beaver by some opposing lawyers. He also represented Al Davis, the maverick, dispute-prone owner of the Oakland Raiders, and discount brokerage king Charles Schwab.

On August 7, 1992, Lencioni replied that the Quattrones' "accusatory" letter was filled with "unfounded allegations, half-truths and innuendo." But he acknowledged their "frustration" and said he aimed to "resolve this in an amicable and expedient manner." He also denied giving the Lurie project a higher priority.[18]

Lencioni blamed the window-brand substitution on the contractor, Pacific Wood Windows, but assured the couple that "a simple smooth sanding" should correct the problem. He disputed other Quattrone accusations, including contract padding, and offered to open his files, referring them to his attorney, Paul Lahaderne.

On January 14, 1993, the Quattrones filed a demand for arbitration, saying they had paid Lencioni more than $1.3 million.[19] "In the spring of 1988, Denise and Frank Quattrone committed their hard-earned savings, energy and spirit to designing a dream home for their young family," the Quattrones said in a brief for the case. "Today, more than five years later, their dream is a nightmare."[20]

○

Colleagues later recalled that the episode had a noticeable impact on Quattrone, as well as on Denise. He had generally left supervision of the project to her, they said, and went ballistic when all the problems emerged. He had to take time off from work to deal with them. And at one point he asked a senior investment banking executive in New York, Robert Scott, to speak with a money-management client at Aetna Life & Casualty, Lencioni's insurance company.

O

In the middle of 1993, Quattrone's lawyer, Ken Hausman okayed an agreement with Aetna to pay for six thousand dollars a month rent plus moving costs.[21] But Aetna balked at paying forty-five hundred dollars for "a Jacuzzi spa or similar spa" for the rental home. In a letter dated May 21, 1993, to Lencioni's lawyer Hausman asked if Aetna could reconsider. The reason for the Jacuzzi: "Because of the stress relating to your client's failure to remedy the punch list and addenda items in a timely manner, Denise Quattrone is now suffering from fibromyalgia," Hausman said. "Part of the treatment for this malady is immersion in a Jacuzzi tub."[22]

The diagnosis of fibromyalgia in February 1993 was a turning point in the lives of both Denise and Frank Quattrone. She would suffer from it through at least September 2004, when it was cited in letters to the judge about to sentence Quattrone. It often prevented her from traveling, causing her to miss both of Quattrone's trials, in 2003 and 2004. It also required her to take a variety of prescribed medicines, including pain and anxiety relievers.[23] According to the Web site WebMD, fibromyalgia "is a chronic disorder that causes widespread pain and tenderness in the muscles and soft tissue as well as sleep problems, fatigue," and other symptoms.

In January 1994, arbitrator Randall Wulff found in favor of the Quattrones. They were basically entitled to the return of almost all of the money they had paid Lencioni. And so the builder's insurer, Aetna, paid them $1,584,060.70.[24] But the legal battle was just beginning.

The same month they received the refund check, the Quattrones asked Lencioni to finish the job. He refused.[25] Eventually, the entire house would be completely torn down and rebuilt from scratch by another builder.

On April 30, 1993, Hausman filed a lawsuit containing the claims of fraud and personal injury to Denise. In response, Lencioni brought in an additional defense lawyer, William J. McLean, who worked in downtown Palo Alto.[26]

The battle then shifted to Santa Clara County Court in San Jose, where the Quattrones filed amended complaints against Lencioni, his wife, and the subcontractors. The charges included fraud, negligence, misrepresentation, and infliction of emotional distress. They asked for damages of $5 million, tripled because they alleged that Lencioni was engaged in "an ongoing pattern of racketeering activity."[27]

Not only had Lencioni substituted inferior "knockoff" windows and built the home with "numerous serious defects," but the Quattrones said he had also fraudulently submitted a $154,151 bill from one subcontractor that was for a higher amount than Lencioni had actually paid.[28]

The impact on the Quattrones, as laid out in the court complaint, was dire. Denise had been "forced to abandon her career, and has spent substantially all of her waking hours in a fruitless attempt to obtain completion of her home." As a result, the lawsuit alleged, Denise had suffered numerous painful and disabling symptoms typically associated with her chronic ailment.[29]

As for Frank, he had "to spend protracted amounts of time away from his work and career," leaving him unable to entertain clients at home and causing him "extreme emotional and physical distress, including marital strife necessitating counseling, sleeplessness, anxiety, headaches, fatigue and depression."[30]

In December 1993, the Lencioni lawyers demanded Denise Quattrone's medical records and details of her condition. In May 1994, she responded in extensive detail, listing the names of specialists consulted, and she listed a dozen medications she had been prescribed.[31]

The records of the litigation fill seventeen thick legal file folders in the court archives in downtown San Jose. Jeremy Fogel, the former state court judge who presided, recalls that the case was unusual for a single-family home dispute in that it resembled "one of these massive commercial construction cases." He recalled that Quattrone himself stood out as "forceful and smart and knowledgeable."[32]

The terms weren't disclosed when the case was finally settled in early 1997. "The bottom line is, the Quattrones won," said McLean, Lencioni's lawyer, who said the epic battle boiled down to a five-thousand-dollar billing error and the window substitution, which the architect had known about. But, he noted ruefully, "it just became a war."

Lencioni and his wife had themselves gotten a divorce—which McLean attributed at least partly to the stress of the case.[33] In one public comment on the case in 2003, Lencioni called Quattrone "a monster."[34]

○

In 1995, the Quattrones signed a new contract with a new contractor to build the house again, this time for $2.3 million.[35] Dick Breaux, the more easygoing contractor who took over the job after Lencioni, got along with Quattrone well enough to finish the home. Breaux had built a house for one of Quattrone's longtime clients, T. J. Rodgers of Cypress Semiconductor, who had been featured in *Fortune* magazine in 1993 as one of the "bosses from hell." Breaux recalls that he thought "foolishly" that if he could keep Rodgers happy, he could handle anyone.[36]

Although Breaux found Quattrone reasonable, he too tangled with his wife Denise. Breaux also wound up in arbitration with the Quattrones.

The front doors were one of the last few items outstanding. But as Breaux sat in Quattrone's office, he told the banker he despaired of pleasing Denise. *She'll be fine*, Quattrone assured him. But when he redid the doors, Breaux recalls, "By God, they weren't acceptable. She wanted me to bring back the [previous] front doors so she could compare." Breaux refused. He told Denise the doors were at his warehouse, and if she wanted to look at them, she could come down there.

Denise responded with a hastily scribbled, angry fax to Breaux: "Would you prefer arbitration?"

Breaux quickly wrote "yes" over the same piece of paper and faxed it back to Mrs. Quattrone. Thus ensued a new arbitration, whose outcome isn't known.

○

The drawn-out war seemed to bring out the worst in Quattrone. True, he was vindicated. But his response showed a relentless, win-at-all-costs side, an impulse to obliterate his enemies. One former colleague of Quattrone's thought the banker's crushing victory in the dream house case, together with the favorable outcome of the Miniscribe case, added to his overconfidence, leading him to believe "he was invincible."

BUILDING A POWERHOUSE

9

AS THE STOCK MARKET took off in the 1990s, so did Quattrone's power within Morgan Stanley. His deals got bigger. His pay soared from $1 million annually to the $6 million level by 1995, colleagues recall. And yet, just as his grievances against home builder Gary Lencioni snowballed into a years-long battle, he accumulated grievances against Morgan Stanley that also snowballed, in a bizarre mirror version of the Dream House dispute.

Each summer, Quattrone would schedule an off-site meeting of the technology group at which both the analysts and bankers would discuss what they thought would be happening in their sectors over the following twelve months. A few of them were held at the Meadowood resort in Santa Rosa in the Sonoma Valley. The analysts would each give presentations for fifteen to twenty minutes, followed by a Q&A. Bankers would talk about private companies that might be going public.

The back-and-forth inevitably included what transactions could be expected and which banks had the inside track—whether based on key relationships with venture capitalists, analysts, or bankers. It was, typically, a bravura performance in which Quattrone would display a matchless command of which venture capitalists and technology executives called the shots and—most important—picked the bankers at companies up and down Silicon Valley.

Quattrone was both master of ceremonies and coach, urging them to find top-quality managements. The buzzwords were "first-class business in a first-class way," and "a boutique in a bulge bracket firm, the best of both." There would be wine tasting, golf, team building, and the inevitable karaoke. Quattrone, who had a smooth, mellifluous voice, still loved singing his college favorite "Rocky Raccoon." He didn't necessarily consider himself a brilliant singer. As Jay Hoag, a venture capital investor and longtime Quattrone fan pointed out, "One of the characteristics of a great karaoki singer is an awareness that your audience doesn't necessarily appreciate you."[1]

In the spring of 1992, one of the Morgan Stanley merger bankers, George Boutros, told his bosses in New York that he was going to have to leave the firm. The reason was that he and his wife, Danielle, didn't like New York City life, and wanted to move back to California. Boutros was a talented banker, and so Morgan Stanley found a way to keep him at the firm—a transfer to California.

The son of a Lebanese diplomat who grew up in Beirut, Boutros attended public school in France, the University of California at Berkeley, and business school at UCLA.[2] At first Boutros complained that there wasn't enough to do, but the next year he worked on two big deals and became Quattrone's right-hand deal maker. As Quattrone liked to point out, merger advice, along with follow-on stock sales, were key parts of what he called the "high-margin downstream business" that a big firm with a broad talent pool—unlike the specialty boutiques—could harvest from companies after their IPOs.[3]

Kessler, and later Meeker, also organized "bus tours" in which a few dozen visiting investor clients would be ferried around to several different companies up and own Route 101 in Silicon Valley. The clients, dressed casually for the outing, would descend on the companies and pepper managements with questions. The first bus tour, in August 1990, visited Intel, Sun Microsystems, Apple, Silcon Graphics, and Adobe. But it was interrupted on the second day by Iraq's invasion of Kuwait.[4]

Meeker also participated in group marketing trips with a half dozen or more other Morgan Stanley analysts, including communications equipment analyst George Kelly, who covered Cisco, enterprise software analyst Chuck Phillips, who covered Oracle, and others, such as Steven Milunovich, who covered big computer companies like IBM. The bonds they forged on these trips became an important factor when Quattrone left Morgan Stanley and they had to decide whether to join him.

As Quattrone and Meeker visited companies, she got to know their managements, but didn't make as much of a splash with stock price predictions or earnings estimate changes, Kessler recalled. Yet her close ties with company managements "enhanced her reputation with institutions," he said. "They figured she knew more about Intuit, for example, than anyone, and would call her to find out how she felt about it."[5]

Kessler believed that Meeker's ties to the firm's banking deals left her reputation hostage to the deals' quality.[6] Meeker disagreed. She felt that Morgan Stanley gave her the right to veto plans to take a questionable company public. She aimed to find perhaps two great companies every year. One of her first IPOs, in April 1992, was Learning Company, which made Reader Rabbit educational software. The company's stock market value increased sixfold by the time it was acquired for $606 million in 1995.[7]

Indeed, Meeker gave a thumbs-down to some winning companies. Although

Quattrone might question an analyst's judgment in such situations, he wouldn't overrule it at that point. He might say, *Are you sure?* But he wouldn't say, *You are wrong.*

For example, Meeker vetoed Morgan Stanley leading the IPO in 1992 of Quantum Computer Services Inc., in Vienna, Virginia, which offered a networking service for personal computers called America Online. Meeker thought it was an interesting little company, but was worried about the competition that it faced from rival services CompuServe and Prodigy. So after Quantum renamed itself America Online, the $26.5 million IPO was led by Alex. Brown & Sons and Robertson, Stephens & Co. Of course, AOL became a runaway success in the 1990s, creating $57.9 billion in shareholder value before it acquired Time Warner Inc. in 2001.[8]

But Meeker's initial lapse did no lasting damage. When the company retuned to the market the next year to sell more stock, Quattrone, Meeker, and New York tech banker James Liang all flew to AOL headquarters to make the pitch. Morgan Stanley won the lead in the $66 million deal, and continued to advise AOL after Quattrone left.

Quattrone was certainly tireless on his own behalf. Just as he had seated Fisher next to Miller of MIPS in 1989, Quattrone managed to sit across the aisle from two executives of client prospect WordPerfect on their way back to Utah from a meeting with Fisher at Morgan Stanley headquarters in New York in late 1992.

Bankers from Merrill Lynch and Donaldson Lufkin & Jenrette Inc. were also onboard. "We had been through a whole day of presentations, and then, there's all the same people," recalled WordPerfect chief financial officer Dan Campbell, who was traveling with another WordPerfect official, Duff Thompson. "Frank was kneeling in the aisle next to Duff for so long that the Merrill guy finally handed him a pillow."[9]

Quattrone had a graphic term for an extraordinary, unforgettable effort to win a piece of business: "The slobber."[10]

Beyond schmoozing and slobbering, Quattrone also forged close financial ties to the key players of Silicon Valley.

In February 1992, Morgan Stanley led a fund-raising effort for two investors, John Powell and Roger McNamee, who left T. Rowe Price to form their own venture fund for health care and technology. Morgan Stanley both led the raising for the $85 million fund, Integral Partners L.P., and also invested in it. McNamee became one of Quattrone's most visible supporters. Another key Integral investor was Kleiner Perkins Caufield & Byers, whose John Doerr became known as the most prominent venture capital investor of the 1990s.

As Meeker's star was rising, Kessler began to feel beleaguered. In 1992, he downgraded a number of the semiconductor stocks he no longer felt like following. And he began to style himself as the firm's technology strategist, writing more about interactive media and visiting big entertainment companies like Walt Disney Company, Paramount Communications Inc., and Time Warner with media bankers.[11]

Then Quattrone called and brought Kessler back to reality. However brilliant Kessler's insights, he thought they were of no use to investors or Morgan Stanley itself because there weren't any public companies in the field. "We're not going to make a penny off any of this multimedia bullshit," Quattrone told Kessler. "Andy, these semiconductor companies are cash-guzzling machines. They need to raise money ALL the time. And we are just the guys to do it for them."

As Kessler tried to listen respectfully, Quattrone continued, "You know, Andy, I just don't understand. We made George Kelly into the analyst he is today, and are about to make Mary Meeker into a top analyst. Why don't you let us do that for you?"

"Got it, Frankie," Kessler replied. After he hung up, he added, "Asshole."[12]

Quattrone also told Kessler's boss, Morgan Stanley research executive Jack Curley, that Kessler's time would be better spent covering an established profitable area, semiconductors, than emerging multimedia. In Quattrone's view, Kessler should have dropped coverage of the semiconductors if he no longer wanted to cover them, instead of downgrading them.

Soon Kessler was summoned to a meeting by two top research executives. Quattrone, they told him, was complaining about him.[13] In early 1993, Kessler made plans to leave. He wasn't the only one to jump ship. Quattrone could be brutally demanding. As a workaholic who e-mailed colleagues at all hours, he recognized few boundaries between work and home life.

Strandberg, who had worked on the MIPS deal, left in April 1991, soon after getting an 11:00 P.M. call after dinner one evening while on vacation in France. It was Quattrone, with a detailed series of questions about data on a spreadsheet.

O

Just as Kessler left, Morgan Stanley won two multimedia deals he had worked on, IPOs for Avid Technology Inc., an audio-video editing systems maker, and 3DO Company, which was developing a new type of video game. The IPO of 3DO became the hottest of 1993.

Pronounced three-dee-oh, 3DO was the brainchild of Trip Hawkins, who had hit a home run in the 1980s with Electronic Arts, a company with the trailblazing strategy of selling video games direct to retailers, including a bestselling John Madden football game. The company aimed to sell an "interactive multiplayer" that would rival those sold by Nintendo and Sega. In January

1993, Hawkins unveiled 3DO's plans publicly, and in March he announced that 3DO would go public.

The reaction was caustically skeptical. *The Red Herring* was a magazine devoted to emerging growth companies, named after the first version of an IPO prospectus that includes red type on the cover. In an open letter to Hawkins in April 1993, the magazine's editors aired questions about the 3DO IPO. Traditionally, they noted, venture-backed companies wouldn't go public until they had revenues and profits. The business risks, they warned, "are so high that it is inappropriate for the company to sell stock to the public market at this time."

Quattrone responded to the *Red Herring* critics after the quiet period ended. The market performance of 3DO seemed to have vindicated him. The stock rose 35 percent on its first day of trading, and within a few weeks had more than doubled, giving the company a market value above $725 million. Taking a company public with no product revenues "was certainly unusual!" he acknowledged in a Q&A for the magazine, "and not something we plan to make a habit of doing."[14]

But then Quattrone displayed his characteristic breezy self-assurance in comparing 3DO to biotech companies like Genentech that went public while their drugs were still being tested. Investors could measure 3DO, he said, by how many development systems had been shipped, or how many CD title development contracts had been signed. "In the end," he said, "it is either going to happen or it's not."

Such questions about companies going public too soon would return after the bubble.

O

Back in New York, Morgan Stanley bankers believed it was the firm's role to act as a mediator between its different groups of customers—the companies that wanted to sell their stock at the highest price possible, and the institutional investors that wanted to buy at the lowest price.

Such debates played out at the Morgan Stanley commitment committee in New York, which had to approve companies being taken public. Its members included McClelland and Robert Scott, another Stanford M.B.A., who was head of capital markets. Scott succeeded McClelland as head of corporate finance in 1992 and became head of investment banking in 1995.

The committee members considered themselves a reasonable proxy for the market. But Quattrone let it show that he considered them too conservative. While other bankers would try to offer balanced presentations, Quattrone often gave them a hard sell. There would be tension in the room as a frustrated Quattrone would make it clear he considered them not just conservative but uninformed. *You don't get it,* he would say.

One of the bankers who witnessed Quattrone's performances before the committee believed Quattrone had, in effect, "gone native" in Silicon Valley. He had become too sympathetic, this banker believed, to the venture capital players who wanted to use the top-notch Morgan Stanley stock-distribution system to sell stocks regardless of quality. In the case of 3DO, such caution was warranted. It was for years one of Silicon Valley's most spectacular flops, erasing $320 million of market value by the time it sought bankruptcy law protection from creditors in May 2003.[15]

To be sure, Morgan Stanley did sell stock in tech companies with more staying power. With Meeker's backing, it led the IPO of Intuit, which sold the red-hot Quicken personal-finance software. The $30 million IPO soared 60 percent in price on its first day of trading in March 1993.

As the IPOs got hotter, the deals got bigger. In 1994, the Quattrone group worked on multiple mergers valued at more than $1 billion. Morgan Stanley advised Novell in a $1.4 billion merger with WordPerfect. And Wellfleet Communications Inc. agreed to pay $1 billion for Synoptics Communications Inc., a Morgan Stanley client, in a networking deal in July 1994.

That year, Quattrone moved the group's offices from downtown San Francisco to Menlo Park, halfway to San Jose. The new offices were in a low-rise office park at 3000 Sand Hill Road, the boulevard on the west edge of the Stanford campus that was home to many top venture capital firms, including Kleiner Perkins.

Quattrone was relentless in promoting his group as number one. When *Red Herring* magazine, in a supplement ranking the investment banks in technology financing, put Lehman Brothers at the top by mistakenly including a big communications deal in Lehman's totals, Quattrone was "furious," recalls Anthony Perkins, then the magazine's publisher and editor-in-chief. Quattrone pulled Morgan Stanley's ads from the magazine for six months, Perkins said.[16]

As his business took off, Quattrone increasingly voiced frustration that he couldn't get the analysts he believed he needed to cover companies he thought warranted the attention. With support from some other bankers, Quattrone wanted the ability to hire more analysts to support the growth of his business.

And so he appealed to the head of equities, Neal Garonzik, who felt pressure to allow the analysts to report to Quattrone. Garonzik believed that the analysts' objectivity would be undermined if they reported to bankers or were overly influenced by them. It was a bruising battle. But Garonzik held the line. He said no.

NETSCAPE

10

IN EARLY 1995, investment bankers at Morgan Stanley attended a farewell dinner for Carter McClelland at the posh St. Regis Hotel on Fifth Avenue. It was an emotional blow to Quattrone. McClelland frequently had backed him in disputes and turf battles with other bankers.

While Quattrone had stayed put in San Francisco, McClelland took the emerging growth company model they had pioneered to headquarters in New York in 1988. Two years later, McClelland became cohead of worldwide corporate finance. He had gotten to know John Mack in the 1970s, when they met by chance on a Caribbean vacation in Little Dix Bay, and their families had vacationed together for a decade. When Mack became president in 1992, he asked McClelland to serve as his head of finance, administration, and operations, taking him further outside Quattrone's universe.

Mack, the son of a Lebanese merchant who played football on scholarship at Duke University, had started out as a bond salesman. He had a lilting, aristocratic Southern accent that strikingly didn't match his olive-skinned Mediterranean looks. Charismatic but impulsive, he earned the nickname Mack the Knife by serving as right-hand man to Richard Fisher. But as he had vied for the top job, he fueled a rivalry between the bond department and investment banking. Several banking stars left, including Joe Fogg, Eric Gleacher, and Robert Greenhill. McClelland himself left when it became clear there wasn't a meaningful role for him.

O

Despite his mentor's departure, Quattrone was about to have his best year ever. Morgan Stanley, which had sold a meager $203 million worth of technology stock in 1990, would sell $5.8 billion in eighteen IPOs in 1995, the most of any underwriter.

Most of them were fairly forgettable. But one was the issue that awakened not just Wall Street but all of America to the potential of the Internet—Netscape Communications Corporation. Netscape would also set the pattern for the frenzy that accompanied scores of IPOs during the dot-com market bubble.

Meeker had read about the company that became Netscape in an article in *The New York Times* on May 7, 1994. Press reports that spring told of an investment by Jim Clark in an Internet browser company called Mosaic. A sandy-haired Stanford engineer with a wide grin, Clark wore wire-framed spectacles but had a taste for adventure, from rides in high-performance jets to open-ocean yachting.[1] He had formed Silicon Graphics to offer three-dimensional computer images for Hollywood special effects and other product designers.

Yet even though the Netscape IPO would put both Meeker and Quattrone on the map, an account of its birth and early days by Clark—contained in a 1999 book he co-authored called *Netscape Time*—suggests some of the credit also should have gone to Dick Fisher, Morgan Stanley's top executive.

"I called Morgan Stanley," Clark wrote, "because they had taken Silicon Graphics public, and I really liked Dick Fisher, the chairman of Morgan Stanley, because he had taken genuine interest in Silicon Graphics when it was going public back in 1986."

Clark soon heard rumors that his rival Spyglass, whose browser was going to be bundled with Microsoft's Windows 95, was going public. Once he knew that Spyglass was in the pipeline, Clark said, "going public as soon as we could was clearly the right move." At that point, he said, "I wanted to move as fast as possible."[2]

"The big risk," Quattrone recalled later, "was that Microsoft would bundle a browser in the next version of its Windows operating system"—which could happen as early as September 1995.[3] Given the commanding presence of Windows in personal computers, such a move threatened to crush Netscape.

On June 27, 1995, the IPO of rival Spyglass surged 60 percent on its first day of trading. Spyglass may have had a contract with Microsoft, but "we had a product that was far better and ten times faster," Clark said. "If Spyglass could score a successful IPO, we had to get our asses in gear."

The soonest they could get to market would be August, the "dog days," when many investors were on vacation. Despite "conventional wisdom [that] no company can go public in August," Quattrone thought investors "would show up for this one."

"Damn the torpedoes," Clark said.

Expectation quickly began building. GOING GAGA OVER TECH STOCKS, *USA Today* said on July 7, warning about the ill that had befallen 3DO investors. NETSCAPE MAY LAUNCH STOCK ROCKET, the Portland *Oregonian* said on July 26. At its proposed price of $12 to $14 a share, the Netscape offering would value the whole company at $477 million. With six-month sales of just $17 million, *Computer Business Review* said on August 1, the IPO "will be asking analysts and fund managers to tear up the textbook on valuation."

When the Netscape road show hit the Grand Ballroom of New York's Plaza Hotel in early August, former Morgan Stanley analyst Andy Kessler dropped in. "If you looked closely before the presentations started, you would have seen a guy in an ill-fitting pinstripe suit, a cheap Casio watch and a mustache in need of trimming. Frankie Q scanned the room, knowing the event was a defining event for his technology group. Arms folded, with a Mona Lisa smirk on his face, he would greet the occasional institutional investor with a quick hello. He knew the only reason they were paying homage is that they hoped to get an allocation of shares in what was clearly going to be a hot, hot, hot IPO, sure to pop after trading began."[4]

Quattrone knew would-be Netscape investors were looking for the next Microsoft, which had gone public nine years earlier. "A lot of people had missed out on the Microsoft IPO because they didn't believe in PCs and they didn't believe in software," he recalled in 2005. Morgan Stanley was happy to position Netscape, as Quattrone put it, as the opportunity to be the standard-bearer, "the Microsoft of this new era."[5]

"Netscape is going to be a monster," an analyst on August 7 told Dow Jones News Service. INVESTORS IN FRENZY, the *San Francisco Chronicle* said August 8. Just before the offering, Morgan Stanley boosted the number of shares being sold to 5 million from 3.5, and raised the price range to $21 to $24.

The runaway investor demand pushed the Netscape offering price to $28, and still the shares soared on August 9 in what the Associated Press called "one of the most stunning debuts in recent stock market history." They first traded at $71 and hit a peak of $75 before closing at $58.25, up an extraordinary 108 percent.

"The closest thing to it that Morgan Stanley had seen was Apple's IPO in 1980," Quattrone recalled a decade later. "Everyone wanted this one. It was a trophy, the thing you had to get to be able to talk at cocktail parties."[6] Tom Brokaw, the TV anchor, said he managed to get two hundred shares through brokers at Morgan Stanley and Allen & Co.[7]

As *The New York Times* noted, the fifteen-month-old company had "never made a dime of profit," yet the $161 million offering valued the entire company at $2.2 billion. *The Wall Street Journal* wryly observed that it had taken General Dynamics Corporation forty-three years to achieve a market value that size.

Yet Quattrone still chafed at the relative lack of status accorded technology at Morgan Sanley. That week, Morgan Stanley was selling a much larger stock issue for a tractor company named J.I. Case, Quattrone said. "And they were having a tough time getting that sold. So even though this event was maybe one of the most important events in the history of the technology industry, at Morgan Stanley it wasn't even the most important offering that day. It was, 'yeah that one is easy, so let's get it out. What we really need to focus on is selling tractors, baby.' "[8]

Unlike many other dot-com stocks that would follow, Netscape made big money for investors. In 1999, it was acquired by America Online in a $4.3 billion stock swap; by the time it closed later that year, the purchase valued Netscape at $10 billion.

O

Netscape had put Quattrone's team at the pinnacle of what would soon become the market's most powerful force. As it did, it also sharpened Quattrone's belief that the organization didn't give him sufficient credit. And, increasingly, he chafed at the controls it imposed on him.

Just as the Netscape frenzy was nearing a crescendo, on July 31, 1995, Carter McClelland joined Deutsche Bank AG. The big German bank was making plans for its securities unit, Deutsche Morgan Grenfell, to expand in the United States, with McClelland at the helm. Deutsche was one of several European banks that wanted more heft in the United States. The reason: That's where the money was. Not only had the U.S. stock market been rising relentlessly in the 1990s, but U.S. mutual funds were surging in size as well.

From the moment McClelland left in January, Quattrone had been complaining more. One time when Kessler ran into him, Quattrone "voiced his frustration with the powers-that-be in New York," Kessler said, "He had this incredibly successful 'boutique-within-a-bulge bracket firm,' he owned Silicon Valley, but he couldn't hire more bankers, couldn't influence their bonuses, couldn't hire the analysts he wanted to bring in more deals, couldn't get the sales force to focus on his deals versus paper companies or all the other industrial crap that Morgan Stanley was deleveraging."[9]

Quattrone believed that the front-office executives didn't understand how fast the market was growing, how winning a small IPO for a client could lead to ten larger transactions over the next five years, and how the number of research analysts needed to expand as the banking head count rose.

On visits to headquarters in 1995 and 1996, Quattrone carried in his jacket pocket a piece of paper that quantified all the revenues he believed his team had generated: fees for underwriting and merger advice; brokerage commissions on technology stocks; and fees Morgan Stanley brokers earned from the wealthy technology entrepreneurs who were his clients. "It was an enormous number," said one executive who saw it.

Quattrone told the firm's executives in New York that he should have a payout based on the revenues he was responsible for. Fisher, Mack, and others all heard versions of the same appeal. And they all told Quattrone that the firm's culture didn't allow such deals. Compensation was subjective, they replied, and would always depend partly on how the entire firm was doing.

Instead, Quattrone wanted all of his team members—bankers, analysts, traders, capital-markets people, and brokers who served the wealthy technology entrepreneurs he brought in the door—to report to him, like a true firm-within-a-firm. But the New York executives believed Quattrone didn't give enough credit to the Morgan Stanley franchise, its great traders and sales people. "He didn't see the world that way," said one banker. "He really believed, and was vocal in articulating it, that it was him."

When he became head of investment banking in 1995, Bob Scott assumed the responsibility of dealing with someone who had by then become a high-maintenance diva. In a series of meetings over Quattrone's last eighteen months at the firm, Scott tried to explain to Quattrone why he couldn't get exactly what he wanted. A couple of times he and Quattrone had dinner at an Italian restaurant in Menlo Park. The bearded Scott, who resembled film director George Lucas, sought to assure Quattrone that his was an important business, and that Morgan Stanley wanted to support it. He was by then the highest paid investment banker at the firm, with his 1995 pay of $6 million.

The firm also had other star bankers in telecommunications, pharmaceuticals, and utilities, and it was annoying to have to spend so much time focusing on Quattrone. Stop asking for a special deal, Scott told him. *We're managing a whole team here. I've got hundreds of really good people. Put yourself in my place. If you were me, what would you do?* Scott asked him.

Quattrone refused to look at it that way. *I'm not you,* he replied to Scott. *It's your problem, not mine.*

A person close to Quattrone disputed this account of the Scott meetings. The Quattrone version was: Quattrone was about to leave for Lazard Freres & Co. when Scott got the job. Scott asked Quattrone "what it would take" for him to stay, the Quattrone associate says. "Frank outlined his concerns and issues and Scott agreed. Frank memorialized the points of understanding in a memo (wanting to be sure there was a paper trail if Scott switched jobs), which he placed in the personnel files. A year later Scott reneged on the deal, and that was the straw that broke the camel's back."

A person close to Scott called the Quattrone account "pure fiction."

Discussing his reasons for leaving Morgan Stanley years later, Quattrone said, "Our group was more efficient and profitable than the other groups at Morgan Stanley, but we were still asked to keep our head count flat." The tech practice added forty to fifty new clients a year, and its revenues had grown from $30 million to $150 million with a flat head count. Yet when Quattrone asked for two more junior associates, he was turned down.[10]

"This was one of the straws that broke the camel's back," Quattrone told Anthony and Michael Perkins, authors of *The Internet Bubble*, published in 1999. He said he had been turned down by "the assistant to the associate drone in charge of new associates." In a separate interview with Robert Lenzner of *Forbes*, he said, "I could not hire the people I wanted because of head counts. I had no direct control over the pay or the promotions of my people. And I spent half my time fending off offers to my team."[11]

Pay was a big issue. Meeker shared the banker's frustration. "There was always some reason our business success didn't translate into personal success," Quattrone said in 1998. "If we did well, another group didn't."[12] At another point he said, "I had a business that was doubling and tripling, and I wasn't getting paid for it."[13]

Interviewed a few years later, at the height of his career, by journalist John Heilemann, Quattrone cast himself as the heroic underdog. Proudly describing how he built the tech practice at Morgan Stanley and his rise in Silicon Valley, Quattrone said, "I was this crazy pioneer pushing this big rock up this really big hill." Describing his demands for autonomy and money, he said, "I told them, our business is real different, our clients are real different, so we've got to approach things differently. But the people at Morgan Stanley just didn't get it."[14]

THE DREAM TEAM

11

IN THE SPRING of 1996, some of Morgan Stanley's real estate people began picking up rumors that Deutsche Bank was negotiating a lease on new space near Palo Alto. Although some thought the space might be for Quattrone's group, they couldn't find out for sure.

Around the same time, Quattrone made a formal proposal to Mack and Fisher in Fisher's office that Morgan Stanley give him a revenue pool that he would control, authority over some tech research analysts, and a share of the trading revenues in stocks whose IPOs Quattrone had brought in.

Fisher, a granite-jawed executive with straight iron gray hair, resembled the actor Rod Steiger. The leg braces and crutches required from his childhood bout with polio enhanced his air of dignity and seriousness. Yet he also had a plainspoken, easygoing candor that helped him address and resolve the thorniest issues.

Fisher felt he didn't have to confer with Mack before replying. *We just don't do that,* Fisher told Quattrone. *It's so far from what we believe in, the way we treat each other. We don't have deals. There's nobody that has a share of their revenues.* When the session was over, Fisher and Mack were pretty sure Quattrone was going to leave.

By then Quattrone had seen so much entrepreneurial activity in the Valley, and so much wealth created, that McClelland's offer to join him at the German bank's securities unit, Deutsche Morgan Grenfell, was almost irresistible. It gave Quattrone's team almost everything he was seeking at Morgan Stanley—a dedicated revenue pool, a 50 percent employee ownership stake in the technology banking group he would create at DMG, and lucrative up-front pay guarantees.

"Frankly, a bunch of us were 35 to 40 years old, and we had seen a lot of our clients start companies and pursue their dreams," Quattrone told the Perkins brothers for their book, *The Internet Bubble*. He added, "It was our time to share in the American dream."[1]

○

Shortly after noon on Thursday April 4, 1996, just before Easter weekend, Quattrone began placing calls to Morgan Stanley executives informing them of his resignation. Some of the bankers later concluded that Quattrone had timed the calls to allow himself the weekend to woo other staffers he wanted to take with him. The following day, the *San Francisco Chronicle* detailed his plans to form what he called a "technology dream team."[2] The name was a play on the 1992 U.S. Olympic basketball team, which featured top pro stars.

"I wanted the flexibility and autonomy to make decisions and build the technology dream team," Quattrone said later. "We're going to create a new kind of investment bank, which has the expertise of a boutique, but is strapped to the infrastructure of a global powerhouse like Deutsche Bank."[3]

The Morgan Stanley headquarters had, only a few months earlier, moved to a blue-and-gray skyscraper located at the north end of Times Square on Broadway and West Forty-seventh Street. Gaudy on the outside, with a giant news ticker and stock quotes running around the lower floors, the building is modern and austere inside, its lobby a mix of polished marble and brushed metal. But the building was emptying out for the holiday weekend, and some executives had already departed.

When Quattrone called Joe Perella, Morgan Stanley's head of corporate finance, early that afternoon, Perella was on a plane to Florida for the weekend. He happened to be phoning the office at the time, and his deputy, Tarek "Terry" Meguid, patched him through to Quattrone.

Are you sitting down? Quattrone asked.

Not only am I sitting down, I'm strapped in, Perella wisecracked.

Guys, I've decided to resign from the firm, and I want to thank you for everything you've done for me, Quattrone told them. He was leaving to join Deutsche Bank, he explained.

Perella breathed a sigh of relief. Because Deutsche Bank had such a slight capability in stock sales and trading, he believed it would be difficult for Quattrone to win IPO business there—a big part of tech banking.

Well, Frank, Perella said, *I'm sure you have high hopes. But I guarantee you it's not going to turn out the way you think it's going to turn out.*

Meguid (rhymes with "agreed") quickly put the call on hold while Quattrone and Perella spoke and made a reservation for himself and another senior banker on the next flight they could catch to California. In quick succession, Brady and

Boutros phoned in their resignations as well. Perella dropped his wife off in Florida and arranged to fly out to California the next day.

O

Meeker and Chuck Phillips, who followed enterprise software and covered Oracle, were attending a Netscape analysts' conference in California when their beepers went off. In rapid succession, Meeker got calls from Quattrone and Fisher. Quattrone was quick to apologize that he had been advised not to solicit too many of his colleagues before the resignation. He wanted her to join what he called "a technology dream team" at Deutsche. As Meeker took in the details of what was happening, she paced in the parking lot. *Does this really have to happen?* she asked.

When Fisher spoke to the analysts, he told them, *If you feel the way Frank does, you need to know we will never do that. The way we run our business is, we all get our turn. Your job is, when your industry is hot, you step up. When your industry is quiet and nothing is going on, one of your partners steps up. Breaking that model as Quattrone proposed,* Fisher said, *breeds instability.* Fisher believed that creating such separate, independent units had a lot to do with problems that emerged at Drexel Burnham Lambert Inc., with the junk bond unit run by Michael Milken.

After piecing the events together, some Morgan Stanley executives concluded later that Quattrone's plan was first to get George Kelly, the elder statesman who covered communications equipment, and then Meeker and Phillips. The analysts were vital to the firm's banking-client relationships with companies they covered, including Cisco, America Online, Netscape, and Oracle.

Kelly had been at a trade show in Las Vegas that Thursday. He was just boarding a flight back to Newark airport when calls came in from Quattrone and then Mayree Clark, the firm's head of research. Clark, who got the news at headquarters at 1585 Broadway, jumped in a car and headed for the airport. Kelly had been working on the largest IPO in history, a $3 billion offering by Lucent Technologies Inc., the former equipment unit of AT&T. Clark's husband, Jeffrey Williams, was the lead Morgan Stanley banker on Lucent, whose IPO *had just been completed that week.* The Lucent deal had been a huge success, and they all knew it meant a lot to Kelly, who had worked at AT&T. Quattrone's chances of snaring Kelly before it was done would have been remote.

Clark sat with Kelly at the airport for an hour. Kelly said Quattrone had reached out to contact him during the previous week. He knew something about Quattrone's deal with DMG, which he relayed to Clark, but he didn't have the whole story. Quattrone had called him just before he got on the plane, but he was a little surprised that he hadn't heard more. Clark urged Kelly to stay in a dialogue with the firm before he made any final decision about joining Quattrone.

Quattrone, who had been in New York when he quit, had dinner with Kelly that night. He said he had been under orders from the Deutsche people not to solicit the analysts in advance. Kelly knew that Quattrone had a vision of creating a boutique within a large investment bank.

The offers to Kelly, Meeker, and Phillips were all in the same ballpark. The offers kept getting better and better as the weekend wore on and Quattrone wasn't getting the quick close he expected. They could expect to double or triple their pay—*at least.*

Kelly was older than the others. He had worked at IBM for fourteen years and for two at AT&T before going to Wall Street, joining Morgan Stanley in 1984. He enjoyed the group marketing trips, the esprit de corps of the research ensemble. He also knew that Quattrone didn't want all of the Morgan Stanley tech analysts.

Kelly told Quattrone he wanted to think about it.

In California, Meeker and Phillips had dinner with Bill Brady at the Hyatt Regency, just south of the San Francisco airport. Brady tried to convince them to join the dream team. Meeker's response: *Is this final? Do you definitely have to do this? Bill, why don't you stay?* Brady seemed taken aback by the reaction.

○

Meguid, the deputy corporate finance chief, flew to San Francisco with Cordell "Cory" Spencer, the chief operating officer of the merger department. Landing at 8:30 P.M. Thursday, Meguid and Spencer took a cab to Palo Alto. The next morning, Meguid and Spencer showed up at the Morgan Stanley tech group offices in Menlo Park, in a crescent on Sand Hill Road.

Meguid was a charming half-Irish, half-Egyptian banker whose father was an economist at the World Bank. First he spent an hour with semiconductor banker John Hodge, a college swimmer from Buffalo who had also attended Stanford. *How can you go to Deutsche Bank?* Meguid asked. *Those guys are nowhere.* Deutsche Bank ranked number twenty in U.S. stock and bond underwriting in 1996. *Frank thinks he can duplicate what we have here at Morgan, but you know he can't.*

Then Meguid introduced himself to Michael Grimes, who had just been recruited eight months earlier from Bear Stearns. He gave Grimes the same pitch. Then he went back to Hodge. Then he spoke with Andrew ("Drew") Guevara, another banker. He felt like an emergency-room doctor doing triage on multiple patients. Although Perella arrived later that day, it was becoming clear that some of the bankers would indeed join Quattrone, Boutros, and Brady.

○

At her weekend house in New Canaan, Connecticut, Clark kept track of each analyst, trying to find a leverage point. *Do you speak German?* she would ask them. None did. With Meeker and Kelly on the fence, it seemed that Chuck Phillips might be the hardest to replace. The good news was, he was aligned with another analyst Quattrone wasn't trying to recruit. But if too many bankers left, the analysts might grow fearful about their own ability to get paid.

By Sunday, Meguid had nailed down Grimes, and Bob Scott had persuaded Jim Liang, an East Cost technology banker, to stay. Paul Chamberlain, a New York capital-markets staffer who had grown up in Palo Alto, also agreed to stay, as did Guevara. Grimes and the others staying helped persuade the analysts to stay, some Morgan Stanley executives believed.

Some of the analysts felt they *were* underpaid. Meeker was sorely tempted, but didn't want to be the only one to leave. She felt there was safety in numbers. At one point Meeker visited the Deutsche Bank offices in midtown Manhattan.

This is a German bank, Meeker thought. *The offer is to work with Frank Quattrone at a bank with headquarters in Frankfurt. What if he starts focusing on revenues at the expense of quality?* When she walked downstairs to visit the trading desk, she noticed people with British and German accents, smoking. It felt like a European bank.

At Deutsche Bank, Meeker could certainly work with great bankers. But Morgan Stanley had a great sales force, research franchise, trading desk, and brand name. She had written a landmark research report on the Internet in late 1995, which was being published as a hardcover book.

Meeker had a pivotal conversation with Perella, who had worked on Wall Street for more than twenty-five years. *The thing that's great about a firm like Morgan Stanley,* he told her, *it has a lot of checks and balances. In any given year, sales and trading, research and banking are not always in perfect alignment. Don't underestimate the power of the culture at a place like Morgan Stanley.*

O

As the analysts spoke among themselves that weekend, they came to an unspoken consensus that they would either all go or all stay. One of the junior analysts called Kelly and said, *Just let me know where I should report on Monday morning.*

On Saturday night, Kelly, Meeker, and Phillips had a conference call. Kelly was adamantly opposed to leaving. He believed that the Morgan Stanley research sales force gave them all a leg up by putting out their views to clients in an organized way. Deutsche Bank didn't have a big sales force, and building one might require a year or two. Without one, Kelly feared, they could get bogged down by too many calls with investors.

As they spoke, the others were inclined to stay as well. On Easter Sunday afternoon, Clark arranged for Kelly to speak with Mack, who asked him for a commitment. *I'm going to stay,* Kelly said.

Kelly broke the news to Quattrone on Easter Sunday night. Quattrone was disappointed. *What would it take? What would I have to do?* Quattrone asked him. Kelly replied that the decision was final. Later that same night, McClelland called Kelly for a postmortem. They spoke twice. *Are we touching all the bases?* McClelland asked.

Years later, Quattrone said that Kelly, Meeker, and Phillips had "chickened out" of leaving with him. "We did DMG partly because these analysts felt so frustrated at Morgan Stanley. I fielded their complaints constantly. If I had known all of them would stay at Morgan Stanley, I wouldn't have left the bank."[4]

AMAZON

12

THE DREAM TEAM landed with a splash at Deutsche Bank in April 1996.

"Our mission is to build the world's premier global full-service investment banking practice for technology companies," Quattrone said. He had "a different vision" than Morgan Stanley. "I've been evangelizing that the technology industry is not like any other in the sheer number of companies, rapid growth rate and the pace of change." He wanted his group to be "a pure play on technology," so they could share more of the rewards and risks of underwriting and merger advice.

The DMG arrangement was "the best of both worlds," Boutros said. "We could do something entrepreneurial but have the infrastructure, commitment and resources of a large financial institution behind us."[1]

The dream team began to live large. Quattrone soon paid $6.3 million for a weekend ocean-view home on the famed Pebble Beach golf course, a ninety-minute drive south. The scenery was breathtaking, and Quattrone's golf-course neighbors included other San Francisco titans, such as discount brokerage boss Charles Schwab and Scott McNealy, the chief executive of Sun Microsystems.[2]

Not only did Quattrone host numerous client events at the course and his house, he also eventually featured the golfing theme in the names of the rooms at his office, with one named the Cypress Room after the Cypress Point course near Pebble Beach.

O

The Quattrone group got off to a sputtering start at Deutsche Bank. In July 1996, they led a $103 million stock offering for a small software developer, Wind River Systems Inc., which was already public. And they launched a $43 million IPO in December of Puma Technology Inc. Their boss, Carter McClelland, said he hoped to make similar group hires in other business sectors, such as health care, media, or financial services.[3]

But they lost the lead on a $301 million follow-on stock sale in November by their biggest calling-card client, Netscape. The browser company stuck with Morgan Stanley as the lead, with DMG relegated to a co-lead spot. Less than two months later, Bill Gurley, a six-foot-nine-inch former Florida University basketball player who covered Internet stocks for Quattrone, downgraded Netscape, sending the stock plummeting 18 percent in a single day. Quattrone didn't try to talk him out of it.[4]

Quattrone would cite Gurley's Netscape downgrade four years later as evidence that his analysts weren't always blindly bullish on clients. But the move could also have been read as a warning shot that his analysts might feel freer to downgrade stocks of companies that didn't stick with his team.

And unlike at Morgan Stanley, where the Quattrone bankers usually refused to serve as comanagers, at DMG they initially accepted such assignments. And even when they did, such as on a $60 million IPO of E*Trade Group Inc., they had to suffer criticism of DMG's weak trading capacity. "Their distribution isn't where I'd like it to be," said Christos Cotsakos, E*Trade's CEO. "They haven't traded our stock as much as we would like."[5] There was also tension with the DMG traders, who had to share some of their revenue with Quattrone's group.

Quattrone won the E*Trade comanager spot with a valuation strategy he often pursued after leaving Morgan Stanley. In the E*Trade bake-off, his group suggested the online broker deserved a valuation much higher than proposed by other investment banks.

Within six months Quattrone had hired ninety people, including twenty from Morgan Stanley. By the end of 1996, the DMG tech group had racked up revenues of just $20 million, while incurring startup costs, including first-year guarantees for Quattrone and Company, of $40 million. Quattrone said his quest was "a long-term goal, a marathon."[6]

But in early 1997, an article in *The Wall Street Journal* noted that DMG's "effort to buy its way into one of the most competitive businesses anywhere hasn't always worked as it was supposed to."[7] One of the story's authors, Anita Raghavan, sparring jokingly with Quattrone on the phone before the story ran, said she would "eat crow" if the group started doing big deals at Deutsche Bank.

O

But then a conflict at Morgan Stanley opened the door for a true marquee deal that would validate the Quattrone group's efforts.

Amazon.com took its name from the fact that the Amazon River, the world's largest, is six times the size of the next largest river. Amazon proclaimed that it offered six times as many titles as the biggest bricks-and-mortar bookstore. Founded in 1994 by a former hedge fund manager, Jeff Bezos, with venture backing from Kleiner Perkins, Amazon signaled in January 1997 that it was preparing to go public.

Meeker wanted to get the Amazon deal for Morgan Stanley. But Morgan Stanley had done banking work for Amazon's biggest rival, the bricks-and-mortar bookstore chain Barnes & Noble Inc. Morgan Stanley's CEO, Dick Fisher, had gotten to know Barnes & Noble CEO Leonard Riggio when the bookseller's largest shareholder, Vendex International NV, wanted to reduce its Barnes & Noble stake, and a Morgan Stanley fund made an investment in the company. Subsequently, in 1993, Morgan Stanley led the bookseller's IPO.

Amazon, of course, represented serious competition to Barnes & Noble. When Fisher called Riggio to see if he had any objection to Morgan Stanley leading the Amazon IPO, Riggio did object. Morgan Stanley's own analyst, Mary Meeker, thought the concept was a good one, Fisher told Riggio. *I bet I can talk her out of that*, Riggio said. Fisher then arranged a meeting in his conference room between Meeker, Riggio, and Riggio's chief financial officer, Irene Miller. There Riggio said he believed he could actually beat Amazon in online book sales. But Meeker, Riggio noticed, was "full of Amazon."[8]

Meeker still wanted Morgan Stanley to lead the Amazon deal even after the lunch, fearing that Quattrone would get the IPO and its associated bragging rights if Morgan Stanley passed. But Fisher and a banking conflicts committee ruled in favor of Barnes & Noble. Morgan Stanley nevertheless tried to keep the Amazon IPO away from Quattrone and Deutsche Bank by offering to serve as comanager . . . as long as Goldman Sachs were chosen as lead. It didn't work. The Morgan Stanley decision making wasn't motivated by sheer idealism: Around the same time, Barnes & Noble chose Morgan Stanley to lead a $62 million stock offering in late March 1997.

Joy Covey, Amazon's chief financial officer, held the Amazon IPO bake-off at the sleek, glass-and-blond-wood offices of Kleiner Perkins.[9] Juliet Wilson, an assistant to Quattrone's Internet analyst, Bill Gurley, came up with a last-minute idea that helped put DMG over the top: binding the pitch book as though it were a real hardcover book.[10] At the pitch, Gurley compared Amazon to Dell Computer, which had taken on traditional personal-computer retailers much as Amazon was taking on bookstores.

For Quattrone, the victory over his former employer was sweet. When Kessler asked him about the rumors that Morgan Stanley had turned down the lead role, Quattrone jeered, "That's funny, when I ran into Mary and those bankers in [the] lobby as we finished our pitch, it sure seemed like they wanted to do the deal."[11]

The Amazon IPO duly surged 31 percent in price on May 15, 1997, its first day of trading.

When Gurley soon announced his departure to join a venture capital firm, Lise Buyer, a petite energetic tech analyst at mutual-fund group T. Rowe Price, in Baltimore, moved to California to take his place. A graduate of Wellesley College and Vanderbilt business school, she would become Quattrone's go-to Internet analyst early in the bubble. One of the first events she attended after joining was an elaborate weekend closing celebration for the Amazon IPO at the posh La Palmilla seaside resort in Los Cabos, Mexico. At one beach dinner for thirty, she recalls, a big wave came in and took out the entire dessert table.[12]

Soon after winning the Amazon assignment, Quattrone sent *Journal* reporter Anita Raghavan a picnic basket. Inside it were cutlery and a plate, a bottle of wine . . . and a stuffed black-fabric crow. Quattrone enclosed a note explaining that he was also including a disposable camera so she could send him a picture of her eating "the fowl meal you volunteered to consume."[13]

THE SENATOR

13

IN LATE 1996, Quattrone met with John Schmidt in his office at the DMG tech group's offices in Menlo Park. Quattrone had gotten word to Schmidt that he was interested in bringing a team of brokers into his group to manage accounts for wealthy investment banking clients. He asked Schmidt how he would go about building such a group.

One of the most upsetting calls Quattrone had ever received at Morgan Stanley, he explained to Schmidt, was from Tom Perkins of Kleiner Perkins, the prominent venture capital firm. Perkins had been irate that his broker at Morgan Stanley had made an obvious mistake on a sell order in Perkins's personal account. The mistake could have cost Perkins tens of thousands of dollars. But because the broker didn't work for him, there was only so much Quattrone could do to resolve the mix-up.

In all, three senior technology executives had had problems with their brokers at Morgan Stanley that hurt their relationship with the firm. As a result, Quattrone wanted to make sure he had control over the quality and responsiveness of such brokerage services.

Schmidt, whose father owned a Cincinnati coal distributor, wound up on Wall Street via the U.S. Treasury Department. After graduating from Georgetown University, where he was a classmate of Bill Clinton, he had managed a $5 billion debt portfolio for the Federal Home Loan Banks in the early 1970s. After managing money at United Airlines and trading bonds at Crocker Bank, he became deputy assistant secretary of the treasury for debt management in the Carter administration.

The bulk of Schmidt's Wall Street career, between 1981 and 1994, had been spent in San Francisco at First Boston Corporation, later known as Credit Suisse First Boston, where he was the regional manager for institutional sales. Schmidt put down roots in the community. His wife, Sharon, was an accomplished horsewoman. And Schmidt became a figure in the local establishment, serving as a governor of the National Association of Securities Dealers in the mid-1990s.

Schmidt left CSFB in 1994 when his branch manager job was eliminated; First Boston had reorganized its management away from geographical lines and more toward business-unit lines. The firm's elimination of the branch manager jobs signaled a weakening of internal controls that would come back to haunt Quattrone. Schmidt then went to Lehman Brothers and ran a group of San Francisco brokers catering to the wealthy, which were known as private-client services brokers.

Schmidt already knew from reading the newspaper that Quattrone was on a roll. During the lunch, Quattrone showed Schmidt the first PalmPilot he had ever seen. *You've got to see this thing*, Quattrone told him. Schmidt agreed that brokers' mix-ups with sensitive clients often generated problems for bankers. The issue was always which department would have to eat the loss if a broker made a mistake in a big client's account.

Schmidt was enthusiastic about setting up a group of brokers to serve Quattrone's clients. The brokers would be able to piggyback on Quattrone's relationships to drum up business. The disadvantage, it would later become clear, was that they couldn't be supervised as easily by the front office in New York.

At Lehman, Schmidt told Quattrone, he had already been able to ride bankers' coattails to get new business. Lehman had led an IPO in November 1995 for Advanced Energy Industries Inc. With an introduction from the Lehman bankers, the Schmidt team had opened personal accounts for some of Advanced Energy's senior officers. The brokers also managed the company's cash balances and a "directed-share" program to allocate IPO shares to investors with commercial ties to the company. During the bubble, such programs became known as "friends and family" shares.

The feedback that Lehman got from the company was "very positive," Schmidt told Quattrone.

In early 1997, Schmidt sat down for a lunch with Quattrone's boss, Carter McClelland, and suggested making a team of private-client brokers part of the technology banking team. McClelland sat back and thought. *That's a very intriguing idea*, he told Schmidt. *I'm trying to think if there's anything wrong with it.*

McClelland's instinctive questions were well founded. Hiring his own group of brokers ultimately backfired spectacularly on Quattrone. Although the manager of Deutsche Bank's existing brokers initially objected to Schmidt working outside his organization, Quattrone eventually got his way.

O

On April 1, 1997, Schmidt reported to the tech group offices in Menlo Park for his first day at work. Tall, distinguished looking, square-jawed, gray-haired, at age fifty he was resplendent in his customary downtown banker's formal, pin-striped suit. As he looked around, he noticed that most of his fellow employees wore jeans and polo shirts and looked like they were in their twenties. Quat-trone himself cultivated his own funky, non–Wall Street style, with jazzy zigzag sweaters instead of pinstripes. It wasn't long before Schmidt became known around the office as "The Senator." Schmidt, who lived in the town of Lafayette across the Bay Bridge from downtown, eventually set up his group in offices downtown, with the analysts, institutional sales people, and merger bankers in-stead of joining Quattrone further south.

Schmidt worked with the Amazon staff on a small directed-share program as part of that IPO. He hired a trio of his former Lehman colleagues—Rob Horning, Dave Leyrer, and Will Weathersby—who brought their own clients as well. Operating outside an existing brokerage organization, Schmidt had to create many documents and systems to build the business from scratch. It was the most fun he'd had in years.

While at Lehman, Schmidt had come into contact with a few semiprofes-sional traders, a genre that became known during the bubble as "day traders." They didn't manage money for others but they traded more actively than if they were just saving for their own financial needs, such as school tuitions and retirement. Schmidt believed such active accounts came in handy for those lean times when he was under pressure to generate trading commissions. They also tended to be steady buyers of new issues.

At the DMG unit of Deutsche Bank, Schmidt began opening accounts with a handful of these traders, including James Lustig. Lustig, a man with a mustache in his forties from Denver, traded under the official-sounding name of United Capital Management, but most of the money belonged to him and his family.

As the year 1997 progressed, the Schmidt group worked on more IPOs. Once a company going public had chosen DMG as its banker, the Schmidt brokers would typically go in and talk to the company's senior management, both about their existing investments and about the eventual sales of their own stock in the company going public. Many of the executives were receptive to opening new accounts.

The Schmidt team eventually opened accounts for several executives of six companies that DMG had either taken public or done other work for. They included: Naren Gupta, vice chairman of Wind River Systems; Brad Rowe, the chief executive of Puma Technology Inc.; and several executives of Artisan Components Inc. All three companies were clients of DMG.[1]

It was this group that eventually mushroomed into some 285 "Friends of Frank" accounts, receiving a stream of sizzling hot IPOs during the bubble. Regulators would later charge that the hot stocks were an improper gratuity awarded as a lure for more investment banking business.

O

Meanwhile, the Quattrone technology banking group was heading toward a $200 million revenue year in 1997 at Deutsche Bank. Not bad considering that they were on a far less impressive platform than the blue-chip Morgan Stanley franchise, and had to live by their own wits. In addition to the Amazon.com IPO, the group led another half dozen IPOs and advised on several sizable mergers. But the instability of the Deutsche Bank platform soon became a problem.

In the spring of 1997, rumors about the size of the tech group members' paychecks started spreading within the rest of DMG. In the summer of 1997, Asian currency markets were roiled by a series of devaluations, starting with a "battle of the baht" in Thailand. Worse for Quattrone, the political star of his mentor, Carter McClelland, began to fade.[2]

In the fourth quarter, the currency turmoil caught up with DMG, cutting in half the $620 million in profit the securities unit had racked up in the first nine months of the year. This caused the parent company's executives to reassess a 27 percent increase in the bank's costs, fueled mainly by the DMG buildup.[3]

At first glance, the technology group's numbers looked excellent. As its head count raced toward 150 people, the group had posted 1997 revenues of $208 million. After costs of $65 million, that left $143 million in profits to be split 50-50 between Quattrone's team and DMG.[4]

But word had gotten around the German bank that Quattrone's guarantee for that year was $7.5 million. With his team sharing a bonus pool of $70 million, there were rumors that his total pay was even higher. There was no doubt that Quattrone's group was doing well. But the Deutsche executives soon determined to reshape his group's contract.[5]

O

In January 1998, Deutsche Bank board member Ronaldo Schmitz sent Quattrone a fax. The board wanted to talk to him, it said, about the group's financial results and "contribution to the performance of the bank." McClelland and Boutros also attended the Frankfurt showdown.[6] Schmitz told them he wanted to renegotiate the Quattrone group's deal.

Boutros replied heatedly. Although he had a heavy-handed negotiating style, he was well respected in the Valley, and regarded as a decent guy outside the office. "I negotiate contracts for a living," Boutros said. "You uphold contracts."

Quattrone chimed in: "All we did was achieve our 2000 results three years early. Instead of throwing us a ticker-tape parade, you're looking at us as villains."

The German executives, Quattrone believed, wanted more of the group's profits. "We didn't pull the wool over their eyes. This deal had been studied to death by senior management," he said the following summer. "It's irrational to me, but it rubbed them the wrong way to see our level of reward. I don't think they ever thought the numbers would go that high." As a result, Quattrone said, the German bank spread the word to its other employees that the technology group's sky-high paychecks were coming out of their pockets.

The bigger blow was that Deutsche Bank abandoned its expensive U.S. buildup and retreated to what Quattrone called a "Europe-first strategy." It also paid some of its highest paid North American employees in stock in a bid to save cash. And it sidelined McClelland. At the end of February 1998, Mc-Clelland quit. The departure led to a firestorm of rumors that Quattrone would go, too; the *San Jose Mercury News* even published a report that Quattrone was shopping the group to other firms.

On March 13, Quattrone cosigned a letter with Schmitz assuring recipients that he didn't have any plans to follow his mentor out the door. Quattrone vowed: "We are here to stay. Please trust us." (When a *Fortune* reporter observed that something must have happened to spark the rumors of his own departure, Quattrone shot back: "Are you calling me a liar?"[7]) And the tech group set a move-in date of July 10 for its new offices just east of the Stanford campus on Hanover Street.

○

In fact, the group would soon mull its options. The last straw came in April, when Amazon chose Morgan Stanley to raise $325 million in a high-yield, junk bond financing. Quattrone was furious, believing he had been handicapped by Deutsche's weak junk bond capability. "I was ripping my lungs out because we didn't have the ability to do this," he said. Worse, the episode had occurred just weeks after the March "trust-us" letter.[8]

○

Quattrone had built his technology franchise during fifteen years at Morgan Stanley, one of the top securities firms in the United States. During just two years at Deutsche Bank, he had shown he could operate that same franchise from a different platform without the Morgan Stanley organization behind him. It was a bumpier ride perhaps, but there was no doubt that he could repeat his earlier success at a lesser venue. The greatest market ever for the kinds of companies he specialized in was approaching. It would offer him the opportunity to realize his ambitions on an epic scale.

THE BUBBLE

BOOK
TWO

CREDIT SUISSE FIRST BOSTON

14

ALL BUT UNKNOWN to average investors, Credit Suisse First Boston had a storied but tumultuous history.

The firm was born in 1932, when the First of Boston Corporation was established as a subsidiary of the First National Bank of Boston. When Congress separated securities and banking after the scandals following the 1929 market crash, the First Boston Corporation severed its ties to the bank and became the first publicly traded U.S. investment bank. In 1978, First Boston swapped shares with Credit Suisse, a Swiss bank, creating a London operation called Credit Suisse First Boston.

But what really put First Boston on the map in the United States was a merger advisory practice led by Bruce Wasserstein and Joe Perella. From DuPont-Conoco to Texaco-Getty to Bendix-Martin Marietta, the two bankers were in the thick of almost every major 1980s takeover battle. In their glory days, the firm's aquamarine glass headquarters in the heart of midtown Manhattan, which towered over the traditional stone facade of the Racquet and Tennis Club next door on Park Avenue, became a secular temple of yuppie careerism.

But by 1998, CSFB had been rocked by a series of debacles. Wasserstein and Perella left in 1988 to set up their own boutique. CSFB then went private in an employee buyout backed by the Swiss bank, Metropolitan Life Insurance Company, and other investors. A number of takeover bridge loans blew up in 1989, inflicting heavy losses. In a rescue by Credit Suisse, the entire firm was renamed Credit Suisse First Boston, and it suffered a humbling move twenty-five blocks south, outside Midtown, to a less glitzy, almost medieval limestone building—owned by stodgy Met Life. Many employees suffered catastrophic losses on the soured buyout; among them was Schmidt, who almost had to sell his house.

The new CSFB headquarters, which covered an entire block between Madison and Park Avenues at East Twenty-fourth Street, had art deco windows, a dramatic three-story marble lobby, and soaring entry archways at its four corners. The building had a series of six different setbacks that ended abruptly in a squat, sawed-off top at the twenty-ninth floor. The reason for this was that 11 Madison Avenue was originally designed to be, at 100 stories, the world's tallest building—until the 1929 stock market crash curtailed those plans.[1] That itself was a recurring pattern at CSFB—vaulting, grandiose ambition cut short by unexpected disaster.

The firm's Swiss parent, Credit Suisse Group, eventually turned to a derivatives expert from Bankers Trust New York Corporation to turn the troubled securities firm around. His name: Allen Wheat. Wheat created a new unit at the firm, Credit Suisse Financial Products, that sold derivatives and swaps—exotic, custom-tailored contracts with high profit margins—and traded them as well. It was so successful that in 1993, Wheat got the job of CEO of CSFB.

Derivatives were usually valued based on formulas, and employees of CSFP were paid based on the unit's results. And Wheat basically applied that formula-based model, which had worked so well for him, to employee compensation in a series of other businesses within the firm. The results were uneven but profitable enough, and a superstar trading culture prevailed.

This model seemed tailor-made for Quattrone. Wheat liked hiring big stars who could ring the cash register—and he put less emphasis on controlling financial or reputational risks. It was, in a way, the opposite of Morgan Stanley's regimented "one-firm" approach.

In the spring of 1998, Quattrone received phone calls from Wheat and Charles Stonehill, CSFB's deputy head of investment banking.[2] Stonehill was an Oxford graduate who had worked with Quattrone at Morgan Stanley, and he had one of the deepest, plummiest voices on Wall Street. Some colleagues called him "The Baritone." He also met with Stonehill's boss, the man who would be his nominal boss, Charles "Chuck" Ward III, a CSFB veteran who was head of investment banking.

At Deutsche Bank, Quattrone had begun to think that the Germans were not only no longer interested in investing in his group's success, they were actually trying to find loopholes in his contract. On May 28, Deutsche Bank CEO Ronaldo Schmitz sent Quattrone an angry fax, scolding him for rescheduling a meeting with a German client. But Quattrone said that in order to attend the meeting, he or one of his people would have had to skip one of the investor conferences for European clients his own tech group had planned.[3]

Even as he planned his departure, Quattrone tried to keep the group's morale up. One May evening, he serenaded tech group members with "Rocky Raccoon," his theme song, at the group's second anniversary party at a hotel ballroom in Redwood City. He was backed by a band led by venture investor Roger McNamee.[4]

○

After being satisfied that CSFB seemed like the best fit for his group, Quattrone turned his own contract negotiations over to Ken Hausman, his personal attorney, who got Quattrone much of what he wanted in talks with Stonehill, his old colleague.

He got shared authority over the technology stock analysts, which Morgan Stanley had refused. Instead of reporting directly and solely to CSFB's research department, the analysts also reported up to him. He and his top deputies could hire and fire them and, most important, set their pay. As competitors would learn to their dismay, this enabled Quattrone to hire more analysts himself and dispatch them personally to visit companies he was interested in taking public.

He also got similar shared authority a few weeks later over his brokers, and eventually even got his own public relations staff.

Quattrone also wangled an unusually sweet economic deal for his group covering 1999 and 2000—a bonus pool of 40 percent of its "incremental contribution" to the firm's revenue above a certain threshold—and a minimum of $10 million annually for himself.[5] The Quattrone team would also get 10 percent of revenues from trading technology stocks: He convinced CSFB that since he reeled in IPOs, he should share in the spoils that flowed from trading the IPOs and other stocks. Further, there would be a $25 million pool for Quattrone, Boutros, and Brady to invest in venture capital deals.

But CSFB tried to retain some control. Yes, analysts and brokers would primarily report up to Quattrone, but they would also have to report, secondarily, to CSFB staff in New York for certain matters, to give headquarters executives some oversight over their transactions and procedures. CSFB called these "dotted-line" reports.

○

Then came the matter of disengaging from Deutsche Bank.

On Tuesday June 30, 1998, Quattrone sent voice-mail messages to his 160 group members, announcing his departure. He said he was contractually prohibited from contacting his former colleagues for thirty days, but pointed out they were free to approach CSFB. "Good-bye for now," he concluded. That night, a CSFB team met with the Quattrone group staffers at a hotel in Menlo Park, California, so they could brief them. By the time Chuck Ward, CSFB's head of investment banking, left three days later, the CSFB team had interviewed almost all of the group members individually.

At their first meeting that same Tuesday evening at Ricky's Hyatt in Palo Alto, Tony Ehinger, CSFB's head of equity sales, told Schmidt: *You'll like working with our private client group. Andy Benjamin [in New York] runs it.*

Schmidt cut in. *Let me explain something about the [Quattrone private client services] group,* he said. *The way it's worked, we structured ourselves as part of the banking team, and that's kind of the way it's going—the way we want it to be.*

But Ehinger didn't accept that. At CSFB, brokers like Schmidt and his team were part of his empire. No major Wall Street firm had brokers reporting to bankers. *No, no, no,* he said, *that's the way we've got it. PCS reports to me. Andy Benjamin reports to me.* Indeed, most Wall Street firms kept their investment banking and brokerage businesses separate.

Can we discuss this with Frank? Schmidt said.

No, he can't recruit [now], Ehinger replied.

Schmidt had knots in his stomach. He was worried that the close relationships he enjoyed with his clients and with Quattrone could come to an end at CSFB. It wasn't clear that CSFB would let him work for Quattrone. And he didn't know whether Quattrone had even included him and his fellow brokers in his negotiations with CSFB.

○

The Deutsche Bank executives were taken aback by the move. Within days, a group of them sat down with Quattrone, Boutros, and Hausman in the twenty-eighth-floor boardroom at Deutsche Bank's U.S. headquarters at 31 West Fifty-second Street. At first, they just wanted to understand what had happened. "This was not about money," Quattrone said later. Using emergency-room lingo for patients who have died, he explained, "We basically 'called the code' on a marriage that wasn't working."[6]

The abrupt departure, so soon after the "we are here to stay trust us" letter, prompted much chatter in Silicon Valley. An anonymous Valley insider joked to *BusinessWeek* that Quattrone was "the Bill Clinton of Silicon Valley." Quattrone insisted that at the time they wrote that letter, they "absolutely had no intention of leaving."[7] "All I can say is things changed quite a bit."[8] But by mid-July, 132 staffers had jumped from DMG to CSFB. "Unlike at Deutsche Bank, where technology was one of many things they had to do, at First Boston, it was the last thing they needed to do," Quattrone said.[9]

In 1996, CSFB had ranked a lowly number eleven in underwriting technology stocks. In 1997, its ranking had slipped to number fourteen. Quattrone and Brady soon met with Scott Smith, an eccentric former lawyer who had helped lead the CSFB tech practice. When Smith started to give them a run-down on who he thought were the best tech bankers at CSFB, they snorted derisively.

How would you know? they asked. Smith quickly left to found his own technology boutique, Viant Group.

O

One of the last to leave DMG was Schmidt. The delay was apparently caused by some CSFB officials who were "uncomfortable" about Schmidt reporting directly to a top investment banker, namely Quattrone. He and his eight-member team sat twiddling their thumbs at their old desks for weeks, as Quattrone negotiated his formal separation from DMG. Finally, near the end of August, Quattrone got word to Ehinger, Stonehill, and the others that he wanted the brokers as part of his team. They started the next day, September 1, 1998.

Under an unusual and detailed contract, the Schmidt brokers worked first for Quattrone and second for CSFB's head of private-client brokers, Andy Benjamin. Both Quattrone and Benjamin had the right to approve changes to head count or expense rates for the Schmidt brokers. The terms gave CSFB's Benjamin responsibility for review of new brokerage accounts, trading reports, new-issue allocations (including IPOs), approval of expenses and personal trades, monitoring of discretionary accounts, and resolving account coverage.[10]

Benjamin initially raised an objection to a few of Schmidt's trading accounts, among them the Denver-based James Lustig. Benjamin was concerned because he recalled that Lustig had in the past opened multiple accounts at CSFB with different brokers—a sneaky way to get more hot IPOs. They agreed that Lustig could maintain an account with the group, but they put him on watch. Schmidt never spotted any such actions by Lustig, who eventually became his group's top commission-paying account.

The Quattrone brokers would have the right to offer brokerage services to executives of banking clients. They also got a valuable written promise of the right to decide who could buy 2 percent to 4 percent of every new stock issue brought in by Quattrone and his band of bankers—an outsize share.[11]

When he was finally able to talk to Quattrone about their new firm, Schmidt warned him: *You signed a deal with the devil.* Based on his own bitter experience, Schmidt was worried about the quality of the management at CSFB. When he had worked at CSFB in the early 1990s, he told Quattrone, things had gotten so bad that some of the staffers had had a saying: *You may get tired of fucking First Boston, but First Boston will never get tired of fucking you.*

The wild ride was about to begin.

THE MULE IN THE LOBBY

15

AS THEY SHARED in the technology group's rising fees, some of the members began to flaunt their wealth.

In the middle of 1998, Bill Brady, the graduate of Princeton, son of a Philadelphia Main Line judge, made an extravagant purchase. He paid $6.3 million for a modern showplace house at 340 Lombard Street on Telegraph Hill, just north of San Francisco's central business district, and steps from the famous Coit Tower. The previous owner, construction executive Steven H. Oliver, was president of the board of trustees of the San Francisco Museum of Modern Art, and he had commissioned architect Jim Jennings to design a place to display his own art collection.

The four-level house, set away and barely visible from the street, had a glass roof terrace that commanded sweeping views of San Francisco Bay and the city. It was featured in an architectural magazine for its "crisp geometries on Telegraph Hill." Its core was a fifty-foot-high white concrete cylinder. Across the resulting cylindrical interior space was a bridge leading to the living room. It had apartments for visiting artists, which Brady turned into quarters for junior bankers. Perhaps most impressive was its garage, which had a ramp that led down underground to a turntable that allowed multiple cars to be parked and then exit without ever having to back out. Visiting tech-group bankers came to refer to the garage as "the Bat Cave."

○

As for Boutros, his lifestyle was sedate compared to Brady's. He lived with his wife, Danielle, and three children in the scenic Sea Cliff neighborhood, at the edge of a bluff with sweeping views of the Golden Gate Bridge. His neighbors included movie stars Sharon Stone and Robin Williams. His Mediterranean-style house had a deck overlooking the ocean and coastal cliffs, with access by stairway to the beach.[1] He also acquired a getaway home in Mexico.

○

Soon after joining CSFB, Quattrone held a gathering for senior CSFB executives at a resort in Napa Valley at which they could get to know his team. As always, Quattrone gave a smoothly polished yet jokey presentation. At another gathering for managing directors, he showed slides listing his top ten reasons for joining CSFB. He flashed a shot of Charles Ward, the firm's sober head of investment banking, who resembled Woody Allen—with his face superimposed over the body of Elvis Presley. *Chuck Ward*, he cracked, *is the most charismatic guy I know.*

Quattrone's timing could hardly have been better. The Internet stock bubble soon began filling with air.

On July 17, 1998, a Morgan Stanley–led Internet IPO for Broadcast.com Inc., a Web broadcaster, set a record by rising 249 percent, more than triple its offering price, on its first day of trading. Two weeks later Quattrone's first CSFB-led IPO, for Carrier Access Corp. on July 30, rose a modest 34 percent on its first day. Carrier Access offered connections for telecom and Internet access. Roger Koenig and Nancy Pierce, the company's husband-and-wife cofounders, opened a personal account with the Quattrone brokers led by John Schmidt.

But a lull followed in new technology issues. In mid-August, Russia declared a moratorium on repaying its debt, signaling a devaluation of the ruble. The impact rippled through other markets, culminating in late September with the collapse of the hedge fund Long Term Capital Management L.P. The impact delayed the IPO of Goldman Sachs Group itself by seven months.

Yet in hindsight, that very crisis sowed some of the seeds of the bubble. The Federal Reserve Bank lowered interest rates sharply, which helped markets bounce back. Online stock trading had become a craze, and online traders favored dot-com stocks. The Internet, it seemed, was changing everything. Fears about the impact of the year 2000 on computer systems sparked a sharp rise in spending on business technology that gained momentum in 1999.

○

At a board meeting on September 23, 1998, Peter Jackson, the chief executive of Intraware Inc., which provided systems for the Netscape search engine, said he thought the time was ripe for an IPO. But some of his advisers counseled caution.

Jackson, a rangy, blond, fast-talking salesman, had attended the University of California at Berkeley on a soccer scholarship. He was the former president of DataFlex Corp., a computer reseller. Intraware was located next to a strip mall in Orinda, California, across the bay from downtown San Francisco. Its revenues were growing fast, from $10.4 million in the year ending in February 1998 to $24.6 million in the nine months ending in November 1998.

The next day, on September 24, shares of online auctioneer eBay Inc. more than doubled in their IPO debut. In mid-November, the IPO of Earthweb Inc. tripled. Then TheGlobe.com rose 606 percent on its first day of trading, and Intraware directors gave the green light for an IPO.

Jackson set the week of November 16 for his bake-off meetings. Bankers from Quattrone's group at CSFB came in Thursday afternoon. The team included Bill Brady and Ted Smith, a blond, clean-cut Midwestern-looking junior banker who lived in one of the extra apartments at Brady's mansion. Also present were Schmidt and Lise Buyer, a petite, energetic Internet analyst who remembered Jackson from DataFlex.

How are you feeling, you poor guy? they all asked Jackson. *Guess you've been through nine of these pitches.* Jackson said that with all of the pitch books the banks were leaving behind, he felt like a mule. The CSFB bankers laughed. Intraware sometimes used a slogan that asked users, "Tired of dragging your ass?" to trade shows and conferences. "Jackson feeling like a mule" became a running joke during the meeting. He would feel like a mule when they packed him up for his road shows, Jackson said. Brady offered his assurance that the IPO would be completed. When Schmidt pitched his wealth-management services, Jackson declined, because one of his best friends was a broker at Montgomery. They left sometime after 5:00 P.M. In the car going back from the pitch, Buyer and Smith hatched a plan to help CSFB stand out from the competition.

Goldman was scheduled to be the last bank to present, on Friday morning. Even before Jackson arrived at the office that day he got a number of voice-mail messages from Intraware employees. *You've got to get in here and see this,* they said.

When he arrived at the office around 7:00 A.M., Jackson saw Ted Smith, the junior CSFB banker, in the lobby. With him was a live mule! Around the mule's neck hung two bottles of champagne and a sign that read: TIRED OF DRAGGING YOUR ASS TO ALL THOSE INVESTMENT BANKING PITCHES? and urged him to pick CSFB. Although Quattrone knew nothing about it at the time, it was an extreme example of his "unforgettable gesture" strategy.

The Goldman bankers urged Jackson to delay going public until he had one more quarter of results to report.

As Jackson reviewed the bake-off results with his directors and venture capital investors, he told them he favored Hambrecht & Quist. But Mark Hoffman, Intraware's chairman and largest shareholder after Jackson, favored CSFB. Hoffman also chose Quattrone for the IPO of his own company, Commerce One Inc., a few months later. Another push for CSFB came from Jay Hoag of Technology Crossover Ventures, which had kicked in $3 million in venture capital funding for Intraware in August 1998.

Some of the other investors and directors asked about Morgan Stanley. Jackson explained that Morgan hadn't been able to present during the bake-off week. Intraware then chose CSFB, sticking with the decision even after Morgan Stanley later offered to lead the IPO.

A few days later Jackson attended a holiday party at the upscale Circus Club in Menlo Park hosted by Kleiner Perkins. He was pulled aside by a Morgan Stanley alumnus who had worked with Quattrone and now worked at an Internet company.

The former banker gave Jackson a harsh wake-up call. *You have proven to me you are one of the dumbest SOBs in the Valley*, he said. *You picked CSFB over Morgan; do you need to have your head checked?*

O

The growing impact of Quattrone & Co. could be seen in the reaction to company presentations at the CSFB annual technology conference, which the banker held at the luxury Phoenician resort in Scottsdale, Arizona, in early December. Comedian Dana Carvey teased Quattrone about whether the firm's name was pronounced "Credit Suisse," which he pronounced with a heavy European accent or "First Boston," with a New England accent. "Which is it, Frank?" Carvey asked.

Cisco Systems CEO John Chambers gave a keynote speech before a two-story screen bearing pithy predictions like "Voice Will Be Free" and "Everything Will Be Connected." When Michael Dell talked up one memory chip designer, its stock rose 9 percent.[2] When Charles Haggerty, chief executive of Western Digital Corporation, said business was getting much better, his remarks sent his stock up 37 percent.[3]

In the next sign of the gathering frenzy, in late December, Henry Blodget, an analyst at CIBC Oppenheimer, predicted that Amazon.com, then trading at 240, would top 400 within a year. Just that prediction sent the stock soaring to nearly 290. Meeker's star at Morgan Stanley was likewise rising even higher. The same month, December 1998, she was featured as "Queen of the Net" in *Barron's*, a financial weekly. And the name stuck.

O

Once they finished work on Intraware's prospectus, Jackson prepared to take his show on the road. He first got some coaching from Tricia Stone, whose company specialized in product and company launches and worked regularly with CSFB. A free spirit, Jackson had trouble sticking to his script, and tended to ramble. Unless Jackson could curb his free-wheeling tendencies, she said, *You're never going to make it to slide six.*

Jackson kicked off his road-show tour on February 9, 1999, in the first-class bar on the upper deck of a Lufthansa 747 from New York to London. Jackson's only contact with Quattrone himself had been to shake his hand at the San Francisco road-show stop. Then he hit Denver before winding up in New York City on February 25.

With the markets faltering, Jackson wasn't sure his deal would get done. It would be humiliating to return without the $60 million the IPO was supposed to raise for his company. The day the deal was finally completed and the stock began trading, his children skipped school to watch in his office, and Jackson appeared on TV with Neil Cavuto on the Fox network. "Well, who said a rocky market is no place for an IPO? Not the folks over at Intraware," Cavuto said. "Despite today's high-tech tumble, guess what? Shares of the Internet software consulting firm surged nearly 15 percent on their first day of trading." Jackson responded that the IPO proceeds would enable him to expand globally. Right behind him was former heavyweight boxer George Foreman, who was promoting his grill.

Suddenly, Jackson was worth $65 million on paper. He was about to hire three hundred people. He rounded the corner from the Fox studios and, alone on the streets of Midtown Manhattan, he burst into tears.

What he didn't know was that over the next two years, he would nearly lose control of his company. Venture capital investors would conclude that Intraware was bleeding money hopelessly. Intraware would come close to running out of cash and being delisted by the NASDAQ stock market. Lise Buyer would leave CSFB, which would stop publishing research on his stock. And the CSFB bankers would stop calling.

THE FLAMING FERRARIS

16

QUATTRONE HAD QUIT Morgan Stanley over his inability to gain control over a semiautonomous technology banking unit. But the shared control he gained at Credit Suisse First Boston over research analysts and stockbrokers would backfire when, as regulators would later charge, he acted too aggressively to use the lure of favorable research and lucrative brokerage accounts stuffed with hot IPOs to win investment banking business. "His structure completely killed him," said a longtime colleague who worked with Quattrone at Morgan Stanley and CSFB.

The regulators might not have cared as much if technology stocks hadn't cost investors so much money when the bubble burst. In 1999 and 2000, there were 529 technology IPOs, according to a 2003 tally by Morgan Stanley. By the end of 2002, near the postbubble bottom of the battered stock market, those IPOs had lost $234 billion in market value from their IPO levels. The damage would have been far worse if calculated from the frothy market peak of each of those stocks.[1]

Thanks to Quattrone, CSFB led 117 technology IPOs, more than any other Wall Street firm, in 1999 and 2000.[2] In his zeal to achieve and then promote his number one market share, he would skillfully and aggressively call attention to himself and his group. So when regulators began sifting the rubble for signs of wrongdoing, they knew the first place to look.

Worse for Quattrone, he wound up pursuing many lesser quality companies, like Intraware, that had been rejected by either Goldman, Morgan Stanley, or both. "He didn't have the platform to compete against Goldman or Morgan," said Scott Ryles, who coheaded the technology banking group at Merrill Lynch in the late 1990s. "So he went after all those type companies that Goldman and Morgan weren't going to compete for."[3]

From the beginning, the in-house lawyers at Credit Suisse First Boston fell behind in getting a grip on the Quattrone group, which didn't have a full-time lawyer assigned to it for most of its first year at CSFB.

Joseph McLaughlin, an Irishman with bushy gray hair, had become the firm's fourth general counsel in five years in 1999. He initially sent two legal and compliance staffers out to the West Coast from New York, senior equities division lawyer Ray Dorado and compliance officer Edward Arnold, to monitor the group's activities intermittently and temporarily.

Although there were legal and administrative staffers on the ground in California who were supposed to monitor compliance with industry rules, their influence varied. When McLaughlin hired Lorraine McDonough, a lawyer from his old firm of Shearman & Sterling, to work there full-time, starting in the fourth quarter of 1999, she left after only a few months to join a dot-com.

And one of the tech group's branch administrative managers, Susan Winegar, quit after clashing repeatedly with Schmidt's assistant, Linda-Louise Lund. The BAMs, as they were known, had a role in managing compliance, but got little respect.[4] Winegar found that if she vetoed something Lund wanted to do, Lund often called legal and compliance officials in New York to try to get permission anyway.

The turnover in the legal and compliance ranks seemed to be part of a larger pattern of valuing profits over controls and compliance. The elimination of Schmidt's old branch-manager job was a possible sign of this. Wheat gave key bankers and traders lots of elbow room and a cut of their profits to keep them pushing hard. So managers had an incentive to drive the numbers as high as possible to get themselves paid, and less reason for concern for reputational risk.

Recalls one former member of Quattrone's technology group: "There was a culture of don't screw with the people who are making the big bucks."

The result of the firm's lax approach to regulatory compliance began to emerge within the first year after Quattrone joined.

In February 1999, CSFB suspended three members of a swashbuckling team of stock traders in London. They called themselves "the Flaming Ferraris," after a cocktail its twenty-something members favored on Friday nights. The group's members had earned bonuses totaling $13 million the previous year.[5] In May, CSFB paid a $210,000 fine to the Swedish stock exchange to settle charges that the suspended Ferraris, who were later fired, broke antimanipulation rules by engineering a phony trade.

Another CSFB gunslinger was Andy Stone, a ponytailed mortgage securities specialist who took big positions and caught the eye of regulators. In February 1999, the Federal Reserve Bank of New York sent CSFB a memo critical of the firm's real estate unit, which was run by Stone. The Fed examiner, Arthur Angulo, notified Wheat that the unit's profits were being front-loaded and expenses being postponed. Provision for losses was "insufficient." The letter questioned "whether this business is being managed in a safe and sound manner."[6] Mr. Stone also left in 1999.

Around the same time, a probe began in Japan of actions by Wheat's former derivatives unit that resulted in the criminal conviction in 2001 of Shinji Yamada, the former head of that unit's Tokyo office, on charges that he had hidden documents from visiting regulators. They were investigating whether the unit helped clients conceal losses.[7] That probe would consume much of McLaughlin's time over the next two years.

THE FRIENDS OF FRANK

17

THE PACE of Quattrone's business soon took off like a rocket. Quattrone's tech group had done eighteen technology IPOs in his best year at Morgan Stanley in 1995. The same group at Credit Suisse First Boston would do nearly three times that many—fifty-three in all—in 1999.

The year started with a bang with the $20 billion acquisition announced January 13 of Ascend Communications by Lucent Technologies. Since the rising stock market lifted the Ascend deal's value to $24 billion by the time it closed in June, the Quattrone group could bill this as "the largest technology merger in history."[1] The deal rained money on Quattrone and the CSFB tech group. The Lucent-Ascend acquisition generated $40 million in fees for Credit Suisse First Boston alone.

But there was more to Quattrone's relationship with Ascend.

Ascend's chief executive Morteza "Mory" Ejabat was one of Quattrone's oldest and best clients. The Quattrone team had taken Ascend public at Morgan Stanley and advised on its acquisition of Cascade Communications at Deutsche Bank.

Ejabat would soon give CSFB even more business. In November 1999, the tech group managed a $500 million private stock sale for Ejabat's next company, Zhone Technologies Inc., and advised Zhone on a $248 million acquisition of Premisys Communications Inc. Ejabat even endorsed the group's work in a CSFB tech group brochure near the end of 1999. "They orchestrated Ascend's merger with Lucent when I was there and have just recently completed a landmark private placement for us at Zhone," Ejabat's blurb read. "They are truly a full service investment banking firm with an outstanding track record."[2]

As part of that "full service," Ejabat had opened an account with the Schmidt brokers who worked with Quattrone. Ejabat's account would be ranked "1," meaning the highest strategic priority.[3] A family trust for Robert Dahl, Ascend's chief financial officer, also opened an account. The CFO job is often vital in both choosing an investment banker and maintaining the relationship between the company and its banks. Although CFOs often received a lower priority than CEOs in such rankings, in this case Dahl received a 1 ranking as well.

As of January 1999, the Schmidt brokers only had a few dozen clients, including about a dozen trading accounts kept by "syndicate players" who sought new issues such as Lustig in Denver, whom Schmidt finally met after joining CSFB.

As the bubble swelled, the Schmidt brokers' right to distribute 2 percent to 4 percent of the stock of all technology IPOs became more and more valuable. Before then, IPO shares typically would rise 10 percent to 15 percent or more in price on their first day of trading. During the bubble, the first-day percentage gains became ever larger, often exceeding 100 percent.

The second tech IPO Quattrone did at CSFB, Pilot Network Services Inc., actually declined slightly when it opened for trading in August 1998, around the time markets were roiled by the Russian debt crisis. But six of the next seven that occurred, between January and April 1999, rose more than 80 percent, and four of them more than doubled. In January, Allaire Corp. rose 119 percent on its first day of trading. In February, Onyx Software Corp. rose 81 percent. In March, Autoweb.com Inc. rose 186 percent. In April, the first-day gains for Informatica Corp., Razorfish Inc., and USinternetworking Inc. were 84 percent, 109 percent, and 174 percent, respectively.

Handing out shares of these IPOs was like giving away free gold coins. Quattrone and the Schmidt brokers found a way to use the lure of such IPOs to win business, the SEC later charged, in IPO bake-offs, where CSFB pitched companies for the chance to lead their deals.

Schmidt would attend the bake-offs, as he had at Deutsche Bank. Some of the pitch was standard industry practice. He would offer to help design a plan to direct some of the IPO stock to individuals having some commercial relationship with the company going public. These directed-share programs, the friends and family stock, were disclosed in the companies' prospectuses. The recipients included executives of key customers, suppliers, or affiliates. The IPO stock was supposed to encourage recipients to give the company going public more business or better treatment. For example, Red Hat Inc., which marketed Linux software, set aside eight hundred thousand of its six million IPO shares in August 1999 for so-called open-source software writers and others as a goodwill gesture.

Schmidt also offered to manage the cash proceeds of the IPO for the company before it was spent. And he would offer to manage the stock sales for executives who owned shares in the companies they were taking public. Such sales were typically subject to "lockups" of six months or longer, to reassure investors that the executives didn't plan to take the money and run.

Most significant, Schmidt would also offer to open brokerage accounts for the same executives to manage their newfound wealth. With this offer at CSFB, Schmidt extended a program his brokers had begun on a much smaller scale at DMG. Although it might have seemed innocuous at the time, this program drew more regulatory heat to Quattrone after the bubble burst.

If a company chose CSFB to lead its IPO, the Schmidt brokers would offer to manage an account for one or more of their executives and directors that would buy shares of each new CSFB-led IPO. The accounts would be discretionary, meaning that the brokers would decide when to buy and sell stocks. Customers weren't allowed to pick and choose which new issues they wanted; it was all or nothing. Accounts were also ranked by the brokers, depending on their job and their ability to award CSFB additional business.

Yet even as they created the accounts, Quattrone and Schmidt knew that questions might be raised about their use of hot IPOs to grease the palms of banking clients. At his second criminal trial in April 2004, Quattrone noted that CSFB lawyers had authorized the accounts, whose holders became known as Friends of Frank. But none of them—not Quattrone, Schmidt, or the lawyers—could have realized in early 1999 how powerful a lure they would become.

An article in *The Wall Street Journal* in November 1997 had described a practice, called "spinning," of steering hot IPOs to potential investment banking clients to help win their business. The term spinning referred to quickly flipping or reselling the shares to lock in the client's profit. Quattrone himself had even been quoted in the article as criticizing one version of the practice.

"At its extreme," Quattrone told the author, Michael Siconolfi, "an IPO is priced Wednesday. Thursday morning, you call 25 venture capitalists and say, 'By the way, XYZ just went public at 15; it's now trading at 30. You just sold the allocation at 29½. I hope you're happy.' That to me is smarmy."[4]

In response to the story, staffers at the Securities and Exchange Commission investigated Wall Street practices giving investment banking clients preferential treatment in allocating hot IPOs. They never brought any charges. But the article and the investigation put the practice on Wall Street's radar screen.

At his trial, Quattrone himself alluded to the fallout from Siconolfi's *Wall Street Journal* article. In his testimony, the banker tried to argue that the accounts were within the rules because his brokers set a minimum account size, gave each account only a limited number of shares of each IPO, and required the accounts to do other trading instead of being solely a receptacle for hot deals. (The posted minimum was $100,000, later raised to $250,000, the SEC said in 2003.) CSFB lawyers felt that such measures "were good, safe harbors that we could rely on so that the allocations Mr. Schmidt was making weren't considered spinning," Quattrone said.[5]

At other firms where brokers worked within a larger organization, hot IPOs were sprinkled more evenly to good clients of all kinds. Investment bankers at those firms could put in a word in to get IPO shares for clients. But at CSFB, the Quattrone-Schmidt brokers designed a program to funnel shares of *every single tech IPO in concentrated doses directly to investment banking clients who could deliver more business.*

Interviewed by regulators in October 2002, Quattrone denied that the purpose of the Friends of Frank accounts was to win more banking business. In that interview, he confirmed that he had been quoted accurately in the *Journal*, and said he thought the practice of spinning was "despicable."[6]

But Schmidt, who administered the program, freely acknowledged to the same regulators a month earlier, in September 2002, that winning more banking business was part of the idea. "The objective," Schmidt said, "was obviously to develop a very good working relationship with the senior officers of our client companies in the hopes of doing additional—both investment banking business and, certainly in our case, private client services business in the future."[7]

Of all the excesses of the bubble, it was the Friends of Frank accounts—with the mere name suggesting an inside group receiving secret favors—that put Quattrone in the regulatory crosshairs after the bubble burst.

Some of the account holders were officers of companies Quattrone had taken public at Deutsche Bank. Executives of Artisan Components Inc., whose $29 million IPO was led by the Quattrone tech group at DMG in February 1998, wound up with several accounts—including for chief executive Mark Templeton, chief financial officer Robert Selvi, and vice president John Malecki.[8]

The number of such accounts eventually reached 285, the SEC said in 2003. They were by no means a "who's who" of Silicon Valley, a wealthier group that would have been less susceptible to such a perk. Instead, they were more of the Valley's up-and-coming entrepreneurs and their associates. Venture capital executives weren't generally included due to regulatory guidance issued after the Siconolfi story.

Here's how the Friends of Frank program worked in practice. In March 1999, Phone.com Inc. chose CSFB to lead a $73.6 million IPO in June. The Quattrone group had already represented the company in two previous venture capital financings. In July, Alain Rossman, the chairman and chief executive officer, opened an account with just $95,773 of his own money. By April 2001, the account had generated $1.3 million in profits before fees. Rossman was joined by twelve other Phone.com executives or officials who eventually established Friends of Frank accounts.[9]

If Rossman and his Phone.com colleagues made money from their CSFB brokerage accounts, the Quattrone group made a lot more from Phone.com. In

November 1999, CSFB led a $1.02 billion follow-on stock offering for Phone
.com. And CSFB also advised Phone.com on three acquisitions as well as a $7
billion merger with Software.com Inc. that closed in November 2000. In all,
Phone.com paid $76.1 million in banking fees to CSFB.[10]

In the group's 2000 brochure, Rossman was the first client quoted on page 5.
"CSFB has done an outstanding job for us, providing a wide range of financing
and advisory services. They really know this market and they make it happen,"
Rossman said. Noting that CSFB had advised on "eight major transactions" for
the company in the previous two years, he concluded: "I guess you could say we
are the consummate satisfied customer."[11]

By the time the bubble ended, two of the biggest winners were the two executives from Ascend, which had chosen CSFB to work on the biggest tech
merger in history. One of the executives had chosen CSFB for two other assignments later in the bubble.

A tally by the *San Jose Mercury News* in March 2003 noted that Mory Ejabat,
Ascend's CEO, received shares of eighty-eight IPOs that generated estimated
first-day profits of $1.9 million. Robert Dahl, the CFO, did even better, receiv-
ing shares of ninety-nine IPOs that generated first-day profits of $2.9 million.[12]

As the pressure to get hot IPOs from CSFB grew, the good news was that
there were a lot more of them, and they were getting larger. There had been
just one in January 1999, two in February, one in March, and three in April.
There were four in May, six in June, and ten in July. One of them, for online broker TD Waterhouse Group Inc., topped $1 billion.

By mid-June, Schmidt was already joking about the Friends of Frank nickname for the accounts, and even suggested that it might appear to be spinning.
On the morning of June 15, he sent an e-mail to Quattrone, Brady, and Boutros
reporting that his unit's May revenues were $2.2 million.[13]

A half hour later, Quattrone replied by offering congratulations on "another
strong month," and asked how the pace of Schmidt's business compared to online brokers like Charles Schwab Corporation. "Our client base is just a bit
more limited than Schwab although our online trading picked up a lot in May,"
Schmidt replied. "We were not able to spin the 'FOF's' as much in May given
market nervousness."

At his first trial, Quattrone acknowledged that Schmidt used the term
Friends of Frank merely "on this one occasion when he was telling a joke."

But another e-mail exchange two weeks later offered a glimpse of Quattrone's role in suggesting candidates for Friends of Frank accounts, and how
the rising pressure to get hot IPO shares was no laughing matter.

On the morning of June 29, 1999, Quattrone's secretary, La Nita Burkhead,
sent an e-mail to Schmidt. "Peter Wolken, AVI Management, closed his ac-

count at DMG and would like to establish a personal account at CSFB. Frank has asked that you please give him a call." She added Wolken's address and phone number in Los Altos.[14]

Schmidt's reply just fifteen minutes later to Burkhead and Quattrone showed the pressure he was under. It was like having box-seat season tickets at World Series time, with lots of long-lost friends and relatives calling out of the blue. "Peter Wolken is an oxygen pirate and wants nothing but new issues," Schmidt fumed. The Quattrone broker expected such private-client accounts to do other trades to generate commissions, not just sit there and receive IPOs. "I have had lunch with Peter and told him our rules on more than one occasion. He refused to do any secondary business. Unless he is a key relationship for the Technology Group, it is a waste of our time and new issues to talk to him."

Quattrone's reply to Schmidt three hours later was succinct and direct: "fine with me. He is not strategic."

Quattrone and his teammates often used the word "strategic" as shorthand to reflect the degree to which an individual was important to building the tech group's franchise. In the context of brokerage accounts, Quattrone told regulators he was only referring to the long-term business strategy of concentrating brokerage services on the technology sector.[15] Schmidt said that he understood the word strategic to mean "individuals who are likely to be the decision makers in the overall relationship with the firm"—including deciding on investment banking assignments.[16]

Eventually, the ability of banking clients to get an inside track on IPO allocations from Wall Street became an open secret. In July 1999, CSFB Internet analyst Lise Buyer said in an e-mail that some IPO shares designated for "friends and family" of the issuing company were routinely being reserved for clients of the securities firm leading the IPO.

"The only unpleasant part of all this," Buyer wrote, "is that some of the F&F shares are reserved not for friends of the company, but for friends of the investment bank. If you take your company public with Bank X, you will most likely receive shares of Bank X's next 5 (a random number) deals. So it becomes something of a 'you scratch my back, I will scratch yours.'"[17]

○

As the year went on, hot IPOs increasingly became part of a highly evolved system of favor trading—in Silicon Valley and beyond. The Quattrone group paid close attention to how shares of tech IPOs were allocated. Quattrone had enough influence within the firm to help other clients and investors get extra IPOs shares outside the Friends of Frank program.

Roger McNamee was one of the Valley's best known venture capital investors.

His firm, Integral Partners, had bankrolled Intuit, Rambus Inc., and Flextronics Inc. He and Quattrone went way back. As a mutual-fund manager at T. Rowe Price in 1991, McNamee had recommended Mary Meeker to Quattrone. The following year, Quattrone had raised money to help McNamee found Integral.

On the morning of Tuesday September 14, 1999, Jill Ford, an equity capital markets staffer in New York, e-mailed Andy Fisher, the tech group equity capital markets chief, about the IPO of Vitria Technology Inc., a business software company. "Integral Partners is in my book—they are initial investors—any special favors there?"[18] One of Quattrone's bankers, Cameron Lester, replied that there were several reasons why McNamee shouldn't get any extra Vitria stock, but suggested they check with his boss, Bill Brady, just in case.

Then Quattrone weighed in. Showing how carefully he tried to calibrate using hot IPO shares as payback for other favors, he asked, "Were they helpful on weed and mdcm?" He was referring to the last two IPOs that CSFB had led—Tumbleweed Communications Corporation on August 5, and Mortgage.com Inc. on August 11—and that had been completed with difficulty in a weak market.

"VERY HELPFUL ON mdcm," Brady replied—suggesting that Integral had bought Mortgage.com stock in the IPO. A few months later, Quattrone bragged that Tumbleweed and Mortgage.com got done "when the market crapped out" because he and Brady had "called in lots of chits with investors we have known for years and have our own money invested with."[19]

Within days, Vitria stock tripled on its first day of trading.

O

Even though the Quattrone brokers didn't include venture capital investors in the Friends of Frank program, he sometimes saw to it that they got some IPO shares.

On September 23, 1999, Linda-Louise Lund, Schmidt's assistant, sent an e-mail to Andy Fisher with a copy to Quattrone, Brady, and Schmidt. "Andy," she said, "Frank and Bill would like 25,000 shares of Interwoven to be allocated to Foundation Capital on the Interwoven IPO."[20]

The Quattrone group had close ties to Interwoven, which made software that helped companies manage their Web site content. Quattrone's team had met the company through Interwoven director Kathryn Gould, who also was the general partner of Foundation Capital, a venture investor in Interwoven.[21]

The Quattrone team had even invested in Interwoven. In June 1999, just four months before Interwoven's IPO, Quattrone and other members of his group bought shares in the company at just one third of what was to be the IPO price. David Allen, Interwoven's chief financial officer, said the company "liked the idea of our bankers having some skin in the game." When Quattrone, Boutros, and Brady sold their shares in October 2000, a year after the IPO, they together reaped sale proceeds of more than $2 million on an investment of $126,000.[22]

After the IPO, which rose 141 percent on its first day of trading on October 8, 1999, the ties between Interwoven and CSFB became even closer. Its chief executive, Martin Brauns, the chief financial officer, David Allen, and four other executives opened Friends of Frank accounts with the Schmidt group brokers.[23] Brauns himself endorsed the CSFB tech group in its 2000 brochure as "our primary public market partner."

○

The intricate, highly evolved system of back-scratching and favor-trading that flourished during the bubble was a smoothly oiled machine when the market was rising. When the bubble burst and it all came to light, the system took on a more sinister cast—designed, it seemed, to grease the palms of insiders at the public's expense.

MONARCH OF THE VALLEY

18

IN APRIL 1999, Jeffrey Dachis was stopped by a security guard in the lobby of the Credit Suisse First Boston headquarters in Manhattan. The flamboyant Dachis was chief executive of Razorfish Inc., a Web site design and systems provider in Silicon Alley in Manhattan, with clients such as online trading powerhouse Charles Schwab and Road Runner, the high-speed online service.

Unlike some dot-com startups, Razorfish was actually showing revenues and modest profits, and had a substantial partnership with advertising giant Omnicom Inc., which had a 37 percent stake at the time of the IPO. However, both Morgan Stanley and Goldman Sachs had declined to pitch for the Razorfish IPO—another indication that CSFB would lead IPOs that rivals might avoid.

One big factor in Dachis's choice of CSFB was the assurance that their Web consulting services analyst, Mark Wolfenberger, would not only attend every road-show meeting but also every sales call. Because Quattrone could field analysts in such numbers, all reporting to him, his team could pay more attention to selling deals than those at other firms.

Dachis, who had an undergraduate degree in dance and dramatic literature from the State University of New York at Purchase, had arrived the afternoon before Razorfish went public for the pricing meeting. There was just one problem: his dog Sophie. *No dogs allowed*, the security guard said. *The dog comes or we don't go*, Dachis said. The security guard backed down.

There was another conflict over the IPO price, and this time Dachis didn't prevail. Dachis wanted $17 a share; CSFB's head of technology capital markets, Andy Fisher, held the line at $16 a share. Dachis didn't fully realize that the deal was heavily oversubscribed, and that the price would more than double on the first day of trading. If the deal had been priced at $17, Razorfish would have received an extra $3 million. The company could have used the money, Dachis thought later.

What galled Dachis years later was that his company got lumped in with dozens of others he considered of lesser quality that were taken public after his, later in the cycle. He found himself and his former company defendants in billion-dollar lawsuits brought by investors who had lost money when the bubble burst. It wasn't just CSFB, Dachis thought—all the Wall Street underwriters had relaxed their standards. "The banking standards went out the window," he said.[1]

○

Indeed, in January 1999, the CSFB tech group bankers hotly debated whether they should scrap an internal guideline that a company going public had to have $10 million in revenues in the twelve months before it went public. It was the IPO of TheGlobe.com—an "online community" company, whose IPO had just risen 606 percent and was valued at nearly $1 billion based on six-month revenues of $1.2 million—that had gotten everyone thinking. One CSFB Internet analyst, Lise Buyer, reacted to that deal—which was led by another firm— by thinking, *The world has gone mad.*

Another CSFB Internet analyst, Bill Burnham, said the revenue debate reflected the new landscape. "Everyone realized the entire market was doing deals like this," Burnham said. "Companies we had relationships with but didn't have any intention of taking public anytime soon announced, 'Hey, if theglobe .com can go public, we can.'"[2]

CSFB ultimately relaxed the revenue yardstick so that a company with *annualized* revenues of $10 million could go public. One company that wouldn't have made it under the old rules was CareerBuilder Inc., an online recruiting firm. When the CSFB tech group took it public in May 1999, its previous twelve months' revenues were just $8.8 million. But revenue in its latest quarter was $2.8 million, giving it an annualized revenue rate of $11.2 million. Such decisions were "emblematic to me of the competitive devaluation of underwriting standards," said Burnham, who left in 1999 to join a venture capital investment firm.[3]

○

With so much control of his own technology banking unit, Quattrone was able to expand quickly, outgunning rivals.

Some of Quattrone's recruits had little actual banking experience. One was Carlos Bohla. Tall, thin, with a youthful, dazzling smile, Bohla had both worked at the Boston Consulting Group and run the venture capital group for Digital Equipment Corporation. Quattrone promptly nicknamed him Soave Bohla, after the wine drink Soave Bolla, and he became the lead banker for e-commerce companies.

In early 1999, e-commerce stocks were soaring. Bohla, commuting between his home base in Boston and Europe, was reading an in-flight magazine on a

transatlantic flight when he noticed an ad for a company whose logo was orange and purple. (Bohla's favorite colors were orange, purple, and green.) It was
for an Internet service provider called Freeserve.

Freeserve was started in September 1998 as a customer acquisition vehicle
for Dixons Group PLC, a British retailer. By early 1999, it had 1.3 million sub-
scribers. In March, CSFB bankers told Dixons's chief executive John Clare
that, with America Online valued at six thousand dollars per subscriber,
Freeserve could be worth billions.

Two weeks later, the CSFB bankers repeated the same pitch to Sir Stanley
Kalms, the founder and chairman of Dixons, in a crowded room with bankers
from Cazenove & Company, a London securities dealer. When the crusty sixty-
seven-year-old Kalms expressed skepticism, based on lower valuations from
another bank, Bohla gave him a breezy reassurance that included the phrase
"Stanley baby." Although CSFB's London bankers cringed, Kalms took their
advice.

Freeserve PLC went public in July 1999 at a valuation of more than $2 bil-
lion, and the stock price eventually quadrupled from there. In December 2000,
even after the bubble burst, Freeserve agreed to an acquisition by France Telecom S.A. at a valuation of $2.4 billion. But the acquisition value later declined
below the IPO price level.

O

By the spring of 1999, the pace of work was so grueling—and yet also
exhilarating—that some of the CSFB tech group bankers would literally sleep
in their offices, under their desks. Bohla slept under his desk three days in a
row in one stretch. He kept in regular touch with Ted Smith, the banker on the
Intraware deal, who was staying in Brady's guest-banker apartment.

Sometimes, taking advantage of the time difference, they would give each
other wake-up calls. At 2:00 A.M. Eastern time in Boston, Bohla would call
Smith to tell him he was going under his desk. Three hours later, at 2:00 A.M.
Pacific time in California, Smith would give Bohla a 5:00 A.M. wake-up call and
tell him he was going under *his* desk. Bohla would wake up and resume his
work, calling Smith back in turn three hours later.

In March 1999, Quattrone took note of the pace in a memo congratulating
the group. They had already brought in $350 million worth of business, double
their previous best year at DMG or Morgan Stanley. But while he noted that
some employees had quit, the good news was, none had joined competitors, and
the group had a strong bench.

"Having said that," Quattrone said, "I am deeply concerned that some of our
best people are working so hard for such long stretches of time that they are
risking 'burnout.' I sincerely do not wish this to happen. As we discussed at our

offsite, we do ask our people to have a very strong work ethic, but remember—it's a marathon, and you have to finish to win the race."[4]

○

Companies were coming out of the woodwork to go public. In the spring of 1999, Audible Inc., based far from Silicon Valley in Wayne, New Jersey, offered spoken versions of books and newspapers on the Web. Audible held a two-day series of bake-off meetings in New York. The CSFB contingent was led by Mike Kwatintez, the *Institutional Investor*–ranked All Star personal computer hardware analyst and head of technology research. The CSFB bankers made sure the Audible executives knew that having "the Kwat" focus on their company was no small thing.

Goldman Sachs didn't pitch for the Audible IPO, a sign that CSFB was being less choosy as it pumped up its IPO totals. Goldman had also turned down another mid-1999 IPO that CSFB led, for Gadzooks Networks Inc.

At the CSFB presentation, one banker went up to a whiteboard and wrote "Amazon" on one side, and "Yahoo!" on the other. In between, he wrote "Audible." Amazon had high revenues per user but low margins, he said. "Yahoo!" had low revenue per user and high margins. Audible, the banker said, had both high margins and high revenues per user.

Audible's chief financial officer, Andrew Kaplan, opened a Friends of Frank account ten weeks after the IPO on July 15, 1999. The accounts hadn't been mentioned in the bake-off. But Kaplan had gotten a call from Schmidt later, offering *an opportunity to invest in a discretionary trading fund.* After Kaplan accepted, he began to get confirmations in the mail, saying he had bought four hundred or six hundred shares of different IPOs, or that he had sold some of the shares a few weeks later.

A few months later, Kaplan mentioned this to Audible's founder and chairman, Donald Katz. Katz himself had already given his personal brokerage business to the private banking unit of J.P. Morgan, the comanager of the Audible IPO. Kaplan mentioned that, with all the IPOs, his account had been making money. Then Katz talked to Schmidt. And Katz soon opened a Friends of Frank account with $100,000.

The Schmidt brokers assigned Katz a strategic priority of 2, one notch higher than they had Kaplan, at 3. Katz got in just in time to get shares in VA Linux, the biggest IPO first-day gainer ever, in December.

○

Even as he sold technology stocks, Quattrone seemed to acknowledge that some might decline in price. In April 1999, he noted that technology stocks had risen to account for 19.4 percent of the market value of the five hundred stocks in Standard & Poor's index, up from just 5.5 percent in 1964. That was triple the energy sector, the onetime heavyweight, he added.

"Everyone deep in their bones recognizes that there is a category of companies called Internet which is changing the world and represents the future," Quattrone said. "And they know that the category of stocks 10 years from now will be worth a lot more than today. Unfortunately there are only a very few stocks they can invest in."

Quattrone noted that the fifteen stocks like Intel in his own "technology hall of fame" were worth $1.3 trillion, and had risen an average of 5,756 times their initial offering price. Even though he understood that some stocks had already been bid up unreasonably, he said some technology investors thought, "If they invest in 20 of them they can make 19 mistakes, and if they get one of them right they think they will make an awful lot of money."[5]

○

By late spring and summer the bake-offs were coming fast and furious, sometimes almost daily. Despite his group's battle fatigue, Quattrone was often able to lighten the mood. CSFB won the bake-off for the May 6 IPO of Latitude Communications Inc., a Santa Clara company offering online video-conferencing, or "virtual meetings." At the end of the pitch, Quattrone piped up, "We've got an attitude . . . about Latitude."

By mid-1999, the CSFB tech group could make a credible claim to be number one in the first half of the year. In a joint press release with CSFB banking chief Ward, Quattrone said his group was number one in technology IPO volume (31 deals for $4 billion), technology merger volume, technology straight-debt volume, technology equity private placement volume, and technology combined financing-and-merger volume (105 deals for $70 billion). Quattrone said he was "proud to be associated with the best technology team there is today."[6]

○

Sometime in the middle of the bubble, Quattrone's publicist, Cheryl Popp, arranged a visit to the CSFB tech group headquarters for Michael Malone, then the editor of *Forbes ASAP*, and one of Malone's colleagues.

Unlike some Silicon Valley offices that had white walls and a spare, open look, the Quattrone offices just east of the Stanford campus had the dark, wood-paneled, shuttered feel of a law firm or a men's club, Malone noticed.

Malone had written a book about the MIPS Computer IPO called *Going Public*, which had culminated with the near disaster of Quattrone's gun-jumping, stock-touting comments in *Corporate Finance* magazine.

A decade later, Quattrone remembered. He proceded to rake Malone over the coals for writing up the episode. *I've had to live that thing down*, Quattrone said. As both Malone and Quatrone's associates squirmed, he continued venting for almost ten minutes. But Malone laughed it off and, eventually, Quattrone relaxed and laughed as well.

Malone was impressed, he recalled thinking. Quattrone really knew his stuff. It was like listening to the shrewdest mind in Silicon Valley. "He seemed to have a deep understanding of the dynamics of what was going on, deeper than anybody I knew," he said. "He was talking to every power player in town on a daily basis."

The banter at the meeting between Quattrone and his associates, Malone felt, was "like rich buddies talking at a country club, a collegial locker-room atmosphere." But, from the tone of Quattrone's initial attack, Malone also got "a sense of the guy that he didn't abide by anything negative. Almost that he had become a sovereign, a monarch of the Valley. And he wasn't going to allow that image to be sullied."[7]

O

One IPO the Quattrone team won that hadn't been rejected by Morgan or Goldman was TiVo Inc., which offered a recording and replay device that helped customers to select and view TV shows tailored to their own schedule.

The CSFB bake-off team included Quattrone, banker John Hodge, and analyst Laura Martin. While some competing securities firms seemed to slap the TiVo name on boilerplate material they had used for other clients, the Quattrone team had clearly done a lot of preparation. While other firms thought of TiVo in terms of devices like cell phones and satellite dishes, CSFB thought of the business as a service with recurring revenues that could be licensed. And they told anecdotes from the Netscape deal when investors didn't know what a browser was either.

Mike Ramsay, TiVo's chief executive, knew and liked Quattrone from his days at Silicon Graphics, starting in the mid-1980s. What impressed him from the CSFB pitch was Quattrone's presence and assurance of his own personal involvement.

O

But the CSFB team wasn't at the top of their game at the bake-off for Quokka Sports Inc. of San Francisco, which offered viewers sports events on the Web, including a choice of varied camera angles as well as supplementary data about the athletes, weather at the ballpark, and such. For example, its Web cast of a round-the-world sailboat race had attracted 1.8 million users in 177 countries. It also had the rights to cover certain auto-racing events, the Olympics, and the 2000 America's Cup sailboat races.

Goldman Sachs didn't pitch for the Quokka deal. Morgan Stanley, which did pitch initially, later backed out, saying they thought it was too early for the company to go public. CSFB presented last. Alan Ramadan, the company's chief executive, had heard that Quattrone was a gifted presenter, able to distill a complex message into something simple and compelling. CSFB analyst Lise Buyer attended the pitch, as did junior banker Ted Smith and brokerage chief John Schmidt.

Quattrone did most of the talking. He said Quokka could be positioned as "ESPN for the Internet." But as they drilled down, some of the Quokka executives concluded that the CSFB bankers didn't fully understand the company's different sources of revenue, ranging from banner ads to embedded sponsorships. Quokka chose Merrill to lead its IPO on August 2, 1999. Less than two years later, in April 2001, Quokka filed for bankruptcy.

Schmidt, listening to the pitch, thought to himself, *You've got to be kidding me.* Schmidt told regulators in January 2002, "I would sit in on a great number of these investment banking presentations to these companies and look at valuations and, you know, scratch my head." Many of the IPOs, he said, "came much too early and never should have come at all."[8]

Schmidt was an old-economy kind of guy, and he would remember this one long after the bubble burst as the height of absurdity, like ordering groceries online or printing business cards online. After they left, Schmidt asked Smith, "Teddy, why in God's name would we ever want to take this company public? They're just putting Web cams on sailboats!"

LEANING ON THE ANALYSTS

19

BANKING BOUTIQUES had been known for tailoring research to banking needs long before the bubble. But now the stakes escalated at a big firm.

Many analysts—inside and outside the technology group—had good reason to succumb to pressure from banking. They could make more money if companies chose CSFB to lead their new stock issues based on the analyst who would cover their stock. Analysts who were respected on Wall Street and commanded attention from top institutional investors could help attract business. And companies hoped that an analyst's involvement, together with the associated fees, would incline them to be more positive on their stock.

Wall Street was already tailoring analysts' contracts to their ability to reel in new business. In one nontech contract proposal, CSFB offered an analyst a three-year deal for 2000–2002 that included banking-related compensation that could total 1 percent to 3 percent of the firm's "net profit per transaction," with a per-deal cap of $250,000.[1] Indeed, most major firms paid analysts at least partly based on their contribution to banking revenues.

Quattrone expanded his research corps after he landed at CFSB. In August 1998, the group hired Erach (pronounced "air rich") Desai from Soundview Financial Group Inc., a technology research firm. As part of the interviewing process, Desai met with CSFB research chief Al Jackson, who worked out of New York.

Just as the executives in charge of brokers weren't happy about Schmidt working for Quattrone, the firm's research chief wasn't happy about analysts working for Quattrone either. *At the end of the day, I have no say in this,* Jackson told Desai at one point. *I'm just a rubber stamp.*

Desai, a 1984 graduate of the Massachusetts Institute of Technology who had grown up in Pakistan, had been recruited by Tony Trousset, a CSFB banker Desai had known when Trousset worked at Alex. Brown.[2] The only contact he had with Quattrone was to discuss what to call his sector, known variously as technical software or electronic design automation. But he was impressed at the banker's understanding of the business at the group's annual get-together that same month in Napa Valley.

Desai had no experience working at a firm where banking was such a big priority. At boutiques like Soundview, research analysts could call them as they saw them, without fear of reprisal from the company in question. Desai didn't know any other way. But Quattrone soon clarified the rules of the road: Treat the clients with kid gloves. In December, Desai downgraded the stock of Cadence Design Systems Inc. from "buy" to "hold," based partly on his view that its revenue would fall short of management's projection of 20 percent growth.

Desai quickly got a call from Quattrone, Desai later testified. *I just spoke to Jack Harding and he's not happy*, Quattrone told the analyst. Harding was the chief executive of Cadence. Quattrone told Desai that Cadence was upset at not getting a heads-up before the downgrade. *That's not how we do business around here*, Quattrone said, according to Desai. He seemed frustrated.

In a meeting in January 1999, Desai said he got a similar piece of guidance from tech banker Trousset about research on banking clients: *If you can't say anything positive, don't say anything at all.* That was the culture of the tech group, Desai understood him to mean.[3]

A similar approach applied to potential clients as well, Desai soon realized. They discussed the tone and wording of a report in which Desai initiated coverage of Autodesk Inc. Desai had given a rating of "hold" instead of "buy," he later testified. Trousset, who had to approve any reports initiating coverage, reminded Desai that CSFB was trying to develop a relationship with the company.[4]

Desai felt a measure of vindication in the spring of 1999. When he downgraded Cadence Design in December 1998, he had received a quick scolding from Quattrone. But in April 1999, Cadence said it couldn't meet its previous revenue forecast for the year. A number of CSFB salespeople called him to say, "You made a great call."[5] Elliott Rogers, who became head of tech research in 2000, said later that Desai had inadvertently kept CSFB "out of a lot of trouble" by ensuring "we were never going to do any business with Cadence."[6]

○

The Quattrone group found creative ways to dangle the lure of favorable research coverage. At a bake-off pitch on July 7, 1999, for the IPO of broadband-access equipment maker Virata Inc., which CSFB won, the tech group presented a slide that said "CSFB Stands By Its Clients." It noted that when bad news hit three technology companies, a CSFB analyst had kept a "strong buy" rating on the company whose IPO CSFB had led, while analysts from comanagers on the same deal had cut their ratings in response.[7]

In theory, research analysts could veto IPOs or other banking deals if they didn't believe in the company's prospects. It was supposed to be an important check on the bankers' natural quest for fees. And it was meant to protect investors, the firm's customers on the other side of the stock sale. However, if one analyst turned up his nose at a deal, CSFB tech bankers might try it out on another, less selective analyst. Analysts who often said yes when others had said no sometimes gained a reputation as "banking whores."[8]

At one point in mid-1999 Quattrone personally pressured his research chief, star personal-computer analyst Michael Kwatinetz, to launch coverage of Gemstar-TV Guide International. A Credit Suisse banker had e-mailed Kwatinetz on June 15, with a copy to Quattrone and senior banker John Hodge, relaying comments from a Gemstar executive that CSFB would have no chance at a pending sale of fifteen million shares of stock unless Gemstar was getting research coverage from the firm.

When Kwatinetz replied that he couldn't begin the process of launching coverage until after July 4, partly due to his need to study for a licensing exam as well as work on "three other banking deals" and other chores, Quattrone shot back a note questioning his decision: "you really damage your credibility with this kind of stuff. take a day off from your test prep and go down [to see Gemstar] this week or next." Quattrone then forwarded his note to senior bankers Boutros, Brady, and Hodge, adding: "trying to shame him into it . . ."[9]

Quattrone later testified that Kwatinetz had committed to launching coverage by a certain date, and "had a history of using those kinds of things as an excuse. And I just wanted to push him on it." Quattrone said that the possible transaction "could have been one of the reasons" for pushing Kwatinetz. "I was blowing off a little steam, to tell you the truth."[10]

O

In the fall of 1999, CSFB recruited star telecom analyst Dan Reingold away from Merrill Lynch. The shape of one offer Reingold received showed that his potential to help win banking business was important: CSFB offered Reingold 2.5 percent of any fees over $150 million CSFB received for telecom banking deals. Reingold declined any percentage deal, believing it would be a conflict that could bias his research.

In October, Reingold met Wheat, and soon got a call from Quattrone. He was "a bit flattered," because "Frank had become arguably the most influential banker in the entire world by now," Reingold thought. "Frank had more money and more power than just about any employee of an investment bank."

Quattrone told Reingold that the technology group was anxious to work closely with the telecom group, partly because telecom companies were such big users and buyers of technology. "He sounded incredibly open and friendly,"

Reingold recalled, but he "couldn't help wonder whether he might somehow try to influence my research."

When he negotiated the final terms in November 1999, Reingold asked for only four amendments to the contract CSFB proposed. The first was to ensure that he would report to Jackson, the research chief. "I did not want to report to Frank Quattrone. I was sure that having a banker as a boss would create more pressure than ever to be bullish on the stocks I covered."[11]

○

In another practice that subtly eroded analysts' independence, the CSFB tech group allowed them to discuss the ratings they were about to publish with the clients' executives, regulators later charged. While this enabled the analysts to maintain closer ties to the company, it also put extra pressure on them to be bullish, the regulators said. As Razorfish was about to close on an acquisition of icube, CSFB information technology services analyst Mark Wolfenberger contacted Jeff Dachis, the Razorfish CEO, on October 29, 1999, and asked his opinion. Should he resume coverage with a buy or strong buy?

"We would have taken you to a strong buy, but given the recent stock run, does it make sense for us to keep the upgrade in our back pocket in case we need it? Either way, I don't care. You guys deserve it," Wolfenberger said. "I just don't want to waste it."

Dachis responded somewhat ambiguously, then conceded that it was "getting hard to justify the valuations." Nevertheless on November 3, 1999, with the stock at $39 a share, Wolfenberger resumed coverage with a "strong buy." He kept that rating until October 27, 2000, when—with the stock at $4—he lowered the rating to a "buy." On May 4, 2001, with the stock at $1.14 a share, Wolfenberger dropped the rating to "hold."[12]

○

In November 1999, Desai made some cautionary comments about the stock of Parametric Technology Corporation, which he had just begun covering, noting that other analysts had been talking it up in advance of a scheduled "analysts' day" at the company. Desai's report warned that a great deal of hype surrounded the company and its stock. *Let's be realistic, this is how we should probably value the company,* he said.[13]

When he arrived at his office, Desai testified, he had a message from the Parametric CEO, Steven Walske. *I've never met you,* he said, *but I don't like you already. I saw your cute little piece about our hyped company, and rest assured we will never do any business with CSFB.*

Then Desai's phone rang. It was Jake Peters, the head of East Coast tech banking for the Quattrone group. *We've been courting the company for years, trying to win the business over from Goldman,* Peters said, according to Desai's testimony. *You sit and get this guy upset.* Desai tried to explain his note. *Yeah, but you used inflammatory words like hype,* Peters said. *Why don't you just go along with the consensus?*

Desai knew he was in trouble. Later that week, he testified, when he was out of the office at a doctor's appointment, he got a curt voice-mail message from Elliott Rogers, a senior semiconductor analyst. *We really need to talk about the tonality of your research,* Rogers said.

At the tech group investment conference the next week, Desai testified that banker Tony Trousset pulled him aside to give him some friendly advice: *You know, the senior guys in Palo Alto don't think you understand how to be banking friendly. People are upset at you.*[14] The remarks hit home, because Desai did feel as though being banking friendly was part of his job. His understanding was that analysts whose companies did the most business with CSFB tended to be the most highly paid.

O

Quattrone was willing to use research not only as a carrot, but as a stick.

In January 2000, as CSFB jockeyed to obtain the lead-manager role for a proposed $400 million stock issue by Aether Systems Inc., Quattrone was informed that Aether wanted Merrill to lead its deal, and planned to offer CSFB only a less lucrative co-manager slot. In an e-mail sent January 26, Quattrone told both CSFB bankers and research analysts that the proposal wasn't acceptable, and that CSFB would drop research coverage of the company if it didn't get the lead role.

Companies wanted extra Wall Street research coverage because it gave them additional informed, credible voices available to discuss the stock. Even if it wasn't always bullish—though it usually was—the research coverage was a sign that the company mattered, an imprimatur of sorts.

"[N]o fucking way do we accept this proposal," he said, adding, "we have agreed on a script, which is books or we walk and drop coverage." In an e-mail the same day, new telecom analyst Reingold endorsed the Quattrone strategy.[15] Aether stuck with Merrill Lynch, and CSFB didn't serve as a co-manager of the offering in March. But Quattrone's lawyers later noted that CSFB didn't follow through on its threat to drop research coverage on Aether.[16]

O

Even at the very height of the bubble, the Quattrone bankers kept the pressure on the analysts, who depended on them for their pay and their very jobs, to be as bullish as possible.

In early 2000, when the tech group pitched to lead the IPO of Numerical

Technologies Inc., Quattrone personally led off. He was followed by Desai. The analyst discussed how he would explain to institutional investors the problem in the electronics chain that the design software company addressed.[17] The research section of the Numerical pitch book was headlined: EASY DECISION ... STRONG BUY! This implicitly promised, regulators later charged, that CSFB would issue a "strong buy" rating when it launched research on the stock.[18] Next came banker Richard Hart, who explained how he would value the company.

On April 8, 2000, Numerical Technologies had risen 154 percent on its first day of trading. Its top two executives, chief executive Buno Pati and chief financial officer Richard Mora had opened Friends of Frank accounts. As the time approached for Desai to initiate research coverage on the stock, he felt pressure to give it a positive rating.

Desai met with the head of marketing at Numerical, who asked him what his thoughts were. Desai explained that because the stock had run up, he would probably give it a "buy" rating, instead of a "strong buy." Within two to three hours he got a call from banker John Hodge, the deputy head of technology corporate finance, asking about Desai's thinking on the Numerical initiation note.

Hodge told Desai that Numerical CEO Pati had just called him, Desai later testified. *He's all upset,* Hodge told him. *He thinks you're going to be a little cautious, that you're not positively inclined to the stock. I just wanted to know where you're at.* Desai was startled that the gist of his conversation had been relayed back to Hodge so quickly.

I can't tell you what your rating should be—"buy," "strong buy," that's your call, Hodge said, according to Desai. *But remember, just because the stock has doubled or something, a lot of stocks have gone on to move to much higher highs, so keep that in perspective.*

Desai's understanding of the ground rules for "strong buy" was that the analyst had to believe the stock would rise 25 percent in the next twelve months. But Hodge encouraged him to look further out, to the company's prospects for the next two or three years.

After reappraising the situation, Desai initiated coverage of Numerical with a "strong buy." The next time he ran into Hodge, Desai says, the senior banker told him, *Good job on the Numerical initiation.*[19]

O

After technology stock research chief Michael Kwatinetz left in April 2000, his successor was semiconductor analyst Elliott Rogers. An e-mail exchange in the fall of 2000 suggested that Rogers gave his own bullish tone to the tech group research.

On October 11, 2000, Bhavin Shah, an Asian-technology research analyst, sent an e-mail to Rogers and Tim Mahon, a semiconductor analyst, saying he was facing some "tough decisions" in setting ratings on two Asian companies that were big CSFB banking clients. Noting some disquieting signs, he asked whether he could launch coverage on one with a "neutral" rating. "Wondering how to approach this based on banking sensitivities," Shah said.

Mahon replied the next day. "Bhavin, Suggest you ask Elliott about 'The Agilent Two-Step.' That's where in writing you have a buy rating . . . but verbally everyone knows your position."[20] The report in question on Agilent, a banking client, was issued in July 2000 with a "buy" rating accompanied by numerous caveats and warnings about losses in some businesses and an earnings shortfall. "Agilent is rated Buy, but only in the most generous sense, though in the short term we would only buy it on extreme weakness," it said.

The report in question on Agilent had been authored by Rogers himself. CSFB lawyers later defended it, saying the text merely highlighted some specific short-term risks and concerns.

But Quattrone's own reaction to another report a month later showed how heavily banking revenue weighed in allocating research coverage. In June 2000, the chief executive of Agile Software Corporation e-mailed Quattrone seeking both "ideas" for possible acquisitions as well as research coverage of his company by CSFB. "We understand nothing happens at CSFB tech until you say so," he joked. In a follow-up e-mail to members of his group, Quattrone asked whether it was worth the effort—only to be warned that Agile had expressed interest in banking ideas before but hadn't followed through by giving CSFB any business.

On the morning of Monday, November 6, 2000, analyst Brent Thill sent an e-mail to Quattrone and another banker informing them of his plans to launch coverage of Agile Software. Morgan Stanley had taken Agile public in a $72.5 million IPO in August 1999, and had led a $435 million follow-on stock sale in December 1999. "Report hits our sales desk after the mkt close tonight. I will be giving a 15 minute teach-in to our worldwide sales force at 1:15 today." Thill's rating on the stock was a "buy."

A few hours later, Quattrone replied: "What have we extracted from them on banking side to get this coverage?"[21]

DENVER

20

JAMES LUSTIG was well known on the Denver scene. He had married into a prominent Denver family. His wife, Debra, was one of the three daughters of Herbert Cook, who ran the Dave Cook sporting-goods retailing chain founded by his father after World War I. After selling the retailer in 1988, Cook shifted into real estate. His HC Properties Ltd. specialized in developing and marketing sites for other fast-growing retailers such as Blockbuster, Office Depot, and Boston Chicken.

The Cook daughters gained their social prominence based partly on their father's wealth, which was estimated at more than $50 million in 1995, and partly on family friendships.[1] Cook and his wife, Gloria, had been close friends with Marvin Davis, the billionaire oil investor turned Hollywood mogul, and his wife, Barbara Davis. Lustig's wife was best friends with the Davises' daughter Nancy. And all three of the daughters and their husbands were fixtures in the society pages of the local newspapers for attending and sponsoring numerous charity galas.

Lustig, a well-dressed man of medium height with a mustache in his late forties, and his wife cut glamorous figures on the charity circuit. In August 1992, Debbie Lustig hosted a lunch at her home with Nancy Davis to promote a charity celebrity ski race. In 1997, they attended a cocktail reception for President Bill Clinton at the home of Sharon Magness, the widow of cable TV magnate Robert Magness.[2]

Steve Farber, who married Cook's daughter Cindy, became a politically connected Denver power broker as a founding partner of the law firm Brownstein Hyatt & Farber. Farber was chairman of the two successful Democratic campaigns of Colorado governor Roy Rohmer. And he represented the former owner of the Denver Nuggets pro basketball team and Colorado Avalanche hockey team in connection with the construction of a new arena, the Pepsi Center. He also represented the Denver Broncos in the construction of a new football stadium. The

Denver magazine called *5280* featured Farber, Lustig's brother-in-law, on the cover in April 1998 as number one among "the most powerful people in Denver."

Lustig and Farber lived on the same boomerang-shaped drive in the Devonshire Heights section of Cherry Hills, an upscale neighborhood south of downtown Denver. The three sons-in-law all had offices in the same downtown office building, at 410 Seventeenth Street, a block from the famed Brown Palace Hotel. Farber's law firm occupied floors 20 through 23. The seventeenth floor housed a suite of offices for HC Properties Ltd., two other family entities, and Lustig's trading operation, United Capital Management.

In 1999, Schmidt sent one of his trading assistants, Scott Brown, out to Denver to verify that Lustig had a bona fide operation and wasn't simply trading out of his bedroom. Lustig would occasionally mention to Wall Street brokers that he knew Tom Marsico, the famous former manager of the Janus Twenty fund. Marsico lived near Lustig in Cherry Hills, and their daughters were friends at school.

Lustig was known as a "syndicate player." The word syndicate was Wall Street jargon for any group of investment banks that served as underwriters for specific stock or bond issues.[3] His entire strategy for making money in this market was simple: He bought and quickly resold, or "flipped," hot IPOs. He always tried to sell any of his stock holdings by the end of the day.

Lustig was one of the many traders who lined up to receive the hot IPOs being offered by Credit Suisse First Boston and other firms on Wall Street. He knew that the Wall Street firms tried to steer some hot IPO shares to their best customers, defined as those who paid the most commissions.

But the underwriters also had to consider the interest of the company issuing the stock in developing a stable base of long-term investors who wouldn't simply flip the stock. The companies that issued the stock abhorred flippers, preferring to see the stock get into the hands of investors they knew truly believed in their companies' futures. Underwriters, too, tried to control flipping, because too much could torpedo a company's stock price. That's why underwriters often tried to crack down on flippers, cutting them off from future allocations if they were detected.

It helped Lustig get more stock to have an official-sounding name, like United Capital Management. That way, on paper at least, he resembled a substantial long-term investment institution that managed a portfolio of stocks— instead of being the flipper he actually was.

Yet Lustig also knew that no matter how many dollars he paid in commissions or how legitimate he appeared, there was a limit to how many shares each individual account could get. The number of shares a "good customer" like Lustig could get would also depend on other factors, such as how many shares of an IPO his broker had access to.

Lustig figured out that he could get more shares of hot IPOs by fielding more than one account with more than one broker at each firm. But if he was too obvious about it, and was detected by the firms' legal and compliance units, he might get cut off completely. So he adopted a series of subterfuges, sometimes with the knowledge of the brokers themselves.

Some traders simply used multiple account names and multiple brokers. But that was risky and might be detected. Lustig developed a more sophisticated system by teaming up with people he knew who could open additional accounts, effectively acting as his confederates. They would get advice from Lustig on how to go about it, and sometimes he would give them seed money; in return, he would get a share of the trading profits. Some traded out of his warren of offices at the Cook family business in downtown Denver. But others operated out of their own offices or homes.

Lustig had a company, JAL Ventures Corporation, that served as a limited partner and investor in the other traders' funds. A JAL affiliate performed administrative services for the other trading operations. And JAL would generally get 30 percent of the trading profits, while the traders themselves kept 70 percent.[4] By the time Lustig had the organization fully developed, he had twenty-one joint ventures with a total of twenty-eight individual traders. Some of the traders made tens of millions of dollars during the bubble.

To an extent, the system required each of the other traders to pose as the same kind of semiprofessional that Lustig appeared to be. So one of their challenges became inventing account names, like United Capital, that masked their identities. The use of account names in "d/b/a" accounts, short for "doing business as" accounts, enabled the traders to "open several accounts at each [investment bank]," according to a lawyer for Lustig.[5]

One trader used the name Energia Global Group Holdings. Another used the name Ascent Capital Corporation. They used only their own money, to avoid triggering additional disclosure requirements. And if they were spotted as flippers and shut down, they would attempt to open new accounts under different names.

The Lustig traders tried to open accounts with brokers at any firm where they might gain access to IPOs. They avidly read a daily report on upcoming IPOs, published by Triad Securities Corporation, located on Broadway in lower Manhattan. Available for twenty-five thousand dollars a year, "The U.S. IPO Consensus Report" offered a look at which deals would be the hottest. It was the *Daily Racing Form* of the IPO market.

The Denver traders had to skirt the rules at times. The standard Wall Street account form to get new issues requires disclosure of any other economically related entities, or affiliates. When these traders filled out these forms, they didn't mention Lustig. Doing so could have given the game away. Some later explained the omission by saying that they misunderstood the question.

The Lustig group members also relied on an intermediary between them and the Wall Street dealers like CSFB to help obscure what they were really doing. In Lustig's case, this was Spear, Leeds & Kellogg, called a prime broker, which processed trades for smaller brokers and traders. The back-office systems and services offered by Spear Leeds allowed Lustig and his other traders to flip the hot IPOs at a profit, without being detected by their brokers or their firms.[6]

In an action that later corroborated the Lustig lawyer's account, an industry regulator fined Spear, Leads $1 million in March 2005 "for creating . . . a system to conceal sales" of IPO shares.[7] Spear, Leeds also offered the traders the ability to "cross-collateralize" their accounts. In other words, the clearing brokers would know the accounts were related but the individual securities firms like CSFB would not. What it all amounted to was "an elaborate effort to disguise our identity from and preserve our anonymity to the [investment banks]," a lawyer for the Lustig traders said in a presentation to regulators in early 2001.[8]

When it was over, one of the lawyers for the group's members expressed amazement at what the Lustig group had accomplished. "In the biggest IPO market the planet had ever known," he said, "this small group of guys accounted for 3% of all the IPO" shares sold during the bubble. Of course, the tactics left the average individual investor who didn't know how to play the game even further out in the cold—unable to get in on the action.

O

Lustig was Schmidt's biggest, most active trading account. He was from a wealthy family, "he had some real money," Schmidt told NASD investigators after the bubble. Lustig had "three or four accounts" with the Quattrone brokers alone, he added.[9]

On November 9, 1999, tech group broker Scott Brown sent an e-mail describing Lustig to a colleague. "Jimmy is a pure trading account, does not hold positions, but can also take very large allocations without causing him any problem," Brown said. "He pays us back for deal allocations on the day of the deal."[10]

The junior tech group brokers Scott Brown and Scott Bushley, sometimes referred to as traders, were just kids compared to Schmidt. Bushley had graduated from Vanderbilt in 1996, and told regulators later this was the only job he had ever had.[11] Brown had a little more experience, having started at Montgomery in 1994.[12]

Lustig would usually place orders with the Quattrone group brokers to buy or sell stocks at the opening price, a practice that enabled him to place offsetting buy and sell trades at other firms at exactly the same price, to hedge his risk, Bushley later told the SEC. "I just learned that over time that's what Jimmy did, and the reason that he did that was to pay us commissions," Bushley said. Lustig and other traders often placed such orders to coincide with IPO allocations, Bushley said.[13]

When Lustig would call, Bushley would give him the names of big, easy-to-trade stocks that were in the news. "Scotty, what's going on this morning?" Lustig would say.

"Oh, GM just reported numbers," Bushley would reply.

"Okay, buy me seventy-five thousand of that on the open," Lustig would say.

Recounting the pattern to SEC investigators in October 2001, Bushley said, "They did market-open trades . . . to give us commissions."

A tech group e-mail in the fall of 1999 listing tech group brokerage trading-account allocations for one IPO indicated that Lustig's United Capital received the most shares, at 30,000. That was followed by Devon Capital at 25,000, Y2K Partners and Rosecliff at 15,000 each, Red Bear at 12,000, Bel Air Capital and an individual named Cal at 10,000 each, Miller Capital and 8,000, Bedford Capital, Poundsbridge and Santa Barbara at 5,000 each, Bentley and a fund called PTM at 4,000 each, and Maxim Financial at 2,000.[14]

Some of the other tech group brokerage accounts were run by traders with ties to organizations that pursued IPO allocations using methods similar to Lustig's. One of them was a trading operation, PTJP Partners, with dozens of traders who used multiple account names to get hot IPOs. Among the PTJP accounts were Devon and Bedford.[15]

During the peak of the IPO frenzy, another CSFB broker, Paul Caan, said the firm's brokers "would get ten calls a day" from would-be traders wanting to open accounts and offering to share their IPO profits. "It seemed like they were reading a script," he said.[16]

Even though Lustig was Schmidt's biggest account, there was never any indication that Quattrone was aware of Lustig's operation and tactics. Yet Lustig and his traders would play an important role when regulators launched an investigation of how the commissions paid by such traders influenced IPO allocations.

MIKE GRUNWALD

21

THE FRIENDS OF FRANK program, designed for Quattrone by Schmidt, offered hot IPOs to clients who had given investment banking assignments to the Quattrone group at CSFB.

And as traders like Lustig became more and more aggressive about their willingness to pay bigger and bigger commissions to get hot IPOs, the commissions came to resemble kickbacks to the brokers in exchange for their IPO profits.

The Schmidt brokers had both kinds of accounts. Now they were about to be joined by a hyperaggressive, highly paid broker who supercharged the way the group did business.

O

Mike Grunwald was a charismatic, dark-haired broker with movie star looks.

His father was an aerospace engineer at NASA and Martin Marietta. His mother was a social worker, and then a probation officer for juveniles. When his parents split up, Grunwald, the youngest of four children, went with an older sister to live with his mother in the Denver suburb of Littleton, Colorado. After graduating from Colorado State University, he attended business school at the University of Texas and became a shopping-center leasing agent at the Dallas-based Trammel Crow Company.

In 1992, Grunwald joined Morgan Stanley, where he became close friends with Bill Brady, Quattrone's head of corporate finance, while working on the same floor of the firm's San Francisco office. In a brief, ill-timed shift, Grunwald left to spend three months at a firm in Greenwich, Connecticut, which marketed hedge funds, just as investor interest in them dried up in 1998 after the Long Term Capital debacle. He then moved to Lehman Brothers.

In the spring of 1999, only two months after he had moved to Lehman, Grunwald was invited to meet with Schmidt and Quattrone at Quattrone's

Palo Alto office. The trio of brokers who had joined the Schmidt group in 1997, who had their own firm called the Nexus Group, was leaving to strike out on their own again, and Schmidt needed help as the pace of business heated up.

In July 1999, Grunwald met with Tony Ehinger, the head of global equity sales, in New York, and the next month he agreed to join. Grunwald was ecstatic. He was going to be joining the leader in the technology banking business at its "epicenter" in San Francisco.[1]

It took two months to draw up his contract. His compensation formula filled three pages of fine print in the eight-page letter from Ehinger, dated October 20, 1999, formally offering him the job. He would receive a $1.47 million stock award from CSFB to offset what he would lose by leaving Lehman. He would be paid a minimum of $1.5 million a year, or $125,000 a month. He would be entitled to 33 percent of all the tech group private-client brokers' commissions, and any amounts over his minimum would be payable monthly.

Grunwald, it appeared, was being brought in to build up some of the businesses Schmidt had begun but not fully developed. For example, Grunwald would be entitled to as much as 50 percent of the corporate cash-management fees from the new economy tech companies CSFB had taken public and whose war chest of IPO proceeds they still had to manage. Grunwald could also receive 10 percent of fees for any banking deal he referred to the technology group, and an additional discretionary bonus to be determined by Quattrone and Brady.[2]

The Grunwald contract terms meant that he would be paid more than Schmidt the following year. There was an undercurrent message in Grunwald's hiring, with Brady's sponsorship, that Schmidt was too laid-back for the younger, more aggressive members of Quattrone's group. Certainly Grunwald's pay was a sign of that.

○

Wall Street traders sometimes refer to easy pickings as "low hanging fruit." One trader later joked that these IPOs were "fruit that was rolling around on the ground."

All across Wall Street, hedge fund managers—those professional traders who manage private partnerships for the wealthy, or for institutions such as pension funds—began focusing on how to get more shares of such IPOs. Some hired extra analysts to attend tech IPO road shows, hoping to convince the underwriters and company executives they were interested in holding on to the stocks and not just flipping them.

At CSFB, brokers throughout the firm devised ways to induce clients to pay higher commissions in exchange for the hot IPOs, regulators would later charge. The firm's institutional brokers, who dealt with mutual funds and other professional money managers, designed a spreadsheet, called a "new-issue performance report," that charted each client's paper profits on their IPO allocations. The report calculated the clients' profits assuming they resold the IPO shares immediately, or held them for thirty days, or held them for three months, or for six months. To varying degrees, the brokers attempted to cite those calculations of paper profits to boost the commissions they received from each customer, making it clear that customers who paid more would get more allocations, the regulators charged.[3]

○

On October 26, 1999, Grunwald met in New York as part of his orientation with fifteen to twenty CSFB staffers, including Andy Benjamin, the head of CSFB's private-client brokers. Benjamin had the dotted-line review authority over the Quattrone brokers' new accounts, trade runs, and syndicate allocations, including hot IPOs. Benjamin suggested that Grunwald meet with his deputy, Paul Caan, the national sales manager who had authority over new-issue allocations for the private-client brokers.[4]

Two and a half years later, Grunwald would give his own version of what had happened. "At that meeting, Caan stated to Grunwald that the firm allocated IPO shares to customers, who were required to 'pay back' the firm for such allocations through secondary commissions," Grunwald said in a 2002 arbitration claim he filed against CSFB.[5]

Caan's description of the IPO allocation practices, Grunwald said, was reflected in spreadsheets maintained in the firm's New York offices that compared commissions paid by hedge funds to the hedge funds' IPO profits. "Brokers and their managers understood that hedge funds generated substantial secondary commissions on 'deal day' in exchange for receiving IPO allocations." Translation: On the day a hot IPO launched, the brokers would steer shares to clients who quickly returned the favor by paying inflated commissions on other trades.

Benjamin said later he was unaware of any such payback program or the instructions by Caan. Nor was there ever any evidence that Quattrone knew about that either. When a broker in another office, Casey Pristou, asked about such a quid pro quo arrangement in September 1999, Benjamin "went ballistic" and said it wasn't allowed. Caan later told regulators that he too had told Pristou that "that is bullshit, we don't do that kind of business."[6] And he denied Grunwald's allegations during the arbitration proceeding brought by Grunwald.

○

In practice, the process of obtaining hot IPOs could be glimpsed in a chain of e-mails between Steve Keller, a CSFB broker in New York who covered hedge funds, and other CSFB staffers.[7]

On Wednesday afternoon September 22, 1999, Keller noted that one client, Sutton Capital, "continues to pay us for deal stock." Sutton had been allocated twenty-five hundred shares of E.piphany Inc., an Internet marketing services company. That day, the IPO nearly tripled in price on its first day of trading. Priced at $16 each, the shares closed at $45.19. That gave Sutton a one-day paper profit of $72,975.

To repay CSFB for the windfall, Sutton paid $28,000 in commissions on other trades—or roughly 38 percent of the first-day paper gain. Keller's e-mail noted that Sutton, a trading client, had engineered a similar payback on an earlier IPO of MP3.com, which had gone public in July.

The same pattern continued with the IPOs of TiVo and Interwoven. Three weeks later, on October 13, CSFB broker Joseph Girimonti told Ted Hatfield, a senior equity-syndicate manager, and other CSFB capital markets executives that Sutton received three thousand shares of TiVo, the TV replay service, which had gone public on September 29 at $16 a share. TiVo's stock price rose $13.94 on its first day of trading, giving Sutton a paper profit of $41,813. And Sutton again had "paid us $28,000 on deal day," Girimonti said.[8]

Sutton also received three thousand shares of Interwoven, a Web content manager. The Interwoven IPO was priced at $17 a share and rose $24, or 141 percent, to close at $41 on its first day of trading, October 8. The first-day paper profit was $72,000, and Sutton "paid us $40,000 on deal day," Girimonti said. Essentially, the brokers were getting paybacks in the form of big commissions.

The next day, Hatfield's reply showed that such commission windfalls were now to be expected, and that CSFB officials knew that such trading accounts were routinely flipping their IPO shares in immediate resales to lock in their paper profits. "[G]reat job," Hatfield replied to Girimonti. "[N]ot to look a gift horse in the mouth, but the account made $170,000 selling on the open."[9]

Regulators never charged Keller, Girimonti, and Hatfield with any wrong-doing.

○

Sometime in the second half of 1999, Schmidt group trader Scott Brown had put together a very rough, homemade spreadsheet tracking some of the trading accounts' profits on the last five or six IPOs. Brown had shown it to Schmidt. They could use it, they agreed, to push the trading accounts to keep the commissions coming. The spreadsheets used this way by the group eventually evolved much further in sophistication. (Schmidt himself had set a guideline that the trading accounts had to do just as much business in "secondary trading" as they did in new issues.[10])

Soon after his meetings in New York, Grunwald later said, he got an e-mail from one of the Schmidt group traders mentioning that the client accounts paid them back for hot IPOs on the day of the deal. And when he returned to California, he was shown spreadsheets by Brown and his colleague Scott Bushley, and was told that they targeted commissions to equal 50 percent of profits."[11]

Whoever had authorized it, the technology group brokers who worked for Schmidt were in the game. Sometime before the fall of 1999, Schmidt's brokers "formed an understanding" that the trading accounts, which by mid-1999 numbered twenty to thirty, would return at least 50 percent of their profits back to the brokers in the form of commissions.[12] Scott Brown and Scott Bushley, the traders, maintained spreadsheets tracking the commissions and profits of customers such as Lustig.

O

When questioned much later by CSFB lawyers, Grunwald said he had no idea that such tactics might violate industry rules against sharing customers' profits, as regulators would later charge. Eight days after his briefing from Caan, he was told that the legal and compliance department was completing a review of the Schmidt group brokers, including its IPO allocation practices for retail accounts, including individuals, hedge funds, and venture capital clients.

The CSFB lawyers were evidently beginning to realize that all the action around hot IPOs might become a problem.

On November 9, 1999, Ray Dorado, the senior lawyer in the equity division, and one of the two CSFB officials who had periodically checked in on the group, summarized the results of an audit of the tech group PCS brokers. His memo promised that the legal and compliance department, known as LCD, "will circulate shortly a draft policy with respect to the allocation process to address certain concerns about the practice known as 'spinning,' as well as appearance problems and general suitability concerns with respect to retail account allocations." He also promised that legal would address some form of review of IPO allocations and record keeping.[13]

O

Back in California, Grunwald set about building up the cash-management business. And he also launched a push for the technology client brokers to get more IPO shares to help expand the number of Friends of Frank accounts.

On November 22, 1999, Grunwald sent an e-mail to Quattrone, Brady, and Schmidt with a to-do list. He wanted to hire ten new staffers and two or three more brokers. As for getting more IPO shares, he said, "since this has been the area that our clients have had the most positive results we need to figure a way to scale it"—meaning, to get more. They were consistently getting the low end of the promised range of 2 percent to 4 percent, Grunwald said, asking that "Frank or Bill make a call."[14]

Grunwald eventually moved into one of the guest apartments at Brady's Lombard Street mansion. He introduced Brady to one of his girlfriends. And he and Brady would have dinner with three or four other friends once or twice a week when they were both in town. The talk was that parties at Brady's house were wild as the peak of the Internet bubble neared, and eventually received their due notice in *Maxim*, a young men's magazine that features photos of scantily clad females.

The *Maxim* author, Ian Mount, first paid homage to the high-tech bat cave and its "nine-car garage that boasts a car-turnaround system, so he never has to back out." Then he quoted an anonymous former coworker of Brady's: "I've done coke in the red suede elevator. I've seen coworkers naked in the hot tub. His parties made *Caligula* look like a Disney movie."[15]

And in a bow to the Hollywood scene, the CSFB tech-team members even stretched the "strategic" goals of the Friends of Frank account holders by including J. Geyer Kosinski, a talent agent, manager, and TV-movie producer. (Kosinski's clients have included Angelina Jolie, Billy Bob Thornton, Forest Whitaker, and Milla Jovovich.) They identified him on their list of clients as "industry ent." and assigned him a priority of 3.[16]

THE HOTTEST IPO EVER

22

THE NEXT four months, December 1999 to March 2000, would bring the climax of the Internet stock bubble, a madly spinning vortex that seemed to spew out the most extreme IPO stock deals and, when viewed in hindsight after the bursting of the bubble, the most extreme conduct.

Quattrone spared no expense at his annual technology investors' conference, traditionally held in the last week of November. For the 1999 conference at the Phoenician in Scottsdale, Arizona, Quattrone spent $3 million and flew in Kevin Zraly, the wine director at the Windows on the World restaurant atop the World Trade Center, as well as four-star restaurateur and chef Daniel Bouloud.

In the middle of Zraly's wine tutorial the first night, as the money managers sipped a 1994 French chardonnay, Robin Williams popped up before the audience from the wings of a stage. "Why don't you download my software so you can upload your hard drive?" he said, launching into ten minutes of comedy schtick.[1]

Williams, it turned out, had come as a guest of Audible, the downloadable spoken media company in which he held stock and options tied to a weekly Internet comedy production deal. After the bubble burst, Williams joked that Audible had paid him in "confederate currency." (Audible's stock eventually rebounded.)[2]

One keynote speaker was Michael Dell, whose candid assessments of specific companies enlivened the proceedings at more than one of the conferences. John Doerr, the renowned venture capitalist, and Yahoo! chief executive Tim Koogle also spoke. Cisco showed off futuristic Web phone booths.[3] Attendees all got a $399 retail value Jornada handheld personal computer made by Hewlett-Packard.

O

In late 1999 Lise Buyer, by then the firm's leading Internet analyst, got a call from Ted Smith, the CSFB banker who appeared so frequently at pitches with

Brady, and who had lived in one of Brady's guest apartments on Lombard Street. Smith told Buyer to get to know Petopia.com, a pet-supply company she had serious doubts about, and prepare to pitch for its IPO. Petopia.com had venture backing from Jay Hoag, a longtime Quattrone ally, and Group Arnault, an affiliate of LVMH, whose chief executive, Bernard Arnault, was also a CSFB client.

Buyer was shocked. Analysts were supposed to be able to veto IPOs of companies they didn't believe in. "He didn't ask me if I was interested in covering it—I was told to, because CSFB wanted the banking business," she recalled later.

The two proceeded to have what she recalled as "a very high-decibel conversation, only because I had the seniority to do that." Ms. Buyer, who made more than $1 million a year, refused the order, and—partly as a result of such disagreements—left the firm in early 2000. Petopia.com, which in March 2000 filed plans for an IPO led by another firm, never made it to market, and closed its doors in February 2001.[4]

○

After the conference, Grunwald fired off an e-mail on Sunday, December 5, 1999, again pushing senior CSFB staffers in New York to allocate more IPO shares for the technology group brokers.[5] Quattrone endorsed the demand, reminding the New York staffers that his group's original CSFB contract entitled his brokers to a target of 2 percent to 4 percent of IPO shares, and 5 percent if they had "quality demand." But the Schmidt brokers had only been getting 2 percent.

When Grunwald pressed New York for assurance two days later on December 7, Quatrone again seconded the demand.[6] "We need to do this at a minimum to accommodate the 60 new clients," Quattrone told the CSFB managers in New York who controlled the allocations. "We should discuss allocations though: want to make sure we are being strategic about this."

○

It just so happened that the repeated demands by Quattrone and his brokers for more IPO shares came on the eve of what became the hottest IPO of all time. It eventually became apparent that some recipients of this particular hot IPO got the valuable shares in exchange for paying oversize commissions immediately afterward.

At 6:00 A.M. on Thursday morning, December 9, 1999, executives of VA Linux Systems gathered at the institutional trading desk on the seventeenth floor of the CSFB offices in downtown San Francisco. Linux was an open-source computer language, available via free download, that challenged the dominance of mighty Microsoft. Those present included the Linux chief executive, Larry M. Augustin, and his friend Linus Torvalds, the inventor of the Linux system. Torvalds was dressed in his customary T-shirt and sandals, and their three toddlers scampered around the trading floor as the grown-ups watched VA Linux start trading.[7]

The VA Linux debut was a milestone for CSFB—for good and bad. Its first-day price gain of 697.5 percent smashed the old record of 606 percent held by the 1998 IPO of TheGlobe.com. And it became one of the most investigated technology transactions of the dot-com bubble. The IPO was priced at $30 a share, and the first trade that morning was at $299 a share, a gain of almost 900 percent. The stock closed at $239.25 on the NASDAQ stock market.

The VA Linux IPO shares had become the most valuable in Wall Street history. Who had received them?

Some of the Denver traders tied to James Lustig scored heavily.

Steve Kris had known Lustig for years. They both played golf at the Green Gables country club on the southwest side of town. Kris had begun day trading during the bubble from his home in Englewood, a Denver suburb. And he had entered into a joint venture with JAL Ventures, Lustig's vehicle for his affiliate traders.

Kris had an account named Ascent Capital with CSFB brokers in Boston. On Monday morning, December 6, a CSFB broker in Boston sent a memo to George Coleman, the head of institutional listed sales trading: "Steve Kris at Ascent Capital has been listening to us, he paid us $150,000 in secondary commissions in November in an attempt to bring the ratio down."

Investigators would later zero in on the use of the word "ratio." It referred to the ratio of the commissions paid by a trading customer to the IPO profits he had earned, as tracked by an IPO profit report. "Bringing the ratio down" meant the customer was paying CSFB more in commissions relative to the customer's profits on past hot IPOs.[8]

At first, Kris was slated to receive only a small allocation of 2,500 VA Linux shares in a preliminary list. But at 2:21 P.M. on December 8, the day before the IPO would begin trading, another CSFB salesman in Boston, Bob Paglione, urged that Ascent get more VA Linux shares. Paglione explained that Kris had paid the firm $100,000 in commissions in the previous week, and was on track to pay CSFB nearly $1 million for all of 1999, his first year as a customer of the firm.

On the morning of December 9, the day trading began, Kris received 12,500 shares of VA Linux—five times the original indication. Based on the first day's trading, those shares generated a paper profit for Ascent of $2.6 million. The same day, Kris repaid the favor. Instead of the standard rate of as little as $.05

a share for easy trades, Kris paid commissions of ten to 50 times that. The commissions totaled more than $500,000—or about one fifth of his profits. It was like paying $100 for a cup of coffee.

The Kris account called Ascent paid $2.70 a share to trade 50,000 shares of Citigroup, a commission of $135,000. Ascent also traded 100,000 shares of Compaq Computer at $1.25 a share, 50,000 shares of K-Mart at $.50 a share, 100,000 shares of Kroger at $.80 a share, and 50,000 shares of AT&T at $2.75 a share. The total commissions Ascent paid CSFB: $502,500.[9]

The next morning, Friday, December 10, Paglione sent an e-mail to the equity capital markets officials, following up: "Ascent ended up doing $500,000 in commissions with us yesterday. Thanks again for your help with this account. Bob."

The Kris trades were all done at commissions that equated to 5 percent of their value, a commonly used benchmark for markups used by brokerage regulators as a ceiling for brokers' profits on a single trade. Regulators have historically found that markups exceeding 5 percent can be evidence that a customer is being overcharged. However, in this case, the 5 percent rate was apparently being used in an attempt to make sure the commissions wouldn't look blatantly excessive.

Another payback trade was so blatant that it would catch regulators' eyes.

Another Lustig group trading account, Energia Global Group Holding, got 13,500 shares of VA Linux, and sold them on the first day of trading at a profit of $3.3 million.[10] The same trader also received 20,000 shares of El Sitio Inc., a Spanish-language Internet network that went public the same day as VA Linux. The El Sitio stock rose 108 percent on its first day of trading, generating $342,500 in additional profit. That same day the trader paid CSFB $1 million in commissions, or 27 percent of the profits on VA Linux and El Sitio.

But this trader didn't go to the trouble of breaking up the payback into several smaller trades, as Kris had. He loaded the entire payback into one gigantic trade of two million shares of Compaq at the rate of $.50 a share—ten times the going rate. His name was Andrew Siegal.

The "sole purpose" of the trading, regulators later charged, "was to generate commissions for CSFB," as payment for the profits on the hot IPOs.[11] In all, customers who did trades with CSFB at "excessive commission rates" got at least 405,000 shares out of the 4.1 million VA Linux shares distributed by CSFB.[12]

Who else got the valuable Linux stock at the IPO price?

CSFB brokers clearly had used the VA Linux IPO to generate extra cash commissions from their trading customers. But the separate group of Quattrone's brokers had also steered the shares to favored investment banking clients in the Friends of Frank program. And one longtime Quattrone venture capital client received one of the largest allocations in the entire deal.

Quattrone's tech-group brokers, led by Schmidt and Grunwald, allocated 92,000 VA Linux shares to 110 different Friends of Frank accounts, regulators charged. The average account got more than 800 shares, nearly half of which were sold were sold, or flipped, within a day.[13] The total first-day paper profit of $6.4 million amounted to an average of $58,000 per account!

At 8:11 A.M. on Tuesday December 14, tech group trader Scott Brown e-mailed one of the Friends of Frank account holders, David Samuel, the founder of Spinner.com, an Internet broadcaster which had been acquired by America Online: "Dave, you received 500 shares of VA Linux at $30 a share. We sold half of everyone's position (meaning 250 shares for you of course), at $226, and not a bad way to make $50,000." Brown added, "Your account is currently valued at $550,000." And he noted that Samuel had initially deposited just $56,000 on August 20, 1999.[14]

But at least one other Friend of Frank got far more. Technology Crossover Ventures, whose partner Jay Hoag was a longtime Quattrone associate, got 50,000 Linux shares—enough to generate a one-day paper profit of $10.5 million.[15] TCV was a "crossover" fund, a category designed to invest in companies both before and after they went public.

Although the degree of Quattrone's influence over initial public offerings was a central focus of debate at his two criminal trials, the CSFB banker had an obvious motivation to see that Hoag was well treated: He regularly doled out investment banking assignments. In an interview with the author, Hoag acknowledged that in 1999 and 2000, CSFB had led six of twenty-two IPOs of companies TCV had invested in, more than any other securities firm on Wall Street.[16] One of them was Intraware.

○

The impact of the VA Linux deal was like a thunderclap.

On the morning of December 16, 1999, just a week after the VA Linux deal had generated $58,000 in average paper profits to each person who had a Friends of Frank account, Quattrone group broker Mike Grunwald sent an e-mail to Quattrone, Brady, Boutros, and three other top Quattrone bankers—Ethan Topper, John Hodge, and Jake Peters—with a copy to Schmidt.

Grunwald was planning to expand the Friends of Frank program, ramping up the number of accounts and ranking them in importance, regulators later charged, based on their title and thus their ability to deliver or influence future banking assignments.

Under the subject line "syndicate distribution to clients and potential clients," Grunwald said he had "a few ideas . . . to make the best use of deal flow."[17] He said he would send the bankers the current list of accounts. Using the same word, strategic, that Quattrone had used before in an e-mail to Schmidt,

Grunwald invited the bankers to flag any account that shouldn't get future hot IPOs. The way he put it was, "anyone that is not strategic or that you believe should not continue, let us know and we will shut down."

Grunwald asked the Quattrone bankers to send him additional names of existing and potential clients who also might want to participate. And he asked them to rank the names on a scale of 1 to 4, with CEOs ranked 1 and CFOs ranked 2, and so forth. Those ranked 1 would get the most stock, those ranked 4 would get the least. "This way we can spread the deals further," Grunwald said. He concluded by renewing his appeal to get more stock. "And gentlemen," he closed, "CONGRATULATIONS on having a great 1999—Awesome! Your loyal servants, Mike and John."

Grunwald's plan to "shut down" accounts that weren't "strategic" would be another fateful move that would affect Quattrone.

O

Within CSFB, the wave of trades with jumbo commissions like Ascent's on Linux's deal day caught the eye of legal and compliance. The firm had a policy capping commissions for some brokers at the lower of 3 percent of the trade value, or one dollar a share. Many of the trades that followed VA Linux allocations had exceeded one dollar a share.

On December 21, 1999, Andy Benjamin, the chief of the private-client brokers in New York, who had dotted-line authority over Schmidt, wrote a memo to brokers that said: "beginning Jan. 1, you may not charge/mark-up/down more than 2% or 75 cents a share without the approval of" Benjamin, or George Coleman or another executive.[18]

The next day, on December 22, 1999, the oversize commissions issue came to the attention of David Brodsky, CSFB's general counsel for the Americas, at a meeting with Ray Dorado, the head of legal and compliance for the equity division. Brodsky, who had just joined the firm in October, was told of trouble between Schmidt, the head of the Quattrone brokers, and Benjamin, who was supposed to oversee the Schmidt brokers' trading.[19]

At the Dorado meeting, Brodsky learned that Benjamin wouldn't supervise the Quattrone group brokers because "John Schmidt won't take direction," according to Brodsky's notes from the session. Brodsky also learned Schmidt's group was receiving "extra" commission dollars from a client who was paying outsize amounts of $2 to $3 per share for trades of IBM stock as repayment for an allocation of VA Linux.

Brodsky promptly asked that the IBM trades be canceled, and instructed that the matter be investigated. But Brodsky then became immersed in another regulatory matter, an investigation of whether CSFB had helped the Ukraine obscure its finances to gain more aid from the International Monetary Fund. A memo by CSFB's outside lawyers in October 2001 seems to suggest that neither Brodsky nor other CSFB lawyers followed up on the larger issues of the Benjamin-Schmidt clash or IPO profit sharing.

Two other CSFB executives who oversaw allocations also took the general question up with CSFB's legal and compliance staff. Tony Ehinger, the global head of equity sales, and George Coleman, head of institutional listed sales trading, both asked whether such big cents per share commissions should be allowed.

But, regulators later asserted, they never told the legal staff about the new-issue performance report and how it was being used to calculate customers' IPO profits, or about the magnitude or scope of the commission payback program.[20]

GRUNWALD'S BLUNDER

23

THE DAWN of the new millennium brought an even faster pace of business, showering riches on Quattrone even as the banker seemed to pull out all the stops to prove he was number one and ring the cash register with marginal deals.

In January 2000, showing his flair for aggressive marketing, Quattrone renewed his claim to being number one in technology banking for all of 1999. The group was number one, he said, in an übercategory he constructed himself; financing and mergers. He also claimed number one status in the volume of his group's tech IPOs and tech mergers. "We are thrilled to have achieved our goal of #1 market share in by far the most active year the technology industry has seen to date," Quattrone crowed in an official CSFB announcement listing fifty-three IPOs the group had led.[1]

Other statistics were only slightly less impressive. Industry arbiter Thomson Financial, which tracks mergers and securities sales, showed CSFB at number three, behind Goldman Sachs and Morgan Stanley, in completed 1999 technology mergers both U.S. and worldwide. And by the yardstick of all technology stock issuance for the year 1999, CSFB also ranked a distant third. The Meeker-led team at Morgan Stanley ranked number one, with $16.2 billion in new tech-stock issues, and Goldman was a close number two, at $15.2 billion. CSFB ranked number three, at $7.7 billion, neck and neck with the next two competitors. Only in the number of IPOs did CSFB appear to beat out rivals.

What's more, some of Quattrone's "reference transaction" clients hadn't followed him to CSFB or relegated his bankers to lesser roles. They included Netscape, which used Morgan Stanley for advice on its 1999 acquisition by America Online, Amazon.com, which used Morgan Stanley as the lead for a 1999 debt financing, and America Online itself. Instead, the CSFB tech group, not alone among underwriters, seemed to be participating avidly in the mad vortex of new issues.

Indeed, the absolute peak of the bubble found the Quattrone tech group offering IPOs that put humdrum old-economy businesses online. On March 7, 2000, CSFB led the IPO of iPrint.com Inc., which offered business cards and office stationery online. A week later, on March 15, CSFB led ImproveNet Inc., which offered home improvement products and services online.

Ringing the IPO cash register paid off for Quattrone personally. In 1999, his pay was $36 million. The year 2000 would bring Quattrone total compensation more than three times that size—$120 million.[2] It would make him the highest paid banker on Wall Street.

O

Everyone, it seemed, wanted to get in on the online mania. In early 2000, Schmidt and Grunwald visited the downtown Chicago headquarters of Playboy Enterprises Inc., whose online business, Playboy.com, had chosen CSFB to lead an IPO that was announced on January 10. They quickly opened Friends of Frank accounts for Christie Hefner, Playboy's chief executive, and two of her colleagues.[3] Grunwald jokingly said they should try to pitch her father, Hugh Hefner, as well. But they never got the chance. And the Playboy.com offering, which was delayed by the SEC, was never completed. It finally got shelved officially in November 2000.

O

Frank Scognamillo, the son of a house painter from the Bronx, had grown up in Pequannock, New Jersey, and attended the University of North Carolina on scholarship. After working in the premium and incentive business in Chicago, he moved in 1990 to Arizona, where he built a customer-loyalty venture, Universal Value Network LLC, that awarded airline miles or discounts to customers who patronized participating merchants. UVN, based in Tempe, Arizona, just outside Phoenix, also had a 49 percent interest in a related credit-card data venture with a subsidiary of Visa USA called Golden Retriever, which Scognamillo founded in 1993.

One of the Credit Suisse IPOs, Netcentives Inc., had an Internet version of the same type of business, including a program called ClickRewards that offered frequent-flyer miles from ten airlines. It boasted access for customers to online giants such as America Online, barnesandnoble.com, and E*Trade.

At the peak of the Internet bubble, Scognamillo met on January 14, 2000, with George Boutros, Quattrone's head of mergers and acquisitions, along with Storm Duncan, another Credit Suisse banker, at the Netcentives office in San Francisco. Netcentives had gone public in October 1999, and its stock price had already soared by six times, from $12 at its IPO to a closing high price of $80.265 on December 22; the day Scognamillo met with Boutros, a few weeks later, it closed at $57.25.

Scognamillo didn't know it, but—according to a lawsuit he filed in 2002—CSFB Internet analyst Lise Buyer, a Quattrone group member, had sent an e-mail to corporate-finance chief Bill Brady and banker Ted Smith in September saying she wouldn't want to cover the stock if CSFB took Netcentives public. She said Netcentives had a "horrible business model," she "wouldn't touch it" if she were an investor, and fretted that "shoving this down investors' throats will reduce my effectiveness" in covering five other stocks she did like.[4] The Buyer e-mail went on to explain that her reservations were based on the difficulty of tracking the company's complex revenue recognition mechanisms, which made analyzing the stock "incredibly complicated." When another analyst who was covering the company quit, Buyer helped out with the firm's preparations for the road shows.

At their meeting, Scognamillo says, Boutros assured Scognamillo that Credit Suisse could vouch for Netcentives, having just taken the company public, that it was moving toward profitability, and that it could achieve its growth plans without additional financing. At that moment, it seemed plausible that the credit-card transactions that lay at the core of Scognamillo's Universal Value Network were going to migrate to the Web. With Netcentives's stock soaring, selling UVN to further its growth plans seemed like a good idea—a marriage of old economy and new, of "bricks and mortar" with "clicks and mortar."

Negotiating vigorously for Netcentives and hinting at more deals in the pipeline, Boutros assured his listeners that Netcentives was a survivor. *We can't tell you what's going on*, Scognamillo recalls Boutros saying, *but this game is already over. Netcentives has already won. There's no competition. We have so many deals we haven't announced.*

Scognamillo had heard of how well the Quattrone group was doing, and that night he went home and cried to his wife because he was going to be "on the same team."[5] He felt, he said, as if he had "made it to the top."[6] Two months later, on March 1, Netcentives at the last minute cut its proposed purchase price for UVN from $34 million to $29 million.

UVN, of which Scognamillo and his family owned 72 percent, would get $17 million in Netcentives stock in the acquisition. But the stock came in the form of unregistered shares—which couldn't be sold for a year. The acquisition of UVN by Netcentives closed on March 3, 2000, with Netcentives's stock price already slipping, at $48.125.

○

The easy profits from the pattern of IPOs' first-day price "pops" were also drawing more and more interest. The frenzy to get them rose to a gale-force roar. Word got around that Hollywood star Barbra Streisand was cold-calling executives of companies going public to get hot IPOs via their directed-share

Friends and Family programs. Mari Tangredi, an executive at Critical Path Inc., a May 1999 (non-CSFB) IPO, took Streisand's call. "At first I thought it was a hoax, but when I heard that voice, I knew it was her," she said. Instead of commissions, Ms. Streisand sent the company balloons, flowers, and four bottles of Dom Perignon.[7]

○

The client shakedowns and cutoffs soon became a problem.

As the bubble neared its peak and threw off epic amounts of cash, the CSFB brokers grew more aggressive about getting payback for trading accounts' IPO profits—and about cutting off accounts that didn't deliver. Among those cut was an account covered by a Boston broker, RSC Latin Management, run by a Long Island trader named Robert Cooper. This move would come back to haunt CSFB.

In California, Grunwald's influence over the tech group brokers was being felt. In January 2000, he hired his former colleague from Morgan Stanley, Jon Jaffe. Grunwald had a mercurial personality, Bushley later recalled: "He's a very hot and cold individual. When he's hot, he can be very intense and very in your face."[8]

Two of the brokers in the Quattrone group—head trader Scott Brown and his successor, Scott Bushley—had begun generating spreadsheets showing the first-day profits trading accounts would have earned on their IPO allocations, and comparing them to commissions they paid to CSFB for other trades. The spreadsheets also included the percentage of IPO profits earned versus commissions paid to CSFB on a year-to-date basis.[9]

Schmidt himself later said he remembered being shown versions of such spreadsheets by Scott Brown around December 1999, for use as a possible "sales tool," but insisted he had never set a goal of IPO profit payback. All he wanted, he said, was for the trading accounts to generate an amount of commissions on stocks already trading that was equal to their commissions on new issues—so they couldn't just receive IPOs without doing other commission business.[10]

Bushley told NASD investigators later that he would make calls at the end of the month at Grunwald's direction, informing the trading accounts of their estimated first-day "flipping" profits, and urging them to boost their commissions as a percentage of that amount. Grunwald would sometimes circle the accounts whose percentages had fallen below the group's target for them, he and Bushley said. When he made the calls, Bushley said, he would gently urge the accounts that "it would be great" if they would raise their percentage. When Grunwald himself made such calls, Bushley said, his tone would be "a little harsher."[11]

In January or early February, Grunwald suggested that the payback required of trading clients be increased, from 50 percent of their IPO profits to 65 percent.[12] The reason, he told CSFB lawyers later: He felt the clients weren't meeting the 50 percent target, and their profits were so huge he felt an increase was desirable. The tech brokers, he believed, were providing a valuable service and deserved to be paid.[13] Of course, cutting off the accounts also made more room for new Friends of Frank banking clients.

Grunwald told the NASD he discussed raising the payback percentage to 60 percent to 65 percent from its previous level of 50 percent at a meeting with Bushley and Schmidt in a glass-walled conference room near their trading desk. "Since there was a 50 percent target," Grunwald said, "we were all there to make money and generate more business, and if the firm makes more money, our group makes more money and I make money." He added, "So, I did suggest that we go higher."[14] Schmidt said he didn't remember any such meeting, adding that he believed "an alarm bell would have gone off" in his head in response to any such suggestion.[15]

All three brokers were asked whether Quattrone knew of any IPO profit payback requirement; not to their knowledge, they all replied. But questioned by his own lawyer near the end of his session with the NASD, Schmidt said he had had "conversations" with Quattrone and two New York CSFB executives, Benjamin and Ehinger, about the tech group brokers' use of trading profits as "a sales tool."

Some of the tech group trading accounts bristled at the higher payback level. When Bushley told Lustig of United Capital about the new higher ratio, the Denver trader was already in "the high mid-fifties," Bushley told the SEC later. "Wow, this is ridiculous," Bushley recalled Lustig saying. "How can this be legal? This is criminal." Although Bushley believed Lustig held an exaggerated view of Wall Street's misconduct, he decided to ask his predecessor, Scott Brown, whether he thought it was in fact illegal.[16]

One trading account whose commission levels proved disappointing was Maxim Financial, whom Grunwald had personally recruited as a customer and had received VA Linux shares. It turned out that a girlfriend of Grunwald's had actually received a finder's fee of about twenty thousand dollars for introducing the account owner to Grunwald, he later told NASD investigators.[17]

On February 10, 2000, junior Quattrone group broker Scott Bushley e-mailed Grunwald to say he had cut off Maxim at the latter's behest: "Basically, I told him that he was very far behind on his commissions and that we expect a 65% return on all money that we make him. I said that he still owes us for the LNUX [the stock trading symbol for VA Linux Systems] deal not to mention the deals that have come since then. I then stated that he can do trades to increase his commissions but he will be further cut off from any syndicate in the future." By "syndicate," Bushley meant new issues, including hot IPOs.

Bushley concluded his e-mail by saying that he wanted to give Grunwald a "heads-up" in case anyone from Maxim called him to complain.

Grunwald's reply confirmed that Maxim was to be cut off. "Out," he said simply.

Bushley responded with equal brevity: "done."[18]

○

On March 8, 2000, one customer of the Quattrone group brokers received allocations of two hot IPOs that would open for trading the next day. The customer received 7,000 shares of Selectica Inc., an Internet sales systems company, that generated a one-day profit of $778,610 when the stock rose 370 percent above its offering price. The same customer also received 15,000 shares of OTG Software Inc., a data storage company, which generated a one-day profit of $557,700. The customer's total one-day paper profit thus exceeded $1.3 million.[19]

The following day, March 10, 2000, the same customer who got the Selectica and OTG shares paid CSFB commissions of at least $166,000 by paying inflated commissions of $.35 to $.75 a share—far above the going rate of $.05 a share—for six trades of 10,000 to 50,000 shares of big, easy-to-trade stocks like Philip Morris and Ford Motor.

○

Sometime in the first two weeks of March 2000, junior tech group broker Scott Bushley placed a call at Grunwald's behest to Cary Brody, an employee of the Colonial Funds mutual-fund unit of Colonial Management Inc. in New York. The name of Brody's account was Y2K Partners LLC. Grunwald had seen the amount of commission business Y2K had done for February, and thought it was "below what he thought it should be," Bushley told NASD investigators later.[20]

Brody had heard some advance word that the call was coming. When Bushley called Y2K around the end of February to say their commissions had come in low, Brody told him that Y2K had suffered losses on some "long-term positions that had fallen apart," Bushley told SEC lawyers later.[21] On the call, Grunwald began by explaining that he was the new leader of the group. February had been a huge month, Grunwald said, and they had expected Y2K's commissions to be a lot higher.

When Brody resisted, Grunwald said, "Come on, man, we made you a lot of money," Bushley told the SEC. And Brody replied, "Yeah, we've made you a lot of money, too." As Bushley put it, "The two dominant personalities kind of started to butt heads on the phone."

The upshot was that Y2K would have to do more commission business to continue receiving new issues, including IPOs. Brody didn't let the conversation go very far. He indicated to Grunwald that he considered the proposal unethical. *We don't do business that way*, Brody said. *We are an ethical firm.* The call lasted just a few minutes. He told Grunwald that he didn't want his commission dollars going to him in any case, and didn't want to do business with CSFB anymore.[22]

Bushley later called his trading contact at Y2K at home to see if the dispute could be smoothed over. Realizing Bushley was upset about the situation, Grunwald even called Bushley at home to apologize, saying he realized the Y2K traders were friends of his. But when Bushley called his trader friend back, he was told that Brody "doesn't want to talk to you guys again." The friend added, "I've seen Cary lose hundreds of thousands of dollars and not be frustrated or sweat about it." But after the Grunwald call, Bushley was told, Brody had "walked out of that office so uptight and mad. And I can understand why he doesn't want to talk to you guys again."[23]

On the afternoon of March 14, 2000, former tech group broker Scott Brown e-mailed Bushley from a personal AOL e-mail account: "Is Y2K shut down? I guess MG wasn't kidding about that 65% thing."

"They voluntarily shut themselves down after MG got on the phone with them," Bushley replied. "He was a total prick and Cary just said he didn't want to do business any more." But Bushley was queasy about what was happening. "Also, and I am serious, is this 65% thing illegal," he asked Brown.

"I don't know," Brown replied. "[I]t probably would not look so good to anyone making an inquiry though."[24]

O

Within eighteen months, such harsh shakedowns of trading clients by the Quattrone group brokers would not only get Schmidt, Grunwald, and Bushley fired, they would also bring Quattrone himself under the microscope of scrutiny from both regulators and the press. There isn't any evidence that Quattrone himself was aware of these actions by the brokers who worked for Schmidt. But he and his group pocketed a share of the commission revenues. So he stood to gain. And the shakedowns became a key link in the chain of events that led to the criminal charges against him.

JOHNDOE526

24

ON THE MORNING of Tuesday, February 15, 2000—five days after Maxim was cut off—CSFB New York broker Paul Caan was summoned to a meeting with his boss and two company lawyers. At six feet tall and two hundred fifty pounds, the heavyset, dark-haired Caan towered over CSFB attorney Karen Crupi, a petite, attractive brunette in her thirties. Crupi sat behind her desk, flanked by her boss, Ray Dorado, a distinguished-looking lawyer who resembled a young Harrison Ford. Dorado was the head of legal and compliance for U.S. stock trading at CSFB.

Caan's boss, Andy Benjamin, a broker with thinning brown hair who wore his tie loosened and his sleeves rolled up, sat in front of Crupi's desk, next to Caan. The two brokers worked closely together: In addition to taking care of his own clients, Caan helped Benjamin manage the firm's cadre of fifty brokers who catered to wealthy individuals and smaller money managers.

Caan, a resident of Greenwich, Connecticut, was making more than $5 million a year based on a roster of big-name clients. They included showbiz types like supermodel Cindy Crawford, record producer Tommy Mottola, and Wall Street titan Larry Fink, the former CSFB bond executive who now ran the fast-rising bond manager BlackRock Inc.

Crupi, Dorado, Caan, and Benjamin had all been forwarded copies of an e-mail sent the day before. The sender was identified only as "JohnDoe526@hotmail.com." The subject line read: "IPO Fraudulent Scheme at Credit Suisse First Boston." The e-mail, one version of which had been sent directly to Quattrone, said in part: "This letter is to inform you of unethical and criminal practices at Credit Suisse First Boston. Paul Werner Cann . . . is in control of allocating IPO's. Mr. Cann allocates more stock to his clients than most brokers receive at CSFB . . . In return Mr. Cann receives illegal kickbacks (payment) from his clients in the form of cash or ridiculous commissions."

The e-mail added that one client of Caan's, "a childhood friend, Mr. Christopher Shempeau, receives more stock on IPOs than some institutions and in turn pays Mr. Cann 50% of the profit back in return." One version of the e-mail, which purported to be from a "concerned" CSFB employee, said other CSFB brokers' allocations had been cut, but not Caan's.

Although the e-mail misspelled the names of Champeau and Caan, it was generally accurate in describing some of the functions that Paul Caan performed in allocating hot IPOs to certain CSFB customers. While Caan wasn't solely responsible for doling them out, he had been given some authority over the IPO shares allocated to the private-client brokers by Benjamin.

The question was: How much of the e-mail was true? As Caan's colleagues watched avidly through the glass wall of Crupi's office, they could see the fleshy broker—he had just started a diet—heatedly denying the kickback accusation. He knew Champeau, Caan acknowledged—but they hadn't been childhood friends. And yes, sometimes Champeau did receive IPO allocations from Caan. But Caan denied receiving kickbacks. He said, in effect, that the accounts that received IPO shares were just good customers.

The CSFB executives who received the e-mail promptly forwarded it to the firm's legal and compliance department, led by Joseph McLaughlin, the firm's global general counsel, and David Brodsky, the general counsel for the Americas, a former prosecutor in the securities fraud unit at the U.S. Attorney's office in Manhattan. The other in-house lawyers who worked for them, including Dorado and Crupi, quickly swung into action. The task was all the more urgent because JohnDoe526 had also sent a version of the e-mail to several news organizations.

Champeau also denied the allegations to CSFB, saying he decided what commissions to pay Caan for his trades. Caan later told regulators some of his colleagues began teasing him. "We will deliver you food in jail," they said.[1]

Meanwhile, CSFB's lawyers also began trying to track down the true identity of JohnDoe526. A lawyer at Schulte Roth & Zabel LLP, where Brodsky had worked for nineteen years before joining CSFB in 1999, tried to learn the name of the e-mail's sender by contacting Hotmail.com, which explained to him that such information isn't given out except under subpoena.

To get a subpoena, CSFB went to court on February 18, 2000, just four days after the e-mail was sent. Based on the denials by Caan and Champeau, Schulte Roth filed a civil lawsuit in Manhattan federal court against JohnDoe526, charging both libel and violation of the federal telecommunications act.[2] The CSFB lawsuit was intimidating. It demanded compensatory damages of not less than $1 million, an injunction against any further acts of the same nature, as well as payment by the unknown defendant for any costs and attorneys' fees.

The CSFB lawyers also enlisted a private investigative firm, the Accetta Group LLC, to try to track down the e-mail's origin. Anthony Accetta, then fifty-seven, was a private eye in the Raymond Chandler style. He wore a trench coat and a fedora, which covered his ample bald spot. An Accetta Group investigator traced the e-mail's origin to a public-access computer in the Nassau County library system on Long Island.

After visiting the Uniondale, Long Island, library that housed the computer, Accetta investigators cross-checked log-in data left by users of the computer around the time the e-mail was sent, records of the computer users' library cards, and records of the firm's own customers. At one point, one of the Accetta agents had to "baby-sit" the computer for several hours to prevent a routine data purge.

By these methods, CSFB identified the likeliest sender of the message to be Andrea Cooper, the wife of Joseph Cooper, who then lived in Inwood, just a few miles from Uniondale. Joe Cooper's brother Robert was a resident of the tony enclave of Sands Point, which sits on Long Island Sound, about fifteen miles from Manhattan. When they checked all the names against CSFB's own records, the investigators found that Robert Cooper had an account, RSC Latin Management, with a CSFB broker in Boston named David Lee.[3] His brother Joe worked with him, Caan later told regulators, adding that the Cooper account had been shut down by CSFB.

Learning the sender's identity made it easier for Caan and Benjamin to explain away the allegations. Since the Coopers had been cut off by CSFB from getting hot IPOs, the complaint could be discounted as sour grapes.

One thing was true: Champeau, Caan's client, certainly did receive hefty allocations of some IPOs, and he paid hefty commissions to Caan, investigators later found.[4] For example, he had paid a commission of $135,000 for a 300,000-share trade of Philip Morris stock on November 18, 1999, a day when he had just received IPO allocations of 8,000 shares of Retek Inc. and 10,000 shares of Symyx Technologies Inc.

Still, lacking access to such trading records themselves, the Coopers had no proof to back up the e-mail's allegation that Champeau paid Caan illegal kickbacks. Confronted by an unexpected $1 million lawsuit against them, and startled that the anonymous e-mail had been traced to them so quickly, the Coopers backed down and hastily withdrew the allegation.

The Coopers not only recanted the kickback accusation but also paid CSFB thirty-five thousand dollars, representing its costs for all the frenzied legal and detective work. It was all over less than two weeks after the e-mail was sent.

At the time, some of the CSFB legal staffers congratulated themselves on averting the potential public relations crisis that could have arisen had any of the news organizations that received the e-mail put the charges into print. None did. But their actions also showed how a powerful Wall Street firm, taking in billions at the height of a raging bull market, could quickly marshal an array of high-priced talent to squelch random criticism or questions from external sources.

A SECRET WEAPON

25

WHILE SOME of the smaller trading accounts were dealt with harshly, questions about allocations to important investment banking customers were handled with kid gloves, particularly when they could lead to more underwriting business.

For example, when Lawrence Bowman, who ran a big $6 billion technology hedge fund, was dissatisfied with his allocation of one IPO in February 2000, he told his CSFB salesman he had been "feeding banking leads to you guys."[1]

When the salesman checked with Quattrone, the banking kingpin "set the record straight" by noting that Bowman had "screwed us" by recommending Goldman in the IPO of Noosh Inc., an online printing company. After that, he recalled, he and Bowman had "a very long and very testy conversation."

But when another CSFB banker wanted Bowman's recommendation for a new underwriting assignment, Quattrone quickly got in touch with Bowman. Drawing the connection between Bowman's requests for bigger IPO allocations and his endorsement on IPO manager selections, Quattrone said, "I think we can be very helpful to one another."[2]

O

Mike Grunwald, the Quattrone group broker, kept pressing for more stock for more new Friends of Frank. On Friday, February 25, 2000, he sent Quattrone, Brady, and Boutros a progress report. The account total had grown rapidly, from 26 in January 1999 to 151 that day, with three more pending. "Our customer list is ballooning based on your great success," he said. Response from clients was "always very favorable and they do believe unique to CSFB." He signed the note, "Grun and Dr. Schmidt."[3]

Quattrone replied via BlackBerry the next day, on Saturday evening February 26, to Brady, Grunwald, and Boutros, with a copy to Schmidt. "Let's review specific names and allocations," he said.

O

One Quattrone e-mail string in February 2000 shows the relentless persua-
sive power behind his success. The recipient was Donna Dubinsky, the chief
executive of Handspring Inc., which made hand-held devices similar to the
PalmPilot. Dubinsky had been chief executive of Palm Inc. from 1992 to 1998.

At 9:15 A.M. on the morning of February 29, 2000, the day after Quattrone
had presented in the bake-off for Handspring's IPO, Quattrone opened up with
a one-word e-mail: "soooooooooooo?"[4]

Dubinsky didn't answer until the end of the day. "Frank," she began, "I
thought you guys were terrific. . . . Mike [Kwatinetz, the ace of the CSFB tech
research staff] was clearly the best thinker on our issues compared to the other
analysts we met." However, she said, Jeff Hawkins, Handspring's chief product
officer, "was concerned that you guys might be too aggressive for us. . . . As
much as we don't want a big 'pop' at the IPO, we also don't want to go out with
a value that we do not feel is sustainable over the long run. You guys clearly
were the most aggressive on the numbers!! I feel that you would work with us
to achieve mutually agreed goals . . . right?"

Dubinsky's question suggests that some business associates had doubts about
Quattrone's judgment, and whether in a pinch he would he would work harmoniously with them. Quattrone had argued, for example, that Handspring deserved a stock-market valuation that was two or three times the multiple of
earnings that Handspring's chief competitor, Palm, already traded at. Quattrone had used over-the-top valuations before in pitching for IPOs—in the case
of E* Trade, for example.

"Donna—thanks," Quattrone replied. "From our perspective it was not just
another ipo pitch. For us, leading your ipo and helping you build the category defining company in this space is a mission, a crusade, a passion. We feel we have the
best analyst, the most experienced bankers, the No. 1 market share in lead managed tech deals, the best track record in pricing deals, the best distribution strategy and the most thoughtful approach to marketing and pricing your offering."

Then the banker went into sales hyperdrive. "Beyond that you have a secret
weapon with us—my personal attention," he said. "I will make absolutely sure
our whole firm focuses on this transaction from start to finish and will not let it
fail regardless of bumps in the market. Last August when the market crapped
out, on the same day, morgan and mary pulled the deal for women.com as we
were getting deals done for tumbleweed and mortgage.com. One of the reasons we were able to do this is that bill brady and I called in lots of chits with
investors we have known for years and have our own money invested with."

Recall that Quattrone, asked whether Integral Partners deserved an extra
helping of the hot IPO of Vitria in September 1999, had checked with Brady

about whether Integral had been "helpful" on Tumbleweed and Mortgage.com. At his second trial, Quattrone acknowledged that Integral was one of the investors he had called on to get the deals done.[5]

"Obviously we would be prepared to do the same and then some for you," Quattrone told Dubinsky. Then he paused to trash his alma mater, Morgan Stanley: "Also it is so clear that mary is out of capacity—askjeeves just switched to goldman and we are about to replace them on another one of her best ipo clients. Finally she really does not have the credibility in this space that mike has, or that she has in the internet."

Since he had been surprised at Mary Meeker's decision not to join him when he left Morgan Stanley nearly four years earlier, Quattrone and his team tended to personalize the competition. They recognized that Meeker was not only Morgan Stanley's top Internet analyst, she was also one of the firm's top tech-business getters as well.

"Donna, this is very, very important to me. . . . I believe in my bones that you and jeff are the real thing. Hope you feel the same about me and mike. To answer your specific question: of course we are willing to work with you to achieve your objectives. We do not wish to be overly aggressive. We wanted to tell you the truth—that we think you could in fact trade at 2–3 times the multiple of palm. If you want to go for it we are with you. If you want to be more conservative we can do that too. You are the client."

Handspring chose CSFB to lead the IPO, which was completed on June 20, 2000.

"A CONCERNED CITIZEN"

26

THE BEST MEASURE of speculative froth that animated the stock market during the bubble was the NASDAQ composite index. It rose from 1,771 at the end of October 1998 to 2,686 by June 1999. But its most explosive gains came in the second half of 1999, when it rose 51 percent, to 4,069. The speculative top came quickly after that. The NASDAQ composite peaked at 5,049 on March 10.

On March 9, just at the NASDAQ peak, the IPO of Selectica, an Internet selling-systems software company based in San Jose, was priced at $30 a share. Demand was white-hot.[1] Selectica became CSFB's second biggest first-day gainer, rising 371 percent in price to a close of $141.23. Fidelity Investments, the Boston mutual-fund gorilla, got 150,000 shares. Munder Capital Management, home of an $11 billion Internet mutual fund that would fall 87 percent in price by 2002, received 25,000. Larry Bowman's fund got 20,000.

Several Lustig traders received Selectica shares, too. Energia Global Group, run by Andy Siegal, received 5,500, as did Ascent Capital, run by Steve Kris.[2] In all—without naming names—the SEC later would claim customers willing to share their profits with CSFB, in the form of outsize commissions, received 324,903 shares out of 3.9 million CSFB allocated.[3]

The following Saturday, in an issue dated March 20, 2000, Jack Willoughby of *Barron's* wrote a sobering and prophetic cover story entitled, "Burning Up: Warning: Internet Companies Are Running Out of Cash—Fast." He noted that without additional financing, 51 out of 207 Internet companies included in a research study would run out of cash within twelve months. One of the first he mentioned was Intraware.[4]

The following Monday, March 15, 2000, the NASDAQ began falling. In the first three days of that week, it fell 10.2 percent, to 4,583, and the 5,000 level eventually became a distant, fleeting memory.

O

On Tuesday, March 21, 2000, Michael Price, a former Morgan Stanley banker, e-mailed Quattrone asking why Selectica stock had fallen 50 percent from its first-day close on March 10: "any insights into the crazy trading?" Price asked.[5] Quattrone, on vacation in Pebble Beach, replied with a Wall Street joke that hinted at an insouciance about investor losses: "'more sellers than buyers.'"

○

Mike Grunwald, meanwhile, had been adding Friends of Frank accounts at a faster pace, more than doubling the size of the list in five months. They included executives of Lante Corporation, which went public February 10, Onvia Corporation, whose IPO was February 29, iPrint.com on March 7, Riverdeep Interactive Learning on March 9, OTG Software Inc. on March 10, eMachines Inc. on March 24, and Numerical Technologies Inc. on April 7.

The pattern was clear. The companies chose CSFB for banking work, then their executives got the hot IPO shares.

On March 21, 2000, Grunwald sent Quattrone and Brady an e-mail update on the accounts, copying Schmidt. The message was the same. They needed more IPO shares for the growing account ranks. "Gentlemen," Grunwald said, "attached is the spreadsheet with accounts as of last week." The number of accounts had risen to 193, with 10 more pending, from under 90 when he arrived.[6]

"Instead of Morganing or Goldmaning them with 200 to 300 shares on every other deal," he said, they needed more stock. "These people love you guys all ready [*sic*] and this account reinforces it. People are genuinely appreciative (well most of them)." He urged that their percentages be increased to 5 percent, and eventually 6 percent to 7 percent.

Around that time, in a move that later won him the thanks of many clients, Schmidt shifted much of the assets of the tech PCS discretionary accounts, the Friends of Frank accounts, to cash—sparing them the worst of the punishing market downturn.

○

A month later, an internal audit of the Quattrone group offered an omen of even worse trouble to come. Dated April 14, 2000, the audit by Credit Suisse Group, the Zurich parent of CSFB, contained a vague but eerily accurate warning: "The Tech Group's relatively autonomous management structure and operating procedures have contributed to insufficient awareness of CSFB policies, procedures and culture among its staff." The level of legal and administrative resources devoted to "support and control [of] the Tech Group's activities must be critically re-evaluated."[7]

O

On the afternoon of that same day, Friday, April 14, 2000, it was becoming apparent that the Dow Jones Industrial Average might suffer a severe pounding. The atmosphere was tense in the cavernous green-carpeted main stock trading room at CSFB headquarters.

Shortly after 3:00 P.M. head listed-stock trader Michael Clark held a quick conference with James Deasy, the head of NASDAQ trading. With the Dow down about 500 and NASDAQ down more than 300, Clark told a visitor, many institutional investors wanted to sell big blocks of stock. Clients, he said, were showing "real concern."[8]

Clark, whose black hair was streaked with gray, sat near the center of two rows of senior traders; their desks, slightly above the floor, resembled the dais at a tribute dinner. He was dressed casually, in a crisp red-and-white-striped shirt, its sleeves rolled up two turns, white pants, and black loafers. But the tension showed as Clark's left leg bounced up and down nervously. The market action was "very, very stressful" for the traders, he said.

At one point, a trader on the north side of the room joked that abandoning the dress-down casual wear that had taken over Wall Street during the Internet mania might turn the market around. "Back to suits, man! Let's get this market going!" Few laughed.

At 3:36 P.M., with the Dow down 600, NASDAQ trading chief Deasy fretted, "It feels like they are going to sell 'em all, right to the end of the day." When another trader called it "the biggest down day ever," Deasy reminded him that 1987 was much worse in percentage terms: "That was twenty-five percent. This is six percent."

That day the Dow Jones Industrial Average fell 618, a record one-day point loss, to 10,306. The damage to the NASDAQ stock market, where most of the new-technology stocks traded, was even worse. The NASDAQ composite fell 9.7 percent to 3,321—down 25.3 percent on the week, and 34 percent below the record of 5,049 it had set on March 10. As Louis Rukeyser noted that evening on his public television show *Wall Street Week*, it had happened on the eighty-eighth anniversary of the *Titanic* hitting the iceberg.

Two weeks later, on Monday May 1, Schmidt notified Quattrone and two other bankers that CSFB's traders had just handled stock sales for two insiders of tech companies the group had taken public. Quattrone's response: "John could we schedule a time to review q1 results and ipo allocations past and future?"[9]

Just then, someone tossed a stick of dynamite in CSFB's direction. It was so detailed, regulators later theorized, it had to have come from an insider, someone who knew the firm well—either an employee or a customer.

On May 5, 2000, an anonymous letter was sent from "A concerned citizen" to the Securities and Exchange Commission, the National Association of Securities Dealers, and members of Congress. The JohnDoe526 e-mail hadn't been sent to regulators, allowing CSFB to keep that accusation quiet. In this case, however, CSFB had no opportunity for damage control, because the firm didn't receive a copy.

"I am writing to bring to your attention a practice at Credit Suisse First Boston ('CSFB') which at least raises serious public policy issues and is possibly illegal," the anonymous letter began. "The practice relates to the allocation of shares in 'hot' initial public offerings led by CSFB's Technology Group to certain investors in exchange for thinly disguised payments to CSFB."

It was an allegation of kickback payments very similar to that made by John-Doe526 in February. When it became apparent that a particular deal would be hot, the letter said, "it is strongly in CSFB's economic interest to set this price range at artificially low levels."

As the pricing date neared for hot deals, "A concerned citizen" continued, "CSFB allocates the shares more slowly than it would in a normal transaction," both for its own customers and for those of other underwriters. "Having withheld these shares, CSFB has undue flexibility as to how to allocate them around the time of pricing." The letter used technical terms, such as "the institutional pot," that no one but a Wall Street insider would have known.

The letter went on: "Institutions looking for shares from CSFB are given 'guidance' about what they have to do to receive an allocation." Then the letter described exactly the kinds of trades that occurred after the VA Linux IPO and so many others. "This usually takes the form of a riskless trade in an unrelated liquid security at a highly inflated . . . commission."

Then the author gave what sounded like it could have been a random, hypothetical example. Except it wasn't. "An example would be a sell order for one million shares of Compaq Computer with a $1.00 per share commission (when the normal rate would be $.05 a share) in exchange for a concurrent allocation in the VA Linux Systems IPO."

The letter concluded, "Through this and other mechanisms, CSFB has earned upwards of $30 million on a transaction in the size range of $150 million, in addition to the underwriters' gross spread. This raises both public disclosure issues as well as concerns relating to the NASD's 'excessive underwriters' compensation' rules."

In closing, the letter said, "I apologize for the anonymous nature of this letter, but as I value my employment in the securities industry, I hope you will understand. Sincerely, A concerned citizen."

The letter was eerily accurate in describing the VA Linux transaction. It was worth exactly $151.8 million. The types of trades were also described accurately. And the estimate of $30 million in extra earnings via the excessive commissions was on-target as well. Although they had their suspicions, regulators never found out who had written the letter.

A LAST HURRAH
FOR HOT IPOS

27

JUST 230 MILES southwest of CSFB's stock trading room in midtown Manhattan, the letter from "A concerned citizen" was received on Friday, May 12, 2000, at the headquarters of the National Association of Securities Dealers. The agency's own office on K Street NW, a power alley for law firms and lobbyists, was just a few blocks north of the White House. The NASD's enforcement chief, Barry Goldsmith, immediately turned it over to the agency's investigative group, believing that its detail, language, and context had a ring of truth.

The NASD wasn't a government agency. Rather it was a "self-regulatory" organization funded by the securities industry itself, and was answerable to the Securities and Exchange Commission. The NASD licensed firms and individuals who work in the securities business, and it had the power to discipline or even expel them from the business if they didn't answer questions or produce documents. But the NASD didn't have subpoena power and couldn't compel testimony from customers, or document production from those outside the business. Those stronger powers resided at the SEC. (NASD's name was changed to the Financial Industry Regulatory Authority, or FINRA, in 2007.)

Goldsmith was graduated from the University of Pennsylvania's Wharton School in 1972, five years before Quattrone, and Georgetown law school. As former chief litigation counsel at the SEC he had worked on the Milken case, and had been brought into the NASD in 1996 to beef up enforcement efforts, eventually doubling its staff. The SEC had required the NASD to spend an extra $100 million over five years on enforcement as part of a settlement of a bid-rigging scandal, in which traders from many Wall Street firms had colluded to maintain artificial price levels, boosting profits at customers' expense.

Joseph Ozag Jr. had worked in law enforcement, as a Capitol Hill police officer, and as a Wall Street broker before joining NASD as a compliance examiner on May 15, 2000. At five-foot-eleven and 240 pounds, the burly Ozag actually resembled a policeman. Ozag was assigned to look into the contents of the letter on Tuesday, May 16, only his second day on the job. Although Goldsmith thought it might be something big, at that point Ozag himself had never actually heard of Credit Suisse First Boston.

On May 17, Ozag sent a letter to Michael Radest, CSFB's compliance director. He asked for all documents related to the allocation of shares of VA Linux "created, sent or received from June 1, 1999, through May 16, 2000," including due diligence and IPO allocation files. He also asked for all related e-mails, notes, voice mails, memos, recordings spreadsheets, and databases. He set a highly unrealistic deadline for all of this—May 26, just a week later.[1]

In the same letter, the NASD also asked for a list identifying the types of "exception reports" that CSFB generated regarding commissions, IPO allocations, sales credits, and institutional sales and trading in the period December 1999 until May 16, 2000. Exception reports usually are generated by Wall Street firms for trades and other transactions conducted outside the normal course of activity. The agency also requested the names of employees in the syndicate, institutional trading, underwriting, and corporate-finance departments from June 1, 1999, to May 16, 2000, and a list of those who had resigned in that period. NASD also asked for the firm's organizational chart on December 9, 1999—the day of the Linux IPO—and May 16, 2000.

Separately, the NASD examiners soon made requests for "blue sheet" data about trading in certain stocks. The blue sheet records, submitted by brokers to a central automated database, list each purchaser or seller, price, number of shares, date, and other data. Available electronically, they could be downloaded into databases, enabling the NASD to mix and match them to check the information in the anonymous letter.

The letter had given an example of a customer who had gotten an allocation of VA Linux and paid a big commission for a trade of one million shares of Compaq. Using the blue sheets, the NASD team looked at trades in VA Linux and Compaq within three or four days of the VA Linux IPO. They noticed a CSFB customer who had received a big allocation of VA Linux and had sold a big block of Compaq the same day. Instead of selling one million Compaq shares at a commission of one dollar a share, as the letter described, this customer had sold two million shares at fifty cents a share. But the result, the payment of a $1 million commission on a Compaq trade by a customer who got a big chunk of VA Linux stock, was the same as described in the letter. The same customer, a few days later, had done trades in Compaq at the rate of just six cents a share.

A number of other accounts, the NASD team noted, that also had done trades in Compaq around December 9, 1999, had paid commissions that seemed to be related to the value of their VA Linux allocations and profits.

Within weeks of receiving the letter, Ozag called Goldsmith into his cubicle on the eighth floor of the NASD enforcement offices. Showing Goldsmith the Compaq trade with the $1 million commission on his computer screen, Ozag said the example in the letter seemed to check out. And so the NASD soon ramped up the probe.

○

Two weeks later, on Friday June 2, 2000, CSFB legal assistant Grace Shentwu sent an e-mail to Quattrone and several other tech group bankers with the subject line "VA Linux Systems Inc. ("LNUX") 12/9/99 IPO—Do Not Destroy Any Documents." It said the CSFB legal department had received an inquiry from NASD enforcement, and had retained a law firm to help respond. "At this time," Shentwu said, "no documents of any kind (including e-mails, computer files, etc.) can be destroyed or altered. Everything responsive must be preserved for review by CSFBC's outside counsel."[2]

The same day as he received the Shentwu e-mail, Quattrone replied: "What is this about?"

The following Monday, June 5, 2000, CSFB compliance attorney Rose Corbett told Quattrone the NASD inquiry on VA Linux "seems to direct its inquiry toward the allocation process. The request is extremely broad and requires production of all documents including e-mails and voice mails relating to the allocation process. Please do not destroy any files related to the IPO."[3] On June 7, CSFB's Shentwu asked Quattrone to send her any responsive VA Linux documents he had by June 12.[4] The next day Edward Loh, a junior tech group staffer, traded e-mails with Shentwu about how to get the material to her.[5]

○

The success of the Quattrone group had been undeniable. CSFB had ranked a lowly number eight in IPOs in 1998. With its top-three share of technology banking, the technology group had boosted CSFB's IPO rank to number four by mid-2000. Yet rumors spread that Quattrone might jump yet again to Merrill Lynch, or launch his own venture capital investment firm.[6]

In March, Quattrone scheduled a meeting with CSFB chief Allen Wheat and his deputy, Charles Stonehill, in Palo Alto "to discuss the structure of our relationship with the firm going forward generally." Promising to sweeten terms of a deferred compensation plan, Quattrone told his bankers, "guys, we are on the verge of global domination in this business," and thanked them for their hard work.[7]

On June 23, Quattrone extended his contract at CSFB, which had been due to expire in 2002, for another three years on sweetened terms. The new deal boosted the tech group's share of the revenues minus costs to 55 percent from 40 percent over certain thresholds. The group's share of tech-stock trading revenues rose to 20 percent from 10 percent. Quattrone's own annual minimum rose to $15 million from $10 million. The new deal also expanded Quattrone's coverage universe to include certain media and telecom companies, and provided for a new high-tech private-equity fund with venture capital. But Wheat had another reason to want to lock up Quattrone. He was considering plans for a big merger.

○

At the Intraware Christmas party in December 1999, CEO Peter Jackson already had a nagging feeling of worry. His company's stock, sold in the IPO at $16 a share, had hit $99 that month, putting the value of his stake at $340 million. But the company was losing $15 million a quarter. He had to spend much of the next year fighting to save it.

By spring 2000, Jackson noticed that Lise Buyer, the CSFB analyst who had followed his company, had left CSFB, and his stock wasn't being followed by any other CSFB analyst. In June 2000, new equity investors pulled away when they saw how the company was hemorrhaging money. With his stock down 50 percent, Jackson raised $25 million in a so-called death-spiral debt offering convertible into stock—a financing of last resort—with advice from Marshall Capital, a CSFB unit, that had the blessing of the Quattrone bankers. But Jackson soon regretted it. Issuing the convertible bonds seemed to drive the stock price down.

The company's cash burn, plus some hard-to-collect payables from other sinking Internet companies, quickly required a payback of almost half the money. In November, Jackson had to lay off 200 of his 420 employees, and later had to lay off 80 more and get the workforce down to about 65. His stock came within hours of being delisted by NASDAQ, and he finally raised enough new venture capital money to repay the convertible bond entirely.

After Jackson had finished retrenching and restructuring, including bringing in a new president and chief financial officer, his company, whose *quarterly* revenues had hit $41.5 million in mid-2000, would shrink to an *annual* revenue rate of just $10 million.

○

Meanwhile, at the SEC, the same "concerned citizen" letter was routed to the Office of Compliance Inspections and Examinations. On July 10, 2000, Ann Griffith, CSFB's deputy compliance director, e-mailed other legal staffers and about a dozen bankers, including Quattrone, that the SEC would conduct an on-site exam of CSFB's equity underwriting process.[8]

Starting Friday July 14, she said, the SEC exam would take up to six weeks and focus on deals where CSFB controlled at least 10 percent of the stock, first-day price gains, commissions for institutional and individual investors, procedures for pricing, and the allocation process.

O

As the stock market continued to weaken, the number of CSFB-led IPOs slowed, from seven a month in late 1999 to just two in June 2000.

July also brought one of the bubble's last great hurrahs for the CSFB tech group, the mammoth $1.14 billion IPO of Corvis Corporation, an optical telecom switching company *with zero revenues* at the time of the IPO. The 7 percent fee level was standard for IPOs of less than $100 million, but was routinely reduced to as low 4 percent or less for IPOs above $1 billion. But Quattrone charged Corvis the full 7 percent, which amounted to a fee of $79.7 million.

Even though Corvis would be five times the size of most of the IPOs of the Internet bubble, jockeying for its stock was intense. The deal's size and timing gave Quattrone what would turn out to be one last chance to play the kingpin role, to pass judgment on allocations to investors such as tech specialist Amerindo Investment Advisers, mutual-fund giants like Fidelity, and CEOs from Bernard Arnault of LVMH to Michael Dell of computer giant Dell.[9]

On July 19, 2000, Quattrone sent an e-mail to Michael Dell. Quattrone and Dell had enjoyed a cordial breakfast in New York in June, and the same day Quattrone had met with officials from MSD Capital, the family investment manager for Michael Dell.[10] Although Dell didn't use CSFB for investment banking, Dell himself was a regular keynote speaker at Quattrone's annual tech group conference.

Quattrone told Dell, "my team has gotten word to me that you are personally interested in having dell ventures receive a meaningful allocation on the ipo of corvis, the optical networking company we are expecting to price in the next week or so. given the intense interest in this space we anticipate this will be a complete zoo, so I wanted to check if your interest was really there and if so what I could tell my syndicate desk about your holding horizon."

With this question Quattrone was making sure the Corvis stock was something Dell personally wanted, and that Dell Ventures wouldn't flip the shares for a quick profit that would put pressure on the market price when trading began. Quattrone also took the opportunity to lock in Dell's commitment to reprise his appearance as a keynote speaker at the CSFB tech conference.

As an afterthought, Quattrone raised one more topic, seeking a reference check that showed how as a banker he influenced the selection of analysts. "[B]y the way, we are still trying to finalize our selection of a pc analyst (slim pickings). how would you react to charlie wolf? best regards, frank." Wolf was a veteran personal-computer research analyst who had worked at First Boston as far back as the mid-1980s, and was known for skeptical, sometimes caustic views.[11]

Dell himself replied a few hours later, and brazenly stated that a big IPO allocation of Corvis for him could help Quattrone win more business from Dell and its customers: "Frank, It was great to see you too. We would like 250k shares of Corvis. I know there have been efforts on both sides to build the relationship and an offering like this would certainly help."[12]

Dell also gave a qualified commitment to appear on November 28 at the CSFB conference, joking that he might cancel if his staff disapproved of the analyst chosen to cover his company at CSFB. Dell also threw his weight solidly against the choice of Wolf: "I asked [Thomas] Meredith [Dell's chief financial officer] what he thought about Wolf and he said 'NFW.'" NFW meant "no fucking way." Dell said he agreed. "You might be better off with a fresh new talent."

The following day, July 20, Quattrone forwarded his e-mail exchange with Dell to Andy Fisher, his stock allocation colleague, urging that Dell be given a generous Corvis allocation out of respect for his personal request: "[R]e corvis, when Michael himself e-mails his interest, i think we should be nice, esp if we want him to keynote."

Fisher quickly cautioned Quattrone against making too many individual promises without first considering the overall picture: "there are an enormous number of pigs lining up at this trough," he explained. First, he said, "we will want to compile the entire list of friends asking for stock."[13]

Five days later, on July 24—three days before the Corvis IPO would be priced—Quattrone received a new appeal for Corvis stock from Glenn R. Fuhrman, the managing principal of MSD Capital, Dell's family office. "We know this is a tough one but we wanted to ask for a little help with our Corvis allocation," said Fuhrman, who added Dell's name to the signature line together with a wish to use CSFB as a banker for other optical deals.[14]

Quattrone replied by cautioning that demand for the deal was "crazy," but vowed to "put in a good word with our syndicate desk."[15]

On Tuesday evening, July 25, senior CSFB equity syndicate executive Ted Hatfield in New York e-mailed Quattrone and Fisher a preliminary list of selected possible Corvis allocations for their comments. The list of fifteen accounts was headed by Fidelity at 1.35 million shares and Putnam and Janus at 625,000 each, so Quattrone could see the size of the largest allocations.

Among the accounts whose executives had appealed to Quattrone for more IPO stock, the list showed Amerindo and Bowman at 200,000 apiece, Dell Ventures at 100,000, and MSD at 50,000. The list also showed Technology Crossover Ventures, which had received 50,000 VA Linux shares, and whose Jay Hoag was a big Quattrone fan, at 75,000. Integral, whose Roger McNamee was a longtime Quattrone associate, was down for 40,000, as was Attractor Investment Management, another venture investor.

TCV and Attractor had been leading venture investors in Intraware, whose IPO had been led by CSFB.[16]

At midmorning the next day, July 26, 2000, the day before the Corvis deal was to be priced and allocated, Fisher e-mailed Quattrone that he needed to "get closure with you on the preliminary allocations we sent you last night."[17] Later that day Quattrone was also told of a conference call to review the Corvis allocations.[18]

After checking with Dell himself on how to allocate the Corvis shares among his different entities, Quattrone recommended to Fisher that MSD get a bigger percentage allocation than in the past.[19] He also asked Tom Meredith, Dell's chief financial officer, and Alex Smith, managing director of Dell Ventures, the computer vendor's venture capital arm, about their interest in Corvis, adding, "gentlemen: long time no see, would love to tee it up with you some time. Mr. Meredith, somebody told me the other day that you grew up in south philly, as i did (i'm from 9th and shunk, stella maris parish, st. joe's prep). is this true, and if so, did you never confess or did my early-alzheimer brain forget this?"[20]

Near the end of the day on July 26, 2000, Quattrone also thought to double-check how the Friends of Frank would be treated in the Corvis deal as well. He e-mailed Schmidt and Grunwald, copying Fisher and Brady: "given high profile nature of this deal I would like to review specific allocations for tech pcs along with andy fisher. Could you pls get them to us asap? Thanks"[21]

On July 28, 2000, Corvis stock rose 135 percent on its first day of trading. Priced at $36 in the IPO—which gave the entire company a stock market value of $12 billion—the stock closed at $84.72 the first day, and kept rising for another few weeks. It hit a peak of $114.75 in August.

With Corvis at a market value of nearly $38 billion, Quattrone gathered a group of online journalists at the Sheraton Palace Hotel in downtown San Francisco in early August 2000. The towering valuation of Corvis seemed plausible as he compared it to the IPO of Cisco in 1990. "I think people have seen how big these companies can become, especially if you become the category leader," he told Adam Lashinsky of TheStreet.com.[22] But Quattrone did concede that while Cisco had priced its 1990 IPO at eighteen times expected 1990 earnings, Corvis had priced its IPO at forty-nine times expected revenues two years in the future.

Then Quattrone was asked whether CSFB had been part of taking too many ill-prepared companies public. "We've been searching our souls about that," he acknowledged fleetingly. Then he seemed to shift any possible blame away from investment bankers and toward venture capital investors. "Everyone is looking to see if the venture guys will repeat their mistakes of the 1980s, when they made lots of me-too investments and returns went to the single digits. We're monitoring that carefully and seeing no evidence yet."

After August, Corvis stock fell steadily amid carnage in both technology and telecom stocks. By April 26, 2001, it had fallen 94 percent from its peak, and 81 percent from the IPO price, to $6.67 a share. That day, CSFB analyst James Parmelee reiterated his "strong buy" on the stock.

Corvis announced staff cutbacks in May 2001, and CNNfn called it a "poster child for fallen IPOs." The stock price hit $1 a share in the fall. By April 2002, quarterly revenues, which had hit $84 million in early 2001, fell to $8.7 million. For the quarter that ended in June 2002, Corvis revenues shrank to $3 million, and its stock hit $.71 in November 2002. By early 2003, its IPO stock market value of $12 billion had melted down to $270 million. By then it ranked as the second-largest money loser for investors among all IPOs for the year 2000.[23]

THE GUMSHOES GO TO WORK

28

ROBERT GLAUBER, a Harvard lecturer who had probed the causes of the 1987 stock market crash for the U.S. government, became chief executive of the NASD's regulatory operations in July 2000, just as the organization was separating from the NASDAQ Stock Market. One of the first run-ins he had with a Wall Street chief executive was with Philip Purcell of Morgan Stanley Dean Witter, who protested that the NASD was about to bring a case against his firm based on ancient history—events that occurred in 1992–94. Glauber gave the green light to the charges anyway, but urged NASD enforcement chief Goldsmith to speed up the enforcement effort.

An NASD exam team, consisting of Joe Ozag and his supervisor, C. Neil Alexander, visited CSFB headquarters in New York for four days, starting Monday, July 31. Shuttling among different rooms each day, one day they found themselves in the basement. The NASD staffers had been frustrated at the slow pace at which the CSFB lawyers produced e-mails, documents, and other data, and felt they were being stalled with excuses and delays.

On Tuesday, August 1, 2000, Brodsky sent a short e-mail briefing on the NASD visit to three top CSFB executives—equities department head Brady Dougan; global general counsel Joseph McLaughlin, vice chairman Richard Thornburgh—and five other CSFB lawyers. Brodsky said the exam appeared to focus on commissions paid by certain trading clients for trades in some "highly liquid" stocks such as IBM or Compaq. The NASD, he said, had identified about twenty customers who had paid much higher commissions around the time they received hot IPOs. If the going rate was $.05 or $.06 a share, Brodsky said, some of the customers had paid "50 to 60 cents a share on the IPO day."[1]

That Friday, August 4, 2000, Brodsky sent an e-mail to a larger group of CSFB officials that included Quattrone. Brodsky told them CSFB had provided the NASD staffers trading records for twenty-one trading clients who had received shares of the VA Linux IPO. He added that interviews with capital markets executives Tony Ehinger and Jeff Bunzel had gone "very well."[2]

To test the assertions in the "concerned citizen" letter, which had described "riskless" trades in unrelated liquid securities, Ozag decided to focus on big, institution-size trades of ten thousand shares or more.[3] When interviewing Ehinger, Ozag asked what the standard commission would be for a trade of a highly liquid New York Stock Exchange–listed stock, assuming the dealer didn't have to put up any of its own money to buy it.

Ehinger replied that the "going rate" was six to ten cents a share, with six cents being more the norm in that period. Ozag then doubled the top end of the range and asked Ehinger about trades done at twenty cents a share or more. The examiner asked: *Would you say that it's fair to say that such a trade with a commission of twenty cents a share or more would be unusual, and even semi-unique?*

Ehinger replied: *Yes, I would.*

When the NASD team members returned to Washington, they asked CSFB for records of trades that met the "unusual, semi-unique" definition—trades of ten thousand or more shares with commissions of twenty cents per share or more, between January 1, 1999, and August 4, 2000. Based on what Ehinger had said, they expected to receive data on a small number of trades.

What they got back was astonishing. The CSFB response included over twelve thousand five hundred trades! Though there had been few in early 1999, the volume had built up that fall, then tailed off again after March 2000, when the market had begun tanking. Thus, they decided to focus on the fourth quarter of 1999, a period that included the VA Linux IPO mentioned in the letter.

Using a computer program, the NASD team tried to correlate the trades with big commissions with the receipt of hot IPOs. Looking at three thousand trades with commissions of twenty cents a share or more in the fourth quarter of 1999, they found that 91 percent occurred within three days of the same customers getting IPOs. Indeed, for some CSFB customers, the pattern resembled the graph of a heart monitor. The trades ran at a consistent six cents a share, then jumped to twenty-five to fifty cents around the receipt of a hot IPO. The agency eventually calculated that such high-commission trades accounted for 22 percent of CSFB's total commissions in one quarter.

On September 11, 2000, the NASD's Ozag asked CSFB lawyers in writing for the names and phone numbers for twenty accounts, plus the names of their CSFB brokers, that had paid big commissions and gotten IPOs. He also asked for their account statements and trade records. Several of the twenty were Lustig-group accounts, including Ascent, Energia, and Lustig's flagship United Capital. Four of the accounts were clients of the Quattrone group brokers, including Y2K Partners, the account that had refused Grunwald's payback demand. Another was

Christopher Champeau, who had been accused by JohnDoe526 of paying "kick-backs" to Caan.[4]

Ozag also asked for the brokers' e-mails mentioning VA Linux and several other stocks, including Compaq, K-Mart, Philip Morris, and Walt Disney. He also asked about the "tech PCS" group, and any e-mails between the twenty accounts' brokers and several key CSFB staffers, including Coleman, Commesso, Ehinger, Fisher, and Quattrone. This request suggested that the NASD was interested in any role Quattrone might have had in allocations.

O

If the NASD probe and visit were the first signs of big trouble for the firm, the market was sending up other warnings as well. Just as the NASD team was wrapping up its on-site visit, a CSFB technology IPO fell flat on its face. Screaming Media Inc., an Internet content syndicator based in Silicon Alley in Manhattan, saw its stock fall 13 percent on its first day of trading, August 3, 2000.

In an e-mail after the market closed that day, CSFB equity capital markets staffer David Hermer sent out a complicated explanation, combined with an appeal for help to the entire CSFB sales force.[5] Ernesto Cruz, the head of global equity capital markets in New York, forwarded Hermer's e-mail to Quattrone the next day: "here is an example of what we try to do to improve a difficult situation."

But Quattrone wasn't impressed: "in the future when a deal like this looks difficult," he answered, "bill brady and or I should get a heads up and get involved in some of the decisions on allocation, as is the case when fisher is running the deal. Not much you can do to improve a deal after the fact." Although Quattrone would later assert he had no responsibility for IPO allocations, such e-mails indicated he got involved in some of the decisions.

O

Despite the periodic updates from Brodsky, the IPO inquiries probably appeared to be a small blip on the radar screen. In August, top CSFB officials decided on a massive new roll of the dice. At the end of the month, Wheat unveiled a $13 billion acquisition of Donaldson Lufkin & Jenrette Inc. (DLJ), another, slightly smaller securities firm.

In an interview the day the deal was announced, Quattrone told the author it was "terrific," something he had been pushing for. CSFB was strong in technology, overseas, in investment-grade debt, and equities, Quattrone noted. As for DLJ, "They're strong in a lot of things, too," he said, "that would really help us get to number one," such as high-yield bonds, online brokerage, prime brokerage and clearing, media and telecom banking, and private-equity, Quattrone said. "It positions us to defeat Morgan Stanley and Goldman Sachs long-term."[6]

○

Despite the flop of Screaming Media, on August 10, another CSFB tech IPO, McData Corporation, tripled on its first day of trading.

A few weeks later, a technology executive who had helped win the Quattrone group an IPO in January 2000 raised his hand for an outsize allocation of another hot deal. The executive was Jim Balsillie, the co–chief executive of Research in Motion Ltd., the Canada-based developer of BlackBerry wireless e-mail devices.

The stormy relationship that eventually developed between Balsillie and Quattrone would eventually be cited disapprovingly by regulators. They believed it showed how Quattrone played IPO allocations, research coverage by analysts he controlled, and a willingness to be "creative" in how he collected fees all together like a symphony orchestra in extracting money from clients.

On September 8, 2000, Jim Balsillie e-mailed his banker at CSFB, Chris Legg, about getting an allocation of the AvantGo Inc. IPO: "Chris; Who at CSFB should I call about an institutional fill on AvantGo? I work very closely with them obviously, and would like to place a nice order on the IPO. Should I call Frank? Jim."[7]

Legg forwarded the request to New York as well as to Andy Fisher, the tech group capital markets chief, noting that Balsillie's request deserved special consideration since he would soon be choosing bankers to manage a new follow-on stock issue. "As Andy knows, we are in the hunt for a large follow on with RIM and our friend Mr. B (CEO of RIM) is looking for a fill on AvantGo (we did the same for him on 724). What kind of special allocation do you think we can get for him? Thanks, Chris." CSFB had led the IPO of 724 Solutions Inc., which had gained a first-day 177 percent in January 2000.

Fisher, who was constantly besieged with demands like Balsillie's, put his foot down on this one. "He got too much on 724 because he helped introduce us to the business and he screamed bloody murder about it. I can't remember the exact number. He should get an allocation through tech PCS that is what the system is for." All those accounts, Fisher said, can "direct business to us."

Fisher's description of the Friends of Frank program suggested what Quattrone later denied—that the accounts were meant for individuals who could give CSFB banking business. Balsillie was already in line to get stock from AvantGo itself, Fisher added. "The guy is a pig and if we give him a direct allocation it should be very small as he has nothing whatsoever to do with this deal."

Four days later, on September 14, 2000, banker Legg took the question to

Quattrone himself. He had spoken with the Schmidt-Grunwald brokers about getting stock to Balsillie. But they couldn't get the RIM boss much more than three thousand shares of AvantGo—far less than the fifteen thousand shares he had received of 724. How far was Quattrone willing to go with a big fee in the offing?

Legg warned Quattrone that Balsillie was likely to complain if he just got three thousand shares. "While his requests may be piggy, thanksgiving is around the corner ('within spitting distance,' according to a conversation I recently had with the CFO) and we are definitely in a feeding mode. I told him I'd give him some indication of his allocation, let me know your thoughts."

Quattrone responded within ninety minutes, with a copy to Grunwald, Fisher, and the New York capital markets desk. His bottom line was that he definitely wanted to get some IPO shares to Balsillie, but was aware that such an allocation risked being interpreted as spinning. Quattrone asked Legg: "How does his personal acct business stack up vz this request? We can't do something where it looks like we are 'spinning.' Would like to be on generous side of what can be defended."

Balsillie's final allocation of AvantGo was never made public. But the stock rose 67 percent on its first day of trading, September 27.

CULTURE CLASH

29

WITH HIS OUTSIZE presence in technology deals, Quattrone had cata-pulted CSFB close to the top of the Wall Street food chain for the first time since the 1980s. So Wheat doubled the bet, hoping to use that bigger market share as a springboard to make the firm's rise more lasting, by strengthening its position in other areas, such as junk bonds and merchant banking. But this time he came up snake eyes.

Wheat's $13 billion acquisition of Donaldson, Lufkin & Jenrette was an-nounced on August 30, very near the top of the historic market bubble. Indeed, it ended up being so poorly timed that it destroyed billions of dollars worth of value for CSFB's Zurich-based parent, Credit Suisse Group.

Quattrone's business footprint contributed to problems with the merger. It influenced the resignation of one of Donaldson Lufkin's top bankers, Ken Moelis, which then forced Wheat to offer rich, multiyear pay packages to re-tain other bankers and traders who also threatened to leave. That left the firm with a bloated, unwieldy compensation structure heading into the long market downturn.

Donaldson, Lufkin & Jenrette, or DLJ, was the creation of Richard Jenrette, a courtly Southerner with a penchant for refurbishing landmark homes and col-lecting Americana. He had cofounded the firm as a research boutique in 1959, and sold it in 1985 to the Equitable Life Assurance Society of the United States. Equitable handed over control of DLJ to a French concern, Group Axa S.A., in the early 1990s, and it was Axa that brilliantly sold DLJ to CSFB at the peak of the market.

A series of encounters between Quattrone and various bankers, executives, and other staffers at DLJ showed how his status influenced the melding of the two firms.

Fred Lane was a veteran DLJ banker who had worked across the table from Quattrone a decade earlier, when Quattrone was at Morgan Stanley. Lane, then cohead of mergers at DLJ, had found Quattrone cordial and competent.

When the CSFB acquisition of DLJ was announced, Lane, then cohead of the DLJ Boston office, called Quattrone. It was midday in Boston and morning in Palo Alto. *We should probably work cooperatively on certain accounts where I have relationships,* Lane suggested. He threw out the names of some companies where he knew key executives, and where neither Quattrone nor his people were active.

That won't be necessary, Quattrone replied. *We don't need your help, and I don't want you calling on any technology companies. These are our companies.* Quattrone ordered Lane not to call on them, and to curtail his relationships with them.

You can't be serious, Lane said.

No, that's the way it's going to be, Quattrone said.

You are an asshole, said Lane, slamming down the phone. Not only was Quattrone territorial, Lane thought, he was so discourteous—rude, really—that it was almost laughable. It certainly didn't fit the collegial DLJ culture as he knew it. Lane soon left and formed his own boutique, Lane, Berry & Co.[1]

○

Lane wasn't the only banker who bumped into Quatrone's special status. One of DLJ's biggest producers was a Los Angeles investment banker named Ken Moelis. A veteran of Drexel Burnham Lambert who specialized in junk bond clients that lacked an investment-grade credit rating, Moelis fit in well at DLJ. But he and other DLJ bankers bristled at checking with Quattrone before contacting their own longtime clients.

Quattrone's contract guaranteed him sole coverage of technology companies, many of them in Moelis's home turf of California. Quattrone's contract, renegotiated in June with Brady Dougan, had given him the right to cover companies in twenty-two technology categories that included communication devices, entertainment, and "other new media." Moelis believed such limits weren't workable.

Like the DLJ bankers, the DLJ brokers would also confront Quattrone's sacred-cow status.

The brokers at DLJ, just like those at CSFB, paid no attention to individual investors with just a few hundred thousand dollars to invest. Like the CSFB brokers, they mainly concentrated on wealthy individuals or midsize institutional investors and fast-trading hedge funds. The biggest difference was size. DLJ had four hundred retail private-client brokers, while CSFB had just fifty.

Mike Campbell, who ran DLJ's brokers, was a gruff, plainspoken native of North Massapequa, Long Island, who had graduated from Adelphi University and later became chairman of its trustees. He was given authority over all of the combined firm's brokers, including those who worked for Andy Benjamin at CSFB.

But when Campbell sought to have the Quattrone group brokers led by Schmidt folded in with the DLJ brokers in San Francisco, the top CSFB executives in New York told him to forget about it.

○

On the weekend of November 10–12, 2000, immediately after the deal closed, the managing directors of both CSFB and DLJ had a bonding, team-building retreat at the hotel Portofino in Orlando, Florida.

The firm rented part of the Universal Studios theme park for an evening of fun after speeches by the top brass. Quattrone was walking around with his coat slung over his shoulder, wearing an open-necked pastel shirt. Schmidt had a beer with Campbell, the DLJ executive who wanted to absorb his group; they later agreed on a way their brokers could work together. An amusement arcade was set up with pool tables, foosball, Ping-Pong, and virtual reality games. There was a small basketball area, with netting around it like a batting cage.

Bennett Goodman, the ranking manager of DLJ's powerful junk bond franchise, was standing around with Moelis and Quattrone drinking beer when they noticed some of the younger bankers playing basketball. They decided to join in. If Quattrone was CSFB's franchise player, Goodman ran the most profitable division at DLJ.

The game quickly ratcheted up in intensity. A crowd of other bankers gathered to watch the two firms' goliaths go at it head-to-head. Larry Schloss, a senior DLJ merchant banking executive, was also on the court, as was tech group banker Hodge, the jock from Stanford. Testosterone was flowing. One CSFB official who happened by recalled that, from the crowd reaction, "You would have thought it was the seventh game of the NBA finals. It was like they were playing for their lives." But the game ended after one of the DLJ players, John Robertshaw, had to get stitches when the basket fell on his head.

○

Ten days after Orlando, Moelis quit to join UBS AG, a European rival of Credit Suisse Group whose initials once stood for Union Bank of Switzerland. At the time, people who knew Moelis said that one factor was the prospective loss of the autonomy he had enjoyed in pursuing clients on his West Coast turf.[2]

His defection so soon after the deal closed rocked CSFB, and—in a scenario reminiscent of Quattrone's own defection from Morgan Stanley in 1996—Wheat personally flew to California to try to save as many members of the Moelis group as possible. The CSFB team was able to save a majority, but at a steep

cost. They did so by giving many of the bankers pay guarantees covering two
or three years.

By the following March, CSFB had given similar guarantees to more than
one hundred senior bankers, plus to about forty managers and traders in CSFB's
own bond department—many of whom almost left to join Barclays PLC in
February 2001, before Wheat made them similar offers.[3] The guarantees would
become a serious, expensive problem for the firm when the stock market continued falling.

O

Despite Quattrone's support for a big allocation of the AvantGo IPO for Research in Motion co-CEO Jim Balsillie, the BlackBerry maker didn't choose
CSFB as the lead manager for its $612 million stock offering on October 27,
2000. Instead, CSFB grudgingly played second fiddle to Merrill Lynch as a
mere comanager instead.

Ordinarily, CSFB wouldn't accept such subordinate assignments. The fees
weren't as lucrative, and it could set a precedent. In this case, however, CSFB did
so based on a belief that Balsillie and his chief financial officer, Dennis Kavelman,
had assured the bankers of a large fee.

But when it came time to collect, Quattrone had to get tough. And the stri-
dent, coercive tone of his e-mails about the situation over the next few months,
together with his proposal that CSFB could be paid for its work on the deal
after the fact, later struck state and federal prosecutors as possibly illegal.

The Research in Motion stock sale offered total underwriting fees of $29.9
million. In an internal CSFB e-mail on October 20, 2000, Jake Peters, the head
of East Coast corporate finance for the tech group, outlined the terms under
which CSFB had agreed to participate. If CSFB didn't get 25 percent of the
fee—a large percentage for a comanager—then RIM or Merrill would "make it
happen after the fact." As Peters noted in the same e-mail, Kavelman "would
not guarantee this."[4]

On November 2, 2000, after Merrill handed out the comanagers' fees for the
deal, Quattrone sent a sternly worded note to Balsillie. "We made it clear during our negotiations that our expectation was that we would receive at least
25% of the overall economics. You agreed to keep an eye on our [fee share] . . .
and told me if we were not satisfied you would write us a check for the difference."
Instead of 25 percent, Quattrone said, CSFB had only received 15.7 percent—a
difference which he calculated at $2.2 million.

"We want to be your partner and work with you on a number of fronts,"
Quattrone said, alluding to an indication that RIM would also send some
merger advisory work to CSFB. "An important reason why we broke our precedent of never participating as a nonbookrunner in a Merrill-led tech deal was

the understanding that our economics would be at least 25% of the overall total. The difference between that goal and where we are on the spreadsheet is
$2.2 million." Pay up, Quattrone said.[5]

In explaining his language to his own bankers, Quattrone said the day before, "just to be clear, jim told me he would write us a check the day after the
deal, so we don't need to be limited by 100% of the deal economics."

What Quattrone was suggesting here, prosecutors would later argue, was
a possible violation of securities rules requiring disclosure of all underwriter
compensation. If RIM paid CSFB the extra money for work done on the deal
that didn't come from deal proceeds, the prosecutors suggested, that could
amount to undisclosed underwriter compensation.

After RIM's Kavelman got Merrill to direct more money to CSFB, Quattrone
sent Balsillie an updated invoice for $2 million on November 16, 2000, just hours
after they had met face-to-face. "When you and I were trying to reach a solution
that got us into the deal, you promised that if I was not happy . . . that you would
write us a check the next day. You asked me to trust you and I did. I still do. I told
you before we took the business on that our minimum expectation was 25% of
the economics, and after dennis's move we are at around 17%. The difference is
about $2 million. We can get creative about how this gets structured, but I feel
strongly that we deserve this incremental amount. What do you propose? Best
Frank."

Balsillie replied the next day, November 17, 2000: "Frank I thought Solectron
would handle this? Merrill assured that here. Please let me know."[6] A few days
earlier, Solectron Inc., an electronics manufacturer, had sold $1.2 billion worth
of stock in an offering led by Merrill in which CSFB had also participated.

Quattrone replied, "Jim I have no idea what you are referring to. Did they
tell you they'd give us an 'extra' $2mm . . . [on Solectron]? Extra over what?
We have zero trust in [Merrill Lynch]. . . . i am quite skeptical about any solution that involves them."

Balsillie shot back: "You're not being reasonable to expect 25 of overall economics, and an accommodation was made with you guys that Dennis Kavelman coordinated. Let's move ahead!" Then Balsillie dangled the lure of possible
additional business to smooth things over. "The deal we talked about in detail
with Chris Legg is very interesting to us."

Quattrone forwarded the exchange with Balsillie to three colleagues. "I am
close to firing this guy," Quattrone said, meaning ending any business dealings
with RIM. "[G]ive me a good reason not to."

Then Quattrone shot back to Balsillie: "jim, the accommodation was nowhere close to acceptable." He added, "it's time to live up to your deal with me.
If you want to do it by paying us $2mm more than our normal scale in an m&a
deal, fine."

Balsillie continued to sidestep the issue. "I am and will continue to live up to my word and more," he replied to Quattrone. "Let's move on."

"[J]ust tell me how and when," Quattrone replied. "can't move on till I know."

Then Quattrone forwarded the e-mail string to his colleagues, with a covering message that added a time element to his threat to "fire" Balsillie: "10 . . . 9 . . . 8 . . . 7 . . . 6 . . . 5 . . . 4 . . ."

O

Seemingly unaware of the fee dispute, on November 16, a junior CSFB technology banker in New York put through a routine request to bankers Boutros and Legg. The banker, John Quinn, asked for approval to send five stylish Tumi carrying bags to RIM's senior management, including Balsillie and Kavelman, to commemorate CSFB's role in the stock sale.

"As a gesture of CSFB's continued support of the company, we would like to give senior management tumi deal bags. We believe that this gesture will create additional goodwill and help to differentiate CSFB from [Merrill Lynch]." Because Merrill "did not give deal bags," Quinn explained, the gifts could "improve [CSFB's] ability to penetrate this account."

With the fee still uncollected ten days later, on November 26, Boutros replied: "NOT approved, unless Frank thinks otherwise."

Quattrone himself seconded Boutros's reply the next day: "Based on the dispute we are having, these bags will cost rimm $400,000 per bag. Denied till payment received. COD."

THE BUST

BOOK
THREE

THE PROSECUTORS

30

IT HAD BEEN six months since the stock market peaked. By the end of September 2000, the Dow Jones Industrial Average had fallen 9 percent. The damage was much worse in the tech-heavy NASDAQ stock market, which was down 27 percent. And the Dow Jones Internet stock index had fallen 44 percent.

The bubble was over. But not everyone knew it yet. For all anyone could tell for sure, the market downturn could have been just a blip, with a rebound to new highs just around the corner. But that isn't what happened. Instead, the market continued to fall, in fits and starts to be sure, but relentlessly, and for three years in all. It would not hit bottom until March 2003.

The investigation of whether Credit Suisse First Boston brokers had received kickbacks or bribes for hot IPOs would be the first in a regulatory wave that gathered momentum as the market continued to fall. Investors, stung by losses, demanded retribution for the myriad ways in which, it emerged, Wall Street seemed to have rigged the game behind the scenes in favor of select insiders and customers, and against the average investor, during the market's epic rise.

For CSFB, the first major Wall Street firm to be investigated for bubble-era misconduct, the stakes escalated rapidly. Investigators from two regulators, the National Association of Securities Dealers (NASD) and the Securities and Exchange Commission (SEC), would soon be joined by a group of the top criminal stock market prosecutors in the country. They ran the securities fraud unit in the office of the U.S. Attorney for the Southern District of New York.

A decade earlier, the same team of the SEC and the Manhattan U.S. attorney's office had pursued junk bond king Michael Milken and his firm, Drexel Burnham Lambert, in a wave of cases that followed a similar era of market excess in the 1980s. That era was marked by epic takeover battles, leveraged debt-financed buyouts, insider trading, and other behind-the-scenes scams. Not only was Milken prosecuted and jailed, some of his customers also went to jail, and his entire firm collapsed.

O

In late September 2000, Caren Pennington, an assistant regional director in the SEC's northeast regional office, which was located in a forty-seven-story, red office tower on the north side of the World Trade Center, contacted the NASD staffers in Washington. A graduate of Williams College and Georgetown's law school, Pennington had worked at a big-name Manhattan law firm, Simpson Thacher & Bartlett, before joining the SEC in 1994.

Pennington, with brown hair and a round face, had a cheerful smile that belied her cynical view of Wall Street and a tendency to speak so quickly that her words ran together. She informed the NASD staff that the SEC was also working on the IPO case arising from the anonymous letter from "A concerned citizen."

Although the two agencies competed for splashy cases, the SEC had a broader mandate than the NASD. Created soon after the 1929 stock market crash exposed a raft of market abuses, the SEC was supposed to root out fraud and scams throughout the market. The NASD was a self-regulating organization funded by the securities industry answerable to the SEC, whose mission was to police conduct by securities dealers. Both agencies had only civil, not criminal, authority.

The SEC prodded the U.S. attorney's office, which did have criminal authority, to get involved. Pennington's boss, northeast regional chief Wayne Carlin, told federal prosecutor Robert Khuzami, chief of the securities fraud unit at the U.S. attorney's office in Manhattan, about the letter's allegations.[1] Khuzami, who resembled a young Al Pacino, was no slouch. He had successfully prosecuted a group of Muslim militants, led by Sheik Omar Abdel-Rahman, who were accused of conspiring to bomb high-profile U.S. targets in a case arising from the 1993 World Trade Center bombing.

The SEC staffers took a different tack than the NASD in pursuing their investigation, but inevitably the two agencies overlapped. While the NASD focused on trading and IPO allocations in the fourth quarter of 1999, the SEC focused on specific IPOs, starting with the two CSFB deals that had the biggest first-day gains.

O

On September 20, 2000, the SEC notified CSFB that its examination of the firm's IPO allocations had been referred to the division of enforcement—a serious step. Pennington's staff asked CSFB for the names of all of its IPOs from 1998 to 2000. Focusing on VA Linux and Selectica, the two biggest first-day gainers, the agency also sought records of what CSFB had told the issuers, any tapes of conversations about IPO allocations, CSFB's policies and procedures for allocations, and other records.[2]

The SEC also asked for documents identifying all recipients of five hundred shares or more of all IPOs, including VA Linux and Selectica, and their contacts at CSFB. The agency wanted all of Robert Paglione's communications on that subject, since he had pressed for more allocations for Kris, the Lustig trader, as well as for those of six other CSFB staffers and *the entire technology group.*

At 6:00 P.M. that evening, CSFB lawyer Michael Radest sent an e-mail giving the bad news about the SEC probe to Wheat, CSFB's chief executive, and nineteen other executives, including Quattrone, Benjamin, Coleman, Ehinger, Hatfield, and Paul Caan, Benjamin's deputy, who had been the subject of the JohnDoe526 e-mail. The SEC had contacted CSFB customers about the case, Radest added.[3]

Sitting in his Palo Alto office at 3:00 P.M. California time, Quattrone's first reaction was to want to to get word to Schmidt. Within two minutes, he fired off an e-mail to CSFB's general counsel for the Americas, David Brodsky, the firm's number-two lawyer. "[I]s it okay to copy john schmidt who runs our tech pcs group?"[4]

Forty minutes later, Brodsky warned Quattrone not to contact Schmidt. Ever since Watergate, prosecutors had a saying—"it's not the crime it's the cover-up"—and Brodsky wanted to avoid any suggestion of one by Quattrone and the Schmidt brokers. "Not advisable," he told Quattrone, "because your conversation with him or anyone other than me or any other lawyer on this matter is not privileged."[5] Not privileged meant any conversation that didn't involve a lawyer could itself become evidence in a court or regulatory proceeding.

The stock market might have declined for a few months, but Quattrone was still the firm's most powerful banker, and Brodsky offered his services personally to get word to Schmidt. "I am happy to call John and tell him and say I advised you not to," Brodsky said. But Brodsky told Quattrone he would advise Schmidt not to discuss the case with anyone, including Schmidt's assistant, Linda-Louise Lund. The reason, Brodsky explained, was that it was "likely" that Schmidt, Lund, and Quattrone himself "will be called as witnesses by the SEC and I don't want there to be any inference whatsoever that anyone was trying to influence anyone else's testimony."

Brodsky also cautioned Quattrone not to discuss the probe with banking clients for the same reason; he offered to have his staff do this as well. "Thus, don't call any 1998–2000 issuer to give heads-up," Brodsky said. "Instead give me list of contacts and we will do so in privileged way." Brodsky added,

"I have done this for many years and know how. Don't worry about this. Regards, David"[6]

Quattrone replied: "thanks."

○

As the probe became an SEC enforcement matter, CSFB upgraded the legal talent working on it, hiring Wilmer Cutler & Pickering, a Washington, D.C., law firm that boasted the top civil securities regulatory practice. Among those assigned to the case were Lewis Liman, son of famed trial lawyer Arthur Liman, and William McLucas, a former SEC enforcement chief.

On October 18, after obtaining subpoena power for the case, the SEC sent one for the same information it had already requested on September 20, and also asking for the names of all CSFB employees involved in IPO allocations, the related chain of command, and documents about valuation and pricing and communications with issuers. One thing in particular Pennington wanted to find out: whether CSFB had deliberately underpriced IPOs to boost its trading profits, as the anonymous letter had suggested.[7]

○

In Washington, D.C., the NASD was also deepening its investigation. After CSFB sent the brokers' names to it on October 5, its staff demanded testimony from ten CSFB people, including brokers with clients who paid big commissions and got IPOs. Between October 31 and November 7, its staff interviewed four brokers in the NASD enforcement offices in Washington, under oath, with a court reporter present.

One of the first brokers to be interviewed, on November 1, was Dominick Commesso, who covered Energia Global Holdings. Energia was the Lustig affiliate whose trader had put a $1 million commission on a Compaq stock trade around the time it received 13,500 VA Linux shares, on December 9, 1999—closely resembling the example in the anonymous letter. Energia trader Andy Siegal also had called Commesso after getting an inquiry from the NASD, Commesso testified.[8]

During a protracted and at times clumsy series of questions about the mechanics of how commissions are set, Ozag asked why Energia had boosted its default commission rate from six cents a share to ten cents, and eventually to twenty-five cents. Commesso said he didn't know, and hadn't asked.

Finally getting to the Energia trade of two million shares of Compaq, a trade worth $51.7 million, near the end of a daylong interview, Ozag asked, "Mr. Commesso, how often do you receive a one-million-dollar commission on a single transaction?" After an objection by CSFB outside lawyer Lewis Liman, Commesso eventually acknowledged that he never had before or since. He said the trade had been "difficult," taking hours to execute in several different pieces. Energia had set the commission just after receiving the Linux shares, Commesso said. Four days later, after paying fifty cents a share for the $1 million Compaq commission, Energia had returned to paying six cents a share for another Compaq trade.

Another NASD staffer, Neil Alexander, asked, "Why did your firm charge Energia fifty cents per share on the ninth, on a listed liquid New York stock?" Commesso replied, "My customers set the commission rate, not me." The broker also replied that the rate of the commission was just under 2 percent—below the guideline set by CSFB management. But Commesso did acknowledge telling Energia that paying more commissions would improve the chances of getting IPO shares.

The answers of Commesso and his colleagues became known at NASD as the "don't ask, don't tell" defense: We assume the customers base our compensation on our full universe of goods and services, including research, they said.

Joseph Girimonti, who had sent e-mails detailing how much Sutton had "paid us . . . on deal day," said he didn't necessarily connect the jumbo commissions with IPO allocations. "I don't ask the client why they're paying whatever rate of commission they're paying us," Girimonti said.[9] When NASD lawyer Steven Kaufman attempted several times to ask Girimonti what he meant by "paying us for deal stock," another CSFB outside lawyer raised objections that seemed to block straightforward answers.

O

The NASD investigators soon realized that some of the traders had opened multiple accounts with different brokers at the same firm, sometimes without the brokers' knowledge, in order to get access to more hot IPOs. For example, Siegal had another account under another name, Horizon, with another CSFB broker, Ladd McQuade in Boston. When McQuade was interviewed the following March, he said he was unaware of any other Siegal account; he said it was the first he had heard of it, and he appeared upset.[10]

The NASD got a copy of the e-mails between CSFB salesman Dan Gilbert and institutional sales chief George Coleman about Steve Kris, the Lustig trader. "Steve Kris of Ascent Capital has been listening to us, he paid us $150,000 in secondary commissions in November in an attempt to bring the ratio down," Gilbert had told Coleman on December 6, 1999, in lobbying for more VA Linux stock for the Lustig trader.[11]

When Coleman was shown the e-mail by the NASD in early November, he didn't remember receiving it. *What does the word "ratio" mean there?* Coleman was asked. The CSFB executive gave a vague answer that referred to an internal

CSFB report. The NASD examiners asked that one of the reports be produced promptly.

Its name was "New Issue Performance Report." It would become the single strongest piece of evidence that the firm's management in New York endorsed the commission-payback scheme. As regulators would later charge, some CSFB sales personnel would use the report to urge customers to boost their payments to CSFB in exchange for allocations.[12]

When the NASD staff tried to reach traders like Kris and Siegal, they found themselves in a hall of mirrors. When they called a California phone number for one account, they got transferred to a phone number in Denver. When they called Lustig, he spoke with them only long enough to say, *Call my lawyer.*

In San Francisco, word got back to the Quattrone brokers that some of their customers had been contacted by the regulators. They included Lustig's United Capital, Devon, and Rosecliff. Bushley and Schmidt had a telephone briefing with Brodsky, and referred the clients' calls to First Boston's legal department.[13]

O

While the NASD was getting testimony from the CSFB brokers and sales executives, the CSFB legal team was also gathering documents subpoenaed by the SEC.

On October 18, 2000, Janine Schampier, a CSFB legal assistant, e-mailed Quattrone and the head of tech capital markets, Andy Fisher, asking for any documents they had about Selectica.[14] Two days later CSFB's Grace Shentwu followed up, asking if Quattrone "worked on the allocation process of the Selectica IPO."[15] Quattrone replied: "had zero to do with it to the best of my recollection." A few minutes later, Shentwu asked Quattrone whether he was "involved with the VA Linux allocation process." Quattrone replied: "same answer."[16]

On October 25, 2000, Schampier e-mailed Quattrone, Brady, and another tech group banker asking for "all documents related to valuation and pricing of Selectica Inc., including notes, memoranda, e-mails on your pc, etc."[17] Quattrone then e-mailed his secretary, La Nita Burkhead, asking her to "pls search email inbox and archives that contain the word 'selectica' and see if we have any files under that name."[18] On October 30, 2000, Burkhead sent Schampier a thirty-five-page batch of Quattrone's e-mail printouts mentioning Selectica.[19]

Like most Wall Street firms, CSFB had a "document retention policy" providing for the routine purging of files two weeks after a merger or underwriting deal closed. Under that policy, files should contain a "due diligence summary" documenting the firm's efforts to check out the backup for facts presented in a prospectus. But loose notes, drafts, and internal memos were supposed to be promptly discarded.

However, the policy stipulated that documents weren't supposed to be destroyed if CSFB became a party to litigation related to the transaction, or received a subpoena for the documents, or if it was "reasonably likely that litigation may be commenced in connection with such a transaction."

The notices to bankers about the VA Linux and Selectica deals contained instructions not to destroy documents. Within CSFB, the legal staff soon debated issuing a broad document-preservation notice that would cover all IPO files. On October 2, 2000, shortly after receipt of the September 20 SEC request for IPO documents, Lisa Czaja, head of CSFB's centralized document-retention group, took note of the unresolved issue. In an e-mail to a subpoena compliance attorney, Czaja said, CSFB's lawyers were still discussing the subject. "There seems to be a divergence of opinion whether it is business as usual or not, whether we send a memo or not."[20]

At Quattrone's trial, CSFB lawyer David Brodksy said he was concerned that a press leak about the probe could do severe damage to the firm's reputation.[21] And of course that would have become more likely if a document preservation notice had been sent to hundreds of employees. Because the SEC staff had allowed CSFB to focus first on producing material about VA Linux and Selectica, the CSFB lawyers decided not to issue a broad preservation notice. The entire firm was still obliged to preserve all the documents in the SEC request, but few employees knew it at the time.

O

Word got back to the SEC and the federal prosecutors that the CSFB witnesses hadn't seemed to be entirely candid with the NASD. One concern the SEC and prosecutors had was that if they did bring the matter as a criminal prosecution any cooperating witnesses who were given immunity in exchange for their testimony could be impeached if they could be shown to have lied to the NASD. Soon, they decided to move.

Prodded by the SEC, an eight-hundred-pound gorilla entered the arena in late November in the form of the securities fraud task force. The prosecutors at the Manhattan U.S. attorney's office were sometimes referred to as the best law firm in the city. They were a militarylike cadre of men and women in white shirts and dark gray or blue suits and neat haircuts who stayed for three to six years and then typically moved into much higher paying jobs in private practice. Not only did they have the power to send individuals to jail, they literally had life-and-death power, as the Drexel Burnham case showed, over an entire securities firm.

Steven R. Peikin was a Rockville, Maryland, native and Harvard Law School graduate who worked for Khuzami as an assistant U.S. attorney in the securities fraud unit. Peikin, whose grandfather was a Jewish immigrant, came from a long line of doctors. His grandmother was an obstetrician. Although he was premed in college, he shifted his sights to law when he realized he couldn't stand the sight of blood. One juror at Quattrone's second criminal trial would describe Peikin as "Sergeant Joe Friday" for his low-key, beat-cop demeanor.

On Tuesday, November 21, 2000, Peikin signed a subpoena summoning eight CSFB employees to testify before a federal grand jury and seeking information on thirteen accounts, many of them the same as those that the NASD and the SEC had asked about. They included several Lustig accounts.[22] Those subpoenaed had various roles in IPO allocations. If there was a kickback scheme, some of them could have known. Many had also been called by the NASD. Among them were: George Coleman, the head of institutional listed sales trading; Dominick Commesso, the broker whose client had paid the $1 million commission the day he received VA Linux shares; and Steve Keller, a CSFB broker who had discussed how Sutton Capital had paid commissions "in return" for deal stocks.[23]

A week later, on Tuesday, November 28, 2000, the prosecutors agreed to meet with Brodsky, his litigation chief, Kevin McCarthy, and two outside lawyers representing CSFB. They met in a conference room on the third floor of One St. Andrews Plaza in lower Manhattan, a squat, oatmeal-colored building. The building sat at the north end of a wide, redbrick plaza surrounded by the landmark Municipal Building, the modern brick police headquarters, and the imposing state and federal courthouses.

Brodsky argued that there was no reason to turn the civil probes by the NASD and SEC into a criminal matter, and urged the prosecutors to drop their subpoenas and withdraw, or at least withdraw the subpoenas to individuals. The subpoenas would also create "disclosure obligations" he would rather avoid, Brodsky said. What he meant was that either CSFB or its parent, Credit Suisse Group, might have to disclose the probe to investors. Even without formal disclosure, Brodsky was also worried about the investigation leaking out.[24]

Khuzami, Peikin, and David Anders, the other prosecutor on the case, stepped out of the meeting to confer privately. It was a no-brainer; they weren't about to accede to the request. Out of politeness, they actually talked about the New York Yankees for a moment to stretch out the conversation, to make it look as though they were taking it more seriously.

Rebuffed at his first sit-down with prosecutors, Brodsky attempted to "repair the damage," as he put it later, by hiring one of the top names in white-collar criminal defense work, Robert B. Fiske Jr., of the law firm Davis Polk & Wardwell.[25] As U.S. attorney himself from 1976 to 1980, Fiske had won convictions of drug kingpin LeRoy Barnes and labor leader Anthony Scotto.

As a defense attorney, Fiske had represented some of the wealthiest citizens and corporations accused of criminal activity. They included Alfred Taubman, the former top executive of Sotheby's Holdings Inc., the auction house, who was accused of price fixing, and Philip Morris Companies, when tobacco companies were charged with deceiving the public.

On December 1, 2000, Brodsky told Karen Crupi, one of the lawyers who had dealt with the JohnDoe526 e-mail alleging kickbacks, that he still hoped to get rid of the grand jury subpoena. On December 3, 2000, Brodsky wrote Liman he was hoping to get the criminal investigation "closed down" until the NASD and SEC probes had "run their course."[26]

Six months had passed since the anonymous letter from "A concerned citizen" had been sent to the SEC and NASD. The drumbeat of notices and requests from the two regulators had escalated from routine inquiries and visits by inspection teams to grand jury subpoenas for a criminal investigation by federal prosecutors. The news of the grand jury probe was about to become public, and soon the entire firm would find itself under siege.

"TIME TO CLEAN UP THOSE FILES"

31

IT WAS THE CALM before the storm. The bubble was over, or seemed like it might be. But nobody could be sure. The worst investor losses actually were yet to come. CSFB and other Wall Street firms eventually would be overrun by regulators and aggrieved investors. But that backlash was still just over the horizon.

In the last week of November, the Quattrone tech group held its annual investor conference at the Phoenician in Scottsdale, Arizona, a resort town outside Phoenix. It was even more star-studded than the year before, with appearances by Tour de France bicycling champion Lance Armstrong and singer Sheryl Crow. At one dinner, guests got a gift set of steak knives and a book on how to cook steak.

After the nightly dinners, Quattrone would hold court for hours at a cigar bar, where drinks were on the house. Cheryl Popp, Quattrone's in-house public-relations officer, liked technology columnist Mark Veverka of *Barron's*, and over cigars and scotch Quattrone took Veverka through the story of his career.

Veverka was fascinated. *Certainly by now you've proven yourself,* he told Quattrone. *What keeps you going to get up and work so hard and deal with all this stuff and the grief you get from CSFB in New York?*

Quattrone smiled briefly at his guest. Many other bankers might answer that question with bland platitudes, but Veverka found Quattrone's answer brutally matter-of-fact. *To fuck Morgan Stanley*, he replied.[1]

○

That weekend David Brodsky, CSFB's general counsel for the Americas, working out of his home office in suburban Scarsdale, New York, turned his attention to advising top CSFB officials, as well as those subpoenaed, about how to handle the probe.

Because Brodsky had been an assistant U.S. attorney in the securities fraud unit himself, McLaughlin and CSFB top management had concluded, once it became a criminal matter, that he should personally take charge of handling the probe for CSFB. The reason, he explained at Quattrone's trial, was "a federal grand jury investigation took this inquiry to a totally new level of danger to the franchise, to the business of CSFB. [A] possible indictment of the bank would essentially put the bank out of business or at least severely threaten the existence of the bank."[2]

Quattrone had returned to California from the conference on Friday, December 1.[3] Shortly after 2:00 P.M. Eastern time on Sunday, December 3, 2000, Brodsky sent Quattrone an e-mail, marked PRIVILEGED AND HIGHLY CONFIDENTIAL, from his home in Scarsdale:

"Frank, As you may know, there has been an inquiry going on by both the SEC and NASD [Regulation] into our allocation processes in the IPO market. There have been some recent developments that are of extreme concern that I need to speak with you about as soon as possible. If you are available today, please call me at [home]. If not today, then tomorrow at [Brodsky's work number]. My assistant knows to interrupt me if you call on Monday. Thanks, David."[4]

In California, where it was still late morning, Quattrone e-mailed Brodsky back from his BlackBerry. "Can you e-mail me some details of your concerns? Tied up all day today but checking blackberry."[5] To reconnect with his family after the conference, Quattrone was planning to take his daughter to a Sunday evening performance of the play *Man of La Mancha*.[6]

Brodsky replied: "Briefly, and this should absolutely not be passed on to anyone else, we have received Federal Grand Jury subpoenaes asking for testimony and documents about the IPO allocation process from the firm and each of the nine people who has so far testified before the NASDR." Brodsky added that the probe could soon extend to Quattrone's banking clients, the tech companies which had issued the hot IPO shares. Brodsky repeated his interest in speaking with Quattrone personally.

"I have retained Bob Fiske to represent us in this criminal investigation and he and I are meeting as early as tomorrow with the U.S. Attorney in NY to try to prevent them from sending subpoenaes for testimony and documents to the customers who received allocations in, among others, VA Lynux [sic], as well as subpoenas to the issuers, because of the inherent possibility of a leak which would be extremely detrimental. Please call me tonight up to 10 pm or tomorrow."[7]

Quattrone fired back a one-line response: "Are the regulators accusing us of criminal activity?"[8] A minute later, he asked: "Who are the nine people?"[9]

At that moment Brodsky was hoping to broaden the regulators' understanding of all the steps in the entire IPO process. By putting the allocations in this larger context, he evidently aimed to make them appear less sinister.[10] Brodsky replied: "The ones I have told so far are George Coleman, Tony Ehinger, and Ernesto Cruz," the main managers of IPO allocations. "Until I tell the others personally tomorrow, I don't want to disclose their names yet. In answer to your other e-mail, they are not formally accusing us or the individuals yet, but they are investigating because they think something bad happened. They are completely wrong, but merely being investigated and having something leak could be quite harmful, so the idea is to get them to back off their inquiry, we educate them as to the entire IPO process, inclusding [*sic*] the allovcation [*sic*] issues and criteria, and urge them to back off."[11]

A few minutes later, Brodsky added a postscript: "But please do not under any circumstances discuss these facts with anyone—however innocently—because everything we say now is going to come under a microscope. I know these people and how they work and I am controlling the flow of information on an extremely tight need to know basis with all sorts of privileges attached. This is serious and unless I can slow it down and curtail what they do, it will spread to others in the firm. That's why I need to speak with you personally."[12]

"Got it," Quattrone e-mailed in reply.[13]

At Quattrone's two criminal trials, the contents of Brodsky's e-mails would be picked over exhaustively for what they did and didn't say and imply about how much the investigations concerned Quattrone and his business. They obviously said nothing about preserving or destroying documents. But Brodsky's heads-up would be the strongest piece of circumstantial evidence underlying the government's accusation that what Quattrone did over the next two days constituted obstruction of justice.

O

The next day, Monday, December 4, Quattrone had a meeting in Oakland, about forty miles north of his office in Palo Alto, with Zhone Technologies Inc. Zhone's CEO, Mory Ejabat, was a charter member of the Friends of Frank, and CSFB was about to take Zhone public. Quattrone returned to the office around midday.

At 3:20 P.M. Pacific time, Quattrone got an e-mail from Richard Char, who had been a partner at Wilson Sonsini, the top tech law firm. Char was head of the execution group, which saw to paperwork and administration. Maintaining files from Quattrone's deals was among his responsibilities. Char had sent the e-mail to his day-to-day boss, John Hodge, head of West Coast technology banking, as well as to Brady, with copies to Quattrone and Adrian Dollard, a lawyer who had just joined the tech group.

The timing of Char's e-mail, a day after Brodsky's heads-up to Quattrone, was a striking coincidence. But prosecutors never found any evidence that it was anything more than coincidence.

"Document Retention" was the subject of Char's e-mail: "With the recent tumble in stock prices, and many deals now trading below issue price, I understand the securities litigation bar is mounting an all-out assault on broken tech IPOs. In the spirit of the end of the year (and the slow down in corporate finance work) you may want to send around a memo to all corporate finance bankers (and their assistants) reminding them of the CSFB document retention policy and suggesting that before they leave for the holidays, they should catch up on file cleanup."

Char added a witty kicker to what he evidently considered a routine reminder, displaying a lighthearted attitude of gamesmanship toward keeping documents away from angry investors and their lawyers: "Today it's administrative housekeeping. In January, it could be improper destruction of evidence. Regards, Richard."[14] If Char had known the contents of the previous day's e-mails between Brodsky and Quattrone, he probably wouldn't have taken such a joking approach. At Quattrone's trial, with his own lawyers sitting in the court room, Char testified that sending the e-mail was his own idea.[15]

Quattrone was out of the office when the e-mail came in. When he saw it on his BlackBerry, he sent a response: "You shouldn't make jokes like that on e-mail!"[16] He didn't mention to Char his e-mails with Brodsky the day before. Certainly Brodsky had warned him against discussing the grand jury probe with anyone. But, Quattrone testified three years later, he didn't connect the Char e-mail about civil litigation with the IPO allocation probe.[17]

John Hodge, Char's boss, then urged Char to send out the file-cleanup e-mail, adding it should be "a top priority." Hodge himself had been warned by an office manager about the messy clutter of boxes in the hallways of the tech-group offices.[18]

About two hours later, at 5:13 P.M. Pacific time that same day, Char sent a revised version of the e-mail he had sent to Hodge, Brady, Quattrone, and Dollard to the entire technology investment banking division. The new subject line was: "Time to clean up those files."

Char expanded on his earlier draft version by including a link to the CSFB Web site that contained the document retention policy and a summary set of instructions: "With the recent tumble in stock prices, and many deals now trading below issue price, the securities litigation bar is expected to [make] an all-out assault on broken tech IPOs. In the spirit of the end of the year (and the slow down in corporate finance work) we want to reminding [sic] you of the CSFB document retention policy."

That policy said that for any securities offering, a designated team member had to create a transaction file containing all SEC filings, the original banking agreement, originals of related accounting letters and legal opinions, and a completed document checklist. No other file categories were allowed.

"So what does it mean?" Char cut through the legalese. "Generally speaking," he said, other documents "should not be left in the file following completion of the transaction. That means no notes, no drafts, no valuation analysis, no copies of the roadshow, no markups, no selling memos, no [Investment Banking Committee or valuation] memos, no internal memos."

Char was correct in anticipating a deluge of lawsuits, and within his rights to remind the group about the document policies. Unbeknownst to Brodsky, he was just doing his job. "Note that if a lawsuit is instituted," Char's e-mail concluded, "our normal document retention policy is suspended and any cleaning of files is prohibited under the CSFB guidelines (since it constitutes the destruction of evidence). We strongly suggest that before you leave for the holidays, you should catch up on file cleanup."

The e-mail was signed: "Bill Brady   John Hodge   Richard Char."[19]

Char addressed his e-mail to "##CSFB Tech IBD," a code for CSFB technology investment banking division. At his trials, Quattrone testified that he didn't realize the recipients would extend beyond the bankers in his group.[20] In fact, the address also included both the Schmidt-Grunwald brokers and the equity capital markets employees such as Fisher, all of whom had played hands-on roles in IPO allocations.[21]

Quattrone immediately began composing an endorsement of the Char e-mail, which he meant to send to all the same recipients by pressing "reply to all." He began typing, "having been a key witness in a securities litigation case in south texas (miniscribe)."[22] Then he stopped without completing the thought two minutes later at 5:15 P.M.[23] His computer e-mail automatically saved the draft after a few moments, and the start of the e-mail remained, unsent, in his draft folder overnight. As the prosecutors debated whether to charge Quattrone with obstruction of justice in the spring of 2003, the fact that Quattrone had time to think about what he was about to do weighed against him. In the next hour, Quattrone worked on a letter to Michael McGrath, the chief financial officer of Accenture Ltd., pitching to lead a $3 billion IPO, his top business objective at the time. He sent that letter at 6:26 P.M.[24]

After returning home for dinner, Quattrone attended a client function in Palo Alto that night.[25]

○

The next day, on Tuesday, December 5, 2000, at 12:43 P.M. Eastern time, Brodsky sent out an alert to top CSFB executives, including Quattrone, that *The Wall Street Journal* was preparing an article on the regulators' IPO kick-back probe. His worst fears about the probe becoming public were about to be realized—far sooner than he might have expected. He and the CSFB public relations staff quickly kicked into damage-control mode, preparing bland statements portraying the criminal investigation in innocuous terms.

CSFB planned to issue a statement confirming its receipt of "requests for information from Government agencies" about IPO allocations, Brodsky's e-mail said. CSFB allocated IPOs based on "many factors," the CSFB statement said, including "the investor's interest in the issue, its demonstrated knowledge of the issuer and the industry, and the nature and extent of the investor's brokerage relationship." The IPOs were allocated in a manner "appropriate and consistent with those in the industry."[26]

A few minutes later, Brodsky sent word of a brief reprieve. The *Journal* wasn't running the story the next day. He added that CSFB public relations staffers were preparing "talking points" on the subject.[27]

But Brodsky was still concerned about the impact of the probe on Quattrone and his golden-goose tech banking franchise, and he wanted to warn Quattrone about the worst-case scenario. He picked up the phone and reached Quattrone at 1:47 P.M. on Tuesday, December 5. Brodsky wanted to discuss the *Journal* article, the impact it might have on Quattrone's business, and Brodsky's belief that it was time for Quattrone to hire his own lawyer in connection with the IPO kickback probe, Brodsky later testified. They talked about how the story might have leaked to the *Journal*.[28] Brodsky also told Quattrone that the investigation concerned whether hedge funds had paid inappropriately high commissions in order to receive IPO shares, Quattrone recalled.[29]

I think this investigation is going to turn in the direction of getting testimony from you, Brodsky told Quattrone, *and I think it's advisable for you to get a personal lawyer as a precaution. The bank can't represent you.* Brodsky then offered to recommend a lawyer to Quattrone.[30]

Wearing a telephone headset as he sat at his computer in his Palo Alto office, Quattrone replied that he was comfortable with his family lawyer, Ken Hausman, who had represented him in the home construction defects case, and on his employment contract with CSFB.[31] He didn't need a recommendation from Brodsky. He then called Hausman, and soon e-mailed Hausman's phone number to Brodsky.[32]

○

Some CSFB staffers quickly sensed that the Char e-mail could spell trouble.

A few hours after receiving the e-mail that Monday, John Bateman, the chief operating officer of the tech group, alerted Lisa Czaja, the head of CSFB's centralized documentation group, who supervised the firm's document retention policy.[33] On Tuesday morning, December 5, Czaja spoke to Kevin McCarthy, the CSFB litigation director, and then forwarded the Char e-mail to Brodsky.

From his office in New York, McCarthy called Char, introduced himself, and asked about his e-mail. McCarthy told Char that CSFB had received requests for documents from regulators that would require some of the recipients of Char's e-mail to keep documents that Char had just advised them to discard. Apologetic, Char offered to rescind his e-mail. McCarthy told him to wait, explaining that the lawyers in New York would take care of it.[34]

As he was leaving his office for a meeting soon after his phone call with Quattrone, Brodsky bumped into McCarthy in the hallway of CSFB headquarters. McCarthy told Brodsky someone in the tech group had sent an e-mail urging a file cleanup. Brodsky, already concerned about the *Journal* article, tensely asked McCarthy to "get in front of this" and send out any necessary counterinstructions. McCarthy said he would.[35]

At 3:00 P.M. Pacific time, Quattrone had a meeting at the Kleiner Perkins office in Menlo Park, a ten-minute drive from his office on the other side of the Stanford campus. He returned to his desk around 4:30 P.M.[36]

O

In his last fifty minutes at work before leaving the office that day, Tuesday, December 5, 2000, Quattrone sent out twenty e-mails.[37] Offered as a defense exhibit at his trial, they gave a glimpse of a master of the universe in action. They showed Quattrone dealing with upcoming meetings with top executives of eBay and AOL, ground rules for a press interview, the group's year-end ads, and personal investments in real estate and venture capital.

At 5:42 P.M. Pacific time on December 5, Quattrone e-mailed Liz Nickles, agreeing to be interviewed for a book on the Internet, as long as he could have "complete control over any quotes." A minute later, he sent an e-mail about CSFB's bid to win the $3 billion Accenture IPO. He discussed a meeting with eBay CEO Meg Whitman about a possible "music space."

At 5:48, he discussed the group's year-end ad listing the biggest deals of 2000. Quattrone suggested the ad "hide the woofers" instead of listing "every transaction." At that point, his wording suggested, investor losses were a concern, but still a matter for humor. (The 2000 year-end promotion was indeed abbreviated; though the tech group claimed sixty-four IPOs that year, the notice mentioned only the five largest by name. The 1999 version had listed fifty-three.)

At 5:55, Quattrone responded to an e-mail from Jay Hoag of TCV, which had received VA Linux shares from CSFB, about talks between General Motors Corporation and Autoweb.com Inc. When Hoag asked for "some flexibility on the fee," Quattrone jokingly agreed "to charge you a higher fee if you'd like, but no more than 100% of proceeds, I promise."

At 5:57, Quattrone talked about getting client quotes for the group's year-end brochure. At 5:58, he asked Hausman about buying the mortgage on a property near his in Pebble Beach.[38] At 6:01, he asked about the agenda for a future meeting at the Technology Museum of Innovation in San Jose, which he sponsored. At 6:04, he told banker Nick Baughan that CSFB wouldn't have to disclose taking a minor assignment from Deloitte & Touche as a possible conflict in the Accenture deal. (Accenture had been part of another accounting firm.) Then he sent a pat on the back to Michael Feder, the banker who got the Deloitte assignment: "nice work, Mikey."

At 6:14, Quattrone e-mailed other bankers about his recent chat with Solectron Corporation chief financial officer Susan Wang at the CSFB tech conference. He suggested "bombarding her" with voice mails and e-mails because "I think she really likes the attention." At 6:15, he e-mailed his own accountant about a personal venture capital investment.

At 6:24, Quattrone e-mailed several tech group bankers about a meeting with AOL in Virginia on December 13, which one banker described as a "going to the throne to kiss the ring meeting." At 6:25, Quattrone sent another e-mail about AOL.

At 6:28 P.M. Pacific time on Tuesday, December 5, Quattrone retrieved his draft response to Char's e-mail with the subject "Time to clean up those files." Quattrone completed the thought he had begun drafting the day before and then retransmitted the e-mail to his entire group: "having been a key witness in a securities litigation case in south texas (miniscribe) I strongly advise you to follow these procedures."

Two minutes later, at 6:30 P.M., Quattrone sent an e-mail to two research analysts, Ray Sharma and Marc Cabi. The subject was "rimm," short for Research in Motion Ltd., the BlackBerry wireless device maker that Quattrone believed still owed him for the Merrill-led stock offering in October. "[W]hat do we need to do to collect our $2mm?" he asked. Then he left the office.

At his criminal trials, Quattrone offered the string of twenty e-mails, showing he was dashing off messages every few minutes, as evidence that he hadn't given much thought to resending the Char e-mail. But the prosecutors countered, by grilling Quattrone about the RIM fee dispute, that he was in fact tackling weighty, serious issues.

O

Within CSFB, the Char "clean up those files" e-mail created a mild stir. It wasn't reported to regulators at the time. Other than Brodsky, the rest of the CSFB legal team didn't know of the description of the IPO probe that Brodsky had given to Quattrone just two days earlier. Nor did they know that Brodsky had called Quattrone just a few hours earlier and advised him to retain a lawyer for the probe.

When Char saw Quattrone's "Time to clean up those files" e-mail endorsing his, he reacted with alarm. Five minutes later, he e-mailed Quattrone, telling him about the call from McCarthy in New York, who had explained that the e-mail would need to be rescinded due to the pending investigations. The legal and compliance department, a frustrated Char complained to Quattrone, had "told everyone except the Tech Group." Char added that the lawyers in New York planned to send out an e-mail advising that "files should be preserved."[39] But by the time Char's e-mail came in, Quattrone was in his car. He didn't see the e-mail for another two hours.[40]

O

Char sent a copy of his e-mail to Adrian Dollard, the lawyer for the tech group. It was news to Dollard, who like Char was new there, that there was an NASD inquiry about VA Linux. The next day, Wednesday, December 6, Dollard spoke to Char, who was concerned that the legal and compliance department (LCD) hadn't issued a corrective e-mail.[41] Char e-mailed Dollard, "I have not seen the e-mail from LCD telling people that the document retention policy has been suspended. Should we call them to find out? I am afraid that on the heels of Frank's message, bankers are earnestly cleaning out files today."[42] Although McCarthy, Dollard, and Char discussed how to do so that day, the corrective e-mail wasn't actually sent until Thursday, December 7.

In fact, the Char and Quattrone e-mails were having the very impact that Char feared. Linda Jackson, a former member of the U.S. Olympic cycling team and a member of Char's execution group, began cleaning out her files after receiving them, discarding notes and drafts of documents related to due diligence and valuation.[43]

Other employees asked for clarifications. On December 5 and 6, Michael Ounjian, a tech group associate in corporate finance, asked about purging computer files. "How does it work with files on the K drive?" he asked Char. "Are you just talking about hard copies or are copies on the system included as well?" Char replied: "We are figuring out a strategy on the K drive. In the interim, best to keep final versions on K but delete intermediate drafts." In his e-mails, Ounjian asked about deleting files for Airspan Networks Inc., @Road Inc., and the Novatel and Handspring IPOs, and asked other colleagues which directories contained files to be deleted.[44]

At the end of the day on Wednesday, December 6, 2000, Dollard sent an e-mail to the same ##CSFB Tech IBD address, with a copy to CSFB lawyers in New York under a subject line reading: "Please Stop Editing Public Offering Files Until Further Notice." He said, "Yesterday Frank and Richard reminded everyone to edit their files to comply with our Document Retention Policy. However, due to a routine regulatory inquiry, we must stop the editing process until further notice."[45]

Char's "Time to clean up those files" e-mail had been sitting in Brodsky's in-box for nearly two days. It had been forwarded to him by Lisa Czaja, head of document retention, early on December 5. Late on Wednesday evening, December 6, Brodsky finally asked about it. "How did we respond to this?" he asked Czaja, CSFB lawyer Bruce Albert, and McCarthy.[46]

O

One reason Brodsky had been too busy to deal with Czaja's e-mail was that he had been doing damage control in connection with the first news story about the grand jury IPO kickback probe.

On Thursday, December 7, 2000, *The Wall Street Journal* published an article about the probe, saying it focused on CSFB and mentioning that Quattrone had enabled the firm to become a leader in technology IPOs.[47]

One of the Brodsky-provided "talking points" that day for CSFB staffers said: "The Wall Street Journal used the word kickbacks and tie-ins to describe the practices employed in the IPO allocation process. Does CSFB accept kickbacks or demand tie-ins for allocations?" The suggested answer began, "It is against firm policy to accept kickbacks or to demand tie-ins."[48]

With the news of the IPO probe now splashed across the top of page C1 of the *Journal*, the cat was out of the bag. There was now no need for the kind of legal tiptoeing that Brodsky had been doing in spreading word of the probe discreetly, as he had with Quattrone. Nor was there any need for further delay in sending the firmwide document-retention notice.

That same morning, December 7, a CSFB lawyer told Brodsky about Quattrone's e-mail advising that employees purge their files of old documents.[49] At 9:59 A.M. Brodsky e-mailed Quattrone from his handheld BlackBerry. "Frank Pls send me a copy of your e-mail regarding document retention. We have to rescind your and Char's memos because they conflict with what the S.E.C. and US Atorney [*sic*] have demanded and what they have a right to demand. I may ask you to send out formal rescission. Please send it to me for review. This is for your own protection. Thanks David."[50]

O

At 1:48 P.M. Eastern time on Thursday, December 7, CSFB lawyers Kevin McCarthy and Bruce Albert sent a formal "Notice of Obligation to Preserve Relevant Documents" to the same CSFB tech group distribution list that had received the Char and Quattrone e-mails entitled "Time to clean up those files." The Char and Quattrone e-mails "should not be followed," they said, for documents about CSFB's IPOs in 1999 and 2000. "Do not destroy any IPO-related documents."[51] A similar notice went out firmwide the next day.

Then it was time for Brodsky to talk to Quattrone. He alone knew the extent of Quattrone's knowledge about the IPO probe at the time the Char e-mail was sent and endorsed. At 1:51 P.M. on Thursday, December 7, Brodsky got Quattrone on the phone. It was, he testified, a "very flat, very hard" call.

Brodsky took a stern tone. He told Quattrone that this was a potentially serious matter that could have repercussions. Brodsky said CSFB had received a subpoena covering the documents addressed in Char's and Quattrone's e-mails. Quattrone told him he hadn't realized that. Despite what Brodsky had told him about the grand jury subpoenas and the criminal probe, Quattrone said, no one had told him the firm had received *a subpoena covering his group's documents.* Brodsky said he needed Quattrone's complete cooperation to make sure nothing bad had happened, and Quattrone assured him he would have it. Brodsky told him the e-mails could create some embarrassment for CSFB if they were misinterpreted by the authorities. Quattrone said he would never want to do anything to embarrass the firm.[52]

Within minutes, Quattrone forwarded Brodsky all the e-mails the CSFB lawyer had requested, including the draft with Char's joke, "Today, it's administrative housekeeping. In January, it could be improper destruction of evidence," and Quattrone's reaction, "You shouldn't make jokes like that on e-mail!"

Brodsky soon replied, "Thanks for reminding Richard. Jokes on e-mail come back to haunt people, even innocent people like us."[53] Brodsky explained in court that he had sent that e-mail as "a sort of soft touch" after their "hard conversation" earlier, suggesting he wanted to mollify Quattrone.[54]

Reporting to his boss, Joseph McLaughlin, on the entire incident several hours later, at 8:10 P.M. on December 7, Brodsky said, "Joe We had to send this out when we learned that Char and Quattrone were advising Tech Group people to clean their files because of expected litigations arising from declining IPOs. I have spoken to Frank and he now understands the ways in which this could have been misinterpreted by the authorities, and he assures me that they will do nothing in the slightest to raise eyebrows."[55]

It was an innocent two-line e-mail, telling his staff to follow the company's policy to get rid of old documents, Quattrone's lawyers would later argue. It was forgotten for more than two years, until January 2003. Then it would become the focus of Quattrone's entire life, blowing a hole in his career, tarring his reputation, and threatening his very freedom.

THE DENVER TRADERS TALK

32

BY NOW investigators at three agencies were following the trail of big commissions to determine if they amounted to bribes or kickbacks. The NASD and SEC had examined records of thousands of trades in which customers had paid up big-time, often soon after receiving allocations of hot IPO shares that had given them instant profits. The trails of order tickets led in many different directions. But often, the investigators saw, they led to Denver. Around the end of the year 2000, a team of SEC staffers who worked for Pennington went to Denver to interview investors at the agency's regional office there.

The SEC team, led by Doria G. Stetch, included two staff attorneys fresh out of law school. Michael Wasserman was a 1999 graduate of New York University's law school, and William Stellmach, who graduated from Harvard Law School in 1998, had just joined the SEC a few months earlier.

Some of the traders were represented by Steven N. Fuller, a partner at the firm of Nixon Peabody LLP in Boston. One after another the traders said they worked in the same downtown building occupied by Lustig and HC Properties, the real estate business of Lustig's father-in-law.

The SEC staffers had confirmation documents showing that the investors had paid unusually large commissions for trades involving big, liquid stocks. Some days they would pay just three cents a share; then, on days when they got hot IPOs, they might pay one dollar a share. The confirmations were placed in front of them. "Why?" they were asked.

The traders generally told the same story. *I felt generous*, said one. *I'm a generous guy*, said another. *For good execution*, said a third. The traders were asked who else worked in the office. None of them mentioned Lustig.

The SEC staff members sent a letter to the traders' attorney, Fuller. The letter threatened a subpoena enforcement action, a civil court action against someone who hasn't complied with a subpoena. The traders had reason to be concerned about regulators taking a close look at their conduct. When he replied to the SEC letter, Fuller sent a copy to a Washington lawyer named Ralph Ferrara.

A former SEC general counsel from 1978 to 1981, Ferrara had a flair for the dramatic. The son of an accountant who grew up in Cohoes, New York, near Albany, Ferrara had carved out a distinctive practice by defending a series of insurance companies accused of sales-practice misconduct by their agents. Representing New York Life Insurance Company, Transamerica Corporation, and American General Corporation, he had won reasonable settlements via an alternative dispute-resolution mechanism he helped devise.

By the end of the year 2000, Ferrara had also represented several companies accused of misreporting their financial results, including Waste Management Inc., MicroStrategy Inc., and Dollar General Corporation.

Lustig's brother-in-law, the politically connected lawyer Steve Farber, had called Ferrara. At first, Ferrara was reluctant. He was busy. Most of his clients were big companies. Head of an "outpost" Washington office for the New York firm of Debevoise & Plimpton, Ferrara's group accounted for about 8 percent of the billings of a WASPY, old-line firm founded by Francis T. P. Plimpton, the father of the late author George Plimpton.

But Farber was insistent. This was his brother-in-law, he told Ferrara. Lustig visited Ferrara in Washington and told him about the netherworld of syndicate chasers who had paid commissions to get new issues during the unprecedented market conditions that prevailed in the bubble. Bit by bit Ferrara learned about an alternative universe, an extended stock-distribution system on steroids that had sprung up around the wild stock action. Lustig even took Ferrara to visit Triad Securities, which had published the *U.S. IPO Consensus Report.*

Both Lustig and Ferrara soon learned that a grand jury was investigating. While regulatory agencies like the SEC and NASD generally focused on broker dealers, rather than their customers, in meting out penalties, the criminal probe opened an array of more ominous possibilities. After all, the prosecutors could view the facts as a case of commercial bribery. While the odds were remote that the Lustig traders would actually be charged with bribery, it wasn't out of the question. Why take the chance?

Ferrara picked up the phone and called Wayne Carlin, the head of the SEC's northeast regional office, who was also Pennington's boss. Ferrara, who wore expensive Brioni suits and enjoyed long-distance cycling on weekends, had an office adorned with opera posters, including one for a French production of *Doctor Faustus. Wayne,* Ferrara said, *you and I are both going to remember this conversation for the rest of our lives.*

O

Just as the kickback investigation was making progress, auditors from the home office of CSFB's parent, Credit Suisse Group, in Zurich, Switzerland, were starting as well to realize that the operation of the Friends of Frank accounts could spell trouble. Between September and December 2000, auditors from Credit Suisse Group reviewed the work of the CSFB San Francisco branch office. It included sales, trading, and other services—other than investment banking—provided to the firm's technology clients.[1] The brokers in the Schmidt-Grunwald technology private-client services group had three hundred discretionary accounts (the Friends of Frank) and eight hundred other accounts.

The resulting report's summary noted the lack of "an appropriate control framework for the branch's PCS Technology Group activities" and "the absence of a developed infrastructure to support retail activities." In other words, the homemade retail brokerage services created by Schmidt and Grunwald lacked needed built-in controls.

The report noted that "only new issue securities" were held in a majority of the PCS technology discretionary accounts, which needed to be reassessed by top management. *Only new-issue securities!* It was beginning to dawn on someone that the Friends of Frank program might not look too good to outsiders. "In the past," the report warned, "there has been scrutiny within the industry regarding allocation of IPO shares to discretionary accounts of executives in a bid to win additional business from their firms." It added: "[T]he use of such accounts for predominantly IPO related activity could result in undue scrutiny which would heighten reputational risks."

Even the firm's own parent could tell that the accounts looked fishy. The report recommended that CSFB "assess the appropriateness" of the way such accounts were used. "Agreed," Quattrone replied, promising to complete that assessment by April 30, 2001. Brodsky also made some vague promise of more "onsite compliance staffing."

Of course it had been Quattrone who insisted that the brokers work directly for him, less connected from the management of other brokers elsewhere at CSFB. But now, in the "comments by management" section, Quattrone pointed the finger elsewhere, suggesting the results weren't his fault. He said, "the PCS Technology activities at the branch grew rapidly, benefiting from market opportunities and the firm's leadership position in the Technology sector. This was done without the benefit of a strong CSFB retail infrastructure."

Quattrone, Schmidt, and Grunwald discussed the contents of a draft version of the report during a half-hour meeting early one afternoon in December 2000 in Quattrone's wood-paneled office on the second floor on Hanover Street in Palo Alto. The news was already out about the government probe of IPO allocations. Schmidt was concerned about the report's implications. He warned Quattrone: *We're being set up.*

O

With the kickback investigations by the NASD, SEC, and federal prosecutors gathering steam, CSFB's lawyers began focusing on the Quattrone group brokers as well.

In December 2000, brokers Schmidt, Grunwald, and Bushley were interviewed, one at a time, in their San Francisco offices, by outside counsel Lewis Liman and CSFB lawyer Bruce Albert. They asked Schmidt basic questions about how he ran the business and where the profits came from. Liman asked Schmidt whether the brokers sought half of the profits from the trading accounts. Schmidt acknowledged that there was a policy requiring accounts to do half their commission business in new issues and half in other trading, but he denied sharing the customers' profits.

Schmidt kept insisting that everything they were doing had been approved by the firm's legal and compliance division; and in truth, this wasn't an area where he had focused a lot of attention. This was an area, he believed, where there hadn't been any problems.

O

As the year 2000 ended, Quattrone renewed his claim of global domination. The group's brochure was filled with bar charts with lines for CSFB, Goldman, and Morgan Stanley; the CSFB bar was always longest. He claimed the most technology IPOs, with sixty-four, compared to forty-one for Goldman and thirty-two for Morgan Stanley. The results, Quattrone said, highlighted "our number one market share position—achieved for the second consecutive year—in the world of technology."

In three years, his group had helped CSFB's investment banking revenue more than double, from $1.47 billion in 1997 to $3.68 billion in 2000.[2]

O

With hot IPO allocations at CSFB the subject of widely publicized investigations, gossip about the "Friends of Frank" accounts soon reached the press as well.

On January 11, 2001, an article in *The New York Post* first revealed the existence of the Friends of Frank program. Details were sketchy, and no names were named. But the article set the tone for the coverage that followed.

The headline was FRANK'S FRIENDS FAVORED: CSFB ACCOUNTS FOR QUATTRONE BUDDIES RAISING EYEBROWS. The story began, "Are you a 'Friend of Frank'? Not sure?" The article asked, "Were you invited to Frank and Denise Quattrone's 20th anniversary party, a black-tie fete at the Palace of the Legion of Honor in San Francisco? Perhaps you've been to CSFB's luxe ski weekends in Aspen, Colo.? Did you get a seat for the U.S. Open at Quattrone's magnificent home overlooking the storied and picturesque Pebble Beach golf course?"

Then the article described the Friends of Frank accounts, quoting an unidentified CSFB client: "It's a pure IPO account where they just buy and sell." The accounts could be considered "incentives" for recipients to do more business with CSFB, the article said. But it noted that there wasn't agreement whether they constituted an impropriety, and quoted CSFB as defending them: "These accounts are entirely appropriate and consistent with industry practice."[3]

The author, Chris Nolan, was something of an authority on Quattrone. She was the same former columnist for the *San Jose Mercury News* who had first printed the rumors in early 1998 that Quattrone was considering leaving Deutsche Bank, prompting the embarrassing "we are here to stay trust us" letter.

Quattrone was indignant. "[I]'d like to sue her for slander," he said in an e-mail to Brodsky the same day. "[S]he is personalizing this to me, when I have done nothing of the kind." Quattrone added that he had had "problems with her in the past. she wrote a gossip column for the sj mercury in which she announced to the world I was planning to leave dmg to join merrill lynch. It was not true, but it planted a seed of doubt in the minds of our clients, our business softened because people feared we would leave, and it became a self fulfilling prophecy."

Brodsky said he understood Quattrone's reaction, but cautioned that such a lawsuit probably wouldn't be able to prove "not only that what she said is false but also that she said it with actual malice," because Quattrone was a public figure. Plus, he said, it would "give her (and the rest of the media world) the satisfaction of knowing that you are sensitive about this issue." What's important, he concluded, was that Quattrone's clients were "standing behind you and think (and say) that you are a person of integrity."[4]

Quattrone wasn't mollified. In mid-1999, Nolan had been suspended and reassigned by the *Mercury News*, losing her column, over her purchase of five hundred friends and family shares of the March 1999 IPO of Autoweb.com Inc., which she had quickly resold at a nine thousand dollar profit. Nolan had obtained the shares based on her friendship with AutoWeb's chief executive, Dean DeBiase. As it happened, AutoWeb was a CSFB tech group IPO, and its chairman and executive vice president, Farhang Zamani and Payam Zamani, both had Friends of Frank accounts.[5]

When Nolan's Autoweb.com stock purchase became widely known a few months later, a *Mercury News* editor said publicly that Nolan's actions "clearly placed us in a situation where the public could perceive The Mercury News to have a conflict of interest." Nolan said she had tried unsuccessfully to get a ruling on the purchase. She left the paper in November 1999, and became a freelancer for the *Post.*[6]

In response to Nolan's Friends of Frank article, Quattrone drafted a letter detailing the conflict allegations to publications that had carried it. After he recounted the episode in a scathing draft of the letter, he concluded, "Maybe someone should be writing a story about Ms Nolan's friends, or her ethics; either way, it would be a short story."[7]

O

On February 23, 2001, about ten prosecutors and SEC staffers gathered in a conference room in a black-clad office building on Third Avenue at the Midtown Manhattan offices of Debevoise & Plimpton. They were assembled for a PowerPoint presentation by Ralph Ferrara on behalf of the Denver traders.

Among those present were prosecutors Rob Khuzami, Steve Peikin, and David Anders from the U.S. attorney's office, and SEC staffers including Wayne Carlin, the director of the SEC's northeast regional office, Caren Pennington, and members of her team. Also, there were a half dozen other lawyers for the Lustig traders. Ferrara spoke for about two hours, and there were few interruptions.

Ferrara was about to offer them a detailed look at the murky netherworld of some of the traders who had paid the outsize commissions to boost their access to hot IPOs. He would explain how they had gamed the Wall Street system during the bubble and won big.

The presentation, he said in an introduction, was an "attorney proffer" that couldn't be used against his clients. Under an understanding he had reached with regulators two days earlier, any clients they wanted to question would be offered "queen for a day" rules. The witnesses couldn't be prosecuted for acts they described, as long as they told the truth.[8] And in the end, the investors and the traders who got the IPOs weren't charged with wrongdoing.

Ferrara's PowerPoint said his purpose was "to explain, not expose" how Wall Street worked. His clients, he said, were "the Buy Side Traders." He asserted that traders who had paid big commissions were only playing by the rules set by Wall Street brokers. His clients operated, he said, under "the Sell Side's 'Rules of the Game.'"

His clients were "entrepreneurs" and "victims," Ferrara said, who were eager to recover any ill-gotten gains Wall Street had wrongfully extracted from them in outsize commissions. When Ferrara used that same line at a repeat performance he soon gave for SEC staffers in Washington, Linda Chatman Thomsen, a top enforcement official, reacted scornfully. She said: *If I hear the word "victim" one more time, Ralph, I think I'm going to puke.*

Ferrara then laid out the structure of the Lustig organization and its ring of affiliated traders. It included "28 individuals (potentially more in the future)" and "21 joint ventures" with Lustig. Each of the joint ventures was "an independent business run by a managing joint venturer/partner . . . trading with their own money."

At the center of the group was "JAL Ventures Corporation, wholly owned by James A. Lustig," who served as an investor and joint-venture limited partner, Ferrara said. A Lustig affiliate performed "administrative functions" for the individual traders, and Lustig generally kept 30 percent of the profits.

The reason IPOs were often underpriced by Wall Street investment banks, Ferrara said, was to attract "regular investors [to] appear in both 'hot' and 'cold' IPOs." But they also provided "a convenient mechanism" for securities firms "to reward favorite clients." The "good customers" who got IPOs, he said, "generate significant commissions."

The traders, Ferrara said, would "control risk" by buying and selling the same stocks simultaneously—purely to generate commissions to pay for the IPOs.

For his presentation, Ferrera had commissioned an accounting of the group's activity by PriceWaterhouseCoopers, and an analysis by Lexecon Inc., a consulting firm in Chicago. For a mere twenty-eight people affiliated with a single individual, the totals he provided for 1999 and 2000 were staggering.

The twenty-eight Lustig traders had maintained more than three hundred portfolios, dealt with more than fifteen hundred brokers at 150 securities firms, and generated 196,000 separate trades totaling more than four billion shares with a dollar volume of $171 billion. In turn, they had received allocations of 918 IPOs, or 90 percent of all IPOs in the two years, with a dollar value of more than $2.9 billion.

The Lustig group's trading had ramped up dramatically during the bubble, from $140 million in the first quarter of 1999 to a peak of $520 million in the fourth quarter of 1999. The group's IPO purchases had represented between 1.5 percent and 2.3 percent of all IPO stock sold in 1999 and 2000.

Ferrara then offered some examples of how brokers had asked the traders for more commissions. The only firm he mentioned by name was CSFB. There, he said, one Lustig "trader [was] told that CSFB was increasing the commission pay-back on IPO profits to 60%." One "trader met with senior CSFB official in NY who benchmarked trader's commissions vs. IPO profits and told him that others would pay more." One "trader [was] told commissions at 15% of IPO profits were anemic and future allocations were reduced."

Then Ferrara offered a graph showing how much more CSFB brokers had been able to convert the tech IPO boom into higher commissions. While other firms' average commissions stayed relatively flat at an average of thirteen cents a share or less, the graph showed CSFB's shooting up to above twenty cents a share in the fourth quarter of 1999.

Then Ferrara offered totals for how much profit the Lustig traders had gained from twelve separate CSFB-led IPOs, including VA Linux, Selectica, and Corvis. On December 9, the first day of trading in VA Linux, the Lustig traders had earned $15.5 million in IPO profits, and paid $2.9 million in commissions to the allocating brokers. He showed similar statistics for IPOs that had been led by Goldman Sachs and Merrill Lynch, but the commissions weren't as big a percentage of the first-day profits.

Then Ferrara summed up how his clients' operation had worked. The key, he said candidly, was "an elaborate effort to disguise our identity from and preserve our anonymity" to the investment banks.

○

Ferrara's offer of cooperation by the Lustig traders was a work of art. While he revealed the tawdry game his clients had been playing, he shifted the blame to the brokers, in the process getting his clients off the hook. For the investigators, it was a clear, authoritative look into the netherworld occupied by, among others, the Quattrone brokers and others at CSFB.

Even after providing testimony, Lustig continued to operate his trading business, with his Wall Street brokers generally unaware of the extent to which he and his confederates had provided evidence against them. The Lustig traders, who were repeatedly ushered in and out of SEC offices by their lawyers in 2001, provided a substantial chunk of the case against CSFB and several other firms charged with IPO-related violations during the bubble. They themselves were never charged.

DAMAGE CONTROL

33

IN CALIFORNIA, the IPO kickback investigation was about to have an impact on the group of brokers Quattrone had made part of his "firm within a firm."

By CSFB's reckoning, Mike Grunwald was a star. In January 2001, he was named a managing director at CSFB. His pay for the year 2000 topped $8 million. He was close friends with Bill Brady, Quattrone's second in command, and lived in an apartment in Brady's $6 million home. Together with a few other friends they would have dinner once a week when both were in town.

In early March, Grunwald got a call from CSFB lawyer Bruce Albert. Could he talk with Albert and other CSFB lawyers a little later in the month?[1]

What's this about? Grunwald asked John Schmidt.

They're talking about the IPO allocation investigation, Schmidt replied.

On March 21, Grunwald endured a lengthy, two-and-a-half-hour grilling from Albert and Lewis Liman, one of the firm's outside lawyers, about the contents of a few documents and e-mails.

The documents were the homemade spreadsheets linking the IPO profits of some of the trading accounts to their commissions. The e-mails spelled out some of the cases in which the tech PCS brokers had engaged in harsh shakedowns of clients, such as Y2K and Maxim, for more commission dollars. Bushley, the group's trading assistant, had produced some of the spreadsheets during his own questioning by the CSFB lawyers.[2] At that time, Bushley had been advised to get a lawyer.[3]

The CSFB lawyers believed the rules were murky in this area. They accepted, initially at least, the view of George Coleman and his colleagues in institutional sales that the use of the "New Issue Performance Report" could have been a benign, relevant benchmark to assure that different customers were being treated fairly. If a customer thought he was being shortchanged in IPOs, his salesman could check to see how he stacked up against other customers.

In their view, it was the kind of aggressive actions Grunwald had taken against customers like Brody that crossed the line.

Within two days of the Grunwald interview, however, CSFB learned that at least one regulator, the NASD, drew the line more broadly.

On March 23, the NASD gave CSFB a Wells notice that it might charge the firm and eight employees with rules violations based on the oversize commissions that the traders had used to pay the firm back for the hot IPOs they received.

The notices of possible NASD charges were given to Coleman, who led the institutional sales force, as well as to Benjamin, who led the PCS brokers. The other recipients at CSFB included Commesso, the broker for the Lustig trader who had put the $1 million commission on the Compaq trade, as well as Ladd McQuade, the Boston broker who covered the same Lustig-group customer. The others included brokers such as Joseph G. Girimonti, who had e-mailed about an account that "paid us . . . on deal day."[4]

Near the end of March, Grunwald got a follow-up call from Albert, the CSFB lawyer in New York. Could Grunwald speak with David Brodsky in about a week's time?

Grunwald was on vacation in Hawaii in early April to celebrate his thirty-fifth birthday when they had the call, which began at 4:00 P.M. New York time and 10:00 A.M. Hawaii time. William McLucas, the former head of enforcement at the SEC and one of the top regulatory lawyers in the country, was also on the line. About halfway through the call, Liman started questioning Grunwald aggressively, as if he were cross-examining him in court. McLucas, in contrast, was playing the role of good cop. Suddenly Grunwald realized he was "on trial" for something serious. By the end of the session, Grunwald said, *I think I need legal counsel.*

I'll e-mail you some names, Brodsky replied.

○

In early April 2001, Schmidt also had an unpleasant, disturbing telephone encounter with the CSFB legal team. His was with David Brodsky, CSFB's general counsel for the Americas. They talked about the spreadsheets tracking customers' IPO profits prepared by Brown and Bushley.

At one point during the call, Schmidt asked Brodsky when the group was going to get a legal and compliance person. Then, without warning, he heard Brodsky yelling at him. Schmidt believed that Brodsky was blaming his assistant, Linda-Louise Lund, for the departure of Susan Winegar, one of the office's compliance-related staffers. Brodsky believed Winegar had had her legs cut out from under her by San Francisco staffers.[5]

David, what's the problem? Schmidt asked. *What are the issues?*

Are you going to cooperate with First Boston? Brodsky asked.

David, I have every intention of cooperating with First Boston, Schmidt replied, suddenly alarmed.

As soon as he hung up the phone with Brodsky, Schmidt called Quattrone to tell him about the call. Schmidt was upset and worried and hoping for reassurance. He got none. It was early afternoon California time. Quattrone seemed distant. *I hired you to keep me out of trouble,* Quattrone told Schmidt.

Schmidt did most of the talking. *Frank, I can look you in the eye, I can look at myself in the mirror, I honestly don't believe anything we did was wrong or in violation of the rules,* Schmidt said. It was the last time he and Quattrone ever spoke.

O

On April 8, 2001, Brodsky sent a seven-page memo to Lukas Muehleman, chief executive of CSFB's parent, Credit Suisse Group. Its subject was "IPO Allocations in Tech PCS Group."[6]

An examination of e-mails, Brodsky said, had led to the discovery of "an apparent agreement between representatives of the Tech PCS Group in San Francisco and hedge fund trading clients" under which allocations of IPOs "were conditioned on an understanding that such accounts would pay back a significant percentage of their profits in the IPOs back to the Tech PCS Group" in the form of commissions on other trades. CSFB planned to suspend Schmidt, Grunwald, and Scott Bushley, their head trader, pending an investigation, Brodsky said.

Brodsky told how, when the Quattrone brokers had come to CSFB in September 1998, they had brought with them about ten trading accounts, which had been "an important source of revenues until mid-1999 when the IPO market had begun to take off." By then, Brodsky said, the number of such trading accounts had grown to between 20 and 30. Starting that year, Brodsky said, such trading accounts had been required to "return" 50 percent to 65 percent of their IPO profits, as calculated by the spreadsheets maintained by traders Brown and Bushley.

Brodsky noted that Grunwald's handwriting had been found on the spreadsheets tracking customers' IPO profits, next to those accounts whose commissions-to-profits ratios were below 50 percent. Brodsky told of Grunwald's call to Y2K, and his e-mail cutting off Maxim. Bushley acknowledged maintaining the spreadsheets, and having end-of-month conversations with customers "to discuss where they stood with respect to the ratio."

Grunwald had acknowledged the existence and enforcement of the ratio, the Y2K call, and the Maxim cutoff, Brodsky said. Schmidt had acknowledged the existence of the rule, the spreadsheets, and the enforcement of the rule, Brodsky said—without admitting to any direct role in the calculations or the enforcement. Neither Grunwald nor Schmidt had told anyone outside the brokers' group—including Quattrone.

As for Quattrone himself, Brodsky said, "he appeared to be shocked by the revelation of such practices at Tech PCS and stated that he had never heard of such practices and would not have condoned them had he known." Brodsky also noted that Grunwald and Scmidt had personally benefited from the practices. The tech brokers received 33 percent of all the commissions they collected—a lucrative revenue stream of which Grunwald got over 40 percent, Schmidt got over 20 percent, and Bushley and Brown lesser percentages. "Thus, by their activities in enforcing and condoning the rule, they were each able to substantially influence their own compensation," Brodsky said.

The Quattrone group brokers believed that many of the accounts were doing trades at rates of fifty cents to two dollars a share simply to generate commissions, Brodsky said. He singled out one account as having generated over six hundred thousand dollars in commissions in a single day. That account was none other than Lustig's United Capital.

The Brodsky memo said that the Quattrone group brokers might have violated industry rules against sharing in the profits of a client's account. They might have aided and abetted fraudulent "wash sales"—the customers offsetting their sales and purchases—he added. And they might have violated firm rules that barred unfair treatment of customers and capped commissions at 3 percent of value, or one dollar a share, whichever is lower.

The need for action was urgent to avoid the risk that CSFB itself might be prosecuted, Brodsky hinted. The U.S. attorney, he warned, was seeking to interview former Schmidt group trader Scott Brown under a grant of limited immunity. When he wrote the memo, Brodsky was thinking that for CSFB to avoid criminal prosecution under federal guidelines, it not only had to show cooperation and rectify any violations, but also had to punish any violators.

○

Grunwald, whose brother David was the head of a nonprofit housing group in Los Angeles, called Los Angeles lawyer Brad Brian of the firm Munger Tolles & Olsen LLP, one of the lawyers on Brodsky's list. He flew down to Los Angeles to meet Brian for the first time on Tuesday April 10.

That evening, he returned to San Francisco for a belated birthday dinner, which was attended by both Brady and Boutros. Though they knew what was coming, neither Brady nor Boutros said anything to Grunwald. Within days he was due to fly to New York for a fete for the firm's new managing directors. He never made the trip.[7]

O

Mike Campbell had become the head of the CSFB private client broker group after his four hundred brokers from DLJ were merged with Benjamin's fifty from CSFB. Campbell had sought, unsuccessfully, to fold the Schmidt-Grunwald group into his empire. In early April, Campbell notified the head of his San Francisco office, Carey Timbrell, that he was coming out there. On Tuesday, April 10, Campbell met with Brady and Boutros. Quattrone's top two deputies were shocked by what was coming. *Gee, Schmidt's a great guy*, they said.

The Quattrone brokers had had no use for Campbell, whom they regarded as part of an inferior retail brokerage universe of cold calls, mutual funds, and financial planning. And to some degree the feeling was mutual. The DLJ brokerage organization Campbell ran believed the Schmidt-Grunwald brokers weren't really offering a true menu of brokerage services, but rather a narrow, unsustainable product line that revolved around hot IPOs. In Campbell's view, if Schmidt and Grunwald had offered a full retail menu, they might have avoided the trouble they had gotten into.

Brady and Boutros were very interested in how clients would be approached by the new team. Campbell and Timbrell were hoping to get their help in reassuring the clients. So Brady and Boutros agreed to make calls to tell clients that Timbrell and his people would be contacting them. *There's a new presentation coming*, the DLJ brokers told them.

Campbell asked Timbrell to arrange a meeting that same Tuesday evening with Jon Jaffe, Grunwald's former Morgan Stanley colleague, who had joined the Schmidt-Grunwald group in early 2000.

At 4:00 P.M. that Tuesday, April 10, Timbrell called Jaffe, asking, *Jon, Mike Campbell's in town, can you meet us for five minutes around 7 P.M.?* Timbrell named a bar downtown. Jaffe was initially reluctant, but agreed.

When Jaffe arrived to meet Campbell and Timbrell, he immediately signaled the meeting's lack of importance to him by taking a call on his cell phone. When Jaffe hung up, Campbell said, *Tomorrow at 12:30, Ray Dorado and Ed Arnold are going to have John and Mike leave the premises.*

Jaffe looked at Timbrell and Campbell with alarm. *Relax*, Campbell said. Jaffe would have a chance to stay and, with another broker he had just hired, take over Grunwald's cash-management business. *Of course, you can't tell anybody*, Campbell added. *If you tell anybody*, you'll *be fired.*

O

The next morning, Wednesday, April 11, Schmidt got a call from a CSFB staffer in New York. His presence was required, along with Grunwald and

Scott Bushley, their trading assistant, at a meeting at 1:45 P.M. at the DLJ offices at 600 California Street, a mile northeast of the CSFB offices downtown.

Schmidt and Grunwald looked at each other. At first, Grunwald thought the
firm was only going to merge their group with the DLJ brokers. But Schmidt
feared the worst. *Mike, they're going to fire us,* he said. *For what?* Grunwald replied.

The three Quattrone brokers took the fifteen-minute walk up along Spear
Street near the water, and uphill on California Street to DLJ. They were ush-
ered into a room with Bill Brady and two CSFB legal staffers, Ed Arnold and
Ray Dorado.

Dorado was the senior equities department lawyer who had questioned Paul
Caan about the JohnDoe526 e-mail in February 2000. He began speaking.
We're here to tell you you're going to be placed on administrative leave, he said.

What's the reason for this? asked Schmidt, seated on the same side of the table
as Dorado. Brady sat across from them—a signal that there was no point in
appealing to Quattrone.

Possible violation of firm policy, Dorado replied.

What policy? Schmidt asked.

Fairness to customers, Dorado said.

Grunwald, in shock, asked whether CSFB would pay their legal fees. Brady
just sat there, silent.

O

At precisely the same time, DLJ's Mike Campbell and Carey Timbrell, with
Jaffe in tow, addressed the remaining Schmidt group troops at the CSFB offices
down by the bay at 201 Spear Street, ten blocks from DLJ. With the staffers
who handled cash management, stock option exercises, and other functions,
there were about twenty people there. They knew what had happened. There
was some weeping.

Campbell introduced himself and Timbrell, and briefly summarized what was
happening to Schmidt, Grunwald, and Bushley. *That's the bad news,* Campbell
said. *The good news is you all have jobs. Stay with us, you'll have a long, rich career.*

O

When they returned to their offices, Schmidt, Grunwald, and Bushley cleared
out their desks. They could feel all eyes on them, and Grunwald noticed it was
more quiet than usual. *I'm sure we'll be speaking soon,* they told Bushley. All
three walked out together.

As they walked out, Schmidt and Grunwald reassured each other. *I don't
know where this is going, Mike,* Schmidt said. *We're going to make it through this,*

they told each other. Grunwald's father had come into the CSFB office at one point and met Schmidt, and physically he had reminded Schmidt of his own father. The visit had had a different impact on Grunwald. He had realized he was just a middle-class kid who had "hit it. I was lucky," he said a year later.

Just before they got into their cars, Schmidt hugged Grunwald. It was the last time they saw each other.

○

When Grunwald returned to the apartment at Brady's home at 340 Lombard Street, he put his head in his hands in his lap. He called his lawyer, Brad Brian, to tell him what had happened and to schedule a follow-up meeting. That night, Brady told him he would have to leave the residence.

There's going to be a lot of bad P.R. here, Brady said. *I don't think you should stay here any longer.*

○

It was only afterward, looking back on it after the passage of a few years' time, that Schmidt could finally admit to himself that he might have been inattentive in not monitoring the actions of Grunwald and the junior traders more carefully. He often repeated a saying that had stuck with him: *There is none so blind as he who will not see.*

○

The following week, Grunwald learned that the U.S. attorney and the SEC had called his lawyers, wanting to speak with him.

At a meeting on April 20, with four attorneys from the Los Angeles office of Munger Tolles, in a thirty-fifth-floor conference room with a view of the HOL-LYWOOD sign, Grunwald heard a worst-case scenario. "We want you to know that if this goes the wrong way, you could go to jail," they told him.

Grunwald asked for a five-minute break, and cried. Ten days earlier he had been on top of the world. Now he didn't know what would happen next. Visiting a relative in Los Angeles, Grunwald stayed up till 3:00 A.M. with him some nights, saying, *I don't believe this. This isn't happening. Why are they doing this to me?* On June 28, he and Schmidt and Bushley were fired.

○

A few months later, near the end of a session with the NASD's Ozag and Alexander, Bushley was able to put it in some perspective. Unlike some of the others who had been interviewed, who had careers to protect, he spoke as if he might not return to the securities business: "Now, in hindsight, it probably is not the most fair way to conduct business; but that's the way the corporate culture at First Boston was, and I did what I was told, and I did my duties to the best of my abilities at the time."

Bushley said he felt the firm had singled out the Quattrone brokers to protect the larger organization, "since Frank Quattrone was a high flyer and one of the most successful technology bankers for the past couple of years, that First Boston was going to take the hit for it." He added, "They're going to try and look proactive, like they're reasserting the structure within the firm."[8]

O

CSFB management decided against announcing the suspension of the Quattrone brokers. When the news broke on April 20, 2001, it appeared to tie Quattrone and his group to the IPO kickback case. However, there was no evidence that Quattrone knew anything about hedge funds like Lustig or the other Denver traders paying oversize commissions for IPOs.

Quattrone of course wanted to distance himself from the brokers and the IPO allocation probe. He wanted some public statement that did that. He had fired Cheryl Popp, his public relations chief in 1999 and 2000, early in 2001, replacing her with a former Morgan Stanley technology banker with little PR experience. He consulted an outside public relations consultant from New York. He called one CSFB official involved in the decision making after 2:00 A.M. Eastern time.

During a conference call with CSFB executives, lawyers, and public relations staffers, Quattrone argued that responsibility for the IPO allocation issues should be clearly laid elsewhere. When one public relations staffer asked about the risks such an approach might pose to the firm's franchise, Quattrone replied: "I am the fucking franchise." The rest of the people on the call were silent.

O

On May 1, Chuck Ward, the global cohead of investment banking, issued a carefully worded statement.

"The decision by CSFB to place certain brokers on administrative leave had nothing to do with the Technology Group's investment banking clients, or their officers or directors," Ward said. "As Head of CSFB's Technology Group, Frank Quattrone is responsible for delivering the Firm's investment banking services to technology clients. He is not and was not responsible for overseeing brokerage accounts or commissions, nor is he or was he responsible for IPO allocations, which are the subject of an industry-wide examination by various regulatory authorities. The Firm is cooperating fully with regulators."[9]

Quattrone had obviously played some role in the IPO allocation process; his influence and input was often avidly sought and at times exercised. Despite that, Quattrone stuck consistently to the Ward statement's general line—that he wasn't responsible for IPO allocations—until October 10, 2003.

THE UNWRITTEN RULES OF RESEARCH

34

WITH THE FIRING of Schmidt, Grunwald, and Bushley, Quattrone had lost control of the brokers who had worked with him in his firm within a firm. Now he was about to lose an even bigger part of his empire—but he wouldn't give it up without a fight.

By mid-March 2001, the NASDAQ market index had fallen 64 percent from its peak a year earlier. The declines were even worse in technology stocks and Internet issues, with the Dow Jones Internet stock index down a devastating 86 percent. The carnage would continue relentlessly for another two years. But much of the damage had already been done.

That month, an investor named Debases Kanjilal filed an arbitration claim against Merrill Lynch, saying he had lost half a million dollars on the stock of Infospace by relying on the "buy" recommendation of Merrill Internet analyst Henry Blodget. Kanjilal asserted that Blodget had kept an overly rosy $100 price target on the stock in hopes of winning investment banking business, while Infospace stock had declined from $140 a share to below $10. (By the end of 2001, the stock traded around $2.) Kanjilal, who was represented by high-profile investors' attorney Jacob Zamansky, won a four-hundred-thousand-dollar settlement from Merrill in July 2001.[1]

As the Char e-mail had warned in December 2000, the plaintiff bar was gearing up for an assault on "broken tech IPOs," with investor actions like Kanjilal's coming out of the woodwork. CSFB had led more than its share of IPOs Quattrone had in December 2000 indulgently called "woofers," and some investors blamed fee-hungry analysts for cheerleading the stocks.

As the SEC later noted, "it was not uncommon" for senior tech group analysts to have been paid $5 million to $10 million, with tech group research chief Elliot Rogers stating that "the starting point" for pay decisions was revenue from banking, trading, and other sources related to companies the analyst covered.[2]

The U.S. House of Representatives Financial Services Committee eventually scheduled hearings on conflicts of interest in Wall Street research for midyear.

O

Even on Wall Street, there was a general recognition that research analysts gave out too many buy ratings and woefully few sells, and had gotten too wrapped up during the bubble in bringing in banking business.

A report entitled "The Issue of Integrity" on February 27, 2001, by Morgan Stanley market strategist Byron Wien, reflected the dawning reassessment of what had gone wrong. Research analysts, he warned, shouldn't "gloss over a negative change in the fundamentals of a company" due to concerns about investment banking relationships. "Investment bankers may believe they will have better relationships with their clients if analysts say nice things about the companies they cover," Wien said. "But they must realize opinions have little value if the person delivering them has no credibility."

Trying to stay ahead of the investor backlash, a Wall Street lobbying group, the Securities Industry Association (SIA), formed a committee to set new "best practices" to curb conflicts of interest in research. Its chairman was Michael Blumstein, a former *New York Times* reporter who had been an analyst of financial stocks at both First Boston and Morgan Stanley and, at the time, headed U.S. research at Morgan Stanley—Quattrone's archrival.

The group's initiatives would include a ban on paying analysts based on a percentage of fees for specific banking deals, curbs on analysts' sales of stocks they recommended, disclosure of their holdings, and a mandate to use the full spectrum of ratings with fewer buys and more sells.

But another of the group's initiatives threatened to peel away a key piece of Quattrone's empire—barring analysts from reporting to investment bankers. At Morgan Stanley, for example, the analysts reported to a firmwide head of research, who reported to the head of institutional securities—insulating the analysts from control, if not pressure, from bankers.

Al Jackson, the CSFB research director, asked one of his deputies, Jack Kirnan, to represent the firm on the Blumstein panel of officials from a dozen big firms. The panel met about ten times, and when the topic of analysts reporting to bankers came up, all eyes would turn to Kirnan. They all knew there would have to be a change at CSFB in order for the voluntary best practices to be adopted universally. Could Kirnan make it happen at CSFB? The CSFB research deputy gamely insisted he could.

When Kirnan returned to brief CSFB executives on the SIA meetings, CSFB research chief Al Jackson supported the proposed change. But Quattrone wanted to fight it. On one of the calls, Quattrone told Kirnan: *You're not trying hard enough.*

Quattrone and his bankers were still unabashedly trying to use analysts to collect banking fees, or to win banking assignments. Sometimes their efforts weren't subtle.

In March 2001, CSFB tech banker Richard Hart asked design software analyst Erach Desai to attend a meeting with Brad Henske, chief financial officer of Synopsys Inc., an electronic design automation company, and the head of investor relations. CSFB had set up the meeting to discuss potential work CSFB could do for Synopsys. Desai, a Pakistani graduate of MIT, had dark curly hair combed straight back. And he favored colorful dress shirts of bright orange, purple, and yellow.

At the Synopsys meeting, John Hodge, the head of West Coast corporate finance, talked about the group's long relationship with Synopsys, dating back to when Morgan Stanley had brought it public, and said the CSFB tech group wanted to continue that relationship. But they weren't discussing specific deals, partly because Synopsys was already flush with about $500 million in cash.

At first, Henske joked that business must be slow if so many people from CSFB could attend the meeting. He then launched into a spiel about his unhappiness with Desai's research coverage. Henske considered Desai a bomb thrower who had a contentious relationship with the managements of many companies he covered.[3] Desai had been wrong about design software trends and wrong about Synopsys's prospects, he said. Desai, who had a buy rating on the stock instead of a strong buy, had been too cautionary, Henske said.

Two days later, while Desai was visiting the West Coast for other meetings, he was summoned to Hodge's office. *You need to figure out a way to get more positive on the [Synopsys] story, because I think we can do business here*, Hodge told him, according to Desai's testimony and e-mails. Desai was shocked by Hodge's blunt demand. He responded that he stood by his macro view of the industry, but would try to keep an open mind. But Desai came to believe Hodge was trying to "compromise" his objectivity.[4]

A few months later, Synopsys hired CSFB to advise on a $700 million acquisition of Avant! Corporation. The deal, announced in December 2001, earned CSFB a fee of $10 million. By then, Desai had left CSFB.

O

Quattrone's authority over research soon helped produce a breakthrough on another front—his tireless efforts to collect on the $2 million IOU from Research in Motion for CSFB's work on its stock offering of October 2000. Not only was there a change in the research analysts who covered the company, but CSFB itself began talks about signing a contract with the company for BlackBerry services.

On March 1, 2001, the CSFB tech group analyst who had covered the Black-

Berry vendor resigned. In an e-mail to Quattrone and other bankers, Chris Legg, one of the Boston tech group bankers, said that another analyst, Marc Cabi, had agreed to "play a more active role" in following the company. Another analyst, Kevin McCarthy, might pick up coverage, Legg added, concluding: "Will collect extra $1.8m" from RIM.

Quattrone's terse reply showed how ready he was to use his tight control over research analysts to win, or in this case collect, banking fees. "Rimm doesn't get cabi or mcarthy unless they pay up," Quattrone replied.[5]

Sure enough, when RIM ponied up the money, the company got the analyst it wanted, and a thaw in its chilly relations with Quattrone. On March 8, Legg updated Quattrone, Cabi, and other bankers: "RIM paid us the extra $1.8M we asked for. That brings our total received from them to $6.5M, which is exactly the 25% we requested as a percentage of the total fee in their most recent financing."

With the fee paid, Legg added, "I would ask that we return them to 'most favored nation' status," meaning he wanted RIM to be treated as well as any other CSFB tech group client to get in the running for the company's next deal. Cabi would be resuming research coverage, Legg said, and he thought CSFB had a shot at RIM's next merger assignment.

And then Legg urged, "Let's make sure they are on the guest list for banking and research events (i.e., they weren't invited to Aspen, let's get them on the list for Pebble Beach or the British Open—Dennis [Kavelman, the CFO] is a scratch golfer and Jim [Balsillie, the CEO] is very enthusiastic)."

Quattrone replied that the group's invitations to the British Open were "very limited, lots of better customers higher up the list. They'll be invited to [the Pebble Beach] outing."[6]

Invitations to the tech group ski outings were among the most coveted, because of its high ratio of luxury fun to business. The Aspen trip of early 2001 offered cooking classes, fly-fishing, and a flight to Telluride one day when the snow wasn't too good. The message was: "Thank you for being a client." Each day seemed to bring a different gift: ski sweater, backpack with water bladder, walkie-talkies, and ski goggles.

One evening there was a dinner at the luxurious private home of a well-known media mogul, who had a swimming pool in his living room. Guests consumed caviar, champagne, and grilled game. An ice sculpture outside was lit up with the words "CSFB Tech Group." At the end of one evening, at the base of a ski run, there were fireworks, more champagne, and cigars. Quattrone personally thanked people for attending.

O

As late as May 2001, Quattrone was still battling the industry group efforts to remove research analysts from his purview. In a lengthy e-mail written on

Saturday, May 12, 2001, Quattrone made a passionate appeal for support to three top executives—the CEO, Wheat, and banking coheads Brady Dougan and Tony James.[7]

Quattrone warned that "it would be a huge mistake to capitulate to our competitors, who are jealous of our success and want to isolate us and make us try to admit that we were doing something wrong when we were not." Quattrone, who had received bad press when his brokers were fired, said he feared "a pr nightmare" if he lost authority over analysts.

His group's reporting structure had been created because research and banking at Morgan Stanley hadn't been "closely coordinated in order to meet the needs of our clients." Having tech analysts report to tech research chief Elliott Rogers, who reported jointly to Quattrone and Al Jackson in New York, "handles potential conflicts better than traditional reporting structures do," Quattrone said.

Then Quattrone paused to attack his archrival, Mary Meeker, as well as telecom analyst Jack Grubman at Citigroup for being "the two most notorious banking-driven analysts on wall street over the past three years." Quattrone said they both had been spotlighted for being overly bullish on their investment banking clients. Meeker had just been featured on the cover of *Fortune* with the headline "Can We Ever Trust Wall Street Again?"

The SIA proposal, Quattrone concluded, "would be a business disaster," risking the loss of tech analysts and bankers: "[T]he partnership between research and banking has been integral to our success. tampering with it in my view would be a huge mistake."

In a call the following Monday morning, May 14, Quattrone urged top CFSB bankers Dougan, James, and Stonehill to "attack" the competition on the issue. But the CSFB executives, already under the gun in the probe of IPOs and commissions, had no taste for such a public brawl.[8]

By the end of the call, Quattrone could tell he might lose the decision.[9] But he still hadn't given up, sending more suggestions to Kirnan. On May 22, 2001, Kirnan said the SIA group wouldn't budge. The SIA group, Kirnan explained, felt Wall Street needed "to state in as explicit terms as possible that 'research should not report to investment banking.' . . . The perception of the public, the regulators and the legislative branch is that analyst independence, quality and integrity is greatly compromised when research analysts report directly to investment banking."[10]

○

On May 25, 2001, design software analyst Erach Desai sent an e-mail to investing clients about the latest quarterly earnings report by Synopsys. From his talks that day with clients, he believed many investors were misinterpreting

Frank Quattrone from the University of Pennsylvania yearbook. *1977 Record, University of Pennsylvania*

Quattrone holds up sign at protest of threatened shutdown of the School of Allied Medical Professions. *University of Pennsylvania*

"The Dream Team": Bill Brady, Frank Quattrone, and George Boutros in 1996, the year they left Morgan Stanley to join Deutsche Bank. *Eric Millette*

Mary Meeker, Internet analyst at Morgan Stanley. *David Lubarsky*

CSFB's Technology Client Services group is a team of experienced professionals with an in-depth understanding of the needs of technology clients.

tech is here to change

2000

CSFB | EMPOWERING CHANGE.™

Mike Grunwald and John Schmidt, brokers who worked with Quattrone's technology banking group at Credit Suisse First Boston, as pictured in group brochure.

Lise Buyer, Internet analyst for the Quattrone group at DMG and Credit Suisse First Boston.
Timothy Archibald

Headquarters of Credit Suisse
First Boston on Madison Avenue
in midtown Manhattan. *Peter Buxton*

Quattrone with Lance Armstrong
and Sheryl Crow at one of his
technology conferences during
the Bubble. *Asa Mathat*

Quattrone golfing near his ocean-side weekend home at Pebble Beach, California. *Gary Newkirk/Corbis*

Copy of anonymous letter from "A concerned citizen" received by regulators, which alleged that CSFB allocated hot IPOs to investors who made "thinly disguised payments" of oversize commissions for riskless trades.

Ralph Ferrara, lawyer for Denver trader James Lustig, addresses about a hundred guests at the posh Le Cirque 2000 restaurant in midtown Manhattan in February 2001—just before his presentation to regulators about how his clients obtained hot IPOs. *Debevoise & Plimpton*

SEC staffers (l to r) Michael Wasserman, William Stellmach, and Doria Stetch, the team probing IPO allocations at CSFB, meet in the Manhattan apartment of team leader Caren Pennington two weeks after SEC offices at 7 World Trade Center were destroyed on 9/11. *Frances M. Roberts*

Federal prosecutors Steven Peikin and David Anders stop to chat outside the federal courthouse on May 3, 2004, during jury deliberations in the Quattrone retrial. *Kathy Willens/Associated Press*

Star prosecution witness David Brodsky, the former general counsel for the Americas at Credit Suisse First Boston, on his way to court during the Quattrone retrial on April 22, 2004. *Rick Malman/Bloomberg News/Landov*

Judge Richard Owen, who presided over Quattrone's two obstruction trials, leaves U.S. courthouse on April 28, 2004. *Rick Malman/Bloomberg News/Landov*

Quattrone holds his head high after the first trial ends in a hung jury on October 24, 2003, as his lawyer John Keker tells reporters, "We are disappointed, because Frank Quattrone is innocent." *Louis Lanzano/Associated Press*

Quattrone's personal lawyer Ken Hausman accompanies Quattrone's mother Rose and sister Mary Ann from the courthouse after the guilty verdict on May 3, 2004. *Kathy Willens/ Associated Press*

Quattrone and his lawyers, Theodore Wells (left) and Mark Pomerantz (right), take a victory walk after prosecutors agree on August 22, 2006, to drop the charges and avoid a retrial. *Louis Lanzano/Associated Press*

the numbers, forgetting that the profits included a one-time gain from invest-ments.[11]

If the Synopsys chief financial officer Brad Henske could sustain that perfor-mance, Desai said in a joking tone, maybe he should be a hedge fund manager instead of a CFO! But Henske interpreted the note as an incorrect prediction that he was going to leave the company.[12]

Not long after, Desai visited Synopsis with two institutional investor clients in tow. He had heard Henske was upset. When Henske walked in and intro-duced himself to the two clients, he told Desai: *I need a copy of that e-mail.* Desai interpreted what Henske said as a veiled threat to get him fired. And Henske complained to others at CSFB about what he considered Desai's "unprofes-sional behavior."

It soon seemed as though Desai was on thin ice. The same day he sent the e-mail about Synopsys, tech research chief Rogers told the analyst he needed to "revitalize his research franchise and rapport with the sales force." They sched-uled a meeting for 11:30 A.M. on the following Wednesday, May 30. The agenda: discuss why Desai had been less visible and less effective with the sales force than other analysts.

Desai knew his job was in jeopardy. In response, he lashed out at how Quat-trone's research analysts were treated. On the morning of May 30, several hours before their scheduled meeting, Desai sent Rogers a lengthy e-mail, copying CSFB New York research executives Jackson and Kirnan.[13]

Desai called his memo "Unwritten Rules for Tech Research." Based on his past misadventures in covering Cadence, Parametric, and Synopsys, Desai said, "I have 'learned' to adapt to a set of rules that have been imposed by Tech Group banking so as to keep our corporate clients appeased. I believe that these unwritten rules have clearly hindered my ability to be an effective analyst in my various coverage sectors."

Desai then recounted several of his scrapes in detail. He said he believed his failure to give Cadence management a heads-up on his 1998 downgrade of the stock was a big part of the reason that he had been denied the chance to cover the more important sector of semiconductor stocks. At the time, he recalled, banker Tony Trousset "informed me of unwritten rule number one: 'if you can't say something positive, don't say anything at all.'"

Next Desai recalled his cautionary comments about Parametric in 1999 that had caused its chief executive to promise CSFB banker Jake Peters that Paramet-ric would never do any business with CSFB. Peters had then spelled out what Desai considered "unwritten rule number two," which was: "why couldn't you just go with the flow of the other analysts, rather than try to be a contrarian?"

Desai said he had also wanted to downgrade Synopsys's rating from a strong buy to a buy in 2000 after identifying "some early signs of business softness."

But he held off, he said, because "banking felt that this might impact CSFB's ability to potentially do business with the company downstream." The company later lowered its earnings guidance, and Desai had regretted not sticking to his guns.

The contents of Desai's e-mail were explosive. The story of how banking had pressured him to hold back on a downgrade of Synopsys eventually became one of the two examples of fraudulent research by CSFB tech analysts cited by the SEC.[14]

As soon as he received it, Rogers forwarded the e-mail to Quattrone, notifying him of the scheduled meeting later that day. He also notified the human resources department—a sign Desai might soon be shown the door.[15] Quattrone replied that Desai was "mistaken about these 'unwritten rules,' as you know." Of course, Quattrone said, he supported "research objectivity" 100 percent. He told Rogers to contact the legal department, too.[16]

Quattrone recalled that past criticism of Desai's "lack of visibility" was due partly to "his insistence on working from boston," plus "his tendency to whip stocks around based on unsubstantiated rumors" and "his lack of 'bedside manner,' or diplomacy, with corporates, which makes his job harder to do."

During the May 30 Desai-Rogers meeting, someone popped in and asked Desai to meet with Brodsky, the CSFB attorney, at 5:00 P.M. At their meeting, Brodsky told Desai that he had discussed his memo with Quattrone. *Frank says this would never happen in his organization.* But Desai stood by his account.[17]

Brodsky noted that the SIA was working on guidelines that meant technology research would be taken out from under tech bankers. Brodsky urged Desai to try to patch things up with Rogers, and asked him if he had sent the e-mail to anyone outside of CSFB. *I'd hate to see this appear in the* [Wall Street] Journal, Brodsky said. Desai said he trusted the recipients not to retransmit the e-mail inappropriately.

O

As some tech analysts jumped ship, some of the stocks they had followed were left in limbo. After Buyer left, for example, CSFB kept a buy or strong buy rating on one of her stocks, online marketer Digital Impact Inc., even as the price fell from just under fifty dollars a share down to two dollars.

But when a new analyst, Jamie Kiggen, who was assigned to cover Digital Impact in May 2001, proposed dropping coverage of it on September 4 because the market was "very competitive," investment banker Ted Smith discouraged the move, saying other bankers would object because CSFB had led the IPO and the company had "good" venture capital backers. Kiggen acquiesced then and left the buy rating unchanged—before finally downgrading the stock to a hold on October 2.[18]

The Digital Impact rating would become the SEC's other example of fraudulent research by the CSFB tech analysts.

O

A year and a half later, lawyers for CSFB and Quattrone defended the tech-group research reporting structure. No rule in effect at the time limited his role in setting analysts' headcount or pay, Quattrone's lawyers said. He had merely wanted to avoid repeating his experience at Morgan Stanley, where the firm was unwilling to employ enough analysts to keep pace with tech industry growth. The contents of research reports, they said, were reviewed and approved not by Quattrone but by supervisory analysts who worked for Jackson.

Quattrone had actually encouraged analysts' independence, his lawyers said, by giving them power to veto IPOs and other securities sales if they had concerns about the companies' quality. Such vetoes had caused CSFB to turn down six IPOs, they said, and Quattrone had even supported Desai's reservations about CSFB underwriting a questionable stock.

But when the SIA's new research best practices were announced in mid-2001, CSFB immediately signaled it would adopt them by changing the tech analysts' reporting, severing their reporting line to Quattrone. The previous reporting structure had been flawed, the NASD said in March 2003, because "it insulated the tech group from CSFB's supervisory systems while concentrating control over the normally distinct functions of research, investment banking and retail brokering in Quattrone's hands, enabling Quattrone to use all these functions to bolster and enlarge his investment banking franchise."

At the end of the year, eight to ten of Quattrone's analysts would leave the firm, at Jackson's behest. The IPO investigation, and the gathering force of an incipient investor backlash against the excesses of the Bubble, were pulling Quattrone's empire apart.

A VOTE OF CONFIDENCE

35

ALTHOUGH storm clouds were gathering over the issue of biased research, the most pressing concern CSFB faced was the now criminal probes into IPOs and commissions by federal prosecutors, the SEC, and the NASD. The firing of the Quattrone brokers had only highlighted the seriousness of the case.

At first the firm had argued that it was only following industrywide practice. In response to the NASD's notice of possible charges in March, the firm was unapologetic. "There is absolutely nothing written in any guideline, rule, regulation, case or speech by a regulatory official that forbids the voluntary payment by clients of large commissions to CSFB to demonstrate that such clients are good enough customers to deserve being given IPO allocations," CSFB said.[1] The indignant tone soon disappeared.

After the Quattrone brokers were fired, Brodsky and the CSFB lawyers had argued to the regulators that those brokers' conduct was isolated. But the regulators asked Brodsky: *Have you read the e-mails you've produced to us?* Richard Walker, the SEC's head of enforcement, told CSFB the agency's interest wasn't confined to the California office.

○

Within weeks of the Quattrone brokers being put on leave in April 2001, Credit Suisse Group began reevaluating Wheat's future as the CEO of Credit Suisse First Boston. On top of the flaming Ferraris, the derivatives unit in Japan, and a big loss on the 1998 Russian debt blowup, some in Zurich said CSFB was "accident-prone."[2] Both Wheat and his boss, Credit Suisse Group CEO Lukas Muhlemann, soon began talking up the need for greater control over the loosely knit organization.

John Mack's sudden departure from Morgan Stanley that January offered a neat solution. It put someone on the job market with the gravitas to deal with the regulatory issues, but who had had nothing to do with generating them himself.

Mack, then fifty-six, had been surprised to find himself marginalized after Morgan Stanley merged with Dean Witter Discover & Company in 1997 to get a retail brokerage network to boost its stock distribution power. Morgan Stanley, home of dozens of pin-striped masters of the universe, had by far the greater prestige on Wall Street. But Philip Purcell, Dean Witter's chief executive, had insisted on the chief executive role, and in fact Dean Witter had the larger stock market value based partly on the steady stream of earnings thrown off by its Discover credit-card business. With Fisher stepping aside when the deal was struck, Mack believed that he would eventually succeed Purcell as chief executive, and he grew embittered as he realized that wasn't going to happen as quickly as he had thought, if ever.

In July 2001, Wheat learned that his time was up. In addition to all of the regulatory snafus, the misbegotten DLJ acquisition didn't help. He was out. On July 12, 2001, Mack was named CEO of Credit Suisse First Boston.

At first, Mack's arrival looked bad for Quattrone. It was Mack who, alongside Fisher, had in 1996 vetoed the kind of structure at Morgan Stanley that Quattrone had gained at CSFB. Mack also peppered his initial interviews with talk about tearing down "silos" and fostering more "teamwork."

Within weeks Mack also began talking about the need to renegotiate the large number of expensive guaranteed pay packages. The guarantees had been struck by the Wheat team to lock in key bankers and traders in the months after DLJ banking star Ken Moelis had left. Quattrone's lucrative group contract was mentioned prominently. Somewhat surprisingly, Quattrone sent out signals that he wouldn't rule out some changes in his own hard-fought deal. His conflicts at Morgan Stanley had been with Scott, not Mack, people close to him said.[3]

Mack, who had played college football at Duke University, was an imposing presence. Image conscious and skilled at getting good PR, Mack also put high-profile public relations strategist Linda Robinson, the auburn-haired wife of former American Express Company chief executive James Robinson, on the team.

One of Mack's shrewdest moves, on August 20, 2001, was to bring in Gary Lynch, the former head of enforcement at the SEC who had successfully done battle with Ivan Boesky and Michael Milken in the late 1980s, to help him wrestle with the IPO probe. Lynch had gone into private practice at a prestigious firm in the 1990s, but the CSFB job was tailor-made for his august authority.

Wheat's ouster reduced CSFB's incentives to defend its IPO allocation practices against the regulatory onslaught. Unlike their predecessors at CSFB,

Mack and Lynch had no connection to the individuals being investigated in the
IPO probe.

O

As of late August, CSFB was still in the crosshairs of the criminal probe.
That month, SEC enforcement lawyers Stellmach and Stetch began a series of
interviews at the agency's New York offices at 7 World Trade Center with four
traders who had paid big commissions and received IPOs. All were represented
by the same lawyers, Michael Trager and Joseph Hartman of Fulbright &
Jaworski, and all cited their Fifth Amendment rights against self-incrimination
when they declined to answer questions.

One of them, Anthony Bruan, was the founder of a hedge fund, PTJP Partners, that recruited traders who obtained IPOs during the bubble, partly
through the use of multiple account names in strategies similar to Lustig's
traders. His nephew Walter, who had boasted that PTJP traders received forty-
five thousand shares of VA Linux, was also interviewed.[4] In 2004, the NASD
fined three Bruan family members, including Walter Bruan, for failing to separate their brokerage firm, Worldco LLC, from PTJP.[5] In his interview on
August 29, the SEC staffers asked Walter Bruan whether Worldco traders had
opened accounts at CSFB using false information, such as misstating their location and overstating their assets. He declined to answer.[6]

The other two interviewees, Richard Calta of Devon and Ronnie Barnes of
Bedford Management, were both PTJP traders and clients of the Quattrone
group brokers. Barnes and Calta were both asked about their business ties to
the Bruan brothers. They were also asked if they knew Schmidt, Brown, Bushley, and Grunwald. Barnes was asked if he had ever made any direct cash payments, gifts, or loans to any CSFB employee. He was also asked whether one of
his accounts had ever been threatened with reduced IPO allocations if they
failed to pay back enough in commissions. Barnes gave no answers. His non-
interview lasted just thirty-nine minutes. The date was Wednesday, September
5, 2001. None of the traders was ever charged with any wrongdoing for paying
inflated commissions to get IPOs.

On Friday Sepember 7, 2001, the NASD's Ozag and Alexander interviewed
Paul Caan, the deputy chief of the private-client brokers, about the JohnDoe526
episode. He said he had only known Chris Champeau, the subject of the letter,
as an adult.[7] He alluded to how the firm had tracked down the senders, sued
them, and made them pay. "There was a lawsuit that was brought against them,"
he said. "They withdrew this allegation and wound up paying a fairly large
amount of money to CSFB."

The NASD investigators asked Caan why Champeau had paid him a commission of $135,000 in November 1999 around the time he got two hot IPOs.

"Do you recall ever getting a commission of $135,000 from any customer in one day?" Ozag asked. "It is possible," Caan said. Why did Champeau pay so much for one trade? Caan's answer was oddly breezy and unapologetic, despite the damage done to the firm, the ouster of its CEO, the firing of the three Quattrone brokers, and the pending criminal probe. "He must have been pretty happy and, you know, wanted to impress me and certainly keep his profile very high," Caan said.

But the investigations would soon wind down.

With the election of George Bush in November 2000, the leadership at the SEC had also changed. Bush had replaced populist chairman Arthur Levitt immediately, on a temporary basis, with a Republican commission member. Levitt's enforcement chief, Richard Walker, announced plans to leave in July 2001. And Bush's more Wall Street–friendly nominee, Harvey Pitt, took office as SEC chairman in August.

Despite all their subpoenas and e-mail searches, the federal prosecutors, Peikin and Anders, weren't convinced that the payment of inflated commissions to get IPOs was criminal. *We have facts in search of a theory,* Peikin told one regulator. They asked CSFB's lawyers to explain why the commissions didn't constitute any one of six possible violations, including bribery and extortion. In a fifty-seven-page memo prepared by Davis Polk and Wilmer Cutler, CSFB's lawyers provided arguments against such charges.[8]

O

The terrorist attack on the World Trade Center on September 11, 2001, changed the face of U.S. law enforcement, lessening the urgency of the IPO kickback probe. For one thing, the northeast regional office of the SEC, which had been housed at 7 World Trade Center, at the north end of Ground Zero, was demolished when the entire building collapsed following the attacks on the Twin Towers.

Not only were the SEC's files destroyed, for weeks the agency's staffers had to work out of their homes. Stellmach and Wasserman convened at Pennington's apartment on the Upper West Side of Manhattan. And Carlin worked out of a makeshift office at his home in suburban New Jersey.

Both Mack and Lynch made clear to SEC officials that they were eager to settle the IPO case. Pitt's deputy, Mark Radke, spoke with Steve Cutler, who at that point was the acting SEC enforcement chief, and hadn't been officially appointed by Pitt. Radke told Cutler he thought CSFB was eager to reach a deal, and urged him to start settlement talks.

The markets, already hard hit by the bubble's aftermath, received another blow from the 9/11 attacks. After a headlong expansion, Wall Street was cutting back relentlessly. In October 2001, CSFB projected a third-quarter loss of

$120 million. "Our most immediate need is to lower our costs," said Mack, when he discussed plans for a cut of 7 percent, or two thousand jobs out of CSFB's global workforce.[9]

The cuts eventually totaled ten thousand jobs. Erach Desai, the disgruntled tech group analyst, wasn't surprised when he got the news that he was being fired.[10] Unlike some others who were cut, however, he was immediately and unceremoniously escorted from his office.

O

When Mack met Quattrone to propose renegotiating his contract, as the firm did with other bankers, it required a special effort. They met midway between Quattrone's home turf in California and Mack's at CSFB headquarters in Manhattan. The neutral venue was the Fairmont Hotel in Kansas City, Missouri.[11]

Mack first threatened to go to court to overturn Qauttrone's contract, then dangled incentives for Quattrone to renegotiate. The group could get an upfront payment estimated at $150 million in company stock. And Mack was prepared to vouch publicly for Quattrone's integrity.[12]

It was a quick, visible PR win for Mack. In exchange, he named Quattrone to the firm's twenty-seven-member executive board. And Mack issued a public vote of confidence in Quattrone's ethics. "Frank has endured months of intense media scrutiny," Mack said in an internal CSFB memo on November 13, 2001. "I know how very difficult that has been for him and his family because there has been no evidence that Frank has done anything wrong or inappropriate. I have complete confidence in his integrity and ethics."

Within eighteen months, the words in that statement and the decision to endorse Quattrone would be reassessed as a mistake.[13]

Mack had gained the symbolic pay deal victory he had sought. But Quattrone tried to minimize it. The next time he ran into Scott, his old adversary from Morgan Stanley, at a two-day meeting of the prestigious Stanford Business School advisory council, Scott asked him how much the Mack renegotiation had cost him. Quattrone reached into his pants pocket and, smiling, pulled out a penny and held it up.

O

At the end of October, the SEC's Stellmach and Stetch interviewed executives of seven companies that had been taken public by Credit Suisse: Onvia.com, Digital think, TiVo, Interwoven, Vitria, Intertrust Technologies, and Digital Impact. Over the course of three days in San Francisco, the investigators asked the executives whether they would have wanted to know about the profit-sharing and allocations to flippers instead of long-term investors.

Some of the executives didn't seem too concerned, if they even understood the pattern Stellmach outlined. But others were. "I would not have been happy about that," said Paul Auvil, Vitria's chief financial officer. He had asked CSFB twice for a list of investors who got the IPO shares but never received one, he said.[14]

At the same time, the regulatory charm offensive by Mack and Lynch was making progress. In talks with the SEC and NASD in November, CSFB agreed to pay $100 million to settle the IPO kickback case as a civil matter.[15] The amount was arrived at partly from calculations of the excess commissions CSFB had earned over six cents a share. The charge, which CSFB would neither admit nor deny as was customary in such pacts, was an improper scheme to share customer profits.

Aware of CSFB's willingness to accept a "hard whack" from the SEC and NASD, Khuzami and the securities fraud unit at the U.S. attorney's office decided not to bring criminal charges in the same case. On November 28, 2001, Peikin and Anders sent a letter to Schmidt and others saying the unit had "closed its investigation" of the matter.

In light of what followed in 2002 and 2003, the IPOs-and-commissions settlement would come to be seen as a bargain. For example, it gave CSFB a pass on any possible charges of "laddering," or requiring investors who got hot IPOs to buy more shares at higher prices once trading began. Goldman and Morgan Stanley had to wrestle with such charges for three more years.

By December, the SEC investigators had already begun to turn their attention elsewhere, launching a series of interviews with clients and former employes of Goldman Sachs Group. They left it to the NASD to interview Schmidt, Grunwald, and Bushley. The SEC's Stellmach and Stetch interviewed Coleman and Ehinger in January in their temporary offices in the old landmark Woolworth building across from City Hall in lower Manhattan.

They asked about a February 14, 2000, e-mail from Ehinger to Coleman. It said one investing client "is on the four to one plan, which is generous." The client "simply needs to be told what we have made him versus what he has paid us, weekly if required." Ehinger said he believed the client was "behind, i.e. six to one or eight to one, but I'm not sure." The e-mail made clear that the New York executives used the ratio of IPO profits to commissions to get clients to pay more. "Someone would say, 'gee is there a target?' And I would say [a] lower [ratio] is better," Coleman said.[16]

O

On January 22, 2002, in the ceremonial meeting room in the basement of SEC headquarters in Washington, officials of the SEC and NASD jointly announced the settlement of charges of "abusive practices" in IPO allocations. "CSFB improperly took advantage of its position as underwriter by allocating

shares of hot IPOs to customers who agreed to share their IPO profits by paying excessive commissions," the SEC's Cutler said in a statement.[17]

Standing next to Cutler, Mary L. Schapiro, president of NASD Regulation,
Inc., called the alleged conduct "a pervasive scheme" that involved "many parts
of the firm." She said, "CSFB's behavior undermines the integrity of the capital-
raising process which is essential to the health of our economy, and shakes the
faith of investors in the fairness of the markets." The commission payments by
about three hundred hedge funds, NASD said, amounted to 22 percent of all
the commissions paid to CSFB in one quarter. None of the hedge funds were
named or charged.[18]

The agencies would share the $100 million penalty. By the SEC's calcula-
tion, it was the second largest amount it had ever imposed for civil misconduct
by a broker dealer, exceeded only by a $122 million penalty against Salomon
Brothers in a 1992 Treasury bond bid-rigging scandal.

Regulators later charged the same kind of commission paybacks were also
paid, to a lesser extent, to other firms. The NASD filed such charges against
Invemed Associates on April 15, 2003, against Bear Stearns Companies,
Deutsche Bank AG, and Morgan Stanley on May 18, 2004, and against Thomas
Weisel Partners on March 30, 2005. Invemed, led by the feisty Ken Langone,
ultimately defeated the charges in 2006.

CSFB itself also took disciplinary action almost immediately against nineteen of its own people. The three employees who paid the biggest fines, a half
million dollars apiece, were Coleman and Ehinger, the heads of global sales and
sales trading, and Caan, the deputy manager of the private-client group.[19]

Benjamin, Caan's boss, only had to pay a quarter million dollars—supporting
the notion advanced by JohnDoe526 that Caan had played a bigger role in the
paybacks. Although the disciplinary actions included temporary suspensions of
a few weeks, none of those disciplined lost their jobs.

For CSFB, the quick settlement cut short the probe and removed the threat
to its franchise. Although the actions of Quattrone's brokers had put him under
a harsh spotlight, he had come through with an endorsement from Mack and
command over a smaller but still healthy empire.

ELIOT SPITZER

36

THOUGH IT HAD BEEN a year and a half since the Internet bubble had begun to burst, the aftershocks were still being felt. In December 2001, Enron Corporation became the biggest U.S. corporate bankruptcy in history. A number of press accounts noted that few securities analysts had been skeptical of the energy company or its stock before Enron blew up.

The finances of several telecommunications companies began to unravel in a bust that paralleled that of Internet stocks; projections of runaway demand weren't materializing for them either. By March 2002, the SEC was probing questionable accounting at Global Crossing Ltd., Qwest Communications Inc., and WorldCom Inc. And star telecom analyst Jack Grubman was taken to task for his bullish ratings on stocks of many telecom companies that were investment banking clients of his employer, Citigroup, including all three of those.

As the economy weakened based partly on aftereffects of the 9/11 terrorist attacks, the stock market began a new slide. The NASDAQ composite, which had already sunk below 1,700 before September 11, 2001, had actually bounced back above 2,000 in December 2001. Throughout 2002, as scandal after scandal emerged, it plunged anew, finally hitting a low of 1,114.11 in October 2002.

○

Around the end of 2001, Hamilton "Tony" James contacted Quattrone. The patrician-looking James, a longtime DLJ banker who was now cohead of investment banking at CSFB, had a request to make. With the markets down and banking business off, he was concerned about the size of the investment banking bonus pool. By comparison, the Quattrone tech group was still swimming in money.

After the markets had weakened in late 2000, Quattrone had agreed to absorb one hundred DLJ tech staffers at no cost to him. Now James asked Quattrone to do him a favor and absorb some costs, taking $3 million out of the tech bonus pool so James could pay others more. Even without the money, the tech group would still be making far more than others. It would be good for the firm, James said. Quattrone could be a team player and help James out of a tight spot. James said he would make it up to Quattrone at a later date.

Quattrone refused.

O

One event that would affect Quattrone's fate profoundly occurred on April 8, 2002, and it had nothing to do with CSFB. New York attorney general Eliot Spitzer released the results of a ten-month investigation into research at Merrill Lynch.

Spitzer was a balding, jut-jawed politician who resembled Fearless Fosdick in the Dick Tracy comics. The son of a New York real estate developer, he had a silver-spoon upbringing that included private school at Horace Mann, Princeton and Harvard Law School, and a stint in the Manhattan district attorney's office.

The office he had won in 1998 had been a backwater whose occupants had more often pursued small-time investment scams instead of the biggest firms on Wall Street. But Spitzer had an entrepreneurial spark, driven by political ambition, and a fearless self-confidence based partly on his family wealth.

The lack of fear was all the more valuable because the national regulators at the SEC and elsewhere were, to a degree, captives of a closed system. They would often serve three to six years at the agency before switching sides and joining a private firm where they earned far more serving and protecting Wall Street. The system didn't encourage breaking too much glass.

While Merrill was an also-ran in technology banking, it boasted the largest number of brokers serving individual investors of any U.S. securities firm. It also had an Internet analyst, Henry Blodget, who had become a media darling for correctly predicting Amazon's stocks' rocket-ship rise in 1998. Blodget had left Merrill after earning $12 million in 2001. He had appeared on TV 123 times during the bubble.[1]

In an affidavit before a New York State judge, Spitzer deputy Eric R. Dinallo asked for an order barring Merrill from issuing new research without disclosing its efforts to win investment banking fees from the companies, and info about the distribution of buy and sell ratings.

If Spitzer was a New York mandarin, Dinallo had a quirkier background. The son of a California TV writer and producer for *Knight Rider* and *Walker Texas Ranger*, Dinallo had an undergraduate degree from Vassar, a master's in public policy from Duke, and a law degree from New York University. Like Spitzer he had worked as a prosecutor for the Manhattan district attorney.

Together he and Spitzer were about to point out that the emperor had no clothes.

Dinallo's filing charged that Merrill had "failed to disclose to the public" that its stock ratings "were tarnished by an undisclosed conflict of interest," namely that analysts were shaping their research "for the purpose of attracting and keeping investment banking clients." The analysts' buy, hold, and sell ratings, therefore, "were neither objective nor independent," as Merrill had purported them to be.[2]

Spitzer and Dinallo had dusted off an obscure section of the New York State general business law, known as the Martin Act, which authorized the attorney general to investigate sales of securities, and prohibited "fraud, misrepresentation, deception, concealment" and other misconduct.

Although Merrill had five different stock ratings from buy to sell, Dinallo noted that Blodget and a junior analyst, Kirsten Campbell, testified that Merrill had never assigned the two lowest ratings, "reduce" and sell, to any Internet stock from spring 1999 to autumn 2001. Instead, they merely stopped rating stocks they no longer favored.

Thus, at the same time that the Merrill Internet analysts were describing some of the stocks in private e-mails as "going a lot lower," or "crap," or "a dog," they never issued ratings lower than "neutral." For example, Dinallo said, on October 5, 2000, Blodget said in an e-mail that the stock of Internet Capital Group Inc., a banking client then at $12.38 a share, was "going to 5." The next day he said privately, "there really is no floor to the stock." Despite these private views, Merrill still gave ICG the intermediate rating "accumulate," and a long-term buy.

To show how banking considerations influenced research coverage and ratings, Dinallo cited an e-mail exchange between Blodget and Sofia Ghachem, another Merrill Internet analyst who reported to Blodget. On October 4, 2000, Ghachem told Blodget, "part of the reason we didn't highlight [a particular risk] is because we wanted to protect ICG's banking business." Yet Merrill had publicly stated that its analysts were "unbiased and objective."

"What we have seen is very, very troubling," Spitzer told the *Wall Street Journal*'s Charles Gasparino. "This is a fundamental deception of the public to place buy recommendations on stocks that the firm knew weren't good investments that were triggered by an ulterior motive of helping the company get investment banking clients."[3] Dinallo's thirty-eight-page affidavit was accompanied by a fat volume of exhibits, including the e-mails.

For twenty-four hours, Merrill stoutly fought the charges, defending itself and denying wrongdoing. "There is no basis for the allegations," Merrill said. The firm was "confident that a fair review of the facts will show that Merrill Lynch has conducted its research with independence and integrity."[4]

However, Merrill beat a hasty retreat the next day. It couldn't risk the imminent threat of criminal charges—a potential death sentence for a financial firm. Instead of hand-to-hand combat and a detailed daily defense, Merrill switched to "no comment." Within days the firm began negotiations to attempt to settle the matter.

It was ironic that Merrill was singled out. The firm's tech banking effort had been pathetically weak during the bubble. An otherwise top firm that ranked number three in stock underwriting in 1999, Merrill had ranked a lowly number nine in Internet IPOs. That very weakness was one reason Merrill had tried to lean on the telegenic Blodget to lure more business.

The Spitzer charges electrified Wall Street. They also humiliated the SEC and NASD, neither of which had spotlighted analysts' conflicts. Worse, the regulators had known of and indulgently accepted them. As one longtime senior regulator put it, they were like salesmen at car dealerships. Of course they were biased! Everyone knew that!

As Merrill and Spitzer attempted to negotiate a settlement, Spitzer at first sought a complete separation of research and banking by Merrill, in a spin-off of its research unit. Merrill Lynch refused, and insisted it couldn't accept such a draconian step if it meant being put at a disadvantage to other securities firms.

The national regulators couldn't sit back and let Spitzer reshape such an important part of how Wall Street operated. Republicans in Congress were already warning about the "balkanization" of securities regulation.

So, in late April, the SEC, the NASD, and the New York Stock Exchange and other state securities regulators joined Spitzer in an industrywide, multiagency research probe of the top ten firms on Wall Street. They would repeat for the others what Spitzer had done with Merrill—a search of their bubble-era e-mails and other documents, to be followed by new rules to reduce the influence of banking on research.[5]

Each major firm, they decided, would be looked at by both a national and a state regulator. At the time, the firms expected to get the closest looks were Citigroup, home of Jack Grubman, and Morgan Stanley, home of Meeker. Like Merrill, both of those firms also had big armies of more than ten thousand brokers, and thus their actions could have harmed more individual investors.

Without a star analyst like a Blodget, Grubman, or Meeker, or a comparable army of brokers serving average investors, it initially seemed that CSFB was barely a blip on the radar screen.

On May 22, 2002, Merrill agreed with Spitzer to pay $100 million to settle the research case, the same amount CSFB had paid to settle the IPOs-and-commissions probe. The firm issued a limited statement of contrition. Republican congressmen groused that Spitzer was dictating rules for national markets by threatening Wall Street with criminal charges. They had a point, but Spitzer had put SEC chairman Harvey Pitt and the other national regulators too far on the defensive for them to resist.

When a group of state regulators met in Washington, the Massachusetts regulators under William Galvin, secretary of the commonwealth, were led by Matthew Nestor, head of the office's securities division. The Massachusetts regulators didn't just draw CSFB because its name had the word "Boston" in its title. They wanted a ripe target.

The Massachusetts staffers had Googled CSFB and found a *Fortune* article in September 2001 focusing on the Quattrone group, then under scrutiny in the IPO probe. As they read the article, they understood there had been some tension over the organization's structure, and some "possible crossing of the line."

The other state regulators knew Spitzer had scored big by unearthing the damning Blodget e-mails. So the group sought a computer system to do e-mail searches. But as the search for a system dragged on, the Massachusetts staff grew impatient, and decided to work by hand. They hired fifteen students from nearby Suffolk University Law School to work part-time at twelve dollars an hour, put them in a conference room with a few computers at an office near the statehouse, handed them computer disks, and told them to start reading.

The first subpoena they sent to CSFB was overly broad and ultimately unproductive. So they decided to focus on the technology group, where they knew Quattrone had overseen both research and banking. Massachusetts then subpoenaed all of the e-mails to and from Quattrone and all of the analysts within his group.

At that point, they found Erach Desai's e-mail discussing the "unwritten rules for tech research." Brodsky's fears about how the e-mail would look to outsiders had come true. When they tried to contact Desai, the regulators were pleasantly surprised to learn that he lived quite close by in Hingham, Massachusetts, on the South Shore about fifteen miles from downtown Boston.

○

Erach Desai was vacationing in Nantucket over the Fourth of July weekend in 2002 when he got a message on his home voice mail to call the Massachusetts regulators. At first he feared that there might be some problem with the new independent research firm he had launched in December 2001, soon after leaving CSFB.

When he got home and returned the call to securities division lawyer Maura Looney, he was elated at what he heard. They wanted to ask him about his e-mail. When Desai received a subpoena, CSFB's lawyers offered to represent him. But Desai declined the offer. Once he had written the e-mail, he realized that he might never again work at a big securities firm that did substantial underwriting business. So he wasn't concerned about jeopardizing his future in that arena by testifying freely—without coaching.

The Massachusetts regulators also contacted former Quattrone Internet analyst Lise Buyer. She had appeared on January 24, 2002, in a *Frontline* documentary entitled *Dot.Con*, produced for the Public Broadcasting System, about the tech bubble and the IPO investigation. In those *Frontline* comments, Buyer had spoken candidly about the pressure on analysts to speak favorably about mergers their firm had worked on, or IPOs the firm had taken public.

"Analysts would often appear on TV," the *Frontline* narrator said, "and Lise Buyer admits they were under pressure to issue positive news to keep their clients happy." Then Buyer came on-screen to say, "If your firm has done banking work for a client, it's understood that the analyst is not going to come out and say, 'Bad idea. Stay away from this.'"[6]

Nestor and the Massachusetts team made plans to fly out to California to interview Buyer, but their flight was canceled due to bad weather. When they finally spoke to her on the phone, with a CSFB-paid lawyer listening in, the results were underwhelming. They had understood her *Frontline* remarks to be an indictment of a rotten system. Yet what she said on the phone that day was much less scathing.

But then Buyer called back the next day—without the lawyer on the line—with a follow-up thought. *The question you want to ask*, she said, *is who has the ability to hire and fire you?* The ability to set pay, she indicated, was another key issue. Without saying so explicitly, she was pointing the finger at Quattrone deputy Bill Brady, who had had that power during the bubble.

O

At 10:00 A.M. on the morning of September 5, 2002, Desai appeared at the seventeenth floor of the state office building in Boston. He testified under oath, with his personal lawyer, Jonathan M. Feigenbaum, present, for four and a half hours. The state investigators, Maura Looney and Bryan Lantagne, the latter the division's chief of enforcement, first walked Desai through his background, how he had come to work at CSFB, and then through the episodes described in his May 2001 "unwritten rules" memo.[7]

Desai told the regulators how he had been recruited to the tech group after becoming one of the top analysts in his sector as measured by *Institutional Investor* magazine. Tech banker Tony Trousset had asked him to meet Hodge at a bar in Palo Alto. "It was very chummy, friendly, get to know each other, you know, what have you done in the business, etcetera," Desai said.

Desai gave the investigators numerous examples of how he believed his research objectivity had been compromised by bankers or banking considerations, including Cadence, Parametric, and Synopsys. The state regulators realized that Desai had an interest in portraying the system as he did, because he had founded his own independent research firm. Yet they also appreciated his willingness to be candid and forthcoming.

As Desai spoke, he made clear that he believed that the perception within the CSFB tech group that he wasn't banking-friendly had not only cost him the chance to cover the higher profile semiconductor sector, but also ultimately his job.

Lantagne asked, "Then some time in October [2001] you were told your employment was being terminated?"

"Correct."

"And did you foresee that coming?"

"I wasn't totally surprised."

"And did you believe it was based in part or in any way on this e-mail?"

"This e-mail, the May?"

"Yes."

"First of all, I think my feeling is that my termination was done under the umbrella of a layoff, which is convenient, but B, raising these issues may have been a factor in it clearly, but in the end the potential banking business spoke louder than anything else."

Lantagne asked, "Had you been willing to change your strategy with Synopsis, had you been more banking friendly, do you believe you would have been terminated?"

"I don't believe so."

Looney asked him about a "Friends of Frank fund," which had been the subject of a few newspaper articles, but Desai knew little of the inner workings of the brokers who worked with Quattrone.

"Can you give me in your professional judgment why, if you can, officers and directors of these companies would be given the benefit of getting into these IPOs?" Looney asked.

"This is just opinion," Desai replied. "I mean, I don't see how it is very different from a bribe."[8]

SPINNING

37

AS THE NATIONAL and state regulators dug into their investigations of the top ten firms on Wall Street in mid-2002, the stock market continued falling as the bubble-era scandals multiplied and morphed in ways that spelled more trouble for Quattrone.

In June 2002 WorldCom Inc. disclosed that it had overstated its past earnings by $3.85 billion, setting a record in that category, just as Enron had become the biggest bankruptcy. WorldCom soon followed Enron into bankruptcy court. And executives of both companies were eventually charged with criminal fraud. The disclosures by WorldCom turned up the heat on Citigroup's star telecom analyst, Jack Grubman, who had been a vocal WorldCom supporter, and was even then already getting his version of the Blodget treatment by the Spitzer team.

In early July, two members of Congress asked Citigroup, WorldCom's lead banker, for information on whether the financial services firm had allocated hot IPOs to WorldCom executives. At a congressional hearing a few days earlier, Grubman had been asked a similar question by Pennsylvania Democrat Paul Kanjorski.

Their questions were prompted by a lawsuit by a former broker from Citigroup's Salomon Smith Barney securities unit, David Chacon. He charged that his former firm had allocated hot IPOs to several executives of investment banking clients, including former WorldCom CEO Bernard Ebbers, former Qwest Communications International Inc. CEO Joseph Nacchio, and executives of three other companies.[1]

Five years after the first *Wall Street Journal* article had introduced the mechanics of spinning, the wreckage of WorldCom and the Chacon lawsuit had put the topic back on the radar screen. And that ultimately led back to Quattrone.

O

In April 2002, Michael Grunwald had filed an arbitration claim against CSFB, alleging wrongful termination and defamation, and seeking $38 million in damages. Despite the firm's assertion that he had violated company policy, he said his firing "was actually the product of CSFB's plan and desire to designate a 'scapegoat' in response to a flurry of regulatory and criminal investigations directed at CSFB's widespread practices" in allocating IPOs to hedge funds and other customers.[2] The case was later settled; terms weren't discussed.

On July 11, 2002, John Schmidt sued CSFB and Quattrone in state court in San Francisco, charging he, too, had been made a scapegoat in the IPO probe. CSFB had fired the three members of his group in an effort "to divert attention from the fact that its practice of demanding kickbacks was endemic at the senior levels in New York. Thus CSFB created a 'rogue operator' strategy to attempt to insulate the firm and divert attention [of regulators] from its own misconduct." Quattrone, had concurred, agreed, and approved of the damage-control strategy, Schmidt said.[3] Schmidt's case eventually went to arbitration, where he received a seven-figure award from the firm for defamation in mid-2006, according to Graham LippSmith, one of his lawyers.

In August, the NASD fined Coleman and Ehinger, who had developed the "New Issue Performance Report," two hundred thousand dollars apiece, and suspended them for sixty days, for their roles in the IPO kickback case. The NASD also imposed one-year suspensions and thirty thousand dollars fines against Schmidt, Grunwald, and the two junior brokers for failing to testify promptly in the case. (Their delay had occurred while the case was a possible criminal matter, and they had wanted to avoid self-incrimination.[4])

But others who had received warnings of possible NASD charges—including Commesso, Girimonti, Hatfield, and McQuade—weren't charged. Nor did regulators ever charge Schmidt, Grunwald, Bushley, or Brown with profit-sharing violations.

It wasn't lost on Schmidt and Grunwald that the responsible New York executives, Coleman and Ehinger, still had their jobs, while they had been hung out to dry. Someone in New York had gone to bat for Coleman and Ehinger, Schmidt believed. But Quattrone, it seemed, hadn't gone to bat for them.

The NASD was the national regulator assigned to investigate and draw up charges against CSFB in the global research probe. The NASD staff decided to include IPO spinning in their investigation, as did the regulators looking at Citigroup.

The NASD soon recalled Grunwald and Schmidt to ask about spinning, less than a year after they had been interviewed about commission paybacks. On September 17, in Los Angeles, Grunwald told Ozag and an NASD attorney the discretionary accounts for banking clients had been set up to build the group's long-term brokerage business—not necessarily to win more banking deals.

In that case, Ozag asked, why had they focused on banking clients? Grunwald recalled that at Morgan Stanley, he had had to make "cold calls to companies and you had to get in the door and tough it out. It was a much longer process." At First Boston, "we had a familiar client base happy with Credit Suisse . . . and we have the ability to call them and say, 'we can help you out in this one area.'"

Grunwald said he hadn't gotten the sense that the discretionary account holders had been favoring CSFB in banking assignments because they received hot IPOs. Ozag asked, jokingly, if the account holders ever offered to return the money. Grunwald's answer indicated that Ozag's background as a Capitol Hill police officer had become known among his quarry. "Never heard that," Grunwald said. "Have you? You were a policeman. No."

They asked Grunwald what Quattrone had meant when he said he wanted the brokers to be "strategic" with the discretionary accounts. Was it about building their business or winning more banking fees? Grunwald said Quattrone hadn't talked about investment banking business with him. "I never had Frank say, 'We just made $4 million from this client; you better take care of him.' That never happened. And so I just would never think that way. Maybe he thinks that; and I am sure he can tell you."[5]

But when they interviewed Schmidt in Los Angeles the next day, he readily acknowledged that one goal of the accounts was getting more banking business. And unlike Grunwald and soon Quattrone, Schmidt said that he understood the word "strategic" to mean "individuals who are likely to be the decision makers in the overall relationship with the firm."

Schmidt's version seemed to be damaging to Quattrone. Schmidt, who had run the program, said they wanted to open accounts for "the individuals who were most likely to take advantage of the various products and services that not only our group could bring to them, but who were also likely to have an expanded relationship with Credit Suisse First Boston, whether it was an m&a transaction, whether it was a debt transaction."

And just as some trading accounts had been cut off, some Friends of Frank account holders were cut out as well. Individuals whose IPO never made it to market or who never expanded their use of other First Boston services, Schmidt said, "were typically the ones that were moved down the list and slowly phased out." If someone was to be cut off, Schmidt said, he would typically check with Quattrone or Brady.[6]

That same month, *The Wall Street Journal* published three articles describing the scope of the Friends of Frank program, including a profile of Grunwald, estimates of the number of account holders, and e-mails in which Quattrone had pressed CSFB executives in New York for more IPO shares. The account holders mentioned included David Ranhoff, then president of Credence Systems, a semiconductor testing concern in Fremont, California, and Dennis Wolf, the former CFO of Credence.[7]

In a front-page *Wall Street Journal* article on September 23, 2002, Ranhoff and Wolf said they didn't realize the accounts were special perks available only to executives who could steer banking business to CSFB. The *Journal* account also cited Alan Black and Alain Rossman of Phone.com, Gary Betty, the CEO of Earthlink Inc., and Martin Brauns, CEO of Interwoven.[8]

The regulatory heat on spinning intensified. On September 30, 2002, Spitzer sued the five executives named in the Chacon complaint against Citigroup, led by former WorldCom CEO Bernard Ebbers and Qwest CEO Joseph Nacchio, to recover $28 million in profits they had garnered from hot IPOs they had received from Citigroup.

Meanwhile, the stock market's meltdown continued into the fall. As a sign of how bad things were getting, Credit Suisse Group CEO Lukas Muhlemann himself lost his job in mid-September, based on the missteps of acquiring Winterthur insurance in 1997 and DLJ in 2000—which had left the parent company overexposed to the market. Mack was given the role of co-CEO.

○

That summer the NASD had unearthed the Quattrone e-mail with the subject line, "Time to clean up those files." The NASD enforcement staff, led by Barry Goldsmith, realized the e-mail had been sent smack in the middle of the IPO commission probe. Goldsmith and the NASD's Gary Carleton thought that any document destruction done in response to the e-mail could violate the rule that securities firms must keep business records and make them available for at least two years.

Indeed, missing e-mails had been a recurring problem at a number of securities firms in the global research probe. In July 2002, the regulators had notified six firms—not including CSFB—that they were to be fined for failure to keep e-mails under the record-keeping rules.[9]

At that point, however, the regulators were unaware that Brodsky had given Quattrone a heads-up on the grand jury subpoena via e-mail and phone in the two days before he sent the e-mail. The Brodsky-Quattrone e-mails hadn't been produced to the investigators because they were considered privileged attorney-client communications. And after Gary Lynch joined the firm, Brodsky himself had left CSFB in April 2002.

○

The three sets of investigators probing the IPO commissions in 2000 and 2001 hadn't ever interviewed Quattrone. Massachusetts had tried and failed to get his testimony in mid-2002. On October 1, 2002, the NASD became the first regulator to interview him. The subject of his first appearance at the NASD's Washington headquarters was research.

Early in the interview NASD lawyer Gary Carleton asked Quattrone about the e-mails that had urged the tech group members to clean up their files in December 2000. He asked about the document retention policy calling for "elimination from the files" of some paperwork.[10]

"I knew that the firm had a document retention policy at the time, I'm not sure of what my understanding of it was in terms of the specifics," Quattrone answered. "I just replied to [Char's e-mail] and forwarded it to the same people who had already gotten it from Mr. Char." He himself hadn't cleaned up any files, he said, because "I didn't have any transaction files."

When asked how his bankers went about seeking business, Quattrone said he began with what he jokingly called "a modest objective." His group "had a mission to make the group the number one supplier of investment banking services to the technology industry." That meant "we wanted to cover companies in every sector of technology, whether it was computers or semi-conductors, software what have you . . . from the very largest companies in their sector to some of the smaller, more promising private companies."

Research coverage was often crucial in the choice of an investment bank, Quattrone said. When VMWare chose a bank to lead its IPO, it was due to the commitment of a big-name software analyst who would follow the stock. Quattrone said his analyst didn't have the same stature.

Asked about the pitch book for 724 Solutions, which promised that a CSFB analyst would "pound the table," and included the phrase "easy decision . . . strong buy," Quattrone said, "what the analyst is trying to convey is that, here's how I would tell the story to investors, and I'm very enthusiastic about it, based on what I know right now, you know. If I were to write a research report, this is what it might look like. It wasn't a commitment to provide research coverage with a strong buy rating."

And about pressing Kwatinetz to postpone exam preparations to pick up coverage on Gemstar with a big stock sale in the offing, Quattrone said, "we were told specifically by this company, as we were told by many companies, that if you don't provide research coverage, then you won't be considered for business. That doesn't mean Mike was forced to pick up research coverage or he was forced to have a specific rating."

Quattrone wasn't asked about Desai's allegations.

During a break in the research interview, Quattrone asked, *What was that all about?* Quattrone said he was surprised at the questions about the file-cleanup e-mails. Four lawyers from CSFB and four from outside law firms had helped Quattrone prepare.[11] But those e-mails hadn't come up in the prep sessions.

One of the lawyers, tech group general counsel Adrian Dollard, said he remembered the episode, and that there had been two e-mails quickly rescinding the clean-up instructions. Dollard wasn't aware of the Brodsky-Quattrone e-mails and phone call in the two days just before Quattrone had forwarded the cleanup e-mail. Dollard reminded Quattrone that no one in the tech group had been told about the investigations at that point.

Quattrone was due to appear before the NASD again two days later for the spinning probe, this time in California. On the plane ride back west, Quattrone and Dollard revisited the subject of the file cleanup e-mails. Dollard told Quattrone that as far as he could tell, Quattrone hadn't known about the grand jury subpoena at the time he had sent the e-mail. It was no big deal, Dollard told Quattrone.[12]

O

At the NASD's San Francisco office, Quattrone was confronted by none other than Joe Ozag, who had led the first IPO probe two years earlier by pursuing the anonymous tip from "A concerned citizen" about IPO kickbacks. Now he would ask Quattrone about spinning.

Despite Schmidt's testimony that the Friends of Frank accounts had been opened at least partly based on the holders' ability to direct banking business to First Boston, Quattrone denied that that was their purpose. Other firms such as Morgan Stanley, he said, had brokers in San Francisco who worked closely with technology executives and other people who happened to be investment banking clients. So did the regional boutiques, he added.[13]

Quattrone said that he and Schmidt had worked to address any possible concerns that the accounts "would be considered spinning," and that Schmidt had told him of "guidelines that he put in place specifically to avoid any impropriety or appearance of impropriety." They included the quarter-million-dollar account minimum, trading in securities other than IPOs, receiving all IPOs and not just hot IPOs, and "modest" allocations.

"Were you ever told that hot IPOs were allocated to discretionary accounts to encourage the account holder to do investment banking business with CSFB?" Ozag asked. "Certainly not," Quattrone replied.

"Did you ever get the sense that was happening?"

"Absolutely not," Quattrone said. "That I would remember because I think that practice of spinning is despicable. And I have been on record as saying that from the very first *Wall Street Journal* article that was written about it. I think the words I used were smarmy. And when you work as long as I have to develop a reputation for ethics and integrity and you achieve some degree of success, the last thing you would ever want to do is compromise that integrity or damage that reputation."

Schmidt's charter had been to build a successful brokerage and asset-management business, and "to be aligned with coverage of companies we were covering on the investment banking side," Quattrone said. But he said he knew of no effort to limit the accounts to CEOs and CFOs, and couldn't recall using the word "strategic" to describe who should get them. What guidelines had he given Schmidt for opening new accounts? "I'm not sure I remember any specifics of conversations related to your question," Quattrone said.

Asked about the system used to rank the accounts, Quattrone said he wasn't involved with the ranking process, and said he wasn't sure that "a person's position" was necessarily relevant. "As I look down at this list there are some CFOs ranked at 1 and some CEOs ranked as number 3. It doesn't seem like it has much correlation," he said.

Quattrone was then shown an e-mail from Grunwald seeking input from him and others for the rankings: "Please rank our list and your list by priority 1, 2 or 3, and we will distribute stock accordingly. Example: CEO 1, CFO 2 etc., 1 receiving the highest allocation." NASD lawyer Steve Kaufman asked, "Does that refresh your recollection as to how the accounts were ranked?"

"No, it doesn't," Quattrone replied. "I think he was using an example of one way in which it might have been ranked. But that doesn't refresh my memory on whether it was in fact used to rank."

Then Ozag asked Quattrone if he was aware that his brokers had routinely sold one third to one half of the accounts' IPO allocations on the first day of trading. No, he wasn't, Quattrone answered. Then Ozag returned to the *Journal* article. "You were quoted specifically," Ozag said, "as saying, [about spinning] 'at its extreme, an IPO is priced Wednesday. Thursday morning you call 25 venture capitalists and say, quote, 'by the way X, Y, Z just went public at 15, it's now trading at 30. You just sold the allocation at 29-and-a-half. I hope you're happy. That to me is smarmy.'"

After Quattrone confirmed he had been quoted accurately, Ozag asked him whether he knew for sure that the pattern he had described as smarmy hadn't in fact occurred in the discretionary accounts. "I don't know what was happening in the discretionary accounts," Quattrone replied. "I didn't see trade runs. I didn't see account information. I didn't review opening or closing of accounts. It wasn't my responsibility. The supervisor responsibilities for that were to John Schmidt and to Andy Benjamin."

Shown the e-mail in which he had urged Schmidt and Grunwald to be "strategic" in opening new accounts, Quattrone said he was only referring to the brokerage group's long-term business strategy of concentrating brokerage services on the technology sector.

○

Once they had assembled their best e-mails and testimony, the Massachusetts regulators were ready to roll by late October with their own set of civil
fraud charges alleging biased research in Quattrone's group at CSFB. The
national regulators wanted Massachusetts to wait, so that charges could be
brought against all the major Wall Street firms at once. Lynch, the CSFB
general counsel, also urged delay, pending an industrywide global settlement.[14]

Nevertheless, William F. Galvin, secretary of the Commonwealth, and the
enforcement staff of the securities division filed the civil fraud complaint on
October 21, 2002. Signed by Matthew Nestor, head of the securities division,
Lantagne, and Looney, the complaint echoed the Spitzer research charges
against Merrill—and spotlighted Quattrone's group.

The brief twenty-page complaint mainly summarized the contents of eighteen exhibits, most of them e-mail strings. "Contrary to the role of an independent research analyst, which is to make objective and informed judgments
about companies based on publicly available information, the research analysts
in the Global Technology Group ('Tech Group') at CSFB worked for and were
controlled by investment banking personnel of CSFB. This reporting structure
and complete control resulted in investment banking exerting undue influence
on the research analyst to give favorable ratings to companies for which CSFB
had done or hoped to do investment banking work."

Near the end, the Massachusetts complaint mentioned "improper IPO allocations." It explained, without qualification, that "individuals affiliated with investment banking deals were bribed with allocations of shares in hot tech IPOs
in exchange for bringing investment banking business to CSFB." The complaint didn't charge CSFB with spinning or even use the word, but it was referring to the Friends of Frank accounts.[15]

The Massachusetts regulators referred the raw material they had unearthed
to Spitzer, in case he wanted to pursue any of it as a criminal matter.

○

On November 22, the coalition of state and federal regulators proposed a fine
of $250 million against CSFB, the second largest penalty among all the Wall
Street firms, behind only Citigroup. On November 25, CSFB hit back at the
Massachusetts complaint, saying it was "riddled with factual mistakes and
flatly incorrect descriptions of documentary evidence . . . that fails to establish
any wrongdoing whatsoever."[16]

CSFB kept fighting when the e-mail from Quattrone to analyst Brent Thill
surfaced in which Quattrone asked him, as he launched coverage of Agile Software, what had CSFB "extracted from them on banking side to get this coverage?" CSFB noted that industry rules didn't bar securities firms from promising

research coverage as part of an investment banking relationship, as long as favorable coverage wasn't promised.

But on November 27, 2002, Massachusetts Commonwealth secretary Galvin
responded by noting that Quattrone's use of the word extracted "shows an element of coercion that's implied that's very troubling." He said the public should
have known that the research might have been "tainted" by the effort to extract
banking business.[17]

In early December, CSFB general counsel Gary Lynch was given personal
responsibility for CSFB research analysts.

Confronted with proposed fines and charges, lawyers for the ten major Wall
Street firms continued wrangling with the regulators. At a meeting in December at the New York Stock Exchange, CSFB's Lynch expressed outrage that
CSFB would have to pay up—again—over research and spinning, after paying
$100 million in the first IPO commission probe. *Why?* Lynch protested. "How
about this?" the NASD's Gary Carleton answered, showing Lynch the Quattrone file-cleanup e-mail. Lynch, who spoke with authority as the preeminent
former SEC enforcement chief, waved it off. "This is done every day on Wall
Street," he said.[18]

As they hashed out charges against the Wall Street firms, the regulators
determined that CSFB would be one of only three, along with Citigroup and
Merrill, that would be accused of fraudulent research. Likewise only Citigroup
and CSFB would be accused of spinning. Citigroup was fined $400 million, and
CSFB and Merrill were fined $200 million.[19] The regulators and Wall Street
firms announced a tentative global settlement just before Christmas. But the
final bill of particulars for each firm wouldn't be made public for another four
months.

The regulators also targeted a few individuals. They brought civil actions
charging Grubman with fraudulent research, and Blodget with aiding and
abetting research fraud. Grubman and Blodget were both barred permanently
from the securities industry, and agreed to pay fines of $15 million and $4 million, respectively.[20] Regulators never found e-mails from Meeker at odds with
her published views; she was, some said, "a true believer."

But Quattrone chose to fight the proposed charges against him instead of
settling like Grubman and Blodget and risking a permanent ban. The NASD
didn't always win. Morgan Stanley, for example, had beaten NASD charges
that it had used inappropriate tactics in marketing risky bond funds to retirees,
the case Purcell had complained to Glauber about.[21] With the legal and financial resources at his command, Quattrone had a fighting chance.

Meanwhile, Spitzer's staff, led by criminal division chief Peter Pope, was still
investigating possible criminal charges against Quattrone based on the material referred by Massachusetts. A graduate of the Phillips Exeter prep school in

New England, Harvard University, and Yale law, Pope typified the East Coast establishment that Quattrone and his clients enjoyed challenging.

The Spitzer staffers drew up a diagram that showed how CSFB bankers won business by conferring benefits on clients that included favorable research and hot IPOs. The diagram had the words "agent of client corp." in the middle with a circle around it, connected by lines showing how "CSFB investment bankers" had directed the use of research and IPOs.

As they considered the material from Massachusetts, the Spitzer prosecutors were struck by the tone of the RIM e-mails sent by Quattrone. They knew favorable research could be a carrot to win banking fees. But they hadn't realized the extent to which withholding research could be used as a stick. When they looked at the Friends of Frank accounts and IPO payback commissions, it was a tempting criminal case.

The Spitzer staffers, led by Pope and Michele Hirshman, the first deputy attorney general, contacted the federal prosecutors, led by criminal division chief Karen Seymour and U.S. Attorney James Comey, to let them know they might be going forward with a criminal case against Quattrone. Peikin and Anders were consulted as well.

The meetings between the two organizations were cordial and cooperative enough, but some of the federal prosecutors were seething. Spitzer had already shown up the SEC in research; Harvey Pitt had actually resigned as SEC chairman in November 2002. Now Spitzer was about to show up the federal prosecutors as well, by bringing a case built partly on acts they had declined to prosecute!

As they investigated the Quattrone group, a group of five Spitzer staffers led by Kevin Suttlehan, Spitzer's deputy bureau chief of criminal prosecutions, made two trips to California. During the first they used the element of surprise by showing up unannounced at subjects' offices and homes in Silicon Valley, hoping to gain interviews before the people phoned their lawyers. Some of those they sought to interview were holders of Friends of Frank accounts.

Suttlehan also interviewed Schmidt and Grunwald, separately, about Quattrone. Schmidt attended a session in New York voluntarily with his lawyer, Richard Marmaro, of Proskauer Rose LLP, in the same downtown conference room that had once been used by TheGlobe.com during the bubble.

Suttlehan was a veteran of narcotics and money-laundering cases at the Manhattan district attorney's office. One lawyer in the case jokingly called him un-subtle-han. During the interview with Schmidt, his tone darkened frighteningly. Outside on the street afterward, Schmidt's lawyer, Marmaro, turned to his client. *You know what that was like?* Marmaro said. *One of those blind dates where you think everything is going great, you like each other, and you go and kiss the girl good night and she spits in your face!*

For weeks afterward, Schmidt was jumpy. Every time his home phone rang, he imagined it would be news that he was being indicted.

O

To be sure, the fraud charges against Blodget of Merrill and Grubman of Citigroup related to bullish research reports they issued that were contrary to some of the more bearish views the analysts had expressed privately around the same time. Quattrone of course wasn't an analyst and didn't actually write research reports himself, and so was at least one step removed from any such allegations. None of the regulators ever asserted that he knew specific reports were biased to favor clients. But his shared oversight of the analysts whose research the regulators later questioned, and of the brokers who created the Friends of Frank accounts, put him more squarely in the regulatory crosshairs. (Quattrone vehemently denied all such claims, and bridled at any comparison with the disgraced analysts.)

All across Wall Street, the hounds of five sets of regulators were in full pursuit of a wide array of bubble-related misdeeds. They were scouring tens of thousands of e-mails. In pursuit of Quattrone, they were literally knocking on doors in Silicon Valley, looking for Friends of Frank who would testify against the technology banker.

OBSTRUCTION

38

BY THE END of January 2003, the regulators were drawing up charges of spinning and fraudulent research against CSFB, most of them based on the actions of Quattrone's analysts and brokers. The NASD, working on comparable charges against Quattrone personally, met with his lawyers in mid-January to give them a preview so they could respond. At the same time, Spitzer's criminal investigators were eyeing some of the same actions, combined with those of the Schmidt brokers in the year-old IPO profit-sharing matter, as a possible criminal case.

To say the least, the different agencies weren't all working together harmoniously. Each had different pieces of the puzzle. More than one of the regulators had obtained Quattrone's e-mail endorsing Char's advice entitled, "Time to clean up those files."

But the actual e-mail had never been made public. That was about to change on the afternoon of January 29, 2003.

That day, two newspapers, *The New York Post* and *The Wall Street Journal*, were both preparing to publish its contents. The reporters called Jeanmarie McFadden, a CSFB spokeswoman, asking whether Quattrone had known about the IPO probe when he sent the e-mail, and whether any documents had been destroyed as a result.

McFadden learned that the e-mails by Char and Quattrone had been promptly rescinded by follow-up e-mails on December 6 and December 7. In the middle of the afternoon, Ms. McFadden contacted Gary Lynch, the CSFB general counsel. As he checked out what had happened, Lynch was told that no one in the tech group was aware of the broader regulatory investigations at the time the e-mails went out.[1]

McFadden, an accomplished and forceful PR veteran who had worked with Mack at Morgan Stanley in the 1990s, clearly wanted to put the best possible face on the incident. And so CSFB prepared a strong statement denying wrong-doing. It said the firm's document policies complied with all laws and regulations, and that CSFB had taken "appropriate steps to ensure that all relevant documents would be preserved and provided to regulators. We strongly believe that CSFB's employees acted appropriately in this matter."[2]

Before the statement was issued, Lynch decided to try to reach Quattrone and discuss it with him personally, to confirm what was going to be said. At 6:00 P.M., Lynch and another CSFB lawyer, Patrick Patalino, got on the phone with Quattrone.[3]

Lynch began by offering Quattrone the chance to issue a personal statement through the CSFB PR department if he wanted. Lynch then told him that CSFB was going to issue a statement expressing support for him and Char, and saying that CSFB believed they had acted appropriately. Before CSFB did so, Lynch said, he wanted to confirm with Quattrone what he had been told—namely, that he, Quattrone, in particular hadn't been aware of the regulatory investigations at the time that he sent his December 5, 2000, e-mail.

Before the call with Lynch began, Quattrone had been sent a string of e-mails, starting with Char's and his own, that culminated with the e-mails rescinding their advice. These e-mails didn't show that he had just been informed of the IPO probes, because they didn't include the December 3, 2000, e-mails from Brodsky that were covered by attorney-client privilege.

Quattrone confirmed to Lynch that he hadn't been aware of the investigations. He suggested that Lynch check with Adrian Dollard, the tech group general counsel, to reconfirm that neither Quattrone nor anyone else in the tech group was aware of the broader IPO probes.

At his first trial, Quattrone said that when Lynch had called him, at 3:00 P.M. California time, he had been at home in bed under heavy medication with pneumonia, and had been awakened from a deep sleep by his wife, Denise, to take the call. He had made a mistake in replying to Lynch, he said, because his memory had been incorrectly conditioned by his talks with Dollard in October 2002, the e-mail string he had been sent that afternoon, and what Lynch had told him about the tech group's lack of knowledge.[4]

But when Quattrone read the stories in both the *Journal* and the *Post* the next day, he noticed that neither story said he didn't know about the investigation when he sent the e-mail. That morning, Thursday, January 30, 2003, Quattrone e-mailed McFadden. "Neither article mentions that we had not been informed of the investigation prior to when the e-mails were sent," he said. "Could you please confirm they were backgrounded on that fact and chose to ignore it?"[5]

O

When Peikin and Anders read the articles about the Quattrone e-mail telling employees to clean up their files, they were surprised, to say the least. Unlike some of the other regulators, the federal prosecutors hadn't seen the Quattrone e-mail before.

When Peikin read the *Journal* article about the Quattrone e-mail entitled "Time to clean up those files," he went back to his desktop computer. He still had a copy of the grand jury subpoena saved electronically, and he checked the date: November 21, 2000. That was just before Quattrone's December 5, 2000, e-mail. Peikin had signed all eight of the subpoenas himself. He couldn't believe the timing: Just two weeks after his firm was slapped with a grand jury subpoena, Quattrone advised his employees to destroy files.

Picking up the phone, Peikin called Carey Dunne, the lead partner at Davis Polk under Fiske who had overseen the firm's work for CSFB on the original IPO kickback case. Peikin asked Dunne: Did Char and Quattrone know about the grand jury subpoena when they sent their e-mails? He also asked whether any documents had been destroyed as a result. Dunne replied, *Our information is they didn't know.*

Peikin told Dunne that his office, the Manhattan federal securities fraud unit, wanted to take a look at that question. He suggested that Dunne and Davis Polk take a crack at it for openers. And Peikin demanded that all communications to and from Quattrone and Char be produced, including any of their communications with lawyers.

Technically, Peikin was asking that CSFB set aside any protection for Quattrone's right to communicate confidentially with the firm's lawyers. He asked CSFB to waive attorney-client privilege and produce all responsive e-mails and other communications, including those labeled "privileged and highly confidential," as the Quattrone-Brodsky e-mails had been.

Government concerns about document destruction had intensified in the wake of the Enron blowup. In June 2002, Enron's auditor, Arthur Andersen, was found guilty of criminal obstruction over the shredding of Enron documents, which had quickly sunk Andersen as a firm. An official government list of factors influencing whether companies could be charged with obstruction prominently included whether they would waive attorney-client privilege as part of their cooperation with government investigators. Dunne had to check with Lynch first, but he believed he couldn't say no.

Davis Polk maintained a massive database of CSFB's e-mails, and it didn't take the lawyers long to find those between Brodsky and Quattrone on December 3, 2000. The next day, early Friday afternoon, January 31, Dunne had Lynch pulled out of a meeting. "Gary, you're not going to like what I'm about to tell you." Lynch muttered an expletive.[6] Dunne informed him of the existence of the Brodsky-Quattrone e-mails about the grand-jury subpoenas and the IPO probe.

Dunne, who had just assured Peikin that Quattrone didn't know of the probe, called Peikin back frantically that afternoon. *Don't rely on anything I said,* Dunne told him. Lynch called some of the regulators at the NASD and Spitzer's office to give them a heads-up as well, then convened a meeting of CSFB's top brass on the twenty-seventh floor where Mack worked.

The executives spent the weekend investigating before making a decision about Quattrone.[7] On Sunday, Lynch and another official called Dollard, the CSFB tech group attorney. They told him that Quattrone had in fact known about the criminal IPO probe when he forwarded Char's e-mail, and they asked Dollard to find out which other people in the group had known at the time as well.[8]

On Monday morning February 3, 2003, CSFB put Quattrone on administrative leave, pending its own investigation of the e-mails. The firm's announcement cited new questions about Quattrone's response in assuring CSFB officials the week before that he hadn't been aware of the probe when he sent the file-cleanup e-mail. It also cited questions about whether Quattrone had in fact acted appropriately in resending the Char e-mail, and in allowing Char to send it in the first place.

Finally, CSFB stuck to its insistence that the firm itself had acted appropriately, even if Quattrone hadn't. After the e-mails by Char and Quattrone, CSFB said, "the firm's legal department acted promptly to ensure that all relevant documents would be preserved and provided to authorities."

That day, Lynch and Dunne went downtown to St. Andrew's Plaza to turn over the e-mails to the prosecutors. Quattrone issued his own statement: "I did nothing wrong. I am confident that the investigation will show that." And his leave was duly noted as a milestone. On CNBC-TV, reporter David Faber called it "the end of an era." Quattrone, he said, had been "the most productive technology banker ever." In 1999 and 2000, Faber added, CSFB had done more Internet and technology IPOs than any other firm.

The production of the Brodsky-Quattrone e-mails touched off a new competitive scramble among the regulators. The Spitzer New York State team promptly added a possible obstruction charge as a fourth leg of its case, which already encompassed research conflicts, IPO spinning, and IPO commission paybacks. But Peikin and Anders also launched their own federal investigation into whether their original IPO kickback probe had been obstructed by Quattrone's e-mail as well.

Quattrone now hired a criminal lawyer, John Keker of San Francisco, a raspy-voiced Marine platoon leader in Vietnam whose left arm swung in a way that showed the effects of a war injury. His defense team also included Howard Heiss and Carl ("Chip") Loewenson of Morrison & Foerster. Quattrone's sidekick Brady retained Reid Weingarten, who also represented WorldCom CEO Bernard Ebbers in battling criminal fraud charges.

In mid-February, both the state and federal prosecutors interviewed Brodsky, who became the star witness against Quattrone in the obstruction case. Initially, Brodsky told investigators that all routine document destruction had been suspended—worsening the possible obstruction in the prosecutors' eyes. He was under the impression at the time that a broad "do-not-destroy" notice had gone out when Char and Quattrone had sent their e-mails. Only later did he remember that the notice was limited to two IPOs, VA Linux and Selectica.[9]

The federal prosecutors were also interested in Char. The timing of his December 4, 2000, e-mail, only a day after Quattrone had been told about the grand jury probe by Brodsky, was obviously suspicious. Had Quattrone somehow gotten word to him about the grand jury? Or had one of Quattrone's people suggested to Char that he send out his December 4 e-mail? Interviewed by prosecutors in February, Char maintained that the timing of his own e-mail had been an innocent coincidence, and he was never charged.

On February 13, Quattrone's lawyers responded to the NASD's notice of possible research oversight and spinning violations. They protested that the proposed charges "bear a striking resemblance to the reform proposals that have arisen from the industrywide settlement negotiations," and weren't based on rules in effect during the bubble. "For the NASD to scapegoat Quattrone, apparently based on his success and fame and not on any actual evidence of misconduct, is neither justifiable nor fair."[10]

The NASD had never applied its ban on "gifts and gratuities" to IPO allocations, Quattrone's lawyers said. The firm's own legal staff had audited the tech brokers' IPO allocations in fall 1999 and left them in place. The allocations were supposed to have been supervised by CSFB New York, the lawyers added.

When Quattrone had urged the brokers to be "strategic" in allocating IPOs, the lawyers said, he was only referring to the strategic goal of building the brokerage business. The evidence didn't show he permitted the brokers to allocate based on the client's ability to direct future banking business.

As for research oversight, any flaws in allowing analysts to report to bankers were CSFB management's fault, not his, the Quattrone lawyers said. "It is both unprecedented and unfair," they said, "to hold an individual, as opposed to a firm, responsible for alleged deficiencies in a firm's chosen structure." It wasn't until May 2002, they said, that the NASD barred bankers from supervising or controlling analysts.

Responding to some of the research specifics, the Quattrone lawyers said the firm had continued to publish research on Aether despite his threat to "drop coverage" if CSFB didn't win the lead on the Aether stock sale. Analyst Kiggen hadn't been pressured to keep a high rating on Digital Impact, nor had Hodge pressured Desai to give Numerical a strong buy. And they denied Quattrone had done anything wrong in urging Kwatinetz to launch coverage of Gemstar.

Nevertheless, on March 6, the NASD charged Quattrone with spinning violations in connection with the Friends of Frank program, and with "undermining research objectivity" by "creating and overseeing a flawed organizational structure," in which analysts reported to bankers. NASD also charged Quattrone with failure to testify about whether his December 5 e-mail was meant to encourage colleagues to destroy documents after he had been notified of the IPO probes.[11]

Quattrone hadn't testified again before the NASD once the obstruction probe began, based on Keker's advice to avoid testimony that could be used against him at a criminal trial. When the NASD barred Quattrone for life for failing to testify, a bar later overturned, Keker displayed a contempt for the regulators in his glass-chewing Marine Corps tough-guy style: "Sanctimonious bastards. Piling on, trying to self aggrandize their little agency."[12]

The following day, in a story evidently timed to heighten the impact of the NASD charges, the *San Jose Mercury News* printed a jaw-dropping list of sixty-three Friends of Frank account holders by name, including the total cost and number of the IPOs they had received, and their first-day profits.

At the top of the list were the CEO and CFO of Ascend, which CSFB had advised on its $20 billion merger in 1999. The next two were the cofounders of Autoweb.com, Farhang and Payam Zamani, who received fifty-six and thirty-eight IPOs respectively, which CSFB had taken public in 1999. The "Merc," Quattrone's hometown newspaper, became one of the most vocal critics against what it later called the greed and venality of the Friends of Frank accounts.[13] But the Friends of Frank themselves, the account holders who received the IPOs, weren't ever charged.

Quattrone officially resigned from CSFB when the charges were brought. Most major firms required employees who didn't or couldn't cooperate with regulators to resign. But one of Quattrone's lawyers, Howard Heiss, said in a statement: "The NASD charges are completely without merit and represent an unprecedented attempt to take punitive action against an individual for conduct that was legal at the time and widespread throughout the industry."

O

A month had passed since the Quattrone e-mail had surfaced in *The Wall Street Journal* and *The New York Post*. For the federal prosecutors, the personal aspect of the situation was unavoidable. Peikin and Anders were investigating whether

Quattrone had obstructed a probe they themselves had conducted. Letting it stand would have been like letting him thumb his nose publicly at them. Yet as late as early March, the Spitzer prosecutors were considering a criminal obstruction charge as well.

James Comey, the U.S. attorney for the Southern District of New York, the politically smooth boss of Peikin and Anders, tried to dissuade Spitzer from making a race of it. *I don't care what you do,* Comey told Spitzer. *If we find obstruction, we're going to charge it—even if you do it first.* Federal charges could preempt the state's. Spitzer eventually ceded the obstruction case to Comey, and handed over the other material his staff and the Massachusetts regulators had turned up, such as the RIM e-mails.

As they weighed whether to bring the obstruction charge, the federal prosecutors knew the case was thin—a single e-mail with only circumstantial evidence of criminal intent. But the market was at its postbubble lows. There was a rising tide of investor and voter outrage at the corporate scandals that had surfaced. Comey found it significant that Quattrone had begun drafting the e-mail, then completed it the next day—indicating he had time to think about it overnight.

As is customary, the Quattrone lawyers had a chance to make a presentation to prosecutors in early April, before the final decision. In addition to Keker and Heiss, the Quattrone team also included Elliott Peters, a partner of Keker's who had once worked in the office next door to Comey's when they were both assistant U.S. attorneys. Quattrone, they said, was merely endorsing Char's e-mail in a frenetic bout of rapid-fire e-mailing, didn't know the files contained documents being sought in the probe, and had a long history of compliance.

On April 23, 2003, Comey charged Quattrone with two counts of obstruction and one count of witness tampering. Noting that regulators don't have the resources to execute search warrants personally when they investigate, Comey said, "we often rely on voluntary compliance" by businesses with subpoenas. "It is an honor system, but one that must and will be guarded with an iron fist." The indictment listed eight separate occasions between May 2000 and December 2000 when Quattrone had been contacted about the IPO probe. Quattrone made a brief court appearance and was released; Keker asked for a speedy trial.

The feisty Keker came out swinging at the government. "Only prosecutors who see the world through dirty windows would take a one-sentence e-mail supporting company policy and try to turn it into a federal criminal case," said Keker, who had prosecuted Oliver North in the Iran-Contra scandal and also represented former Enron chief financial officer Andrew Fastow.

Keker battled Comey on the PR front as well. At his news conference, Comey had said Quattrone had urged "subordinates to clean out their files, despite the fact that he knew that a grand jury and the SEC had asked for documents that were in those files." Yet Keker said one prosecutor had conceded in a phone call that there wasn't any evidence to show that Quattrone knew the subpoenas' contents.[14]

But Quattrone and Keker got a bad break when the first judge assigned to the case recused herself without giving a reason. Her replacement, Richard Owen, was regarded as one of the most government-friendly judges in the district. Having him on the bench, one journalist later wrote, "is like having another prosecutor" in the courtroom.[15]

O

Six days after the indictment, on April 28, 2003, the regulatory coalition led by Spitzer unveiled specific civil charges in the global research settlement. Although Quattrone wasn't party to the settlement, and Credit Suisse like the nine other banks neither admitted nor denied wrongdoing, many of the charges against CSFB related to conduct by Quattrone and his group. The SEC noted that CSFB's investment banking revenue had risen from $1.47 billion in 1997 to $3.68 billion, "fueled primarily by the technology sector offerings completed under Quattrone's leadership."

CSFB was charged with issuing fraudulent research on two companies, Digital Impact and Synopsys, both of which involved Quattrone clients and analysts; Synopsys was based on Desai's testimony. Digital Impact was based on a Quattrone banker pressuring an analyst not to drop coverage on a banking client. And CSFB was charged with issuing exaggerated research on four other stocks, two of them tech group clients. The latter were Numerical, based on Desai's testimony, and Agilent, based on one tech analyst's account of what he had called "the Agilent two-step."

The global settlement also slammed CSFB for spinning in the PCS tech group, handing out hot IPOs to corporate executives based on their ability to steer future banking business to CSFB. Without mentioning the phrase Friends of Frank, the complaint said executives of Egreetings, El Sitio, Next Level Commnications, Phone.com, and iPrint.com received profits on hot IPOs of $585,000 to $1.3 million each over periods of twelve to seventeen months.

The headline of the first section of charges said "The Supervisory Structure of CSFB's Technology Group Created Conflicts of Interest for Equity Research Analysts and There was Insufficient Supervision of the Technology PCS Group." The SEC charges mentioned Quattrone two dozen times, and noted that, until his arrival in mid-1998, "no equity research analysts were supervised by or had any reporting obligations to anyone in any investment banking department."[16]

After being investigated for more than three years for IPO kickbacks, spinning, biased research, and finally obstruction, Quattrone was no longer the Teflon banker. The full weight of the bubble's aftermath was bearing down on him.

JUDGMENT

BOOK
FOUR

THE COURTHOUSE STEPS

39

THE FIRST CRIMINAL trial of Frank Quattrone took place in the same courtroom where Julius and Ethel Rosenberg were convicted of spying for the Soviet Union in 1951. The ceremonial courtroom on the main floor of 40 Foley Square, an imposing stone building with long, wide steps, had thirty-foot ceilings, yet had an intimacy because it could seat only about 110 on seven rows of wooden benches.

Quattrone was the most prominent Wall Street banker to face a criminal trial in forty years, since J. Truman Bidwell, the former chairman of the New York Stock Exchange, was acquitted on federal tax evasion charges in 1963. The once mighty junk bond king Michael Milken had agreed to plead guilty to six felonies in 1990, and appeared in court for a lengthy sentencing hearing. But Milken never faced a jury charged with deciding his guilt or innocence.

There were striking similarities between the two. Both Milken and Quattrone had operated quasi-independent fiefdoms in California, far from their home offices in New York. They both had financed upstart competitors who challenged the status quo. Milken had financed 1980s corporate raiders who launched hostile takeovers of established companies, or had accepted above-market greenmail payments for their shares. He also bankrolled upstarts that became giants, such as MCI Communications Corporation and News Corporation. Just as Quattrone had offered hot IPOs to corporate executives who could give him business, Milken had offered warrants or equity kickers to money managers who invested in the junk bonds sold by his operation. And supporters called both financiers scapegoats for their eras' excesses. Some wanted to see Quattrone's prosecution, like Milken's, as a kind of East Coast establishment retribution against a scrappy California pioneer.

T. J. Rodgers, chief executive at Cypress Semiconductor, accused CSFB of cowardice for throwing Quattrone to the wolves: "Quattrone's real crime is that he violated the 'Bill Gates law'—his competence made him too much money too fast. Big, new money creates resentment among some, and there's always a prosecutor . . . ready to move up the food chain to 'protect America.' "[1]

Quattrone's prosecution was "a travesty of justice," Rodgers said later. "What did he do for my company? His group raised $1.6 billion. I built plants in Minnesota and hired people. I built plants in Texas and grew Cypress up and did it with money that came from investors through that banking firm."[2]

There was no question that the criminal trial reflected some measure of political backlash against those who had operated the bubble-making machinery that produced such epic investor losses. Even Quattrone's critics questioned why the banker was being tried for the e-mail and not his practices in research or his Friends of Frank program.

Indeed, the timing of the criminal charges coincided with a broad regulatory crackdown on Wall Street conduct during the dot-com era. A full three years had passed since the paroxysm of stock market frenzy had peaked in March 2000, and the market remained near its postbubble low.

The obstruction case was Quattrone's fourth scrape with regulators. In 2000 and 2001 the commission paybacks in exchange for hot IPOs were investigated, with Quattrone's brokers heavily involved. In 2002, Spitzer-led allegations of industry-wide biased research and spinning, practices in which Quattrone and his firm had also pushed the envelope, resulted in massive fines. The crescendo in early 2003 was the allegation that Quattrone had personally urged document destruction just days after an update about the first IPO probe.

The witch-hunt view wasn't universal. "Quattrone insists he's innocent, and who knows, maybe we'll learn that he is," said author John Heilemann after the indictment, in a June 1, 2003, article entitled "The Sacrificial Lion," in *Business 2.0*, a new-economy publication. "But the system that he helped devise and profited so handsomely from has, in a way, already been proven guilty. It has undermined confidence in the fairness of the public markets, convincing people, with good reason, that during the Internet era, the game was rigged so insiders would profit while everyone else got taken to the cleaners."[3]

By this logic, the trial Quattrone now faced was a proxy for the rigged system Heilemann described. Other Wall Street players—from research analysts to investment bankers—faced civil charges for their actions during the bubble. But Quattrone and his empire had operated at the red-hot center of the dot-com mania. He thus embodied the entire market's rise and fall. And so his day of judgment became a referendum of sorts on the kind of conduct that had taken place across all of Wall Street.

The twenty-two-page criminal complaint, dated April 22, 2003, charged Quattrone with three felonies. The first two were for obstructing the grand jury probe of IPO kickbacks and the related probes by the SEC and the NASD.

The third charged Quattrone with impairing the availability of evidence, which became witness tampering at the trial.

The prosecutors sketched out Quattrone's role as a powerful leader of a major IPO underwriter. They explained how CSFB's document-retention policy called for employees to get rid of old files, with one important exception: if the firm was sued or received a subpoena for those files. And they laid out the timetable under which CSFB and Quattrone had been asked for documents related to the IPO probes.

There were two key pieces of evidence showing that at the time he encouraged his staff to destroy old documents Quattrone had just received communications about the IPO investigation. The first was the e-mail exchange on December 3, 2000, when Brodsky told him about the grand jury phase of the IPO probe. The second was Brodsky's warning, in a phone call on December 5, that Quattrone needed to retain his own counsel in the IPO case.

The charge quoted Quattrone's endorsement e-mail on December 5, 2000, in its entirety: "having been a key witness in a securities litigation case in south texas (miniscribe), I strongly advise you to follow these procedures." To show the e-mail had had real impact, the criminal charge listed examples of employees who had either destroyed documents in response, or who had sent such instructions to others.

O

On May 27, 2003, Quattrone made his first appearance before Judge Richard Owen. After he exited the elevator, he paused to confer with his legal team before entering the small courtroom Judge Owen used for his routine cases. Wearing a double-breasted blue suit, a light blue shirt, and a red tie, Quattrone seemed impassive and glassy-eyed. The fabled charm and sense of humor were nowhere to be seen.

More than three years after the excesses of the bubble had begun to subside, it seemed incredible to see one of the foremost masters of the Wall Street universe forced to submit to such routine minutiae of the justice system. His immobility made him seem like a fish after a session with the taxidermist.

Just before prosecutors and his lawyers debated the best start date for the trial, Quattrone spoke in a barely audible voice. All he said was: "I'm innocent."[4]

He was more animated by the time the trial actually began.

As eighty jury candidates filed into the courtroom just before 11:00 A.M. on September 29, 2003, Quattrone—in a blue blazer, blue shirt, red tie, and tan slacks—turned around to his right and smiled, searching their faces, eager to make eye contact.

The case was simple enough. Would twelve jurors chosen at random agree beyond a reasonable doubt that Quattrone wanted files wrongfully destroyed in the absence of evidence showing that that was actually his intent and not just an innocent plea to clean up their in-boxes? It seemed like a long shot. Yet federal prosecutors convey such authority just by showing up that they win the vast majority of their cases.

Judge Owen, age eighty-one, a short, bespectacled man with a frequent squint and a shock of thinning white hair, displayed a kindly demeanor toward the jurors. A Quaker who carried a gun outside the courtroom (he had presided over a big mob trial in the 1980s), he wrote operas in his spare time. But his flinty side emerged as he tangled with the lead defense lawyer, John Keker, who had a deep, raspy voice like former senator Bob Dole's.

The atmosphere was generally subdued throughout the marble-floored courthouse. Spectators queued up for a daily trip through a metal detector. Then they had to check their cell phones with court officers before proceeding down a long, wide corridor past a half dozen pay phones in old-fashioned wood booths before entering the hushed, carpeted courtroom.

Quattrone had a small but staunch group of family members present, who generally sat in the front row on the left as the spectators faced the judge. They included his mother, Rose, her husband, Walter Schulke, and his younger sister, Mary Ann. Quattrone's personal lawyer, Ken Hausman, and his wife attended daily, as did Boutros and his wife, Danielle.

Also often on hand were Brady and other tech group members such as banker Ethan Topper and former research chief Elliott Rogers. In addition to a legal team of seven or more lawyers and additional support staff, Quattrone also fielded a public relations team of Bob Chlopak and an assistant. The courtroom was also a magnet for Wall Street lawyers: Spectators included some of CSFB's outside lawyers from Davis Polk plus a dozen or so lawyers for witnesses and other interested Wall Street firms.

During breaks, a generally genial Quattrone would often greet his friends with smiles, hugs, and claps on the back. One of the junior staffers from Keker's firm would carry a bag containing plastic bottles of Poland Spring water for the legal team, Quattrone, and his family. The second morning, Quattrone gently informed one friend that he was sitting in the rows reserved for the jury pool.

Beyond the gate of a light-wood railing, in the well of the courtroom, prosecutors Peikin and Anders sat at the front table closest to the judge. With them were FBI agent Kathleen Queally and Adam Forkner, a paralegal. At the defense table behind them, farther from the judge, sat Quattrone, Keker, two other defense lawyers, and jury consultant Julie Blackman.

After just a day and a half of questioning, a jury of six men and six women was selected.

The prosecutors had a tough nut to crack: get into Frank Quattrone's head and prove that he meant to obstruct justice, namely, the regulatory probes that touched on his group. They needed to educate the jurors in the technicalities of the Wall Street underwriting process so they could see how seriously the IPO kickback probes could have hurt Quattrone's business, thus establishing his motive to destroy evidence.

The main difficulty for the prosecution was that there was no smoking gun showing that Quattrone intended to obstruct the probes; he had never told or written anyone that this was his goal. The entire case was purely circumstantial, based on the sequence of e-mails and nothing more. Still, it was a plausible story. Would the jury buy it?

○

Day one. Just before 3:00 P.M. on Tuesday, September 30, Peikin rose to begin the government's opening statement. Pale and lanky, Peikin wore the prosecutors' government-issue drab gray suit. But he had a wolfish grin the jury seldom saw. "Good afternoon, ladies and gentlemen," he began.

"This case is about a criminal scheme to obstruct justice and destroy evidence. It's about how a powerful and successful Wall Street investment banker tried to interfere with federal investigations, investigations that were looking to see whether his business violated the laws that protect investors in the stock market." Pointing out Quattrone at the defense table, Peikin said that the banker was worried that the IPO probe threatened his business and reputation, and thus told hundreds of people to "clean out their files before federal investigators got a chance to see what was inside of them. He told hundreds of people to destroy evidence." Although the effort didn't get very far, he said, "it got far enough to be a serious federal crime."

Peikin then paused to introduce himself before launching into an overview of the case. CSFB was "one of the most important financial institutions in the world," he explained, and Quattrone was "one of the most senior, one of the most important, and one of the most powerful executives at CSFB." CSFB's public offering of VA Linux, he said, was "the hottest in the history of Wall Street."

The prosecutor explained that CSFB's document retention policy barred destruction of documents under subpoena. He noted that Quattrone had been one of the first at CSFB to learn about the NASD probe, and had also been told he might be called as a witness. The defendant knew, Peikin said, that investigators were "interested in examining his business, the business of the tech group, and wanted to examine and collect the IPO documents that they created."

Then Peikin walked the jurors through the chain of actions over the two-day period during which the obstruction allegedly occurred. He displayed Brodsky's first e-mail to Quattrone on December 3, 2000, alerting him to "some recent developments that are of extreme concern." He then itemized what Quattrone had learned from Brodsky that day about the investigation, then said Quattrone had soon been "presented with an opportunity . . . to interfere with and obstruct" the probes.

The prosecution then showed tech group paperwork boss Richard Char's first e-mail the next day, on December 4, 2000. With many tech IPOs in the tank, Char had suggested the staff be urged to "catch up on file cleanup" before an expected burst of investor lawsuits. Char's e-mail, Peikin recalled, concluded jokingly, "'Today, it's administrative housekeeping. In January, it could be improper destruction of evidence.'"

Peikin said, "Now, when Frank Quattrone got the e-mail you just saw, he had a choice." Knowing what he did about the three IPO investigations and the documents being sought, "he could easily have decided not to give his approval to Mr. Char to send this e-mail. But Frank Quattrone chose another path. A path that violated the law and a path that would eventually lead up the steps to this courthouse and into this very courtroom."

Displaying Quattrone's first reply—"You shouldn't make jokes like that on e-mail"—Peikin said that by that comment, Quattrone had "told Mr. Char that it was okay to send out this memo, but that he should sanitize it by taking out—"

Keker cut in. "Excuse me, your honor. I'd say that's a little argumentative and I would object on that ground," he drawled.

"It's overruled," Judge Owen replied.

"—taking out the references to improper destruction of evidence," Peikin continued. "And that's exactly what Mr. Char did." It didn't stop there, Peikin said. Quattrone "made another choice. He chose to put his full weight and power of position behind this document destruction effort."

Peikin then displayed Quattrone's first draft endorsing Char's e-mail. It began, "having been a key witness in a securities litigation case in south texas (miniscribe)." But after beginning that draft, Peikin said, Quattrone had "stopped long enough to think good and hard about what he was doing."

After learning of an imminent news story about the probe, and that he should retain his own lawyer, Quattrone "turned back to the message he'd begun to draft the previous evening," Peikin said, and added the phrase, "I strongly advise you to follow these procedures."

Peikin's argument had been tightly organized, controlled and practiced. Keker now opened up with a totally different style—conversational and freewheeling, but occasionally veering toward disorganized. At one point, one of his aides displayed the wrong exhibit.

If the government prosecutors had an almost military style of dress and demeanor, Keker himself was more colorful. While the prosecutors wore blue or gray, he often wore jackets of olive green or brown. His raspy drawl could sound like a drill-instructor's bark. And after tangling repeatedly with the judge, his air of defiance grew to resemble that of a sailor returning to the ship after liberty call on a Saturday night.

After a quick introduction, Keker quickly jumped back into the heart of the prosecution case, displaying the first Quattrone response to Char's draft e-mail. "I'm pulling this back because what I want to do is go right back to what you've just heard was supposedly a criminal scheme. The criminal scheme that has been explained to you by the prosecutor, who is supposed to prove this case beyond a reasonable doubt, is two things.

"The first part of the criminal scheme is Mr. Quattrone on December fourth writing to a colleague saying, 'you shouldn't make jokes like that on e-mail.'" Keker pointed out that the Char-Quattrone exchange had also been sent to Adrian Dollard, the tech group general counsel, plus to Brady and Hodge, Char's boss, and had been endorsed by them.

"So point number one is, you'll have to ask yourself at the end of this case whether or not somebody [is] trying to read a lot into somebody saying, 'you shouldn't make jokes like that' on e-mail, and then turning around and calling that authorization or permission or anything else, is evidence? Or is it speculation about what's in a man's mind?"

Then Keker displayed the key Char e-mail Quattrone had re-sent by hitting "reply to all" on December 5. "If we could go to the next and last piece of the criminal scheme," he said, oozing scarcasm, "that is the e-mail of the next day," addressed to the technology banking group. All Quattrone was doing was to urge his group members to follow company policy, Keker said. "Now the government says, 'Oh, that's a criminal scheme because there were investigations going on.'"

But Keker said Quattrone never saw the actual grand jury subpoenas; he relied on the lawyers at CSFB for information about the investigations. They told Quattrone the probe was about a different part of the bank than his, about IPO allocations and extra commissions, "and that is done in parts of the bank that Mr. Quattrone doesn't control," Keker said.

Quattrone didn't have criminal intent because he merely advised employees to follow company policy, and Char was the tech banker responsible for carrying out the document policy, Keker said. If Quattrone had wanted to see documents destroyed, he could have simply allowed Char's message to stand without his endorsement.

At that point, prosecutor Peikin objected that Keker's opening was "argumentative," and Judge Owen agreed. He lectured Keker near his bench, in a sidebar conference out of the jury's earshot, that he should be using phrases like "we expect to prove," or "we come to prove." At first, Keker acquiesced. "Yes sir, I will adjust," he said.

Keker then engaged in a bit of theatrics that telegraphed his plans in advance and later appeared to have hurt his case. "You will hear from Frank Quattrone, who will tell you what was going on in this period and what he thought and what he understood so that you can better—you will get to know him as a man."

From that point on, the prosecutors knew they could leave unchallenged the defense assertions that Quattrone had little to do with IPO allocations, because they could bring it up when he took the stand. That they were hanging back on that point emboldened Keker to stake out the banker's distance from allocating IPOs as a major pillar of the defense. That meant that when it was cracked or toppled, it would hurt Quattrone's credibility all the more.

Keker then flashed slides that minimized Quattrone's power and importance within Credit Suisse Group, with its eighty thousand employees, and the CSFB banking division, with its three thousand employees. He showed a slide with the different investment banking divisions, with the technology banking division at the bottom. A "remarkable investment banker" who had worked on the IPOs of Amazon.com, Netscape, and Cisco Systems, Keker told the jury, Quattrone had "never been in any kind of trouble."

At this point Judge Owen interrupted Keker a second time, instructing the jury to "disregard that last comment."

Keker resumed, and Judge Owen interrupted him a third time.

The judge's repeated interruptions of Keker's opening statement were interpreted by some courtroom observers as an early sign of his pro-prosecution tilt.

To minimize Quattrone's alleged motive for interfering with a probe of commissions paid by hedge funds to get IPOs, Keker told how the management of IPO allocations was far removed from Quattrone's part of the bank. So were brokerage commissions, so were subpoenas, he said. Compliance with subpoenas was managed by the legal and compliance division, Keker said.

So when Quattrone "seconded" the Char e-mail, Keker said, he didn't make the connection between its contents and "an allocation commission investigation [and] a different part of the bank." On the day he sent the e-mail he was dealing with "a vast number of subjects" and "about 6:28 in the evening finally dashed off that e-mail that you have seen and that has been called a criminal scheme."

As for Brodsky's phone call to Quattrone just before the banker sent the e-mail, Keker said, the CSFB lawyer "didn't say anything about saving documents," and even after Quattrone's e-mail had gone out, CSFB treated the matter as "no big deal."

The first prosecution witness, Jeffrey Bunzel, an equity capital markets executive at CSFB, took the stand around 4:00 P.M. on September 30, 2003, to explain the various phases of the IPO allocation process. The goal was to pave the way for testimony showing how the original IPO investigation might have delved into Quattrone's part of the business—to show Quattrone's possible motive for obstructing the probes.

Day two. On Wednesday October 1, three regulators—Roger Sherman of the NASD, Caren Pennington of the SEC, and former federal prosecutor Robert Khuzami—all described their agencies' roles in the IPO kickback investigation up through December 5, 2000. All three witnesses told how their investigations could have moved in Quattrone's direction, and definitely called for documents in his group's possession.

The NASD's Sherman said the probe had begun in May 2000 with the receipt of "an anonymous tip"—the "concerned citizen" letter. Several of the twenty accounts looked at in the probe, he noted, belonged to brokers who worked with Quattrone. But Keker pushed back, getting Sherman to acknowledge that the Quattrone brokers reported to New York and not Quattrone for customer trading matters.

The SEC's Pennington explained her agency's subpoena for documents related to VA Linux and Selectica. She said that the SEC wanted to know whether the technology companies that issued the IPO shares had been told about the extra commissions the firm was receiving as compensation in the IPOs, and whether CSFB had deliberately underpriced the IPOs as a way of attracting more commission payments.

Although the regulators described their cases as they stood on December 5, 2000, they weren't allowed to divulge their outcomes, due to a pretrial ruling by the judge. The ruling generally barred testimony about events after December 5, 2000, as irrelevant to Quattrone's state of mind. Thus, the jury never heard that the Quattrone brokers were fired, a point for the prosecution. However, Keker was able to say that Quattrone was never called as a witness in the case.

O

Just before the lunch break, after the jury had left the courtroom, Keker had the first of numerous dust-ups with the judge. He had seen press commentary about how often Judge Owen had interrupted his opening, and may have wanted to serve notice that he wouldn't meekly accept such rough treatment. One of Quattrone's team later compared it to a baseball manager kicking dirt while arguing with the umpire.

Keker asked the judge for permission to show an organization chart that CSFB had eventually provided to the SEC, showing that Quattrone didn't have any supervisory role over the VA Linux and Selectica IPO allocations. Prosecutors were raising "a lot of smoke . . . by showing a very broad subpoena," but the IPO case ultimately led elsewhere within the firm, he said.

"I know," Judge Owen replied, "but I am going to have to wait on that until your case. Am I not?"

"I don't think so!" Keker suddenly shouted. His rising voice startled spectactors who had begun drifting out of the courtroom for lunch. When

Owen resisted, Keker loudly protested "the complete absence of government proof."

Judge Owen replied mildly that the case had "just started."

Day three. On Thursday, October 2, prosecutors got several CSFB legal staffers to walk the jury through the e-mail notices Quattrone had received about the investigations in June 2001 about VA Linux and in October 2001 about the Selectica allocation process.

The next prosecution witness, Kevin McCarthy, CSFB director of litigation for the Americas, explained each bit of Wall Street jargon in the Char e-mail, as well as in the Quattrone e-mail endorsing it. As the "Time to clean up those files" e-mail from Quattrone lingered on a video screen across from the jury, the group of his supporters led by Hausman and Boutros sat grim-faced and silent.

When Keker tried to show the jury e-mails in which CSFB lawyers debated when to send out a more extensive document preservation notice, Owen rejected them as irrelevant: "The issue in this trial is, what did your client know and when did he know it?"

Day four. On the morning of Friday, October 3, the prosecution offered evidence that Quattrone's directive had resulted in document destruction. Linda Jackson, a former member of Char's execution group, was asked about her response to the Char and Quattrone e-mails. "I started to clean out my files," she said.

At midmorning, the government's star witness was sworn in. The balding, gray-bearded David Brodsky was thin and distinguished looking, almost professorial. He had left CSFB in April 2002, after Lynch's arrival, and at the time of the trial was a partner at the law firm of Latham & Watkins.

David Anders, a handsome young prosecutor whose wavy black hair gave him a Frankie Avalon look, took a turn with a witness, leading Brodsky through the CSFB document retention policy. As Brodsky spoke, Anders displayed notices Quattrone had received in July and August 2000 about the NASD and SEC probes of IPO kickbacks.

Brodsky was shown the September 20, 2000, advisory that the SEC's IPO exam had been referred to enforcement, and Quattrone's e-mail asking Brodsky if it was okay to copy John Schmidt. Brodsky had answered that it was "not advisable," since both Quattrone and Schmidt were "likely" to be called as witnesses.

Anders showed Brodsky the SEC subpoena of October 18, 2000. He got Brodsky to spell out to the jury how Quattrone's e-mail urging employees to clean out their files might have deprived investigators of documents in a majority of the twelve categories listed in the subpoena. Brodsky said he had taken personal charge of the response to the criminal subpoena because of the "totally new level of danger to the franchise," one that could have put CSFB "out of business."

Then Anders presented the most damaging evidence against Quattrone. He showed e-mails that documented the briefing that Brodsky had given Quattrone on the IPO investigation by the grand jury, just two days before Quattrone sent his "time to clean up those files" e-mail.

Again and again, Brodsky described the degree to which he believed the investigation posed a direct threat to Quattrone. "Many of the IPOs that were the subject of these subpoenas had come out of the technology group personnel," he said. "So this was CSFB's business that was being threatened, but it was very largely Frank Quattrone's business that he had spent a lot of time working on, building up, potentially threatened, and I wanted him to know about it."

Brodsky's testimony dramatized the importance of the IPO probe, and thus suggested why Quattrone might have had reason to interfere. Keker objected that Brodsky's *thoughts*, which hadn't actually all been conveyed to Quattrone, were irrelevant to the banker's state of mind. But Judge Owen overruled him.

Anders then introduced a government exhibit showing Quattrone's pay for the years 1998, 1999, and 2000. For his half year at CSFB in 1998, Quattrone had received total compensation of $9.9 million. For 1999, he was paid $35.2 million. For 2000, Quattrone had received $250,000 in salary, a cash bonus of over $72 million, and stock worth over $47 million, for a total of $120.1 million.

In the courtroom, there was a buzz. What did the jurors think? How did they react? No one could tell. But Keker, who had objected unsuccessfully to Anders bringing up Quattrone's pay in the middle of Brodsky's testimony, later denounced the move to reporters outside the courtroom. Keker called the timing, just before a three-day Yom Kippur holiday, "a cheap shot" by prosecutors to keep the jury thinking about Quattrone's paycheck all weekend.

Brodsky then described his telephone contact with Quattrone on the afternoon of December 5, just before Quattrone had re-sent Char's e-mail. "I think this investigation is going to turn in the direction of getting testimony from you," Brodsky said he had told Quattrone. "And I think it's advisable for you to get a personal lawyer."

Day five. The following Tuesday morning, October 7, in a three-hour cross-examination, Keker repeatedly attacked Brodsky for taking on the responsibility of handling the grand jury subpoenas and then failing to send out a wider notice to suspend the document retention policy. If that had been done, the defense suggested, Char wouldn't have sent out his e-mail, because he would have known files couldn't be purged.

Then Keker staked out the ground Quattrone and CSFB had first claimed in May 2001 after his brokers were suspended—that he wasn't responsible for IPO allocations, and thus wouldn't have had any reason to fear the probe: "You knew, Mr. Brodsky, did you not, that Frank Quattrone was not responsible for overseeing brokerage accounts or commissions; nor was he responsible for IPO allocations?"

When Brodsky began to give a qualified answer, noting Quattrone's "supervisor relationship" over some Schmidt group functions, Keker cut him off triumphantly. He threw in his face the words that had been crafted for CSFB investment banking chief Chuck Ward in May 2001.

"Mr. Brodsky," Keker said, "have you said in the past that, 'As head of CSFB's technology group Frank Quattrone is responsible for the firm's investment banking services for technology clients. He is not involved in making decisions about IPO allocations for any accounts, or in discussions with any clients about commissions'?"

"I have," Brodsky acknowledged. "And I would . . . resay it today."

It was this defense position, so carefully established by Keker, that later appeared to backfire against Quattrone.

○

Quattrone did get one break. His involvement in the Miniscribe case, which he cited in his brief e-mail endorsement of file cleanup, was summarized only briefly. In a statement read into the record, the jurors were told that an investor's fraud complaint alleged that the company's bond prospectus had been falsified, that Quattrone had testified as Morgan Stanley's banker, and that the firm hadn't been found liable. But the summary didn't mention any questions about document destruction, much less about brick shipping.

Day six. On Wednesday, October 8, top CSFB lawyer Gary Lynch became the last prosecution witness. Tall, gray-haired, and distinguished looking, he resembled a Catholic priest, some at CSFB said. In thirteen years at the SEC, as he rose to enforcement director, he had gained fame pursuing the insider-trading cases of the 1980s. After twelve years at Davis Polk, he had been hired by CSFB CEO John Mack in mid-2001.

Lynch told of the call he got on January 29, 2003, from CSFB's public relations staffer, Jeanmarie McFadden, alerting him to the news stories being prepared about the Quattrone e-mail. When he got on the phone with Quattrone, Lynch testified, the banker confirmed that "he was not aware of the regulatory investigations at the time that he sent out his December 5 e-mail."

○

The government then rested its case after the equivalent of only about four days of testimony.

The government's case was that Brodsky had given Quattrone a thorough update on the IPO kickback probe just before the banker had been given an opportunity to encourage document destruction. But the prosecutors could only reconstruct events through e-mails and a handful of witnesses. They had no hard evidence that Quattrone had set out to undermine the investigation.

It was all a circumstantial case. Quattrone's supposed motive was that he had to protect his business and his lavish pay. He had been told enough about the case to know it could have threatened him if investigators took a hard look at the inner workings of his team. And he had known his group had raw material that investigators might have wanted to see.

QUATTRONE TAKES THE STAND

40

AFTER THE PROSECUTION rested at midmorning on Wednesday, October 8, the defense called four witnesses who attempted to put Quattrone's e-mail in an innocent context. Individually, they were each plausible. But even together, they were a sideshow. Because now the jury would be waiting to hear from Quattrone.

Richard Char, author of the "Time to clean up those files" e-mail, had joined Quattrone's tech group in 1999 after thirteen years at the Silicon Valley law firm Wilson Sonsini. As head of global execution, Char was responsible for much of the paperwork for the group's deals. With jet-black hair and Asian features, Char appeared to be in his early forties.

Char said he had drafted the file-cleanup e-mail because the group had been very busy. Tech group staffers had gone from deal to deal without closing out their files, discarding unneeded material, and sending the final deal files to the file room.

The e-mail had predicted an "all-out assault" by lawyers for investors who had lost money, and Char was asked about the joke he included in the draft: "Today it's administrative housekeeping. In January it could be improper destruction of evidence." Quattrone had scolded him for the joke, but Char said he didn't interpret that as Quattrone's permission to send the e-mail, as the prosecutors contended. Instead, he said, he had sent the e-mail on the instructions of Hodge, the senior tech banker.

On cross-examination, Char said he didn't know about the IPO investigations when he sent the e-mail, and "felt pretty stupid" once he realized it would have to be retracted. He said he knew it was "wrong" once he knew there was an investigation. The implication: If Quattrone knew about the investigation—which he did—he should have known it was wrong to send it, too.

The next defense witness, John Hodge, had a blond, California surfer look. He was the banker who, Desai had testified, had pressured the analyst to initiate coverage with a buy on Numerical, resulting in regulatory charges against CSFB of exaggerated research. And on the stand he displayed a flippant, wise-guy attitude toward the prosecutors.

Explaining the need for the file cleanup, Hodge recalled having received an e-mail from one of the office managers complaining about "boxes in the hallways." But Hodge disputed the premise of several simple prosecution questions during his cross-examination. Asked whether he and other tech group members generally followed Quattrone's instructions, he said he didn't know, or couldn't remember. "Sometimes, sometimes not!" he said, grinning at Quattrone.

The third defense witness, tech group lawyer Adrian Dollard, explained that he and other tech group members hadn't known about the IPO investigations when they first received the Char and Quattrone e-mails. Once he found out, he recalled, he had sent out a corrective e-mail himself.

Dollard also sought to explain why Quattrone had told Lynch he wasn't aware of the probes when he endorsed Char's e-mail. The e-mails had come up during Quattrone's interviews with the NASD in October 2002, he said, and after he researched the matter, he told Quattrone the tech group members hadn't known about the IPO probes at the time.

Day seven. On Thursday, October 9, 2003, the jury then heard from two defense character witnesses. Rosario "Rusty" Lamberto told of their childhood in South Philadelphia, and Russell Hall, a Stanford classmate, made a point of noting that the Hall and Quattrone families were both active in the Girl Scouts. Both of their wives were Scout leaders, he said. The testimony appeared to be an appeal to juror number twelve, Arlene Vrabel, a Girl Scouts executive in Westchester.

○

Throughout the first week and a half of the trial, Quattrone had displayed an eerie calm, a spring in his step and an upbeat manner that had defied circumstances that might have shamed or mortified others. He had nothing to be ashamed of, his bearing suggested.

Quattrone's composed demeanor was almost certainly the result of a determined effort. He was a master at salesmanship, and skillful beyond even his fellow masters of the universe at exactly the kind of presentation he would now be called on to make when he took the stand. He routinely made and won high-stakes IPO pitches for a living. His self-confidence was supreme.

His decision to testify was risky, to be sure, exposing him as it did to questioning by the prosecution. As Keker said, it gave him a chance to provide a convincing window into whether he really had criminal intentions when he sent the e-mail.

O

Before Dollard's testimony had resumed that morning, Quattrone had practiced the walk to the stand, marking off the number of steps in a careful rehearsal.
At 12:22 P.M., Keker said, "Your honor, the defense calls Frank Quattrone."

Quattrone looked bright-eyed and upbeat in his blue blazer, blue shirt, tan
slacks, and black penny loafers. "Be seated, sir, and state and spell your name
for the court reporter," said June Hummel, the deputy clerk.

"My name is Frank, F-R-A-N-K, P, as in Peter, Quattrone, Q-U-A-T-T-R-
O-N-E." His lawyer began. "I would like to direct your attention to December 4,
2000. Did there come a time that you received an e-mail from Richard Char?"
Keker asked that the e-mail exhibit be shown on the screen.

"Yes," Quattrone said.

"And on December 5, did you reply to that e-mil?

"Yes, I did."

Keker asked that Quattrone's December 5 e-mail be shown. "When you made
that reply on December 5, 2000, were you intending to obstruct an SEC investigation?"

"No, I was not."

"Were you intending to obstruct a grand jury investigation?"

"No, I was not."

"Were you intending to tamper with a witness to an SEC or grand jury investigation?"

"No, I was not."

"Mr. Quattrone, why did you send that e-mail on December 5, 2000?"

Richard Char was responsible for making sure that the technology banking
group's files "complied with the firm's document retention policy," Quattrone
said. "And I was simply seconding or encouraging people to follow the document retention policy after he did so." The e-mail he retransmitted didn't relate
to the grand jury probe he had heard about, or to the SEC investigation, Quattrone said.

As he continued from this punchy beginning, Quattrone's voice was soft but
confident, addressing his answers to the jury members on the right side of the
courtroom, making eye contact with them, moving his hands expressively as
he spoke, and drinking occasionally from a Styrofoam cup. One lawyer who
had reviewed Quattrone's e-mails, in which he sounded like an omnipotent
master of the universe, was surprised at how soft-spoken he was.

Then Quattrone engagingly told the story of his rise from the pants presser's son in South Philadelphia to his perch atop the investment banking world
in Los Altos Hills, California. Quattrone lived with his wife of twenty-three
years and their daughter. When he had joined CSFB in 1998, one hundred

people had followed him. By the peak in 2000, his group had five hundred employees.

Guided by Keker, Quattrone tried to show that he didn't have complete authority over the brokers in his group—another executive oversaw matters such as daily trading reports and "syndicate allocations." Those matters included both commissions and IPO allocations, Quattrone explained.

"Did you have any responsibility for making decisions about IPO allocations?" Keker asked.

No, Quattrone answered. Technology investment banking, he said, "had *no* responsibility for deciding IPO allocations." Records of IPO allocations and commissions were kept by the equities division, he said, not by the investment banking division.

Then Keker walked Quattrone through a series of ten notices Quattrone had received about the IPO probes by the NASD, SEC, and grand jury, leading up to the Brodsky e-mails on December 3, 2000. He considered them the province of other divisions such as equity and equity capital markets, he said.

Of course, Quattrone *had* exercised big-time influence over allocations, even if they were literally managed by other divisions. After all, his brokers had designed the Friends of Frank program, which by then had been cited by regulators for the improper spinning of hot IPOs to win banking business.

But the investigation Quattrone was on trial for obstructing concerned commission paybacks by traders, where he had exercised less direct oversight. True, three of his brokers had been fired for cutting off a few trading clients who refused to pay back 65 percent of their profits. But there was never any evidence that Quattrone knew about such practices.

Keker asked: What about the warning that Quattrone might be called as a witness by the SEC, and should avoid any appearance of trying to influence the testimony of others? "I didn't understand it," Quattrone said. "It was a lot of legal mumbo jumbo." At that point, word had spread that Quattrone was on the stand, and about twenty people were standing in the back of the courtroom.

Even when Brodsky e-mailed him around 11:00 A.M. Pacific time on Sunday, December 3, 2000, about the grand jury subpoena, Quattrone said, he didn't feel threatened, because he thought regulators were focusing on the other divisions that allocated the IPOs. The crowd in the back had grown to about thirty.

When he got Char's e-mail at about 3:00 P.M. Pacific time the following Monday, December 4, 2000, Quattrone testified, it didn't remind him of the previous day's e-mails from Brodsky because "it was about civil litigation. Didn't really mention anything about grand jury investigations or anything like that."

The disconnect Quattrone described was perfectly plausible. Char was talking about civil lawsuits by investors who had lost money. Brodsky was talking about a grand jury subpoena for a criminal investigation.

When Char had joked about "improper destruction of evidence," Quattrone explained why he had reproved him, in a way that tried to make light of his own trial. "I thought that Mr. Char was using some inappropriate language," Quattrone told the jury, "and that e-mail was a medium that lasts forever and could come back to bite you. I guess I was right about that."

Keker then asked Quattrone to explain the Miniscribe reference in his "reply-to-all" e-mail. Quattrone didn't mention shipping bricks or questions about whether Morgan Stanley had destroyed documents. Instead, he recalled, his side had won because "we had saved all of the key documents from years ago so that we were able to prove that we had done good due diligence."

Even after he got the phone call from Brodsky advising him that the investigation might move in his direction, and that he should hire his own lawyer, Quattrone said he didn't connect the grand jury probe with Char's file-cleanup e-mail. To support this, he pointed out that the lawyer he hired, Ken Hausman, was "my family attorney," and wasn't a criminal lawyer.

Keker then persuaded Judge Owen to let him show the contents of each of the twenty e-mails that Quattrone had replied to in the forty-five minutes before he forwarded the Char e-mail. Keker said the e-mails were "a very important snapshot of what's in his mind . . . what he was thinking about within minutes before and after this alleged crime."

While Keker flashed each one rapid-fire, Quattrone explained his thoughts about it in a few words and then jumped to the next. They showed he was juggling tasks, from helping collect documents for the year-end advertisement, to trying to win the mandate for the big Accenture IPO, to trying to win more business from AOL Time Warner.

The point was that his reaction to the Char e-mail was just a knee-jerk reflex. He was merely responding to the dozens of e-mails in his in-box, and gave little thought to any single one. When they got to the Char e-mail, Quattrone repeated that he hadn't intended to obstruct justice.

Day eight. The next morning, Friday, October 10, Keker questioned Quattrone for another half hour. After learning that the Char e-mail and his would have to be rescinded, he said, "it looked like people had caught it, and were going to do something about it, and so it was no big deal." The courtroom was even more packed than before, with dozens of people standing in back, awaiting the start of the cross-examination.

The last issue Keker raised for Quattrone was why he had told CSFB's top lawyer, Gary Lynch, that he didn't know the firm was being investigated when he forwarded the e-mail. The reason: He had been ill with pneumonia and awakened in bed. Further, Quattrone cited the incomplete e-mails he had received from CSFB, the phrasing of Lynch's questions, and Quattrone's own recollection of his discussion with Dollard during the break in the October 2002 NASD testimony. He had honestly forgotten the Brodsky e-mails, Quattrone said.

As the lawyers wrangled at the bench over a question Keker wanted to ask, Quattrone smiled. It was 10:45 A.M. The crowd of standees waiting in back for the cross examination to start, many of them other prosecutors, had grown to about forty.

In conclusion, Keker asked, "Did you think that following the policy, the document retention policy on December 5, would cause people to destroy subpoenaed documents?"

"Not for a minute," Quattrone replied confidently. He had been told that the investigation concerned hedge funds paying high commissions to get IPOs, which had "no relevance whatsoever between what was in the investment banking files."

Just before 11:00 A.M., Keker said, "I have no further questions." It seemed that Quattrone, at the top of his game, had delivered.

○

Viewers of TV courtroom dramas like *Perry Mason* are accustomed to expect the prosecutor to try to "break" the defendant, destroying his story so thoroughly that he confesses on the spot. That did not happen when Peikin questioned Quattrone on Friday morning October 10, 2003. Yet the confrontation was no less dramatic.

Peikin's approach was to attack the defense Keker and Quattrone had voiced most often—that because he had no oversight of IPO allocations, he wouldn't have had any reason to interfere with the IPO probe.

More shocking was the way Peikin questioned Quattrone on the stand—dropping the courtroom decorum and treating him as the criminal he was accused of being. There was anger in the way Peikin attacked Quattrone; after all, at the very least it looked like Quattrone had played it cute with an investigation Peikin and Anders had personally pursued. It probably reflected Peikin's competitive, pugnacious personality. But it also seemed aimed at persuading the jury to look past Quattrone's slick talk and carefully parsed story.

Peikin, wearing the usual government-issue gray suit and white shirt, stood at a lectern roughly twenty feet from Quattrone, who wore a gray suit, blue shirt, and red tie. As he brought up questions about specific deals or e-mails, he pulled government exhibits from two reddish accordion legal-file folders, advancing to the witness stand and placing them before Quattrone like a picador at a bullfight.

"Mr. Quattrone," he began, "yesterday on direct examination, you were asked the following question and you gave the following answer, page 1123 at line 13, by Mr. Keker. 'Question: Did you have any responsibility for making decisions about IPO allocations? Answer: No.' Do you recall that portion of your direct examination?"

"I believe so," Quattrone ventured.

"Isn't it a fact, sir, that you did participate in the process of making IPO allocations at Credit Suisse First Boston?"

"Yes."

"And your role in making IPO allocations varied from deal to deal, didn't it?"

"Yes, from nothing to something," Quattrone said.

"And in some deals you were involved, as you say, not at all, correct?"

"Correct."

"And in some deals you were quite involved in the IPO allocation process, isn't that fair to say?"

Here Quattrone drew the line. "No."

"Well, there were some deals in which you communicated information from clients about IPO allocations to the equity capital markets group, correct?"

"Yes."

"And there were some deals in which you reviewed IPO allocations that had been made on a preliminary basis before they were made final, correct?"

"It's possible that I looked at a partial list of allocations before final decisions were made, yes."

"For the purpose of reviewing them, correct?"

"I don't know for what purpose, Mr. Peikin."

"And in fact, sir, there were some IPOs that were done at Credit Suisse First Boston in which you participated in making the IPO allocation decisions, isn't that correct?"

"I might have participated in some discussions," Quattrone said in a quiet voice. "I did not make any decisions."

By the time Peikin first reached into his files for an exhibit, Quattrone's breezy self-confidence from the day before had vanished, and now a look of fear seemed to flicker across his eyes. Of course, Quattrone's brokers had routinely awarded hot IPO shares to his investment banking clients during the bubble. Now it was suddenly being thrown in his face to attack a key element of his defense.

The prosecutor showed Quattrone the August 2000 e-mails between him and the CSFB equity capital markets staffers about the debut of Screaming Media, the IPO which had tanked on its first day of trading. Peikin asked Quattrone to read the e-mail he had sent to Ernesto Cruz, the equity capital markets chief: "In the future, when a deal like this looks difficult, Bill Brady and or I should get a heads up and get involved in some of the decisions on allocations, as is the case when Fisher is running the deal."

"You can stop there," Peikin said. "Now, Mr. Quattrone, by this e-mail, you were requesting that you or Mr. Brady participate in allocation decisions, correct?"

"When a deal was very, very difficult. When there was not enough demand for it to get done."

The tone of Peikin's questions darkened. "Mr. Quattrone, just listen to the question I'm asking you. By this e-mail, you were requesting in some situations you or Mr. Brady participate in allocation decisions?"

"In some situations."

"The answer to my question is yes?"

"That's what I said."

Peikin then showed Quattrone the e-mail in July 2000 in which he told Schmidt and Grunwald that he wanted to "review specific allocations" of the Corvis IPO earmarked for the Quattrone brokers' clients. "By this e-mail, Mr. Quattrone, you requested to review specific allocations of shares in Corvis that were being made by the Tech PCS group, right?"

"Along with Andy Fisher, correct."

Then Peikin reviewed Quattrone's top-tier education, and sought to show that Quattrone had risen to the top in a competitive business. But Quattrone, apparently smarting, refused to play ball. "Is there competition among employees for a promotion?" Peikin asked.

"I don't know."

"You never experienced any competition among employees for promotions during the time you worked in investment banking?"

"How would I observe that?"

"I'm asking you a simple question. A yes or no, sir."

Quattrone asked for the question to be repeated. Then he replied, "And I said, I don't know."

Then Peikin sought to establish how powerful Quattrone was within CSFB, to support how much influence he could exercise over IPO allocations, even though that wasn't technically his job. Quattrone was the only CSFB banker with research analysts and brokers reporting to him, the banker acknowledged.

Peikin questioned Quattrone about the Tech PCS brokers, exploring how Schmidt reported to Quattrone, also with a dotted line to Andy Benjamin. And he asked whether Quattrone knew that many clients of the Schmidt brokers were executives of technology companies. Quattrone replied that he did.

"Were you aware of any colloquial name used at CSFB for these accounts?"

"I've seen it in the press," Quattrone said.

"And tell us what the name was?"

"Friends of Frank," Quattrone said.

"And the Frank's you, right?"

"I believe so."

"Mr. Schmidt used that term with you, didn't he?"

"I can't recall."

The tone of the questioning grew even nastier as Peikin confronted Quattrone with the contents of his e-mails. "Take a look at government exhibit 2061 and tell me whether that refreshes your recollection as to whether Mr. Schmidt ever used that name with you."

"He used it on this one occasion when he was telling a joke."

"I asked you whether that refreshed your recollection as to whether Mr. Schmidt ever used the name Friends of Frank in referring to the accounts maintained by the technology private client services group. Yes or no?"

"And I gave you my answer."

"I'm not sure you did, sir," Peikin said. "My question is, Does that refresh your recollection as to whether Mr. Schmidt ever used that term with you?"

"And I said that it refreshes my recollection. I will say, it refreshes my recollection that he used it on this one occasion."

It was nearly 11:30 A.M. Despite the crowd, the courtroom was completely silent. Following a midmorning recess, Peikin continued grilling Quattrone about the Friends of Frank accounts, and how he had negotiated to obtain 2 percent to 4 percent allocations of technology IPOs, which the Schmidt group brokers could allocate.

Peikin asked Quattrone to review the March 21, 2000, Grunwald e-mail listing the names of more than two hundred Friends of Frank account holders. In the e-mail, Grunwald was pushing to get more IPO shares for Quattrone's clients. When an IPO was completed, Quattrone acknowledged, the company's executives would get a chance to open an account that would get hot IPO shares.

Peikin asked Quattrone about the ranking of the Friends of Frank accounts with a number from 1 to 4. "You understood that Mr. Grunwald and Mr. Schmidt and the people in the Tech PCS group were ranking these accounts in order of their importance, right?" Yes, Quattrone said.

"The more important the person, the more IPO stock they got, right?"

"I don't think so." Quattrone's reply here matched his NASD testimony in 2002.

"You don't think so?"

"No."

"You think it was the less important the person, the more IPO stock they got?"

"I don't really know what 'important' means, or how you would define that."

Again and again, Quattrone tried to duck the effort to tie him to the IPO allocations that had triggered the regulatory charges of spinning, and which might persuade the jury that he had reason to obstruct the IPO probe.

Peikin asked whether Quattrone's strategy in steering IPOs to the Schmidt clients was that they would "think well of CSFB and perhaps direct additional investment banking business to CSFB?"

"Not exactly," Quattrone said.

Didn't Quattrone intend to "use Tech PCS to build a relationship with the executives?"

"No," Quattrone said.

"Did you ever tell anybody that you wanted to use IPO allocations in these Tech PCS groups as part of a strategy?"

"I don't recall. I might have."

"Did you ever tell anyone that part of the strategy of using these IPO allocations was to convince executives of technology companies to direct additional investment banking business toward CSFB?"

"I don't recall saying that."

Peikin showed Quattrone the e-mails from December 2000 in which Quattrone had endorsed Grunwald's push for New York to send the tech group brokers 3 percent of all IPOs.

Peikin asked Quattrone to read aloud what he had written in the exchange: "We need to do this at a minimum to accommodate the 60 new clients. We should discuss allocations, though. Want to make sure we are being strategic about this." As Quattrone spoke, some of the people in his section of the courtroom, on the left, turned around to look at the clock on the rear wall. Their faces were anxious. The entire room remained quiet.

Reviewing Quattrone's e-mail exchange with Grunwald, Peikin asked, "And you were asking Mr. Grunwald whether he could discuss allocations of new issues with you, correct?" Correct, Quattrone said. "And you said that the purpose that you wanted to discuss allocations was to ensure that you were being strategic about those allocations, right?"

"That CSFB, we, are being strategic," Quattrone answered.

After spotlighting Quattrone's effort to use IPOs to win business, Peikin stepped back to cast doubt on the larger point in his defense. "Now, Mr. Quattrone, you testified that IPO allocations were not the responsibility of the investment banking department, is that right?"

When Quattrone replied that "the investment banking division didn't make allocation decisions," Peikin asked him to confirm that the Schmidt group brokers had made such decisions. Quattrone agreed.

Peikin hammered away at Quattrone's assertion that he had little to do with doling out hot IPOs. He showed Quattrone e-mails in which he had reviewed preliminary allocations for the Corvis IPO, or asked Schmidt if they could review past and future IPO allocations. He showed Quattrone the series of e-mails with Michael Dell and Amerindo about IPO allocations.

After a lunch break, the tension seemed to ease as they slogged on through the e-mail strings, and Peikin continued his effort to tie Quattrone to allocations.

Peikin showed Quattrone the proposed Corvis allocations that included Amerindo, both of the Dell accounts, as well as Technology Crossover Ventures and Integral. "Mr. Quattrone, what we've been talking about in these e-mails is the IPO allocation process, right?" In some cases, yes, Quattrone replied. "And that's what you understood the SEC and grand jury investigations to be focused on in the year 2000, correct?"

Quattrone tried to escape the implication that he would have had reason to obstruct the investigation. "My understanding on December 4 was much narrower than that," Quattrone said. "My understanding varied in the year 2000 as to that issue."

As Peikin circled back to Quattrone's December 2000 e-mails, Quattrone acknowledged that the investigations posed a threat to CSFB's business. Then he grew punchy. When Peikin quoted from a long e-mail certifying that Quattrone had "conducted a diligent and comprehensive search" for VA Linux documents, and then asked, "right?" Quattrone said he wasn't sure what he was being asked.

"I'm sorry, your Honor. I'm fuzzing out here," Quattrone said. Owen declared a midafternoon break at 3:25 P.M.

After they came back Quattrone tried to suggest that he hadn't paid much attention to the stream of incoming notices about the IPO probe. But Peikin noted that Quattrone responded within two minutes to the notice on September 20, 2000, that the SEC's exam was being referred to enforcement, asking Brodsky if he could talk about it with Schmidt.

Peikin then mocked Quattrone's characterization of part of Brodsky's reply as "a lot of legal mumbo jumbo." Was Quattrone referring to "he and she as well as you will be called as witnesses by the SEC"? (The "he" and "she" referred to Schmidt and his assistant, and "you" was Quattrone.)

No, Quattrone said.

"So is it fair to say that the part you described as legal mumbo jumbo was the other part of the e-mail of that sentence: 'I don't want there to be any inference whatsoever that anyone was trying to influence anyone else's testimony'?"

"Correct."

"Is that the part you considered to be legal mumbo jumbo?"

"Right."

"You don't know what influencing testimony is?"

"I didn't at the time. I didn't take any meaning from that at the time. . . . I didn't understand the legal technicalities of influencing testimony."

○

The cross-examination was overwhelmingly seen as a disaster for Quattrone. One reporter, Allan Chernoff of CNNfn, said Quattrone had first said he "was really not involved," but that "evidence came out that in fact Mr. Quattrone was involved in IPO allocations." The *Financial Times* said Quattrone's admission "undermines a central pillar of his defense." *The New York Times* said Quattrone "appeared to contradict his earlier testimony, acknowledging for the first time that he participated" in IPO allocations.

Keker came in for some criticism for leaving his client so vulnerable, that they should have acknowledged Quattrone's involvement up-front. Indeed, it seemed that Peikin had fooled the defense team with a version of the "rope-a-dope" strategy boxer Muhammad Ali had employed against George Foreman. In that fight, Ali had tricked Foreman into tiring himself out by laying back passively on the ropes; then he knocked Foreman out with just a few punches. The prosecutors seemed to have tricked Keker by not challenging the repeated defense assertions that Quattrone had no responsibility for IPO allocations. Knowing he would testify, they could afford to hang back and surprise Quattrone.

But as damaging as the cross-examination seemed, it was not a knockout blow.

Day nine. When the trial resumed the following Tuesday, October 14, 2003, Peikin tried to cast doubt on another pillar of Quattrone's defense—that he wasn't very worried about the IPO probes, and thus wasn't thinking about them when he forwarded Char's e-mail.

Peikin took Quattrone through the contents of Brodsky's e-mails on December 3, 2000, and their serious implications. Brodsky had never before contacted him over a weekend, Quattrone acknowledged. Peikin read the first part of Brodsky's e-mail notifying Quattrone that CSFB had "received federal grand jury subpoenas asking for testimony and documents about the IPO allocation process."

To underscore the seriousness of this, Peikin asked if Quattrone knew what a grand jury was.

"I'm not sure I did, no," Quattrone replied.

Peikin seemed stunned. "Are you telling us that you didn't know what a grand jury was at the time you received this e-mail?" Quattrone said he didn't think he did. But he hadn't asked Brodsky what a grand jury was, Quattrone acknowledged. And he did understand the meaning of the term "criminal investigation," also used by Brodsky.

Peikin took Quattrone through the Brodsky e-mails, line by line. When he got to Brodsky's warning that "everything we say now is going to come under a microscope," Peikin sarcastically asked Quattrone if he knew what a microscope was. (He did.)

When Peikin finally got to the Char e-mails, Quattrone continued fencing with him. Peikin asked Quattrone if he realized that "it might well be illegal to destroy documents after a subpoena had been served, right?"

Quattrone replied, "If they were for documents that you were going to destroy, yes."

And when Peikin asked Quattrone whether he thought Char would have sent the e-mail if Quattrone had told him not to, Quattrone gave a flip rejoinder. "Are we dealing in the category of ifs in general?" Quattrone replied. "If the legal and compliance department had told us that the document retention policy was suspended," Quattrone said, "none of this would have happened."

When the cross-examination ended at 11:15 A.M., Keker tried to repair the damage. He asked Quattrone to explain what had been so widely interpreted as a contradiction—as he put it, "the difference between participating in the process and having responsibility for making decisions about allocations?"

He didn't make decisions, Quattrone insisted. All he did was occasionally "forward a few client requests." All the e-mails prosecutors had shown him, he said, referred to only three different IPOs—Corvis, Screaming Media, and Interwoven—out of the more than one hundred the tech group had worked on at CSFB.

O

That morning, Michael Siconolfi, the deputy editor of the Money and Investing section of *The Wall Street Journal*, visited the courtroom. There were superficial similarities between Siconolfi, then age forty-seven, and Quattrone, who turned forty-eight that day. They had similar brown mustaches. Both were Italian, aggressive, and competitive. And both were polished, engaging public speakers with charm and wit. But years of covering the securities beat had given Siconolfi a keen appreciation of how big Wall Street firms stacked the deck against the average investor.

Siconolfi and Quattrone had tangled in the past. In his 1992 exposé of how Morgan Stanley bankers had pressured analysts to write more favorable research on investment banking clients, Siconolfi had spotlighted Quattrone, saying he had "prodded" an analyst to put out "a favorable report." Quattrone had acknowledged pressing for research coverage, but denied demanding favorable comments. Siconolfi had also popularized the term spinning in a 1997 article explaining how some investment banks allocated hot IPOs to potential clients to win more financing business.

Since becoming an editor in 1999, Siconolfi had directed the *Journal*'s coverage of the postbubble regulatory crackdown against Wall Street by Spitzer, the SEC, and the NASD. His view of the world carried undeniable clout: Stories he edited about spinning and biased research were read by every top regulator in

Washington and New York. He and Quattrone had even clashed personally in June 2000 over whether the *Journal* should include Quattrone's 1999 pay level in one story.

So there was an edgy undertone as Siconolfi introduced himself to Quattrone in the courtroom aisle during a break. They had never met in person before. Quattrone smiled, the two men shook hands, and Siconolfi might have even wished the banker a happy birthday. Having broken his right hand playing basketball a few months earlier, Siconolfi suddenly found himself wincing in pain. He couldn't tell for sure. Maybe his hand was just extra sensitive because of the old injury. But it seemed to him as if Quattrone was intentionally squeezing his hand hard enough to inflict pain, all the while maintaining the even, friendly smile.

○

After lunch that Tuesday, October 14, the jury heard the start of closing arguments. Anders said there was no way a superstar banker like Quattrone could have misunderstood the seriousness of the situation. "Frank Quattrone, just like Derek Jeter, he was at the top of his game, the top of his profession. Nothing gets by them. Anyone in Frank Quattrone's position understood the significance of a grand jury subpoena on document retention, even if it wasn't spelled out for him by the lawyers."

In his own closing, Keker used a high-tech scanning device to display bites of the trial transcript on a screen. He used a chart headlined "Reasonable Doubt: Why You Know Frank Quattrone Is Not Guilty." He attacked the prosecutors, repeating his pretrial line that they "look at the world through dirty windows," seeing wrongdoing everywhere, even when it doesn't exist.

Keker also sought to blame the prosecutors for Quattrone's performance on the witness stand. He called the government effort to prove Quattrone's intent "mostly conjecture, speculation, false logic, putting together what must have been."

All that was left was a rebuttal by Peikin. Quattrone and Boutros seemed in high spirits. Smiling at each other, they each repeated a catchphrase from Keker's closing argument, "Where's the beef?"

○

In the end, at least three jurors said the prosecution had failed to make its case. One of them was Michael Roman, a silver-haired graphics designer from Ossining, New York, and father of two. He said it was up to the prosecutors to paint the whole picture. "It was like a picture of dots I had to connect," Roman said later, "and I thought a few of those dots were missing."[1]

On Friday, October 17, the jury told the judge they were deadlocked. On

Monday, October 20, Keker began making motions for a mistrial. The deliberations were then interrupted for two days by the birth of the first child of one juror, Stuart Siegel, a thirty-six-year-old software developer at IBM. On Wednesday, October 22, Judge Owen read the jurors an Allen charge designed to break deadlocks by encouraging jurors to reconsider their views.

On Friday, October 24, Siegel, a Ph.D. from Tarrytown, New York, and two others shifted their votes on counts one and three, obstruction of the grand jury and witness tampering. Siegel concluded that Quattrone "should have been aware" that the grand jury's probe could encompass documents held in his unit. That left the votes at 8–3 for conviction on counts one and three, and 6–5 for acquittal on count two. But Roman told other jurors he wouldn't change his votes under any circumstances.

When Owen declared the mistrial at 12:43 P.M. on Friday, October 24, Quattrone stood motionless, his hands clasped before him, showing no emotion as his mother and sister hugged his defense lawyers. In a statement, Keker said, "We are disappointed, because Frank Quattrone is innocent."

Quattrone had dodged a bullet. The damaging cross-examination hadn't been enough to convict him on an obviously thin, circumstantial prosecution case. Three jurors had held out till the end for acquittal. Although some observers questioned how Keker had put Quattrone on the stand, they also said that that problem was now fixable.

JUROR NUMBER 1

41

AFTER THE MISTRIAL, the prosecution and defense held talks about a settlement. But Quattrone wanted to clear his name completely and get back in the business. So there was no deal. Just as he had felt confident enough to testify in the first trial, winning the votes of three jurors despite a flawed appearance, Quattrone still felt he could ultimately prevail.

But the Quattrone team lost a bid to get a higher federal court to replace Judge Owen, citing his alleged proprosecution bias. If anything, that seemed to harden Owen's attitude toward the defense during the second trial. And that in turn prompted more loud groaning at the judge by the Quattrone side of the courtroom.

Still, because Keker and Quattrone had a chance to repair the flawed strategy of the first trial, much of the courtroom betting was that Quattrone would be acquitted or, at worst, get another hung jury. For the same reasons, the prosecutors made a decision to be more aggressive in the use of additional material against Quattrone.

○

Six months later, on Tuesday, April 13, 2004, jury selection began for the retrial. This time, jury selection was held in the much larger ceremonial courtroom of the new, modern courthouse at nearby 500 Pearl Street. To protect jurors' privacy, more of the candidate questioning took place in a conference room outside the courtroom.

One pool member, George Doty, was quickly excused after volunteering that his wife was a tech analyst at J.P. Morgan Investment Management who had purchased or followed many of the Quattrone IPO stocks, "and I have a full set of steak knives from various conferences that Mr. Quattrone sponsored in the past."

On paper, Jonathan Miller might have been an ideal juror for Quattrone.

The forty-one-year-old resident of Waccabuc, New York, was a technology entrepreneur! He had founded iClick Inc., a provider of online human resources material, in 1995. The business was sold in early 2000 to a larger company, Consumer Financial Network, a unit of iXL Enterprises Inc.

Miller didn't spell this out, but CFN was later renamed ProAct Technologies Corporation. Like many dot-coms, the stocks of both iXL and ProAct collapsed when the bubble burst. Miller had left the company in March 2004, and as the Quattrone retrial began, he had been doing consulting work with some of his former colleagues.

The father of two boys, then eight and ten years old, Miller was dark-haired, alert, and slightly nerdy looking. On the morning of Wednesday, April 14, Judge Owen began the questioning in open court. He asked the same basic questions of all prospective jurors, which are aimed at eliciting any obvious bias.

"What is your employment?" asked Judge Owen.

"I'm a business technology executive and an entrepreneur," Miller said. "I start and manage software and technology services companies. My last position, which ended at the end of the first quarter, was chief technology officer for a small, privately held software company."

Judge Owen asked whether Miller knew about IPOs or had had any involvement in them. "No, we didn't take our firm public," Miller said. "We raised several rounds of equity capital and decided to sell the firm to another privately held company instead."

"Did you know or hear anything about this case before you came into this courtroom?" the judge asked.

"Yes, I did," Miller said.

The questioning then shifted into the small conference room, where Miller faced Owen out of earshot of other prospective jurors and the public. Also jammed into the room around a rectangular table were the court reporter, Owen's two law clerks, two members of a press pool, the two prosecutors, the defense lawyers, and Quattrone himself.

Judge Owen asked Miller what he had heard about the case. Just a little bit, Miller said, adding that he believed he could be fair.

"Apart from this case itself, do you know anything about Mr. Quattrone in any way?" Judge Owen asked, at Keker's suggestion.

"No," Miller said. Could Miller decide the case solely on the evidence no matter what he might remember? I don't think I would have a problem, Miller said.

Now Keker took up the questioning himself. After getting the name of the company Miller had started, iClick, Quattrone's lawyer asked whether Miller had come into contact with investment bankers. Yes, Miller said. "And do you have views about investment bankers generally that would affect your judgment in this case?" Keker asked.

"I have opinions about their role in the process and the amount of—you know, as an equity owner and as a person who started a company, and put his own money in, and then raised more money, and put more money into my own company, *I always felt that the commissions and fees that we paid were higher than I would have liked to, and . . . I looked at the private placement agents and the investment banks as . . . necessary but not always pleasant parts of the process of building a company,*" Miller said. (Emphasis added.)

Keker quickly and lightly made a joke of the remark. "And you're probably not alone in that," he said.

Quattrone then picked up on the joke himself. "I object!" he said to Keker in mock indignation. It was obviously an unusual opportunity for Quattrone to display his charm.

As both sides tried to size Miller up, Keker turned more serious. "Mr. Quattrone is an investment banker. There will be a lot of testimony about investment banking. What we need to know is whether those views generally would affect your ability to give him a fair trial in this case."

"I don't think so," Miller said.

The defense was allowed to remove ten jurors, the government six. Neither side removed Miller. He was just too tempting to the defense. He was an Internet entrepreneur, and both Quattrone and Keker had had a chance to warm him up with a little light repartee. The first juror selected, Miller sat in seat number one.

Many of the other jurors also had white-collar jobs. They included a buildings engineer at a local university, an unemployed executive assistant, the owner of a small marketing and design company, a doorman, and a freelance television director. The six men and six women also included a receptionist at a public relations firm, a human resources employee, an office worker at a cancer research organization, an office assistant at the United Nations, a travel agent, and a radiology marketing consultant.

The last juror selected, Bryan Russo, had directed Martha Stewart's TV show, and even knew the family of CSFB chief executive John Mack from a series of what he described as "meditational weekends" that both families attended three or four times a year.

Day one. When the retrial began on Thursday morning, April 15, 2004, many of the participants followed the same script. They included Peikin's opening statement, which he repeated almost word for word from the first trial. By the time he got to the part that said "Frank Quattrone had a choice" but "chose another path, a path . . . that would eventually lead right up to the steps of this courthouse," one of the reporters present was reciting the same catchphrases under his breath.

Peikin's core argument remained that Quattrone knew that by forwarding the e-mail he might deprive the IPO investigators of documents that could have linked him to IPO allocation abuses.

A few elements changed. Quattrone wore wire-framed spectacles instead of the contact lenses he wore during the first trial. The specs gave him a nerdier look, less like a master of the universe. And the opening defense statement was made not by Keker, but by Jan Nielsen Little, a female partner of his. Little, age forty-six, was tall and thin, and often wore a subdued gray pin-striped suit. Her statement was lower key and with fewer sound bites than Keker's had had at the first trial. As she spoke, she spread her arms wide apart to show the distance between Quattrone's operation and the areas of CSFB that managed IPO allocations.

This time around, Little didn't promise the jury that Quattrone would testify. So the prosecution had to adjust to make sure the jury would hear the damaging, contradictory testimony about IPO allocations. They did so by reciting excerpts from Quattrone's testimony from his direct and cross-examinations from the first trial. Peikin played himself, minus the hostile demeanor, and Anders sat in the witness box reciting what Quattrone had said.

Unlike in the first trial, when jurors slept or wrangled over trivia, this group formed a cohesive, collegial bond. They often discussed which actors resembled the key players. Movie buff Sheldon Silver, the public relations receptionist who was himself a former actor, thought Keker resembled James Caan, and that Judge Owen looked like Jason Robards or Lionel Barrymore. He also thought Quattrone resembled Kevin Spacey, or maybe Dylan McDermott.

Miller, juror number one, kept some notes of his reactions. When Peikin stood to deliver the government opening, he reminded Miller of Sergeant Joe Friday from the old TV series *Dragnet*. Miller thought, "He is brilliant. I like him right away. He is crisp, clear and confident, without any arrogance." His remarks were organized "just like high-school English class."

When defense attorney Little gave her opening statement, Miller found her argument "fragmented and weak." He and and a few other jurors thought she looked like actress Glenn Close.

Little began by setting the scene. "Over three years ago on December 4, 2000, in an office in Palo Alto, California, a bank employee named Richard Char sent an e-mail to everyone in his banking group, several hundred people." Little described Char's e-mail, and noted that Quattrone was also working at his office that day when he read the e-mail. "Mr. Quattrone clicked on the 'reply to all' button, and began typing a reply to everyone in the group to endorse the subordinate's advice to follow standard required company policy."

When Quattrone returned the next day, Little said, he finished the e-mail "typing the words 'I strongly advise you to follow these procedures.' . . .

Members of the jury, this trial is about that one-sentence reply e-mail sent by Frank Quattrone, in which he endorsed the recommendation of one of his employees to the rest of the banking group to follow company procedures about documents. As I will now outline to you, the evidence in this case will show that that e-mail is exactly what it says it is, an endorsement of Mr. Char's reminder about bank policy—no more, no less, and not a crime."

When Little finished, the same government witnesses paraded through the courtroom, starting that same afternoon with Bunzel, the CSFB capital markets executive, who sketched the steps in the IPO process.

Day two. April 19, 2004. Although Little had given the opening, Keker resumed the lead role for the defense, and quickly sought to redraw the line to distance Quattrone from IPO allocations. Instead of stressing that Quattrone had no responsibility for them, as he had in the first trial, his new line became that Quattrone didn't make the "final decisions."

"Now, you mentioned investment bankers sometimes have input into and make suggestions about IPO allocations?" Keker asked.

"Yes, I did," Bunzel replied.

"Do they ever make that final decision about who's actually going to get them?"

"No, they do not," Bunzel said.

Day four. Brodsky's testimony, which began on Wednesday, April 21, 2004, was less dramatic this time around. Keker objected more frequently, and the effect was to break the rhythm of the star witness. Keker's objections also limited how much Anders could get Brodsky to explain or elaborate on the words in his e-mail exchange with Quattrone.

Day five. One big difference was the retrial's uglier mood, which boiled over after the lunch break on Thursday, April 22, 2004. As Keker cross-examined Brodsky, Judge Owen sustained a prosecution objection to a question aimed at showing the IPO kickback probe wasn't of great concern. When Keker persisted with a new version of the same question, Judge Owen cut him off, saying, "I sustain the objection. This is within the court's prior ruling." But Anders hadn't made an objection. This prompted a round of double takes and raucous groans from the Quattrone section.

Judge Owen wasn't calling them all for the prosecution. Moments later, he overruled an Anders objection when Keker asked Brodsky whether he thought Quattrone had "done anything wrong" when he forwarded the Char e-mail. No, Brodsky said.

But then Judge Owen blew up at Keker again when he asked Brodsky whether he wouldn't have advised anyone in a situation like Quattrone's, where he might be questioned by the government, to get a lawyer. Owen asked Anders: "Are you objecting to that? I will sustain an objection to that. You can't have a general question."

In sustaining another objection Anders hadn't made, Owen prompted a new round of moans, coughing, and laughter from the Quattrone supporters. The atmosphere was beginning to resemble that of a baseball game in which the umpire has made a series of big calls against the home team.

Peikin whirled around and glowered angrily at the Quattrone section. "May we come up to the sidebar briefly, your honor?" he asked.

"For what?" Keker protested. "There is no question pending, your honor."

At the sidebar, out of jury and spectator earshot, Peikin told the judge that the spectator section "occupied by Mr. Quattrone's lawyers and friends and former employees" had three times generated "audible reactions [to the judge's rulings] that have to be obvious to the jury."

An SEC lawyer in the crowd, George Demos, had informed prosecutors that Hausman, Quattrone's personal lawyer, was prominent in the loud groaning. Peikin told the judge, "since I can identify some of those people as counsel, I think it's particularly outrageous."

After excusing the jury, Owen addressed the hostile crowd. The jury could hear their laughter and comments, he said, which was "impermissible at a trial." The noise making had "to stop forthwith," he said, or he would take "appropriate steps to see that it does."

O

Three or four days into the trial, two jurors, Miller and Denis Crosley, found themselves heading out of the courthouse together, and decided to have lunch in Chinatown a few blocks north. The fifty-seven-year-old Crosley, a resident of White Plains, New York, was a longtime advertising man. He had worked in account management for some of the great names of Madison Avenue, including J. Walter Thompson, Doyle Dane Bernbach, and Amil Gargano. Miller considered the more easygoing Crosley, who was bald with gray hair, his main rival for the status of the jury's "alpha male."

At lunch they talked about families and careers. As they left the restaurant, they eyed a man behind them who seemed to be listening to everything they were saying. When they got outside, they lingered on the corner of Mott Street, then took a left to see if the man took the same route. He did. They wondered if they were being followed by someone connected with the trial. (They never found out for sure.)

Crosley, who sat in seat number four, also got to know the man on his left, Felix Santos, who lived on the Grand Concourse in the Bronx and worked as a doorman near Union Square in Manhattan. They would chat during breaks or when the lawyers were wrangling at sidebars with the judge. Santos's mother was sick in the hospital. Crosley figured her condition was serious, because relatives were flying up from the Dominican Republic to visit her.[1]

Unlike those in the first trial, these jurors interacted harmoniously—which set the tone for the possibility that they could reach a unanimous verdict. Some jurors promised others who had trouble following the case that they would help them along the way. When juror number twelve, Susan Toth, who worked in radiology marketing, had a coughing fit one day that briefly halted the courtroom proceedings, five or six jurors brought her cough drops or cough syrup the next day. Because there were two Susans on the jury, she became known as Coughing Susan.

Day six. Friday, April 23, 2004. In the jury room down the hall from the courtroom, some jurors were stifling giggles over one of Michael Dell's e-mails. When Quattrone had asked Dell about Charlie Wolf as a possible CSFB computer analyst, Dell had replied, "NFW." But alternate juror Kim Jupiter didn't know what the letters stood for. Crosley decided to breach the instruction that jurors weren't to discuss the case. He whispered the words "no fucking way" in her ear, and a shocked Jupiter almost fell off her chair.

○

The rest of the defense testimony generally followed the same lines as in the first trial. The first defense witness, tech group lawyer Adrian Dollard, repeated his explanation for why Quattrone had told Lynch he didn't know of the IPO probe when he forwarded Char's e-mail. Char reprised his testimony that it had all been an innocent misunderstanding. His appearance began late Friday, April 23, and continued Monday morning April 26.

Day seven. That Monday, the Quattrone side got a big morale boost with the news that CSFB had been chosen as one of the two lead managers, alongside Morgan Stanley, for the IPO of Google Inc., the search-engine provider.

Hodge was dropped as a defense witness. He had come off as a fun-loving jokester and Quattrone's golfing buddy. He was replaced by Charles G. T. Stonehill, the distinguished-looking Harrow and Oxford graduate and Morgan Stanley alumnus with the plummy baritone who had negotiated the terms of Quattrone's contract at CSFB.

Keker got Stonehill to explain that Schmidt, the Tech PCS brokerage chief, reported to Andy Benjamin—and not Quattrone—for the purposes of IPO allocations, with the goal of distancing Quattrone from allocations. But when confronted with the e-mails in which Quattrone had weighed in on specific allocations,

Stonehill conceded that, as Peikin put it, he had "no idea what was actually done in practice."

Keker next made the point that Quattrone was so busy, he couldn't have given that much thought to the file-cleanup e-mail. He put into evidence a three-ring notebook exhibit of thirty-five pages that contained a color-coded display listing time, subject line, and sender or recipient of all the e-mails, plus cell phone calls, that Quattrone sent and received during the three-day period between the first Brodsky e-mails December 3, 2000, and the Quattrone e-mail that forwarded Char's on December 5, 2000.

The defense handed a copy of defense exhibit 520 to each juror to inspect. In his closing argument, Keker would encourage the jurors to request copies of the exhibit to peruse as they deliberated. (When they did, juror Patricia Graham noticed that the subject line of one of the other outgoing e-mails on December 5 was "Lunch with Gov. Davis"—the California governor.)

The next Quattrone witness was Peter Giles, president of the Technology Museum of Innovation in San Jose. He had known Quattrone for ten years. Quattrone was on the Tech Museum executive committee. (Giles wasn't asked, but Quattrone had given $1 million to the museum, and helped raise another $13 million.[2])

Rusty Lamberto and Russell Hall repeated their character testimony from trial one—minus the material about the Girl Scouts, apparently since this time there was no Girl Scout executive on this jury. Then Keker notified the judge and prosecutors that he planned to call Quattrone, but wanted him to take the stand the next morning so he could start fresh.

It might have backfired in the first trial. But because the prosecutors had already been able to highlight the contradictions in that testimony by reading it aloud to the jurors, there was no point keeping him off the stand for the second trial. What's more, the prosecutors had lost the element of surprise, and Quattrone was better prepared to address the subject of IPO allocations.

A NEW ATTITUDE

42

DAY EIGHT. The defense was expected to make substantial changes in Quattrone's retrial testimony, and it did. More surprising was how much the prosecution changed in cross-examining Quattrone.

The biggest change in Quattrone's direct testimony was that Keker incorporated a better explanation for the e-mails that had been thrown in Quattrone's face by Peikin, showing him reviewing requests for allocations of Corvis and other IPOs. In the first trial, the big defense theme was that Quattrone and the investment banking division had "no responsibility" for IPO allocations. This time, Quattrone retreated slightly. Although he had input into the allocation process, he said, he didn't make the "final decisions."

Beyond his testimony, Quattrone also seemed to try to appear less slick, less like a Derek Jeter or a master of the universe. It seemed to go with the shift from contact lenses to the nerdy wire frames. At one point, when he got tangled up in reading an e-mail, he said, "Sorry, I keep messing up this microphone." A little later, as he searched for one of the Char e-mails, he said, "Sorry, bumbling around here trying to find it."

As he took the stand wearing a slate-gray sports jacket on the morning of Tuesday, April 27, 2004, Quattrone's opening lines echoed those from the first trial. He was aware of the SEC and grand jury probes when he forwarded the Char e-mail, but didn't connect the two because he believed the investigations concerned hedge funds paying very high commissions to get IPOs, and "didn't have anything to do with the documents Mr. Char was referring to."

Keker again handed the jury copies of the new three-ring binders listing his e-mail and cell phone calls during the three days from December 3 through December 5, 2000. He took Quattrone through the ten different notices he received about the IPO probes.

Quattrone sipped water as Keker introduced a new defense exhibit showing that between May 2000 and December 2000, Quattrone received 15,042 e-mails and sent 7,768. Then he showed the first Brodsky e-mail of December 3, 2000, telling Quattrone that there had been "some recent developments that are of extreme concern," and the second, informing Quattrone that the firm and some of its people had "received federal grand jury subpoenas asking for testimony and documents about the IPO allocation process."

Then Keker carefully had Quattrone explain his understanding of what a grand jury was, and what he did and didn't know about grand juries at the time. He was obviously expecting the prosecutors to bring up Quattrone's incredible testimony at his first trial that he didn't know what a grand jury was. This time, Quattrone acknowledged, "I had heard the term grand jury before."

Shown the second version of the Char e-mail that he forwarded, Quattrone said, "I wasn't thinking about the grand jury investigation. Mr. Char's e-mail was talking about civil securities litigation." Char's e-mail had focused on documents that had to be discarded at the end of a banking deal, Quattrone said, and so he wasn't thinking about hedge funds and commissions.

As he exited the courtroom for a morning recess, Quattrone waved to friends.

Back on the stand, Quattrone repeated the lesson he had learned from Miniscribe, about keeping documents required to prove due diligence while discarding "extraneous documents that had handwritten notes in the margin." He had been interrupted in drafting his first "reply to all" message, he said, by work on a letter pitching for the $3 billion Accenture IPO. And he said he "wasn't thinking about an investigation" when he re-sent the Char e-mail.

Then Keker brought up Quattrone's first-trial testimony that Peikin and Anders had read the previous Friday. Allocations, Quattrone said, were made in the last two days of the three- to four-month IPO process. Keker then led Quattrone to the new position, which he had already staked out, that would allow room for the e-mails that had been shown during the first trial, in which investors had besieged him for help in obtaining hot IPOs.

Guided by Keker, Quattrone said that in the year 2000 "the final decisions" on IPO allocations were made by the equity capital markets group and the equities division. He and others had input from time to time, Quattrone explained, because those making the decisions were weighing many different considerations. When corporate executives called him, he said, he would have merely referred the call "to the appropriate people."

When Quattrone had e-mailed Michael Dell to ask how important it was to him to get shares of the Corvis IPO, he had merely sent word of Dell's interest to the equity capital markets group. And out of three hundred IPOs CSFB had led, one hundred of which were technology group deals, Quattrone had only had input into the allocations on about ten of them. And he hadn't made "the final allocation decisions" for any of them.

Although the Schmidt group brokers in Tech PCS did have the right to allocate 2 percent to 4 percent of some IPOs, Quattrone said, the brokers themselves made the "final decisions." Was there "anything in any of those e-mails that you were ashamed of on December 5?" Keker asked. Absolutely not, Quattrone said.

O

The cross-examination of Quattrone in the retrial was done by Anders instead of Peikin. It contained no dramatic fireworks like Peikin's had. If anything, it was the opposite—quiet, methodical, and unemotional.

Anders had a completely different style from Peikin—and, he told people, a better winning percentage. Peikin seemed like a high-school athlete, with a jocklike manner, quick to make jokes, and highly competitive. Anders, who had grown up in Scarsdale, New York, and graduated from Dartmouth College and Fordham Law School, was more methodical and organized. When he first went to sleepaway camp as a youngster, he had asked his parents for a map.

He had never lost a case, he joked with Peikin, until they had teamed up. And indeed, a year later, he would go on to gain a guilty verdict in the trial of WorldCom"s Bernard Ebbers, who was accused of the greatest corporate fraud in U.S. history.

Anders was more earnest, a genuinely nice guy, and the difference showed in the way he questioned Quattrone. If Peikin had mauled him like a jungle animal, Anders treated the defendant with deference, patience, and respect. If the results were less dramatic, the tone was probably less distracting, and might even have created less sympathy for Quattrone.

As he questioned Quattrone, it didn't appear that Anders was drawing blood the way Peikin had. But he did two things well. He exploited Quattrone's retreat to the new stance that he didn't make "final decisions" on IPO allocations by connecting his activities more closely to the subject of the original IPO kickback probes.

He also highlighted Quattrone's denial in his previous trial that he didn't know what a grand jury was. Quattrone seemed to realize that that denial had hurt his credibility, and may have wanted to avoid a similar mistake. So as Anders patiently asked Quattrone if he understood each phrase of the e-mails informing him about the IPO probes, it became harder for Quattrone to hold the position that he hadn't recognized the probes were serious.

In all this Anders was helped by Judge Owen, who repeatedly ordered Quattrone to answer Anders's questions yes or no instead of launching into flights of explanation. That reduced Quattrone's ability to dance away from the questions, as he had a decade earlier with tort lawyer Joe Jamail in his Miniscribe testimony.

O

Keker had finished questioning Quattrone at about 3:30 P.M. on Tuesday, April 27. Anders adroitly filled the remaining hour and a half of courtroom time by mapping out the dimensions of Quattrone's role in allocations.

Anders began, "You have testified at a prior proceeding that you were not involved in decisions regarding IPO allocations, is that right?" Yes, it is, Quattrone said. "You testified in direct examination today that you are not involved in decisions regarding IPO allocations as well, is that right?"

"Actually, what I think I said is that I didn't make IPO allocation decisions," Quattrone said.

"You didn't make the final decisions."

"I didn't make the decisions."

"Okay," Anders said. "Now, as I think you might have acknowledged a moment ago, you were involved in the allocation process while you were at CSFB, isn't that fair?" From time to time I was, Quattrone said. Then the banker acknowledged that the allocation process extended beyond final decisions.

The first prosecution witness, CSFB banker Jeffrey Bunzel, had outlined the different phases of an IPO—from the bake-off pitch for the business all the way through the allocation of shares and completion of the deal.

Anders asked about "indications of interest," the phase in which clients would seek IPO shares without making a formal bid at a set price. Quattrone agreed that such indications were a part of the IPO allocation process in which he sometimes participated.

"Sometimes you would receive indications of interest, right?" Anders asked.

"There were probably a few occasions where I got . . . something you would call an indication of interest."

Next Quattrone acknowledged that he and other bankers sometimes reviewed preliminary allocations—the first rough draft of an allocation plan.

The prosecutor then displayed the e-mail in which Hatfield sent Quattrone a list of "indicative," or "preliminary" allocations for the Corvis deal. "This is an example of you being asked to review preliminary allocations, right?"

A very small number, but yes, you're right, Quattrone said, still smiling confidently and nodding his head. "And you're being asked to review them?" It's fair to say I did review them, Quattrone said.

Anders then displayed the notice that Quattrone and other tech group bankers had gotten of the conference call to review the Corvis "book." The book is a collection of indications of interest, a starting point for preliminary allocations, Quattrone agreed.

"And these are investment bankers who are participating in a call to review the book, right?" That's correct, along with equity capital markets, Quattrone said. "And this is, fair to say, another example of investment bankers participating in the allocation process?"

Here Quattrone tried to draw the line. "I don't think it is, because I think this is just to review the people who were demanding it." This wasn't the first step in the allocation process, Quattrone said. This was before the process began.

Anders counted off the phases of an IPO—indications of interest, preliminary allocations, setting the price, and final allocation decisions. "As you said, this wasn't your job to do these final allocations, right?" That's correct, Quattrone agreed.

"Isn't it fair to say that there are at least a few instances when you did get involved in making decisions on allocations?"

"I got involved in some discussions that led to decisions that were made by other people," Quattrone said. "But I never made the decisions."

"Well, let's look at a couple of e-mails," Anders said. He displayed the Quattrone e-mail about Screaming Media, the IPO whose stock had fallen on the first day of trading. In the future, when a deal looks difficult, Quattrone had written, he or Brady "should get involved in some of the decisions on allocation, as is the case when Fisher is running the deal."

Anders patiently took Quattrone through each phrase of the e-mail and forced him, with some difficulty, to acknowledge he had written each phrase. "And then you used the phrase, 'as is the case when Fisher is running the deal.' Is that right?"

When Quattrone tried to explain what he meant, Anders cut him off, trying to keep him to yes or no answers. "Did I read those words correctly?" Anders said. "I read the first part of that—'involved in some of the decisions on allocations'—and you agree that's what you wrote?" That's right, Quattrone said. "And you continued, 'as is the case when Fisher is running the deal.' Those are the words you wrote, right?"

"In that particular part of the sentence, those are the words, yes," Quattrone said.

"Okay. And isn't it true that what you're referring to is, when Fisher is running the deal, you get involved in some of the decisions on allocations?"

"In those limited number of cases, as I said in the very first part of this, when a deal like this looks difficult, that's what I meant."

After another bout of wrangling, Anders asked, "So it's a fair conclusion from that that there are instances when you've been involved in decisions on IPO allocations?"

Quattrone grudgingly agreed. "It's a fair conclusion because I wrote it that I was involved in some discussions that led to decisions by other people. So if you want to say that that means that I was involved in decisions, fine."

Why don't we look at another e-mail? Anders said, his hands clasped confidently behind his back. He displayed Quattrone's February 29, 2000, e-mail to Handspring chief executive Donna Dubinsky, in which he mentioned that

CSFB was tops in a number of categories, including having "the best distribution strategy."

Anders stopped. "'The best distribution strategy.' That refers to the allocation process, doesn't it?" At first, Quattrone said no. Then he acknowledged that the distribution strategy was part of the allocation process.

Then Anders asked about Quattrone's promise of his "personal attention," and his vow to make sure the whole firm focused on it "from start to finish." Start to finish meant "from the beginning of the IPO, the mandate, through allocation, final allocation, isn't that right?" That's correct. "And you're pledging . . . you're going to give your personal attention to those topics, start to finish, right?" That's correct.

Then Anders asked Quattrone about telling Dubinsky how he had "called in chits with investors we have known for years" to get other deals done. "You helped out getting people to buy the stock?" Yes, we were involved in some calls to investors, Quattrone said. So Brady and Quattrone, two investment bankers, had helped out "that last stage of an IPO, right?" Quattrone grudgingly agreed.

Anders then displayed the post-transaction summary that showed the allocations for Handspring, listing all accounts that received twenty thousand shares or more. The document would have been in investment banking files? Potentially, Quattrone said. It contains allocation information, right? Yes, it does.

"These different things you've been talking about," Anders asked—indications of interest, preliminary allocations, pricing, and final allocations—"it's fair to say that you and other bankers have participated on occasion in various phases of each of these steps, right?"

"Yes, except for making the final decision," Quattrone said, sticking to the newly defined boundary line of his involvement.

"Participate in discussions leading to the final decision, right?" Anders asked. Yes, in some very small number of cases, that's correct, Quattrone said.

Anders then moved in to compare the roles Quattrone acknowledged playing in the allocation process with what he had been told about the investigations. He wanted to show that Quattrone knew the investigators had been interested in the entire allocation process, including the parts Quattrone had played a role in.

"I'm handing you government exhibits 102, 201, 400, and 605," Anders said. He displayed the e-mail Quattrone had received from Rose Corbett on June 5, 2000, about VA Linux and the NASD probe of that IPO. "Am I right that the word 'decisions' appears nowhere in this e-mail?" Nowhere at all, Quattrone agreed. "It refers to 'the allocation process,' right?" That's correct, the banker said.

Anders displayed an e-mail notification to Quattrone about the SEC underwriting examination. It "talks about CSFB's equity underwriting process," the prosecutor said. "Am I correct the word 'decision' doesn't appear anywhere in this e-mail?" Doesn't appear to, Quattrone said. "The phrase 'allocation process' appears a couple of times at least, right?" Yes, it's there.

Ditto two other e-mail notifications Quattrone had received about the probes. Hadn't both referred to "the IPO allocation process"?

The courtroom was dead silent as Anders asked one last question about the December 3, 2000, Brodsky e-mail. "The word 'decisions' doesn't appear anywhere in this e-mail, isn't that correct?"

"I don't believe so," Quattrone said.

Anders suggested to the judge it was a good time for a break, and the trial recessed for the day.

"YOU DID A FINE JOB"

43

DAY NINE. Wednesday, April 28, 2000. The next morning, Quattrone wore a blue blazer and pleated tan slacks, and continued sipping Poland Spring water from a plastic cup. He and Keker showed some concern about the impact of Anders's cross-examination technique, with Quattrone trying harder to break the prosecutor's rhythm by explaining e-mails showing his role in allocations. That sparked another clash with Judge Owen.

Anders, in a blue suit, returned to the Dubinsky e-mails and Quattrone's story about calling in chits to get deals done. Anders asked whether many of the documents saved in a deal file came from sources outside the firm, such as outside counsel and accountants.

As Quattrone began elaborating on a yes or no question, Judge Owen cut him off: "The answer is yes. You have answered his question. Go ahead." When Quattrone protested that "it's not a complete question," Owen said, "You answered the question. It's answered and go forward." Keker asked to approach. "No," Owen said.

"I object to your interrupting his answers when he is trying to answer a question," Keker said. But Owen told Keker that Quattrone must confine himself to yes or no answers when called for. If he wanted to elaborate, he would have to ask, Owen said. The stance made it harder for the banker to explain away the e-mails.

Anders sought to establish that Quattrone understood the document retention policy, and that it included instructions in case of litigation or subpoena. "And you knew in December 2000 that this provision prohibited bankers from destroying any documents that were called for by the subpoena or requested in the litigation?"

When Quattrone again gave a qualified answer—"If they knew that, yes"—Judge Owen summoned the lawyers to the sidebar at 10:12 A.M.

He ordered Keker to tell Quattrone to stop volunteering qualified answers, but Keker balked and said that Quattrone's answer "was completely appropriate for that last question." Owen said, "The government is entitled to put a question and get a responsive answer and not a volunteered answer by the witness."

Keker disagreed. "What you say calls for a yes or no doesn't call for a yes or no. . . . You want them to be able to manipulate him without being able to answer the question and that is totally improper," Keker said. Owen said, "They are entitled to get their yes or no and go on, and the witness is not entitled to throw in something that he feels softens up that yes or no, which is what we are hearing."

Keker agreed to pass on the judge's warning, rolled his eyes, and summoned Quattrone after the jury left. After they conferred, Quattrone laughed as if enjoying a joke, and returned to the stand.

When the questioning resumed, Anders walked Quattrone through a series of e-mails, as Peikin had done, showing how involved the banker had been in allocations.

The prosecutor asked whether it was true that Quattrone would review IPO allocations for Tech PCS from time to time. Quattrone said he "looked at some lists that had priority systems," but it wasn't part of his responsibilities to review the group's allocations.

"I am not sure that is the question I asked," Anders said. "Isn't it true that from time to time you reviewed allocations of IPOs done by Tech PCS?" I can't give a yes or no answer to that, Quattrone said, apparently following Keker's instructions, based on the judge's warning.

"Let's look at some documents and see if that helps," Anders said. He displayed Quattrone's e-mail to Schmidt and Grunwald asking to review the Corvis allocations. "So this is an example of you reviewing allocations for Tech PCS on a deal, right?"

Not exactly, Quattrone said. This is an example of asking to do so.

Owen broke in again. "Sir, please, is that an example or is it not?"

"This e-mail does not show me actually reviewing them," Quattrone said. The e-mail showed him merely asking to review, he added, and he couldn't remember whether he had actually followed up and done so.

Anders showed Grunwald's February 2000 e-mail asking Quattrone's help in boosting the number of IPO shares the Tech PCS brokers would get for clients. "It's fair that you understood this to mean he wanted your help in getting more of the total pot for the Tech PCS group, right?" Quattrone agreed that was a fair assumption.

Anders next displayed Quattrone's reply. "You said, 'let's review specific names and allocations.' That is what you said?" Quattrone agreed. "And you were asking to review allocations for clients of Tech PCS regarding new issues, right?" Yes, I was, Quattrone said.

Anders got Quattrone to acknowledge that he knew some Tech PCS accounts got IPOs and paid commissions on other trades. He showed him Schmidt's e-mail using the phrases "Friends of Frank" and "spinning." Quattrone protested that "the entire e-mail was a joke." At Anders's request, Quattrone defined spinning as "a specific type of flipping that was done for the specific purpose of influencing an executive's decision making on investment banking business."

When Anders asked Quattrone about some e-mails that had been shown when Anders had reread Quattrone's testimony from the first trial, Quattrone jokingly congratulated him on his performance. "You did a fine job impersonating me," he said.

Anders thanked him briefly, then pressed on. "Those examples weren't the only times that you played a role in the IPO allocation process, right?" There might have been others, Quattrone said.

Then Anders showed the series of e-mails outlining the effort by Research in Motion chief executive Jim Balsillie to get extra shares of the AvantGo IPO, and the tech group's efforts to weigh whether that could help win a role in RIM's next stock issue. Included was Fisher's tart response, "The guy is a pig," and Quattrone's caution that he wanted to be generous, but didn't want to do anything that would "look like we are 'spinning.'"

"You said you can't do something where it looked like you were just giving Mr. Balsillie an IPO allocation in order to win the business, right?" That's absolutely right, Quattrone said. "And the business is the follow-on offering for RIM, right?" Correct. "You're saying allocation . . . as generous as possible, as long as it doesn't look like it's spinning?" That's my suggestion, yes, Quattrone said.

"That's input you're putting into this particular allocation, right?" That's correct. "Not making a final decision, right?" Correct.

Then Anders slowly roasted Quattrone for testifying at his first trial that he didn't know what a grand jury was. He recapped what Quattrone had said on the subject the day before, namely that he had "heard the term," and knew it listened to testimony. Then he showed him the transcript from his first trial, in which he said, "I believe that I did not know what a grand jury was at that time."

"You told the truth during that prior testimony, didn't you?"

"I did my best to, but on that particular occasion, I—"

"I'm sorry, just yes or no, Mr. Quattrone. I'm sorry to interrupt you. You told the truth during your prior testimony?"

"I tried my very best to." Later, the banker added, "I may have misspoken."

After Anders showed Quattrone early notices he had received of the various stages of the NASD, SEC, and grand jury IPO probes, he reached the heart of the prosecution case: Brodsky's e-mails and phone call to Quattrone about the IPO probe, followed by Quattrone's endorsement of Char's e-mail.

Again Anders painstakingly took the banker through each phrase. "You understood that 'extreme concern' meant that it was something important, right?" Yes, Quattrone said. He knew what a subpoena was, and a grand jury, a criminal investigation, and a leak.

Anders then showed Quattrone the first Char e-mail on December 4, 2000, and read Char's line, "In January, it could be improper destruction of evidence." Then he asked, "You understood this to mean that once there was litigation or a subpoena, if you threw away documents, it would be improper, right?"

"I think that is a fair assumption, yes."

"It's fair that you knew about a grand jury investigation at this time, December 4, right?" Yes.

Anders displayed Char's second e-mail. As he drafted his endorsement, Quattrone had stopped after typing the word "miniscribe."

Quattrone said he had been the banker for the financing for Miniscribe, and, as Anders noted, "it turned out later on that the company was engaged in securities fraud." When Quattrone testified before the Miniscribe trial, Anders asked, "Do you recall during that deposition there were some claims that Morgan Stanley had destroyed documents?" Quattrone said that might have been the case.

"You testified yesterday that you observed how the lawyers in that case had fun with documents and twisting people's words, do you recall that?" Anders asked. "It's fair to say that you and the other witnesses didn't have fun while that was going on, right?" No, Quattrone said. "In fact, isn't it fair to say that it was an unpleasant experience for you and the other witnesses while that was going on?" That is very fair, Quattrone said.

When they deliberated, some jurors pointed to that Miniscribe testimony, brief as it was, as a compelling insight into Quattrone's state of mind—because he had cited the case in resending the e-mail. He was thinking about litigation and keeping documents from lawyers, the jurors noted.

Anders and Quattrone recapped the Brodsky phone call at midday on December 5, 2000, and Quattrone's earlier testimony about it. Brodsky had said that the investigation focused on an improper link between large commissions and IPO allocations, right? And Quattrone had testified that he wasn't concerned because he didn't think this had anything to do with his area? Quattrone said that that was correct.

But wasn't it true that the Tech PCS brokers gave out IPOs to hedge funds? Yes, Quattrone said. And they earned commissions on securities trades, right? Yes, the banker said.

○

The prosecutors had decided to throw the kitchen sink at Quattrone this time out, and the last dirty dish was the $2 million fee Quattrone was trying to collect from Research in Motion right after he seconded the Char e-mail on

December 5, 2000. This was something Spitzer's prosecutors felt showed Quattrone at his worst, holding up a company for millions as a quid pro quo for supposedly objective research coverage.

Outside the jury's earshot, Anders told the judge that it knocked down the defense theory that "he was just dashing off e-mails which had little consequence and he ran out the door." Over Keker's objections that it was designed to "dirty Mr. Quattrone up," Anders got Quattrone to admit that the RIM fee wasn't disclosed to investors.

After a break, Anders showed Quattrone government exhibit 625, his e-mail endorsing Char's. "And you testified on direct examination you wrote this e-mail in a rush because you were leaving work, right?" Correct, Quattrone said. "After you sent this e-mail at 6:25 but before you left, you sent one more e-mail, didn't you?" Yes, I did, the banker said.

At Anders's prodding, Quattrone acknowledged that CSFB hadn't been paid as expected for its work on the RIM offering. Quattrone believed that the RIM CEO, James Balsillie, had orally promised to write a check to CSFB for certain fees related to this underwriting. That was the money he was trying to collect in that last e-mail.

Noting that the prospectus for securities offerings must reflect "how much money is going to the underwriters and how much goes to the company," Anders asked Quattrone whether he knew that "when there's secret, undisclosed compensation that's a violation of the securities laws?" Quattrone said he knew it could be.

Anders hammered at the point: The $2 million fee Quattrone was seeking wasn't disclosed to the other bankers, wasn't mentioned in the underwriting agreement, and "wasn't disclosed to investors who purchased these securities, right?" Quattrone didn't dispute him.

In their appeal brief, Quattrone lawyers said no extra fee disclosure was required because RIM was a Canadian company and the dispute concerned only the division of underwriting fees, not their total. In any case, they added, any disclosure responsibility rested with RIM and not Quattrone. In their own brief, prosecutors said they hadn't meant to suggest at trial that Quattrone himself had violated fee disclosure rules.

O

Just before 4:00 P.M., Keker rose for less than a half hour of redirect. He asked a quick series of questions that returned to the defense point that Quattrone didn't supervise his own brokers' IPO allocations, New York did.

Was there "anything wrong" with giving executives of technology companies hot IPO allocations through Tech PCS? No. The CSFB legal department had declared such accounts "would not be considered spinning" if the brokers followed certain guidelines, Quattrone said. "Tell the jury what you meant about the lawyers had given you guidelines," Keker suggested.

"Well, as Mr. Anders referred, there was a topic called spinning that became of interest in the late 1990s, and that was when it first really became known about the widespread practice in the industry of executives getting IPO allocations from Wall Street firms," Quattrone said. "And while the investigations into it never went anywhere, there were never any charges brought, there was a heightened level of scrutiny about the practice. And so, during that time frame, our lawyers made sure that [the Schmidt group's allocations] did not constitute spinning."

Quattrone continued, "Mr. Schmidt then explained to our lawyers the guidelines that he had come up with. And it was minimum account size, it was a certain number of shares in an IPO. The fact that they couldn't just buy IPOs; they had to have some trading commissions and secondary commissions as well. Those were some of the things that our lawyers felt were good, safe harbors that we could rely on, so that the allocations Mr. Schmidt was making weren't considered spinning."

"Was anything wrong with these guidelines as far as you knew?" No. "In December of 2000?" No.

Of course, CSFB had been charged with spinning in April 2003 in the global research settlement, based on the very program Quattrone had just described. And Quattrone personally was charged by the NASD with spinning in March 2003, based on the same facts; the NASD later dropped the charges, citing the delay caused by the trials. But under the rules of evidence at the trial, that was all irrelevant to Quattrone's state of mind when he sent the e-mail in December 2000.

Keker was done at 4:22 P.M., and Owen told the jury they were likely to get the case after closing arguments on Friday, at about 2:30 or 3:00 P.M. At his suggestion, they agreed to come in early Friday to get a jump on the process.

THE VERDICT

44

DAY TEN. After a one-day break on Thursday to allow one prosecutor to attend a funeral, the jury got the case at 3:40 P.M. on Friday April 30, 2004, after closing arguments and instructions from the judge.

"He knew about the ongoing investigation, and he told his employees to destroy documents anyway," Anders said. "He did it to obstruct justice, and he did it to protect his lucrative business and livelihood."

Keker, in his summation, mocked the government for trying to criminalize "this 22-word little bureaucratic snippet." He urged the jurors to ask for copies of the three-ring binder listing Quattrone's calls and e-mails for December 3 through December 5, 2000.

In a forty-five-minute set of instructions, Judge Owen said the government had to prove that Quattrone had acted with "corrupt intent," which required a nexus or connection between Quattrone's actions and the pending grand jury proceeding. As he read, the judge juggled several scraps of paper containing what seemed to be legal boilerplate. The nexus requirement would be satisfied, he said, if Quattrone directed the destruction of documents called for by the grand jury subpoena, or if he directed destruction of documents he had reason to believe were within the scope of the subpoena.

The jurors could take into account whether Quattrone deliberately chose to avoid making sure that his e-mail wouldn't cause a problem, the judge added, a concept known as "conscious avoidance." The prosecutors had asked a number of witnesses, including Quattrone, whether he had asked anyone, including Brodsky, any questions before forwarding the Char e-mail. He hadn't.

As they began their deliberations inside the jury room, juror Felix Santos, the doorman, suggested choosing a foreman. Crosley, the White Plains ad man, and two others expressed interest. But by acclamation the group asked Miller to take on the task, partly because he had been seated in the number one seat, in the first row, closest to the judge.[1]

The jury members quickly took a straw poll. The result was 7–4 for conviction, with one undecided. One vote for acquittal came from Crosley. Another was cast by Sheldon Silver, the public relations receptionist. The third was by Oscar Marin, the engineer who managed eleven dormitories for New York University. The fourth came from Susan Poryles, a human resources employee at Thomson Financial, which provides data to Wall Street. The undecided vote was cast by Bryan Russo, the freelance TV director who knew the Mack family.

Then the jury members who felt strongly about their votes went around the table, giving some of their thoughts.

Miller was among the first to speak. He mentioned that he had worked with bankers; it hadn't always been the most pleasant experience. He found it hard to believe that Quattrone wouldn't have been able to connect the dots. These people are very intelligent, he said. People are constantly demanding their time, so they are always multitasking.

Crosley said he wondered whether the whole incident could have been an accident, whether Quattrone's actions might have been an oversight.

Patricia Graham, the unemployed executive assistant from the Upper East Side of Manhattan, explained her guilty vote. As a former employee of the Industrial Bank of Japan, Graham knew that major financial institutions are audited routinely. Within her group at IBJ, Graham had sometimes served informally as the "auditor babysitter," and was always being asked for documents. She told the other jurors document retention policies are everyone's responsibility.

She knew the big producers didn't exactly welcome such requests with open arms. And when she heard the NASD's Sherman and the SEC's Pennington testify about documents they had been seeking, she believed the attitude of someone like Quattrone would have been "leave us alone, we're busy making millions of dollars." When Graham had heard Brodsky testify about his phone call to Quattrone, she concluded that Quattrone had made an obstruction attempt.

Some of those who voted against conviction objected that it wasn't a crime to be rich and arrogant. Among them was Bryan Russo, the TV director. Russo said Quattrone's body language indicated that he was a good guy, a stand-up guy. He told others he was concerned about whether Quattrone had acted out of ignorance—had it been accidental or deliberate? He just didn't know.

Oscar Marin, the university buildings engineer, said he needed more of a "smoking gun" to vote guilty. Shelly Silver, the public relations receptionist, observed that the jurors were being asked to add up all the e-mails together to determine what was going on in Quattrone's head.

Rosey Rudnick, a travel agent from Harrison, New York, cited her husband's work as a regional manager for First Investors Corporation, a securities firm where he had worked for twenty-five years, in explaining her guilty vote.

When the trial began, she had been inclined to believe Quattrone wasn't guilty, because she believed that securities executives "often get picked on" by regulators. But she told other jurors that she didn't believe Quattrone could get contacted by the firm's chief counsel on a Sunday and still "be so cavalier to think it wasn't important."

The jurors generally agreed that the three different charges were so interrelated that they didn't take separate votes on each. None of the jurors split their votes, voting guilty on some charges and not guilty on others, which had happened in the first trial.

Susan ("Coughing Susan") Toth, the medical marketing consultant from Sloatsburg, New York, talked about Miniscribe as a key to Quattrone's state of mind when he drafted his forwarding e-mail. It showed by Quattrone's own words, she believed, that he was thinking about document destruction and being a witness. It had been an unpleasant experience, he had said.

Several of the jurors said they thought Quattrone's varying answers at the two trials, about his knowledge of what a grand jury is, hurt his credibility.

Before they left for the day, the jurors took another vote. Susan Poryles switched her vote to guilty, bringing the count to 8–3–1 in favor of conviction. At one point, she was alarmed at something she thought she heard Silver say—namely, that he wasn't open to changing his vote. In a tense exchange, he tried to reassure her that he was open. But in fact, to some jurors Silver's body language did show some impatience at how much testimony the jurors were asking to hear, and about the idea of deliberations the next day, Saturday. Silver had plans for the weekend, and he quickly objected to returning before Monday.

Several of the jurors wanted to see not only particular bits of evidence but testimony, and had questions they wanted asked of the judge. Crosley, for example, wanted to know whether the jurors could make any inference about the lack of other charges against Quattrone. As the foreman, Miller assembled the requests, and he thought it best to err on the side of including them all rather than risk offending some jurors by omitting any.

At 5:50 P.M. on Friday, the jury's requests were sent into the courtroom, and the jury returned as well. "We thought we'd break at 6:30," Miller told the judge. Owen said he would try to get them some of the requested items, such as an easel, immediately. "We realize some of the requests will take a while. So we'll take them on Monday," Miller said. Then the jury left the courtroom.

Some of the requests were extensive. All the e-mails sent to and from Quattrone, for example. The document retention policy. Defense exhibit 520 listing Quattrone's calls and e-mails. All of the testimony by Brodsky and McCarthy, and some of Quattrone's. Peikin said he thought the jurors were expecting to be given transcripts; they were. But Owen's practice was to have testimony read aloud in open court. He summoned the jurors.

When they returned, Owen said, "You've asked for certain testimony. Generally, the way we do that is we read it to you. Okay? And there's apparently what, three or four or five hours of stuff in there to read?"

"We can narrow it," Miller said, and Owen suggested they do so. The notes were returned to the jury to amend.

Then Keker and Owen wrangled over how many copies to provide of defense exhibit 520, which listed the calls and e-mails. Keker suggested twelve; Owen said one would be enough. The jurors quickly got an easel, the document policy, and one copy of defense 520. At 6:35, the jury asked for two more copies of the document policy and several more copies of defense 520.

They also narrowed their requests for testimony. They asked to hear what Quattrone had said when "he was asked about his experience with the Miniscribe lawsuit and how that experience influenced his decision to send his endorsement of the Char e-mail." They also asked for Brodsky's testimony on both direct and cross about his eleven-minute conversation with Quattrone on December 5, 2000.

The jurors said they would return to deliberate at 9:00 A.M. on Monday. The judge sent them home. "Now, instructions on that for the weekend: From the minute you break here, do not discuss the case, obviously, with anybody. Do not read anything about it. Do not do anything with regard to it. Don't even think about it, okay?"

When he returned to his home in Waccabuc, about twenty miles north of Manhattan, Miller couldn't sleep, tossing and turning and wishing he could talk to his wife about the case. At the end of the day Friday, he and Susan Poryles had gotten the sense that one of the "not guilty" votes, Shelly Silver, might be digging in, based on things he had said and his body language as he pushed away from the table. Silver had been one of the few jurors to oppose Saturday deliberations. *Oh man*, they said, *he's going to be the holdout.*

When he awoke at 8:00 A.M. on Saturday morning, Miller wrote out what he compared to his own "opening argument," six long, legal-size pages with his own thoughts and answers to possible objections.

Silver, age fifty-nine, spent a sleepless weekend as well. He knew he had to come to grips with some of the reasons for his sympathies for Quattrone. Silver had talked about his partner of fifteen years, John Simon, in open court. John resembled Quattrone. Silver came from Philadelphia; his father's family had come from South Philadelphia. Silver's best friend grew up in Quattrone's neighborhood. He knew the streets of Philadelphia mentioned in Quattrone's e-mails. Silver's own late mother had looked so much like Quattrone's mother, Rose, that he had to look away when he saw her in court.

Silver had initially felt that Quattrone was "too smart to have done this." A veteran of several juries, he also believed that it was easier to begin with a "not guilty" vote. After he heard the other jurors' thoughts on Friday, however, he kept telling himself that he really wanted to "do the right thing with this."

O

On Monday morning, May 3, 2004, Felix Santos told Crosley that his mother had died, and the two men hugged. The funeral was scheduled for the following day, Tuesday. Santos told June Hummel, the deputy clerk, that he had to leave early on Monday, and would be absent on Tuesday. When Hummel checked back with him at Owen's request, Santos said he had to leave at 3:00 P.M. Monday. He said he could deliberate until then.

Crosley told Miller he would like to address the jury for a few minutes. He wanted to bring up some issues he had thought about, and depending on the reactions from other jurors, he said he might be able to change his vote. Miller said that was fine; he had some things he wanted to say, too. He wrote out a schedule of speakers for that morning on the easel.

When Crosley began, he confessed that he had been doing a lot of thinking about the case over the weekend. When others said they had, too, they all laughed that so many had ignored the judge's admonitions. Crosley said he was nearly at the point of changing his vote, but he just wanted to raise some issues.

He was trying to understand what Quattrone had done by accident versus by intent. And he was trying to understand what Quattrone knew when. He was amazed that the document retention policy was treated like an act of Congress. He also challenged some of the people who were voting guilty to voice specific reasons.

As he spoke, Crosley had with him a set of written questions that suggested "reasonable doubt." For example, Crosley wrote, "endorsing Char e-mail was just normal course of business." Quattrone was "being made a scapegoat by the gov't: because they couldn't solve the bigger alleged crime of kickbacks." He noted, "there is no evidence of a 'pattern' of actions beyond the incidental endorsement of an e-mail message." And, he said, "you can't convict someone of obstruction for endorsing a reminder to destroy documents that (he and the gov't knew) were already supposed to be destroyed, can you?"

On the whole, the thrust of Crosley's comments was to explain why he was on the fence. Although many of his points tilted toward "not guilty," they were couched as questions or issues and not arguments.

Then Miller spoke for about twenty minutes from the notes he had prepared.

As Miller saw it, there were eleven important facts. He counted the numbers aloud as he made the points. One, Quattrone was aware of atypical investigations by the NASD and SEC. Two, these investigations, focused on CSFB, were unusual and of concern, based on Brodsky's note in August 2000. Three, the investigations did cover Quattrone's areas, and Quattrone was senior enough to be concerned. Four, the referral of the SEC's investigation to the enforcement division was a warning sign or red flag to any intelligent business person.

Five, a threat was conveyed to Quattrone personally by the chief counsel's e-mail about a matter of extreme concern that he needed to speak to him about personally. Six, it wasn't reasonable to think that Quattrone forgot about the warning, because he was used to multitasking and high e-mail volume. Seven, he was thinking about document destruction and being a witness when he composed the draft.

Eight, Quattrone had come back and finished the e-mail the next day. This involved rereading the sentence he had begun writing and the body of Char's e-mail. It didn't matter how the draft got saved. Going back to it meant it wasn't a casual act. Nine, he finished the Char response after the final call with Brodsky, and after flagging his own lawyer. The issue was still fresh in his mind. He was also concerned about the *Wall Street Journal* article.

Ten, Quattrone had made no attempt to retract his e-mail or Char's once he received Char's e-mail about his notice from legal and compliance that their e-mails might be in conflict with the document retention policy. He didn't even confer with Brodsky; he just let things lie. Eleven, Quattrone lied to the new chief counsel two years later.

Borrowing a phrase from the prosecutors, Miller strongly urged the four jurors in the not-guilty camp to "use your common sense" to determine Quattrone's intent. There was no reason to doubt he knew what he was doing, Miller wrote.

Then Miller addressed some of the objections. One, why would the banker have put the file-cleanup message in e-mail if he was so smart? His answer was that Quattrone's response was *soft and vague*, simply reiterating the document policy. *He was very smart*, Miller had written. *He masked his intent, as evidenced by your doubt now.*

Two, *don't be swayed by how nice a person he was on the stand. He was well rehearsed. He faced us, he was gentle and soft, putting on a show. This is not the real Quattrone. The real Quattrone had to be a savvy shark to make his way so high in the cutthroat financial services world.* Use your common sense, Miller said. For there to be reasonable doubt about his intent, Quattrone would have to be really stupid or forgetful—and that's not reasonable.

Instead, Miller said, Quattrone could be supersmart by acting dumb, sending an e-mail that looked casual and innocent, but worked, and caused some documents to be destroyed. *Don't let this highly intelligent, savvy deal maker snow you, too, and get away with breaking the law,* he said.

Finally, Miller concluded by urging the jurors to reach a unanimous verdict. *A mistrial would be a disservice,* he said. *We owe it to the U.S. government and Mr. Quattrone to reach a decision.*

After Miller spoke, Silver and Crosley said they were willing to consider changing their votes. But they wanted to be reassured that those voting guilty would be willing to reconsider as well if they felt the evidence warranted it.

Susan Toth, "Coughing Susan," spoke next. She considered the testimony about Miniscribe the most damning, particularly since Quattrone had clearly been thinking about it as he forwarded Char's e-mail. She was the one who had asked for the Miniscribe testimony to be read back. If any of the jurors in doubt heard it, she said, it could make all the difference.

At 10:55 A.M., the jury took a new vote, and Shelly Silver had switched to guilty. The new count was 9–1–2 in favor of conviction, with one not guilty and two undecided. The last three holdouts were Crosley, Russo, and Oscar Marin, the juror who wanted the smoking gun.

At that point, the jurors returned to the courtroom to hear the testimony they had requested. The court reporter read Quattrone's direct and cross-examination about the Miniscribe case. It began, "Miniscribe was the only time I'd ever been involved in securities litigation before." And it ended, "Question: Isn't it fair to say it was an unpleasant experience for you and the other witnesses while that was going on? Answer: That is very fair."

Then the court reporter read the direct and cross of Brodsky about the eleven-minute call with Quattrone. Then Owen gave them a copy of government exhibit 60, the phone log record of when the Brodsky call had occurred, at 1:47 P.M. At Keker's request, Owen reminded the jury that that was Eastern time, and thus a greater amount of time before Quattrone forwarded the e-mail.

Then Owen told the jury the answer was no to the question of whether they could consider the lack of other charges against Quattrone as circumstantial evidence of intent or motive. And he cautioned the jury against speculating on the reasons why other charges hadn't been brought.

After the read-back of the Brodsky call testimony, Crosley said, *I'm really hearing that Brodsky called him [that day] and told him. Well, then, I guess it's guilty. Yes, you can turn around and blame the CSFB attorneys for not being more on the ball, for not suspending the document retention policy. But they're not on trial here.* And he changed his vote.

When Bryan Russo changed his vote shortly thereafter, he said he had become convinced that Quattrone really had to know the consequences of his inaction in not telling Char to stop. That left Oscar Marin as the last holdout.

At 12:45 P.M., the jurors heard Quattrone's direct and cross-examination about his understanding of the content of the call with Brodsky. It took just five minutes. The jury ordered lunch brought in.

As they all sat around the table, Marin asked Shelly Silver why he had switched his vote to guilty. They had sat near each other during the deliberations. Silver explained to him that there wasn't the kind of smoking gun in this case that Marin was seeking. This was something where the jurors had to get inside the person's head to decide what he was thinking.

Silver said that he had concluded that Quattrone was too smart; sometimes smart people do stupid things, or get so arrogant they don't think they're going to be caught. Quattrone, who was used to doing several things at once, had started and stopped in midsentence, resuming a day and a half later, after the call from Brodsky. Silver thought Quattrone must have been thinking, "I've got to save my ass." He told Marin he didn't think Quattrone had acted innocently.

At around 1:20 P.M. on Monday, May 3, 2004, Miller asked whether they should take another vote. When they all voted "guilty," the room was quiet. They waited several minutes for it to sink in. They were in no hurry to return to the courtroom.

O

Quattrone had appeared confident before the verdict, chatting up the courtroom sketch artists and other trial observers, and stepping out for coffee just before noon.[2]

Some time after 1:30 P.M., word spread that the jurors had reached a verdict. There was a general feeling that, given what had happened in the first trial, a verdict reached this quickly was likely to be an acquittal—all the more so since Anders hadn't attacked Quattrone on the stand the way Peikin did. However, when the jurors entered the courtroom at 1:50 P.M., none looked at Quattrone— the classic signal of a guilty verdict.

"Ladies and gentlemen," Owen said, "you've given me a note saying you've reached a verdict?" Marin, the last juror to vote guilty, answered the judge: "Yes, sir."

The crowd in the courtroom was relatively sparse, as a verdict had come with little warning. Quattrone remained seated, his hands flat on the defense table.

"Do you have the note? Thank you. All right. Your verdict is that you have found the defendant guilty on each of the three charges. Is that correct?" Yes, Miller answered.

Quattrone seemed to shudder, and gulped visibly.[3] He continued staring straight ahead, blinking repeatedly and reddening as he seemed to be fighting back tears. Juror Rosey Rudnick, the travel agent, noticed that he was biting his lip, and seemed in shock.

As June Hummel, the deputy clerk, polled the jurors individually, Quattrone glanced over at them.[4] Boutros's lips could be seen moving angrily. Jan Little, the defense lawyer who had given the opening statement, closed her eyes and appeared to grimace slightly. Quattrone's mother, Rose, and sister, Mary Ann, were crying.[5]

As he waited ten minutes or more for a car to be called, Quattrone grew teary-eyed as he comforted his mother, saying, "It's going to be okay. It's going to be okay."[6] Hausman exited the courthouse with Quattrone's mother and sister, his face clenched in anguish.

Outside, Quattrone remained silent as Keker vowed to appeal, citing the judge's biased pro-government rulings. "There's an awful lot of evidence the jury didn't hear," Keker said, "and if they'd heard it, maybe they would have come out differently and we will be filing an appeal. If we have to do this thing again, till we get it right, we will do it again until we get it right."[7]

REVERSAL

QUATTRONE'S defenders in Silicon Valley said he had been the victim of a witch hunt.

"Frank's a great man," Roger McNamee of Integral Capital Partners, whose IPO allocations had been featured at Quattrone's trial, said on CNBC-TV. "I can't imagine Silicon Valley ever becoming the great engine of growth that it became in the eighties and nineties without Frank. He's literally one of the people who built Silicon Valley." He added, "On the finance side, Frank had no peer. He was the first investment banker at a major firm who bet his career on Silicon Valley."

McNamee acknowledged Wall Street's excesses, but blamed regulators. "It's a horrible outcome in a situation where, you know, I don't think anyone pretends that Wall Street was a perfect situation in the late nineties. I think it was totally out of control, but I think the regulators were asleep. And the rules in place at the time could have prevented a lot of what happened, and bad regulation was a big issue." McNamee also said CSFB should get its share of blame—which, of course, the firm had.

Responding to a question from *Kudlow & Cramer* show cohost James Cramer, McNamee said, "The issues that we were dealing with here were systemic. The industry got completely wrapped up in a mania, investors got wrapped up in a mania, and the news media and the regulators. Everyone was wrapped up in a mania. And it seems to me that when the market collapsed, everyone was looking for someone to blame. And I think it became very convenient to point at one person as though somehow one person was responsible for a mania that involved, you know, tens of millions of people."[1]

Two of Quattrone's hometown newspapers took the opposite view, that even if Quattrone had been singled out, somehow justice had been served.

"Star financier Frank Quattrone was once seen as Silicon Valley's Midas. Now, he's more likely to be remembered like Icarus, illustrating a cautionary tale of how far mortals are meant to go—and not go," said Carolyn Said of the

San Francisco Chronicle on May 4, 2004, the day after his conviction. "Quattrone's two trials brought to light a culture of cronyism that prevailed in Silicon Valley and Wall Street during the Internet boom. Testimony made it clear that the norm was insider wheeling and dealing that favored investment-bank clients and institutional investors with shares of hot initial public offerings, which they could then flip for massive profits. Regular folks could buy stock in companies only after they had opened for trading and soared to stratospheric prices."[2]

At the south end of Silicon Valley, the *San Jose Mercury News* weighed in with similar sentiments. "What Quattrone and his colleagues at Credit Suisse First Boston did wasn't pretty," the *Mercury News* said, in an editorial entitled, "Into Quattrone's Life, Some Jail Time Must Fall." "They doled out access to hot initial public offerings to favored clients in a practice known as 'spinning.' Those so-called 'Friends of Frank,' a few dozen individuals, many of them well-paid Valley executives, reaped big rewards while facing no risk. Their gains came at the expense of less sophisticated investors and the companies whose IPOs were routinely underpriced."[2]

Even if other Wall Street firms have engaged in less overt spinning, the newspaper said, that didn't make it right. After all, the banks had paid $1.5 billion in penalties for such "reprehensible conduct" in research and spinning, the editorial said, and "Quattrone's CSFB was among those that paid the largest sums."

That settlement didn't close the books on the matter, the editorial said. "The banks behaved badly because people in them behaved badly, and Quattrone was the poster child of bad behavior. As such, he deserved to be the target of prosecutors. So what if he ultimately got nabbed for obstructing justice, rather than for spinning?" Obstruction was still a "serious offense," the *Merc* said.

"Quattrone's sentencing closes a venal chapter in Valley history. While many others will go unpunished, he will pay a heavy price for the greed and excesses of an era that left the Valley with a brutal hangover."[3]

O

At Quattrone's alma mater, one student took a more indulgent view. "Frank's conviction was the result of a witch hunt," wrote Joseph Graham, perspectives editor of *The Wharton Journal*, a student-published weekly, in September 2004. "Trillions of dollars had been lost in the deflating of the technology bubble and somebody needed to suffer for the suffering of our portfolios. But, much like the teenage girls in old Salem, Frank was not the cause of the mania he was tied to. Is touting some poor investments a crime? . . . Frank sold portions of exciting companies to droves of very sophisticated, very willing buyers. The supply demand imbalance was not Frank's fault. Sure, Frank took advantage of it . . . but that's what businessmen do . . . the good ones anyway."[4]

O

On May 16, 2004, two weeks after his conviction, Quattrone's wife, Denise, drew her husband's attention to an article in the *San Jose Mercury News* about a man who had been released from prison after serving twenty years for child molestation. He had been released after several witnesses recanted their testimony. The article told of the financial plight of the agency that had taken up the man's cause, the Northern California Innocence Project—which had just lost four hundred thousand dollars in state funding due to a budget crunch.[5]

When Quattrone contacted the agency, which worked to free the wrongfully convicted, he learned that its executive director, Kathleen Ridolfi, was from the same street in South Philadelphia that he was. And he soon wrote a check from a Quattrone foundation to keep the organization afloat, then recruited a raft of his associates in Silicon Valley to contribute a combined half million dollars.

Quattrone's altruism, of course, happened to serve his own PR point, that he too had been wrongfully convicted. In October 2005, he hosted a cocktail reception to raise more money for the group, which included a dance performance called *Barred from Life*, at the Mountain View Center for the Performing Arts. Speaking from a staircase above guests gathered in an atrium, he read from notes with his hands shaking with emotion. He described himself as the "victim of a flawed legal system," and said his experience bonded him to the project. "If this could happen to me," he said, "it could happen to anyone."

O

On June 24, 2004, John Mack was ousted as chief executive of Credit Suisse First Boston. The executive chosen to succeed him was Brady Dougan, a long-time colleague of Wheat's who had led the equity division at the time of CSFB's alleged "pervasive scheme" to pocket fat commissions in exchange for IPOs. Mack, it seemed, had served his purpose for the Swiss, stabilizing what had been a foundering ship.

After Mack left, many of those who had overseen and been disciplined for the alleged IPO abuses—including Coleman, Ehinger, Benjamin, and Caan—remained. As for Dougan himself, the lanky Midwesterner received another promotion in February 2007 when he was named chief executive of the parent company, Credit Suisse Group.

O

In a letter dated July 5, 2004, to Judge Owen asking for mercy, Denise Quattrone noted that she had been "battling the ravages of a chronic illness and its complications and disappointments for the last ten years." Her husband, she said, is "not the 'Master of the universe' whom the public and press is looking to punish."

Quattrone, she noted, had made a large donation to a CSFB fund for families of the 9/11 rescue workers after the World Trade Center attacks. Even when informed he was going to be indicted, she said, Quattrone was assisting his daughter in "putting together care packages for our troops in Iraq." Even after that bad news, she said, Quattrone "had the presence of mind to write our soldiers a heartfelt patriotic thank-you letter for their service to our country."

As she painted it, Denise's condition was in a way the reverse of Quattrone's— as much success and adulation as her husband had achieved in his work, she had been equally afflicted with the ravages of her disabling illness at home.

Any lengthy absence by Frank would be "absolutely unimaginable," because "the physical realities of my illness are inconsistent [and] unpredictable," and for her the everyday activities most people engage in were not possible.

Throughout her ordeal, she said, "Frank is always there for me, taking over whatever needs to be done in my absence for our daughter. . . ." She described in detail the physical toll her illness had taken, the distress it caused her, and the care and comfort she relied upon Frank to provide.

In her plea to the judge, Denise concluded, "I honestly know and believe that I won't survive a continued and prolonged separation from Frank. . . ."[6]

○

On July 22, 2004, about ten of the jurors had a reunion dinner at Café Centro, an upscale restaurant in the Metropolitan Life building above Grand Central terminal. It began at 6:30 P.M., and all of those who attended stayed until 10:30 P.M. The waiter took group photos with a camera owned by one of the jurors, who later circulated them via e-mail. Miller announced that he was leaving the area to join a dot-com on the West Coast. Rosey Rudnick, the travel agent, urged the jurors to stay in touch.

○

On September 8, 2004, in Judge Owen's own smaller courtroom in the tower of the old federal court building, Quattrone appeared for sentencing. His team had pulled out all the stops and arranged for letters to the judge from 495 of his supporters—family members, childhood friends, Wall Street colleagues and competitors, venture capital executives, and trustees and employees of his daughter's school and the Tech Museum. Denise herself wrote three letters and her daughter, one.

But Judge Owen was unmoved, for the first time openly giving his unvarnished view that he considered Quattrone guilty. He granted an upward departure from the sentencing guidelines to give the banker eighteen months in prison, because he found that, based on the guilty verdict, Quattrone had lied on the stand.

"If you get on the stand and you say no, no, no, never happened, and it is absolutely in my opinion crystal clear that this was untruthful, it is appropriate to conclude," Owen explained, "that this is terribly damaging to the administration of justice if this kind of thing goes unremarked and un–dealt with."

Although Owen ordered Quattrone to begin serving his sentence immediately, a federal appeals court allowed him to remain free pending his appeal. His supporters, including a who's who of Silicon Valley that included some of the letter writers, later gathered at a surprise birthday party at a local club. But in November, the NASD barred him from the securities industry for life for failing to testify in its civil case, in which he was charged with spinning and flawed research supervision. (In 2006, the SEC overturned the ban, and the NASD dropped the charges.)

O

In January 2005, CSFB was renamed, dropping the "First Boston" and becoming simply "Credit Suisse." As the stock market continued to surge, Credit Suisse launched a new corporate-image campaign. Full-page ads showed a man in a business suit, hands in pockets, in the middle of a vast empty office space. Some distance away stood a lone desk, chair, and desktop computer. The headline read: "Some people think start-up. We think IPO."

The ads prompted a caustic commentary from *New York Times* columnist Floyd Norris. "In the winter of 2000, the greatest boom in initial public offerings was cresting. Companies with no revenues, let alone earnings, were being sold to the public at high prices, then doubling or tripling on the first day. At the center of it all was Credit Suisse First Boston, where Frank Quattrone, the powerful investment banker, was underwriting hot stock after hot stock."

Unknown to most at the time, Norris recalled, CSFB had received more than commissions for the IPO shares. "Customers who wanted in were expected to provide additional compensation, either through sky-high commissions or steering business to the firm. When the great bubble deflated, those left holding the stocks lost most or all of their investments. Jokes were heard that First Boston's customers should have known they would get clipped. Why else have a clipper-ship logo?"

The new ads, Norris noted, risked reminding Credit Suisse's customers "of its old ways of underwriting flimsy companies."[7]

O

Quattrone's appeal, filed on January 27, 2005, said the government had "failed to demonstrate that Quattrone knew what documents had been subpoenaed." And Judge Owen had rejected a defense bid to instruct the jury that this was

required. Owen had compounded this by giving the "conscious avoidance" instruction, allowing the jury to find guilt if Qauttrone deliberately hadn't checked.

The appeal added that Judge Owen had interfered with Quattrone's testimony, improperly limiting the banker to yes or no answers on cross-examination,
without letting him explain or elaborate. Owen had also, with the RIM cross-
examination, allowed the prosecution to raise "a baseless and highly prejudicial
accusation that Quattrone had committed an unrelated and uncharged securities law violation" in seeking $2 million in undisclosed underwriting fees.

The appeal added that Owen had improperly admitted inflammatory evidence such as Quattrone's pay, while excluding other exculpatory evidence,
such as why Quattrone forgot the sequence of events with Lynch in January
2003, or the CSFB lawyers' debate over a wider document retention notice.

In its opposition brief, dated April 29, 2005, the government said the judge
had the discretion to exclude evidence that could have confused the jury, and
any errors were harmless.

O

On March 15, 2005, Anders won a conviction of Bernard Ebbers, the former
chief executive of WorldCom, on nine criminal counts, including conspiracy and
securities fraud, for his role in the $11 billion accounting fraud that sent the
telecom giant to bankruptcy court. It was just one of a string of successful government prosecutions of bubble-era misconduct. Martha Stewart, like Quattrone, had been found guilty of obstruction in March 2004. The two former top
executives of Tyco International Ltd., Dennis Kozlowski and Mark Swartz, were
convicted of larceny, conspiracy, and securities fraud in June 2005. And Kenneth
Lay and Jeffrey Skilling, the former leaders of Enron, were convicted of fraud in
May 2006.

O

But on May 31, 2005, the U.S. Supreme Court voided a criminal conviction
of Arthur Andersen LLP, the former accounting giant that had collapsed under
the weight of its alleged role in shredding documents during an investigation
of the collapse of its audit client Enron.

The charges against Andersen bore some similarity to those against Quattrone. They stemmed from Andersen partners having urged subordinates to
comply with the firm's document retention policy by destroying documents
while the SEC was investigating Enron.

The successful appeal was based on the Andersen trial judge having told the
jury they could convict on a witness-tampering charge even if the Andersen
employees believed their conduct was lawful. The ruling buoyed Quattrone's
defense hopes of winning the appeal.

O

On July 12, 2005, Anders personally appeared before a three-judge appeals court panel hearing the oral arguments for Quattrone's case in the new federal court building in back of Foley Square in Manhattan. Once again Quattrone's mother, sister, dozens of former colleagues, and his own large legal team showed up in his support.

The judges questioned both prosecution and defense lawyers sharply. When Quattrone's chief appeals lawyer, Mark Pomerantz, argued that Quattrone didn't know that documents from his group were being sought by the grand jury, the presiding judge, Richard Wesley, raised the Brodsky e-mails alerting Quattrone. To say Quattrone was "unaware" was "a bit disingenuous," Wesley observed.

But Judge Wesley also scolded Anders for his rough use of the Research in Motion fee dispute to try to suggest Quattrone had violated securities laws. Any good trial lawyer tries to "push the envelope," Judge Wesley said. "You really blew the side of the envelope out, didn't you?"

O

Many of the regulators involved in the IPO cases wound up working for big Wall Street firms.

Richard Walker, the SEC enforcement chief when the IPO probe was launched, and Robert Khuzami, the head of the prosecutors' securities fraud unit, went to Deutsche Bank AG—a big German rival of CSFB's Swiss parent Credit Suisse Group.

Pennington, who had supervised the SEC IPO kickback case, and Dinallo, the Spitzer deputy who led the case against Merrill, went to Morgan Stanley. In the fall of 2004, prosecutors Peikin and Karen Seymour went to Sullivan & Cromwell, the lead outside law firm for Goldman Sachs.

In late 2005, Anders, too, joined a top law firm, Wachtell Lipton Rosen & Katz, that was best known for its work on big mergers and acquisitions. It had also represented Martha Stewart. There he joined Wayne Carlin, the former head of the SEC's northeast regional office, who had helped oversee the agency's original IPO kickback probe in 2000 and 2001. That law firm would soon win a case that, in hindsight, marked a shift in the regulatory tide against Wall Street.

O

With Spitzer still leading the way, regulators had made cases against other leading Wall Street figures. In the fall of 2003, the New York attorney general pursued charges of allowing improper mutual-fund trading against several top fund managers. He brought charges in May 2004 against former New York

Stock Exchange chief Dick Grasso over a lavish pay package that had cost Grasso his job. And he forced the ouster of Maurice "Hank" Greenberg in 2005 as the chief executive of insurance giant American International Group over charges that AIG had helped itself and other firms misstate their earnings.

Spitzer had been aided in his anti–Wall Street crusade by a New York state law that helped him negotiate settlements of such charges under the threat of the kind of criminal prosecution that can be fatal to financial firms. But among white-collar defense lawyers, a backlash was also building against such tactics.

On March 3, 2006, a hearing panel threw out an IPO kickback case brought by the NASD in April 2003 against Invemed Associates LLC, whose chief, Ken Langone, had mounted an expensive defense led by Wachtell Lipton. Although other firms had chosen to settle such charges, Langone had vowed to fight them, saying, "if other people want to roll over and admit they did something, if they did something, good for them."[8] Spitzer had also charged Langone for his role in approving Grasso's pay at the stock exchange.

The NASD had obtained expert testimony from mutual-fund pioneer John Bogle, who called such oversize commission payments "payola," and a "pay-to-play kind of arrangement," which he called "clearly on the wrong side of the ethical line." But the panel found that while Invemed brokers tracked customers' IPO profits, and their commissions were correlated with those profits, that wasn't the same as an explicit agreement to share profits, which both the brokers and customers denied. Both the customers and Invemed said the commission rates were set voluntarily by the customers. Unlike the brokers at CSFB, the evidence didn't show the Invemed brokers had coerced or cut off customers who hadn't paid.[9]

A few weeks later, several dozen NASD staffers gathered on the second floor of a downtown Washington, D.C., restaurant, Smith & Wollensky, for a farewell party for Barry Goldsmith, the agency's head of enforcement. Goldsmith had succeeded in building a more aggressive enforcement effort in his ten years in the job. Among the attendees was Ozag, the former D.C. cop who had led the IPO kickback probes of CSFB and Invemed.

In one of the send-off toasts, top NASD executive Robert Glauber seemed to allude to the Langone setback by noting that it was important for the agency to pursue difficult, challenging enforcement cases, and not just the easy-to-win ones. The remarks would soon take on even greater resonance.

○

On Monday March 20, 2006, the federal appeals court overturned Quattrone's conviction, citing faulty jury instructions and other errors by Judge Owen, and ordering that any retrial be handled by a different judge. The panel acknowledged that "the evidence is sufficient to support Quattrone's conviction on each count," and that "a rational juror" could have concluded that the banker "was aware that the grand jury sought documents" in his group's possession.

But it turned out that the Andersen shredding decision had been a huge break for Quattrone. The Supreme Court had ruled the Andersen jurors were told erroneously that they could convict on witness tampering even if Andersen employees believed their conduct was lawful. The Quattrone appeal panel noted that Judge Owen's instructions similarly failed to require a connection. When he had summarized the requirements for counts one and two, obstructing the criminal and civil probes, he said the jurors could vote guilty if Quattrone merely "directed the destruction of documents that were called for" by the subpoenas. The summary "eviscerated" the requirement to find that Quattrone connected his e-mail with the investigation, said Judge Richard Wesley, writing for the majority.

The panel also took issue with other Owen rulings, such as restricting Quattrone to yes and no answers during his cross-examination and allowing prosecutors to characterize the RIM fee dispute as possible rule breaking. But they ratified Owen's decisions to allow Quattrone's pay into evidence, and to exclude defense evidence of the debate among CSFB lawyers about suspending the document retention policy.

The appeals court's order for the case to be assigned to a new judge explained that some of Owen's remarks "could be viewed as rising beyond mere impatience or annoyance."

The Quattrone team hailed the decision as "a significant victory." Quattrone himself said, "For over three years during this difficult ordeal, I have held my head high knowing I was innocent and never intended to obstruct justice."

The news would quickly get even better for Quattrone. Four days later, on Friday, March 24, the SEC set aside the NASD's November 2004 order barring him from the securities industry for life. Quattrone had appealed the ban to the SEC, arguing that the NASD should have allowed him to avoid testifying because at the time it was acting as a quasi-governmental agency in probing research-bias charges and spinning in conjunction with the SEC. In overturning the ban, the SEC said only that the NASD should have given Quattrone a hearing on the issue—which hadn't been the NASD's practice. Instead, the NASD had imposed such bans automatically to keep out those who wouldn't address charges of misconduct.

Two months later, the NASD was forced to retreat, dropping the last remaining civil charges against Quattrone, of spinning and flawed research oversight. Too much time had passed to make the case, the agency concluded, partly because some witnesses weren't in the securities business any longer and therefore couldn't be compelled to testify.

Quattrone's lawyers had argued that so much time had elapsed since the conduct charged had occurred between 1998 and 2001 that witnesses' memories might be impaired, and that in any case the rules in effect at the time—which had later been strengthened—didn't bar his actions. But after the Langone defeat and Quattrone's own back-to-back wins from the appeals court and the SEC, it seemed as though the agency didn't have the stomach for a protracted new battle.

O

Quattrone allowed the lawyers who had won the appeal, led by Mark Pomerantz of Paul Weiss and his partner Ted Wells, one of the top trial lawyers in the United States, to negotiate with the new set of prosecutors who had inherited the Quattrone case. Wells would later lead former White House aide Scooter Libby's unsuccessful defense against charges of perjury and obstruction during a probe of the leak of the identity of a Central Intelligence Agency operative.

Comey's successor as U.S. attorney, Michael Garcia, had made fighting terrorism a bigger priority than white-collar crime. That summer, Richard Owens, the cohead of the securities fraud unit and one of the last senior prosecutors who had overseen the Quattrone prosecution still in the office, announced his departure. Some legal observers believed that the new judge assigned to the case, George Daniels, would allow the Quattrone defense far wider latitude than Judge Owen had.

On the morning of Tuesday, August 22, in the courtroom of Judge Daniels, a subdued scene played out. Although some of Quattrone's die-hard partisans attended, including Bill Brady and lawyer Ken Hausman, it appeared that they were deliberately avoiding any victory dance.

Quattrone embraced one of the courtroom artists who had sketched him at his trials, and grinned when Judge Daniels asked whether he had any questions about a deferred prosecution agreement, under which the charges would be dropped if Quattrone stayed out of trouble for a year. "No, your honor," he said.

Riding the elevator down, Quattrone asked Wells how he had done. "You did great," Wells said. "You were worried, weren't you?" Quattrone joked. Outside, the mood became more jubilant, as Quattrone marveled at the "sunny day," and walked in an almost formal procession on the sidewalk of Worth Street, flanked by Pomerantz and Wells. He read a brief prepared statement, saying he was "very pleased that the case will be concluded," and said that he looked forward to resuming his career.

"Like a championship boxer or a celebrity at a movie premiere, Frank Quattrone was swarmed by photographers who wanted to capture the look of a man who just won his life back," wrote Associated Press reporter Larry Neumeister.

"Give us that winning smile," one of them shouted as the millionaire in a gray suit happily obliged.

"You betcha!" Quattrone said.

But Neumeister noted that Quattrone's victory wasn't unequivocal. He quoted Harvard Business School investment banking professor emeritus Samuel Hayes, a longtime arbiter of Wall Street folkways: "He's a convicted person whose case was dismissed on a technicality, and the things he was accused of are serious crimes," Mr. Hayes said. "You can't put a scrambled egg back into the shell."[10]

Some months later, Quattrone hosted an elaborate "thank-you" celebration for his entire legal team. He flew the lawyers and their spouses or guests, a party of eighty to one hundred, to Pebble Beach for a weekend that included dinners at his home and the golf course resort. And he gave a humorous "awards" tribute in which he thanked each team member by name.

O

The Quattrone reversal was just one element of the ebbing enforcement tide. In securities fraud cases against fifteen New York Stock Exchange "specialist" traders accused of cheating investors, Manhattan prosecutors lost several trials, and Garcia decided to drop charges against five individuals. And a big tax-shelter prosecution was largely thrown out by a federal judge, who ruled that prosecutors improperly pressured KPMG LLP, the defendants' former employer, to cut off payment of their legal fees.

In mid-2008, after a four-year battle, a New York State appeals court threw out the Spitzer case against former NYSE chief Dick Grasso, ruling that Grasso could keep his entire $187.5 million pay package.

The most ignominious downfall, of course, was suffered by Spitzer himself. After serving just fourteen months of a four-year term as New York governor, an office to which he had been catapulted by his anti–Wall Street crusade, he resigned in March 2008 after the news broke that he had patronized a prostitution service.

But after the debt-market meltdown of 2007–2008, the pendulum began swinging back toward more regulation again. Amid a debate over how regulators hadn't acted to rein in risk-taking by financial institutions, two individuals who had played roles in the first kickback probe of CSFB gained two top jobs at the SEC. Mary Schapiro, who had announced the profit-sharing charges in January 2002 as president of NASD Regulation, became the SEC chairman. And she named Rob Khuzami, the former federal prosecutor who had led the criminal probe of the same matter, to be the SEC enforcement chief.

O

And what about Quattrone? Did he deserve the legal ordeal? Had he done anything wrong? The questions aren't easy, and the answers depend both on one's perspective, and on the date of the question.

Quattrone was obviously a talented, charming, hardworking banker, and a devoted family man. He set his own path at blue-chip Morgan Stanley, defying the firm's demand to absorb its values by starting in New York, and having the nerve to stand out with his funky sweaters and dinky deals in a sea of pin-striped Ivy Leaguers.

Among the characteristics that seem to have gotten him in trouble were a tendency to bully, coerce, and control, a win-at-all-costs mentality admittedly common on Wall Street, and a lack of humility verging on arrogance and hubris. His own visions of his greatness seemed to have blinded him to the risks that the powerful market tide he rode could turn against him.

When technology took off in the mid-1990s, Quattrone gave little credit to the strength of the Morgan Stanley organization in helping him land the deals he brought in. Like Milken before him, Quattrone became so confident, and had such economic power within his organization, that he became exempt from some of the routine checks and balances, rickety as they might have been at CSFB, that had been designed to promote compliance with the rules.

By following a banker's natural impulse to try to win a bake-off or obtain a favorable analyst's report, Quattrone pushed the envelope in research through the power he exercised over analysts—by having them report to him, and through his setting of their pay. Having his own small crew of brokers put him into the picture in the first profit-sharing probe, particularly after three of them were fired in mid-2001 for violating firm policies related to the issues being investigated.

But it was the Friends of Frank accounts, with their distinctive name and structure, that more than anything landed Quattrone in hot water. True, their original purpose was simply to prevent Quattrone's banking clients from getting cold-called randomly by brokers in his own company but outside his control.

Intentionally or not, however, the accounts quickly became similar to "bribes," in the word of former analyst Desai and the Massachusetts regulators, as they were offered only to executives who chose CSFB, and were stocked with hot IPOs. While other securities firms certainly had brokers who got hot IPOs to banking clients, Quattrone had done it in an organized, systematic way.

While Quattrone could truthfully say that the accounts were cleared by CSFB's legal department, that wasn't enough cover against the force of the postbubble regulatory backlash, which took two years to gather strength in 2001 and 2002 as the market floundered and Spitzer scored with his research probe. His denials that the accounts weren't meant to win banking business were ultimately unconvincing to regulators.

For the average investor, Quattrone's most consequential action might have been a lot simpler. He engineered the most IPOs of Internet and other technology companies at the height of a market mania, many not ready for prime time, costing investors billions when the stocks subsequently plummeted when the bubble burst.

In comparison to the way Quattrone pushed the envelope in spinning, research, or IPOs, sending the "time to clean up those files" e-mail was almost trivial. But the timing of its appearance, just as other regulators were preparing to charge him with research and spinning violations, forced the hand of the federal prosecutors.

Quattrone was simply too big to ignore when it emerged that he had sent an admittedly ambiguous message calling for document destruction. By then, the very high profile Quattrone sought when doing battle with Morgan Stanley and Goldman Sachs made him too tempting a target for all the regulators, from Massachusetts to New York. The rising force of his chest-beating, "we're-number-one" braggadocio might have made sense in chasing business. But it was a two-edged sword.

O

In high school, Quattrone had been fascinated by Odysseus, the intelligent, resourceful soldier who devises the Trojan horse to win the siege of Troy. Though his men are all killed in a shipwreck during a difficult ten-year journey home in Homer's *The Odyssey*, he finally arrives safely to reclaim his crown as king of Ithaca and to kill dozens of his wife's suitors.

In his own career, Quattrone became an unequaled leader in building a team to raise money for technology companies, good and bad, in the boom years. When the bubble burst, he lost his own banking army and suffered through a difficult five-year battle against regulators and prosecutors before finally besting them in court—emerging legally unscathed from what his defenders called a witch hunt.

Yet other myths also seemed pertinent—the fall of Achilles, the warrior who tempted fate by desecrating the temple of Apollo, or even Icarus, who built wings of feathers and wax and gained the ability to fly. As one cynical Wall Street lawyer put it after the case was closed, Quattrone "flew too close to the sun and his wings melted."

ON MARCH 2, 2002, Frank Scognamillo, the Arizona marketing entrepreneur who had sold his customer-loyalty business to Netcentives at the peak of the Internet frenzy two years earlier, in March 2000, filed a lawsuit against Credit Suisse First Boston, Boutros, and another CSFB banker; Quattrone was later added as a defendant.

Unable to sell his Netcentives stock initially under a one-year lockup agreement, Scognamillo had seen its price plunge along with the rest of the Internet market. By the time the lockup expired, a year after the merger, the stock had fallen 95 percent from its merger level of $48.125 a share, to just $2.563 a share. On September 6, 2001, after its stock had closed at just $.12 a share, Netcentives was delisted from the NASDAQ stock market. On October 9, the company filed for bankruptcy; its assets were liquidated two months later, in December 2001.

The Scottsdale, Arizona, law firm retained by Scognamillo, Beus Gilbert PLLC, had an opulent office suite covering the top floor of a six-story, bronze glass office building in Scottsdale—not far from the Phoenician resort where the tech group had held its annual conference in its heyday. Lead partner Leo Beus preferred to avoid some mass-tort cases such as Enron, where he couldn't hope to control the course of the case. But he had helped clients win big recoveries. He had represented British bank Standard Chartered PLC in a negligence case against Price Waterhouse arising from the bank's purchase of United Bank of Arizona, which was settled in 1999 for an undisclosed sum after a 1987 jury verdict of $341 million was thrown out.[1] The Scognamillo lawsuit, originally filed in Superior Court of Maricopa County, Arizona, was transferred to Northern California Federal Court in May 2003.

The first Beus Gilbert lawyer assigned to the Scognamillo case, Quinton Seamons, an alumnus of the SEC, had to bow out around the end of 2005 due to illness. The second lawyer, Kenneth Mann, joined the firm in 2005 after moving to Arizona from Florida to live near his daughter and her family. In a fifth amended complaint filed in November 2005, Scognamillo charged that Credit Suisse had improperly boosted the Netcentives stock price via favorable equity research and other "manipulative conduct," including IPO allocation practices. By 2008, although Quattrone had been dismissed as a defendant, the plaintiffs had staved off some of CSFB's efforts to get the case thrown out, thereby winning the right to extensive document discovery and interviews with Boutros, Buyer, and other CSFB bankers.

At his deposition on February 8, 2008, Boutros tried to put the IPO carnage in perspective. "A lot of companies were taken public by every single underwriter on Wall Street in that period of time, and frankly, there are companies that are taken public all the time which, with hindsight, maybe weren't as good as people felt at the time," Boutros said. "That happened a lot during the 1999–2000 time frame, because a lot of companies went public during that period of time, as you well know, and frankly, it happens all the time. No one can make perfect judgments about companies. And with hindsight, hindsight is twenty-twenty, as they say."[2]

Scognamillo attended the interview with Boutros, and recalls Boutros indicating how tiny the Netcentives deal was compared to CSFB's whirlwind of bubble-era business. "He said to him we were a nit," said Scognamillo.[3] A lawyer for Boutros noted that the merger banker wasn't involved in underwriting IPOs, but did echo Scognamillo's account by asserting that UVN was "a very small acquisition" for Netcentives.[4]

Of course Netcentives was just one of many IPOs handled by CSFB and other big firms that went down the tubes after the bubble burst. A consolidated class-action federal lawsuit against all the big firms, which had underwritten more than three hundred IPOs during the bubble, wasn't settled until spring 2009. But Scognamillo's was unusual, with damages sought by one investor who had lost millions on a single stock, in a process that included extensive contacts with Credit Suisse bankers.

In July 2008, Mann asked the court's permission to file a seventh version of Scognamillo's complaint. The proposed new complaint charged that Credit Suisse executives knew that many of the companies they were taking public during the bubble were destined to fail, but withheld that knowledge from investors. As evidence, the lawsuit cited analyst Lise Buyer's comments about Netcentives's "horrible business model," as well as her never-published projections of future losses that Scognamillo hadn't seen during the merger talks. (Buyer says that these numbers were mechanically generated projections, not "real estimates.")[5] In November 2008, presiding Judge Thelton Henderson denied the motion to amend the complaint. In January 2009, claims against Boutros and another CSFB banker were dropped. In April, Credit Suisse agreed to pay a small sum to settle the case.

In fact, the vast majority of the tech companies taken public by CSFB cost investors money. At this author's request, an analysis of eighty-six IPOs claimed by the CSFB tech group, by IPO expert Jay Ritter, professor of finance at the University of Florida in Gainesville, found that they raised $10.4 billion from investors in their initial offerings. By the end of 2002, the value of those dollars had shrunk to $4.1 billion, for an indicated loss of 61 percent.

Ritter calculated returns for eighty-three IPOs of U.S. companies, plus three IPOs of non–U.S. concerns that traded on U.S. exchanges. (The CSFB tech group did another eight IPOs of non-U.S. companies that didn't trade in the United States.) The names of the IPOs claimed by the tech group were obtained mainly from two end-of-year brochures prepared for 1999 and 2000 by tech group marketing staffers. The calculations didn't include a few tech IPOs that were led by another firm, Donaldson Lufkin & Jenrette, before it was acquired by CSFB in late 2000. Nor did they include gains or losses after a stock was bought out in an acquisition.[6]

Quattrone at times showed some awareness that the losses might look bad. At a meeting with journalists in August 2000, he had tried to deflect the responsibility toward the companies' venture capital backers. And during his legal ordeal, his public relations representative, Bob Chlopak, sent out a fact sheet noting that IPOs he had overseen over his entire career, including Cisco Systems and Amazon while at Morgan Stanley and Deutsche Bank, had generated $200 billion of investor wealth.

At his two obstruction trials, Quattrone's lawyers introduced exhibits into evidence aimed at showing he had dashed off his file-cleanup "reply to all" endorsement in the process of firing off a total of twenty e-mails to suggest that he wasn't giving deep consideration to obstructing the IPO probe. As it happened, one of those e-mails asked a marketing executive whether the group could "hide the woofers" in its year-end ads listing its accomplishments for 2000 by not mentioning the IPOs that had plummeted in price. Indeed, the final version of the group's press release did just that—listing only five of the group's fifty-plus IPOs.

Ritter's analysis showed that fifty-two of the eighty-six tech group IPOs for which returns could be calculated using U.S. market prices had fallen by 80 percent or more in price from their offering date through the end of 2002, when stocks had reached their low point after the bubble. Nearly one third, or twenty-eight of them, had fallen by 95 percent. Only eight of the group actually delivered positive returns to investors.

The biggest dollar losers were: Corvis, the optical switching company, which saw 98 percent of its IPO value of $1.14 billion melt away; TD Waterhouse Group, the online broker, whose $1.01 billion IPO sank by 61 percent; Gemplus International SA, a French smart-card maker, whose $382 million IPO fell by 79 percent; McData Corporation, a switch maker whose $350 million IPO

dropped 75 percent; and Intersil Holding Corporation, a wireless communications chip-set provider, whose $500 million IPO slipped by 44 percent. Four of
those occurred during or just after February 2000, when Internet stock prices
were just reaching their peak.

The biggest gainers were: Software.com Inc., an Internet e-mail provider,
whose $90 million IPO rose nine times in price; AppNet Systems Inc., an
e-commerce services company, whose $72 million IPO rose more than four
times in price; and Silknet Software Inc., an online order-management software provider, whose $45 million IPO rose nearly four times in price. All three
of those IPOs occurred before the end of June 1999, before Internet stocks sky-
rocketed in the fourth quarter, setting the stage for the crash. The next biggest
gainers were Integrated Circuit Systems Inc., a silicon timing device maker,
whose $162.5 million IPO rose by 40 percent, and Virata Corporation, an In-
ternet phone-line systems provider, whose $70 million IPO rose 80 percent.

Mergers before the bubble burst bolstered the gains by Software.com and
Silknet, and Virata was acquired in 2001, before the bloom was totally off the
rose.

The loss of value for the CSFB technology stocks wasn't radically different
than for tech IPOs led by other Wall Street firms, Ritter said. Of course, CSFB
boasted that it led the most. Along with a collapse of telecommunications
stocks that closely followed the Internet bust, he says, it was "one of the biggest
booms and busts in the history of the developed world's financial markets."

But because the rapid rise and fall of the tech and telecom sectors occurred
over a brief period of time, and represented "a paper gain followed by a paper loss,"
Ritter said, "the economic consequences weren't as severe as if it had been a long-
standing gain that had built up over time and had been widely shared by investors throughout society"—as had been the case with the Great Crash of 1929.

Ritter himself served on a fourteen-member IPO advisory committee convened at the request of the SEC by the New York Stock Exchange and NASD,
which in May 2003 recommended reforms in the IPO process. One of its proposals, aimed at curtailing "spinning," would have barred allocation of IPO
shares to officials of companies with an investment banking relationship with
the underwriter, or as a "quid pro quo for investment banking business." This
reform was never adopted, although the NASD has taken the position that spinning violates its prohibition against gifts and gratuities over certain limits.

When Quattrone returned to the securities business on March 18, 2008, by
announcing the launch of Qatalyst Group, a technology-focused merchant bank
in San Francisco, Ritter was quoted in a story about Qatalyst by Aaron Rica-
dela of *BusinessWeek*'s online edition.

"His reputation in Silicon Valley is based upon two facets," Ritter said. "The
positive side is, as an investment banker, he and his team were involved in

financing many prominent companies. He was one of the most important players in the financing of Silicon Valley," he said. "The negative is, some of his
procedures for attracting business were ethically questionable."

Ritter, the article added, had studied companies that went public between
1996 and 2000 and found that only 5 percent of those whose executives received IPOs from their underwriters switched investment banks when they
returned to the market to sell additional stock. Of those whose executives
weren't "spun," as the article put it, Ritter said a much greater proportion—31
percent—switched underwriters. As a result, Ritter said, "it was a successful
business strategy at attracting deals."

On March 24, five days after the *BusinessWeek* article, Quattrone's lawyer,
Ken Hausman, sent Ritter a letter demanding a "retraction" of the "libelous
statements" Ritter contributed to the article, saying they "paint a false and de-
famatory picture of Mr. Quattrone and his conduct." Hausman said he doubted
whether the Florida-based Ritter had actually studied Quattrone's reputation
in Silicon Valley, and noted that the NASD had withdrawn the "spinning charges"
against Quattrone.

The three-page letter went into detail disputing the original NASD charges,
saying "there was no evidence presented that any IPO allocations were made to
attract banking business, and ample evidence that Mr. Quattrone was not responsible for making or supervising IPO allocations."[7] But of course Schmidt's
testimony in September 2002 to the NASD that getting more banking business was one goal of the Friends of Frank accounts could have been viewed as
evidence of that.

Adding impact to the demand, Hausman sent a copy of his letter to the University of Florida board of trustees, which Ritter called "a further attempt to
intimidate me." A university lawyer followed up by contacting Ritter, and they
discussed whether the statement might be libelous. Ritter believed not, on the
theory that to be libelous, a statement had to be "knowingly false, and ethics
are quite obviously a judgment issue." Ritter didn't retract or correct the statement, and hadn't heard back from Hausman as of summer 2009.[8]

CAST OF CHARACTERS

Frank Quattrone—technology investment banker at Morgan Stanley (1981–96); Deutsche Bank (1996–98); and CSFB (July 1998–February 2003)

South Philadelphia

Rose Quattrone—Quattrone's mother

Denise Quattrone—Quattrone's wife

Rusty Lamberto—Quattrone's childhood friend

Wall Street Bankers and Brokers

Morgan Stanley

Richard Fisher—head of capital markets when Quattrone joined firm in 1981; became president in 1984; died December 2004

Carter McClelland—head of San Francisco office in mid-1980s; hired Quattrone at Deutsche Bank in 1996

Andy Kessler—semiconductor research analyst

Joseph Fogg—head of investment banking in late 1980s and early 1990s

Mary Meeker—star Internet analyst

John Mack—head of bond department, then president; left in 2001 and became CEO of Credit Suisse First Boston

Bob Scott—became head of investment banking, 1995

Mayree Clark—head of research, 1994–2001

George Kelly—communications equipment analyst

Joe Perella—head of corporate finance, 1996

Terry Meguid—deputy head of corporate finance, 1996

Credit Suisse First Boston (titles as of 1999–2000)

Allen Wheat—CEO until July 2001

Charles Ward—cohead of equities and investment banking, 1994–2000; cohead of equities and investment banking, 2000

Charles Stonehill—deputy head of investment banking; negotiated to hire Quattrone, 1998

Brady Dougan—global head of equities, 1996–2000; cohead of equities and investment banking, 2000–2004; president, 2004.

J. Anthony ("Tony") Ehinger (pronounced "Anger")—U.S. head of equity sales, May 2000; global head of equity sales, May 2000 on

George W. Coleman—head of institutional listed stock sales

Ernesto Cruz—head of global equity capital markets

Quattrone Tech Group at CSFB

George Boutros—head of technology mergers

William J. B. Brady—head of corporate finance

John Hodge—deputy head of corporate finance

Ted Smith—junior banker who stayed in Bill Brady's guest apartment

Andy Fisher—tech group equity capital markets chief; umpired allocations of hot tech IPOs for Quattrone

Richard Char—head of execution group

CSFB Technology Private Client Services (Tech PCS) Brokers

John Schmidt—head of Quattrone group brokers who ran Friends of Frank program

Michael Grunwald—pursued commission "payback" program in Quattrone's group

Linda-Louise Lund—Schmidt's assistant

Scott Bushley—trading assistant

Scott Brown—trading assistant; left firm in early 2000

CSFB Legal and Compliance Department

Joseph McLaughlin—global general counsel, through August 2001

Gary Lynch—global general counsel, after August 2001

David Brodsky—general counsel for the Americas, 1999–2001

Kevin McCarthy—head of litigation for the Americas

Ray Dorado—head of legal and compliance for North American equity division

CSFB Brokers

Andy Benjamin—head of Private Client Services brokers, catering to individual investors and small hedge funds

Paul Caan—Benjamin's deputy head of PCS; had authority over some IPO allocations; subject of original JohnDoe526 anonymous kickback complaint

Dominick Commesso—broker for Lustig trader Andy Siegal

Ladd McQuade—head of PCS brokers in Boston; Siegal also had account with him

CSFB Research Analysts

Mike Kwatinetz—head of technology research; left in early 2000

Elliott Rogers—head of tech research starting in 2000

Lise Buyer—Internet

Erach Desai—design software

Donaldson Lufkin & Jenrette

Hamilton ("Tony") James—investment banking chief; became cohead of banking at CSFB

Ken Moelis—head of Los Angeles office until November 2001

Bennett Goodman—head of high-yield bond unit

Mike Campbell—head of private-client brokers

Clients
Venture Capital

Roger McNamee—cofounding partner of Integral Capital

Jay Hoag—Technology Crossover Ventures

John Doerr—Kleiner Perkins Caufield & Byers

Corporate Executives

Peter Jackson—CEO of Intraware

James Balsillie—co–chief executive of Research in Motion Ltd.

Michael Dell—CEO, Dell Computer

Thomas Meredith—CFO, Dell Computer

Donna Dubinsky—CEO, Handspring

Jim Clark—chairman and founder, Silicon Graphics; chairman Netscape Communications

Q. T. Wiles—CEO, Miniscribe, 1985–89

Jeffrey Dachis—CEO, Razorfish

Friends of Frank

Morteza Ejabat—CEO, Ascend Communications, Zhone Technologies

Alain Rossman—CEO, Phone.com

Don Katz—CEO of Audible

Martin Brauns—CEO, Interwoven

Investors and Traders

Larry Bowman—technology hedge fund manager

Glenn Fuhrman—manager of MSD Capital; Michael Dell's "family office" money manager

James Lustig—United Capital Management

Steve Kris—Ascent Capital

Andy Siegal—Energia Global Group Holding

Chris Champeau—identified in JohnDoe526 e-mail as friend and client of Paul Caan

Bob Cooper—client of CSFB Boston broker; related to sender of JohnDoe526 e-mail

Joe Cooper—Bob Cooper's brother, CSFB client; his wife, Andrea, sent JohnDoe526 e-mail

Cary Brody—Y2K Partners

Silicon Valley

Gary Lencioni, contractor for Quattrone's dream house project

David Terpening—Quattrone's architect

Dick Breaux—second contractor for dream house

The Regulators

National Association of Securities Dealers (NASD)

Robert Glauber—chief executive, NASD Regulation Inc.

Mary Schapiro—president, NASD Regulation Inc.

Barry Goldsmith—enforcement chief

Roger Sherman—prosecution witness at Quattrone trial

Joseph Ozag—led commission kickback probe

Securities and Exchange Commission

Harvey Pitt—chairman, 2001–02

Richard Walker—enforcement chief through mid-2001

Steve Cutler—enforcement director after October 2001

Wayne Carlin—head of northeast regional office

Caren Pennington—assistant northeast regional director

Doria Stetch—branch chief northeast regional office

William Stellmach—staff attorney northeast regional office

U.S. Attorney's Office for the Southern District of New York (Manhattan)
James Comey—U.S. attorney who decided to charge Quattrone

Karen Seymour—head of criminal division

Rob Khuzami—head of securities fraud unit during IPO kickback probe

Steve Peikin—conducted criminal IPO kickback probe, 2000–2001; prosecuted Quattrone for obstructing IPO kickback probe

David Anders—conducted IPO probe with Peikin; prosecuted Quattrone for obstruction

New York State Attorney General
Eliot Spitzer—elected New York attorney general in 1999

Eric Dinallo—head of investor protection unit

Peter Pope—chief of criminal division

Kevin Suttlehan—attorney in criminal division

The Lawyers
Ken Hausman—Quattrone's family lawyer

William MacLean—represented contractor Gary Lencioni

John Keker—Quattrone's chief criminal defense counsel

Ralph Ferrara—James Lustig's lawyer at Debevoise & Plimpton

Steve Farber—James Lustig's lawyer and brother-in-law; "the most powerful man in Denver"

Joe Jamail—Texas tort lawyer in Miniscribe case

Robert Wise—represented Morgan Stanley in Miniscribe case

Mark Pomerantz—led Quattrone's successful appeal

Judge and Jury
Judge Richard Owen

Jonathan Miller, retrial jury foreman

Denis Crosley

Sheldon Silver

The Press
Michael Siconolfi—reporter and editor, *The Wall Street Journal*

Chris Nolan—*San Jose Mercury News, The New York Post*

Mark Veverka—*San Jose Mercury News, Barron's*

NOTES

KEY TO COURT CASES AND REGULATORY ACTIONS

FS/CSS: *Frank Scognamillo, et al., v. Credit Suisse Securities (USA) LLC etc., et al.,* CO3-02061 TEH (No. Cal. D.C.)

INVD: *NASD Department of Enforcement v. Invemed Associates LLC (CRD No. 6728),* Disciplinary Proceeding No. CAF030014.

JS/CSFB/FQ: *John Schmidt v. Credit Suisse First Boston, Frank Quattrone,* 410207 (Calif. Sup. Ct. 2002) Does 1–100.

LCI/AAA: *Denise and Frank Quattrone, and Gary Lencioni, Lencioni Construction Inc.,* 74-110-0053-93 (American Arbitration Association, San Francisco, Calif.).

LCI/CSC: *Denise Quattrone, also known as Denise Foderaro, and Frank Quattrone, v. Gary Lencioni, Lencioni Construction Inc., Barbara Lencioni, et al.,* and related cross-action, 731055 (Calif. Sup. Ct.).

MASD: Commonwealth of Massachusetts, Office of the Secretary of the Commonwealth, Securities Division, In the Matter of: Credit Suisse First Boston, No. E-2002-41, Administrative Complaint, October 21, 2002; exhibits.

MIN1: *Feivel Gottlieb, Thomas R. Bloom, LeRoy B. Mott et al. v. Q. T. Wiles, Gerald W. Goodman, William R. Hambrecht, et al.* C.A. 89-M-963 (Co. D.C.), deposition of Frank P. Quattrone, vol. I (Miniscribe case).

MIN2: *U.S. National Bank of Galveston, et al. v. Coopers & Lybrand , et al.* 89-CV-1081-A (D.Ct., Galveston Cty., Tex. 212 J.D.). (Miniscribe trial)

MSG/CSFB: *Michael Scott Grunwald, v. Credit Suisse-First Boston Corp.,* 74 160 460 02 JAS (American Arbitration Association, April 3, 2002).

NASD/CSFB: NASD press release, dated January 22, 2002: "NASD Regulation Charges Credit Suisse First Boston with Siphoning Tens of Millions of Dollars of Customers' Profits in Exchange for 'Hot' IPO Shares."

NASD/FQ: NASD press release dated March 6. 2003: "NASD Charges Frank Quattrone with Spinning, Undermining Research Analyst Objectivity, Failure to Cooperate in Investigation." NASD Office of Hearing Officers, Disciplinary Proceeding No. 030007, Dept. of Enforcement, Complainant, v. Frank Peter Quattrone, March 6, 2003.

NYSC: Affidavit dated April 8, 2002, by Eric R. Dinallo, Assistant District Attorney General, State of New York, seeking reforms in research practices by Merrill Lynch & Co., et al., before Judge Martin Schoenfeld, index no. 02/401522, New York State Court.

RSB/CSFB: *Richard Scott Bushley, v. Credit Suisse First Boston Corp.*, and Does 1–25 and related cross-claims (Judicial Arbitration and Mediation Service, San Francisco, Calif., Case no. 1100038544).

SEC/CSFB1: *Securities and Exchange Commission v. Credit Suisse First Boston Corporation*, 02 CV 00090 (RWR) (D.D.C.).

SEC/CSFB2: *Securities and Exchange Commission v. Credit Suisse First Boston LLC, f/k/a Credit Suisse First Boston Corporation*, 03 CV 2946 (WHP) (S.D.N.Y.).

SEC/IPO: *In the Matter of Certain IPO Allocations*. NY-6752. Securities and Exchange Commission (SEC) order directing private investigation and designating officers to take testimony, October 6, 2000.

USA/FQ: *United State of America v. Frank Quattrone*, 03 CR 582 (RO) (S.D. N.Y.).

BOOKS

Andy Kessler, *Wall Street Meat: Jack Grubman, Frank Quattrone, Mary Meeker, Henry Blodget and Me* (United States: Escape Velocity Press, 2003).

Spencer E. Ante, *Creative Capital: Georges Doriot and the Birth of Venture Capital* (Boston: Harvard Business Press, 2008).

Jim Clark with Owen Edwards, *Netscape Time: The Making of the Billion-Dollar Start-Up That Took On Microsoft* (New York: St. Martin's Press, 1999).

Michael Lewis, *The New New Thing: A Silicon Valley Story* (New York: The Penguin Press, 2001).

Lowenstein1: Roger Lowenstein, *Origins of the Crash: The Great Bubble and Its Undoing* (New York: The Penguin Press, 2004).

Lowenstein2: Unpublished drafts of portions of above book provided to the author by Lowenstein.

Michael S. Malone, *Going Public: MIPS Computer and the Entrepreneurial Dream* (New York: HarperCollins Publishers, 1991).

Anthony B. Perkins and Michael C. Perkins, *The Internet Bubble: Inside the Overvalued World of High-Tech Stocks—And What You Need to Know to Avoid the Coming Shakeout* (New York: HarperCollins Publishers, 1999).

Thomas Petzinger, Jr., *Oil & Honor* (New York: G.P. Putnam's Sons, 1987).

Dan Reingold with Jennifer Reingold, *Confessions of a Wall Street Analyst: A True Story of Inside Information and Corruption in the Stock Market* (New York: HarperCollins Publishers, 2006).

1. Bubbles

1. Christina Dyrness, "VA Linux Rises Almost 700 Percent in First Day of Trading," *The News & Observer (Raleigh, North Carolina)*, December 10, 1999.

2. Terzah Ewing, Lee Gomes, and Charles Gasparino, "VA Linux Soars a Record 698%," *The Wall Street Journal*, December 10, 1999.

3. Frank Quattrone e-mail to Credit Suisse First Boston technology group members, March 14, 2000.

4. SEC/CSFB2, April 28, 2003.

5. Ante.

6. Al Jackson testimony to National Association of Securities Dealers (NASD), March 13, 2003, FS/CSS.

7. Andrew Benjamin testimony to NASD, April 1, 2003, FS/CSS.

8. Qatalyst launch press release, March 18, 2008.

9. Deborah Gage, "Quattrone Is Starting Firm in S.F.," *San Francisco Chronicle*, March 19, 2008.

10. Richard Waters, "Quattrone at Centre of Data Domain Bid War," *Financial Times*, June 18, 2009.

2. South Philly

1. Frank Quattrone e-mail to Tom Meredith, July 26, 2000, USA/FQ, government exhibit 1062.

2. Mark Veverka, author interview, August 6, 2004.

3. Richard Shaffer, author interview, August 11, 2004.

4. Henry V. Bender letter to Judge Richard Owen, May 27, 2004, USA/FQ, urging leniency after verdict.

5. Monsignor James Connelly, author interview, August 19, 2004.

6. Susan Pulliam interview of Rusty Lamberto's mother, April 2001.

7. Josephine Hirsch letter to Judge Richard Owen, May 27, 2004, USA/FQ, urging leniency.

8. Mike Ciocca, author interview, August 3, 2004; Susan Pulliam and Randall Smith, "Silicon Touch: For Frank Quattrone, With a Fief at CSFB, Tech Was a Gold Mine," *The Wall Street Journal*, May 3, 2001.

9. Francis Rabuck, author interview, September 2, 2004.

10. Mike Ciocca, author interview, August 3, 2004.

11. Rose Quattrone Schulke letter to Judge Richard Owen, June 1, 2004, USA/FQ, urging leniency.

12. Ciocca interview.

13. Roger Kashlak, author interview, August 22, 2004.

14. Henry Bender, author interview, October 26, 2004.

15. Bender interview and letter to Judge Richard Owen.

16. Bender letter.

17. Bender interview.

18. Schulke letter to Judge Owen.

19. Marlene Markel letter to Judge Richard Owen, August 20, 2004, USA/FQ, urging leniency.

20. James Keeley, letter to Judge Richard Owen, July 19, 2004, USA/FQ, urging leniency.

21. Lindsey Cronk letter to Judge Richard Owen, July 24, 2004, USA/FQ, urging leniency.

22. Joseph N. DiStefano, "Accused Former Credit Suisse Tech-Stock Salesman Had Humble Beginnings," *The Philadelphia Inquirer,* March 16, 2003.

23. Ciocca interview.

24. Kevin Vaughan, author interview, September 3, 2004.

25. University of Pennsylvania yearbook, 1977.

3. Morgan Stanley

1. Frank Quattrone direct testimony, April 27, 2004, USA/FQ.

2. Donald R. Kendall and Diane S. Kendall letter to Judge Richard Owen, Summer 2004, USA/FQ, urging leniency.

3. Richard Brust letter to Judge Richard Owen, August 23, 2004, USA/FQ, urging leniency.

4. Jack McDonald interview, cited in Lowenstein2.

5. Nancy Rutter, "How to Nab an IPO," *Forbes,* August 29, 1994.

6. William Hambrecht, author interview, September 27, 2004.

7. Denise Quattrone letter to Judge Richard Owen, July 5, 2004, USA/FQ, urging leniency.

8. Terry Vance letter to Judge Richard Owen, June 21, 2004, USA/FQ, urging leniency.

9. Ibid.

4. The Prince of Silicon Valley

1. Frank Quattrone testimony, April 27, 2004, USA/FQ.

2. Jack McDonald, author interview, July 2004.

3. Allen Morgan, author interview, spring 2001.

4. Lowenstein2.

5. Adam Lashinsky, Oliver Ryan, and Patricia Neering, "Remembering Netscape," *Fortune,* July 25, 2005.

6. Anthony B. Perkins, "Dan Case and Frank Quattrone on Riding the Technology Market," *Red Herring,* July 1, 1993.

7. Richard Shaffer, author interview, August 11, 2004.

8. Frank Quattrone e-mail to Credit Suisse First Boston technology group members, February 5, 2001.

9. Nancy Rutter, "How to Nab an IPO," *Forbes,* August 29, 1994.

10. Lowenstein2.

11. Rutter, *Forbes,* August 29, 1994.

12. Alec Ellison, author interview, April 1, 2009.

13. Kessler, p. 97.

14. Perkins, *Red Herring*, July 1, 1993.

15. Kessler, pp. 71–85.

16. Ibid.

5. Miniscribe

1. Frank Quattrone deposition for MIN1, April 3, 1991; USA/FQ, government exhibit 81.

2. Andy Zipser, "Cooking the Books," *The Wall Street Journal*, September 11, 1989.

3. Michael Miller, "Dr. Fixit," *The Wall Street Journal*, June 23, 1989.

4. Executive summary of report to Miniscribe board by Fried, Frank, Harris, Shriver & Jacobs, released September 12, 1989.

5. Stuart Zipper, "SEC to Ex-Miniscribers: Pay $10m," *Electronic News*, August 19, 1991.

6. Stipulation between prosecution and defense dated April 16, 2004, USA/FQ, government exhibit 900.

7. Petzinger Jr., p. 371.

8. Frank Staggs, author interview, August 2, 2004.

9. Quattrone deposition for MIN1, April 3, 1991; USA/FQ, government exhibit 81.

10. Quattrone testimony at MIN2; USA/FQ, government exhibit 82.

11. Andrew Mytelka, author interview, August 17, 2004.

6. An Early Brush with the SEC

1. Gary Rivlin, "George Boutros Likes It Rough," *The Standard*, December 25, 2000.

2. The bake-off, together with the entire IPO process, was chronicled in a book by Michael Malone, a former *San Jose Mercury News* reporter, called *Going Public: MIPS Computer and the Entrepreneurial Dream*, published in 1991. The MIPS part of this chapter is based largely on that account.

3. Nancy Rutter, "How to Nab an IPO," *Forbes*, August 29, 1994.

4. Malone.

5. Ibid.

6. Ibid. Someone from the group tape recorded the call, which was excerpted at length as the climactic cliff-hanger in Malone's book.

7. Amendment No. 3 to the S-1 registration statement for the IPO of MIPS Computer Systems Inc., on file with the Securities and Exchange Commission, December 21, 1989.

7. Tech Takes Off

1. Quattrone interview, cited in Lowenstein1, p. 107.

2. Kessler, p. 104.

3. Ibid., p. 116.

4. Nancy Rutter, "How to Nab an IPO," *Forbes*, August 29, 1994.

5. Ibid.

6. Michael Siconolfi, "At Morgan Stanley, Analysts Were Urged to Soften Harsh Views," *The Wall Street Journal*, July 14, 1992.

7. Kessler, p. 119.

8. The Dream House

1. Quattrone brief, October 12, 1993, LCI/AAA.

2. Denise Quattrone deposition, March 27, 1996, LCI/CSC.

3. David Terpening, author interview, October 6, 2004.

4. Nancy Chillag, lawyer for Sabina Marble & Granite Company, author interview, September 17, 2004.

5. Quattrone brief, October 12, 1993, LCI/AAA; Dick Breaux, author interview, November 22, 2004.

6. Quattrone brief, October 12, 1993, LCI/AAA.

7. Quattrones' letter to Lencioni, July 27, 1992, LCI/CSC.

8. Ibid.

9. Ibid.

10. Quattrone brief, October 12, 1993, LCI/AAA.

11. Ibid.

12. Quattrone letter to Pacific Wood Windows, April 13, 1992, LCI/CSC.

13. Quattrone brief, October 12, 1993, LCI/AAA.

14. Quattrone first amended complaint, December 17, 1993, LCI/CSC.

15. Quattrone brief, October 12, 1993, LCI/AAA, and Dick Breaux, author interview, November 22, 2004.

16. Ibid.

17. Quattrones' letter to Lencioni, July 27, 1992, LCI/CSC.

18. Gary Lencioni reply to Quattrones, August 7, 1992, LCI/CSC.

19. Quattrone demand, January 14, 1993, LCI/AAA.

20. Quattrone brief, October 12, 1993, LCI/AAA.

21. Ken Hausman letter to Paul Lahaderne, May 21, 1993, LCI/CSC.

22. Ibid.

23. Denise Quattrone response to interrogatories, May 1994, LCI/CSC.

24. Paul Lahaderne letter to Kenneth Hausman, January 18, 1994, LCI/CSC.

25. Ibid.

26. William McLean, author interview, September 17, 2004.

27. Quattrone first amended complaint, December 17, 1993, LCI/CSC.

28. Ibid.

29. Ibid.

30. Ibid.
31. Denise Quattrone response to interrogatories, May 1994, LCI/CSC.
32. Jeremy Fogel, author interview, September 20, 2004.
33. McLean interview.
34. Christian Berthelson and Reynolds Holding, "High Flying Financier on the Way Down," *San Francisco Chronicle*, February 9, 2003.
35. Denise Quattrone declaration, February 22, 1996, LCI/CSC.
36. Breaux interview.

9. Building a Powerhouse
1. Jay Hoag, author interview, September 1999.
2. Gary Rivlin, "George Boutros Likes It Rough," *The Standard*, December 25, 2000.
3. Frank Quattrone e-mail to Credit Suisse First Boston technology group, February 5, 2001.
4. Kessler, p. 108.
5. Ibid., p. 126.
6. Ibid., p. 127.
7. Mary Meeker, *The Technology IPO Yearbook*, Morgan Stanley, October 3, 2003.
8. Ibid.
9. Nancy Rutter, "How to Nab an IPO," *Forbes*, August 29, 1994.
10. Ibid.
11. Kessler, p. 139.
12. Ibid., p. 140.
13. Ibid.
14. Anthony B. Perkins, "Dan Case and Frank Quattrone on Riding the Technology Market," *Red Herring*, July 1, 1993.
15. Mary Meeker, *The Technology IPO Yearbook*, Morgan Stanley, October 3, 2003.
16. Anthony B. Perkins, author interview, March 11, 2005.

10. Netscape
1. Lewis.
2. Clark, p. 209.
3. Adam Lashinsky, Oliver Ryan, and Patricia Neering, "Remembering Netscape," *Fortune*, July 25, 2005.
4. Kessler, p. 150.
5. Lashinsky et al., *Fortune*, July 25, 2005.
6. Ibid.
7. Brett Fromson, "Buyers Drive Up Netscape Stock Price," *The Washington Post*, August 10, 1995.
8. Lashinsky et al., *Fortune*, July 25, 2005.
9. Kessler, p. 150.

10. Perkins and Perkins, p. 113.

11. Robert Lenzner, "Get It While You Can," *Forbes*, May 6, 1996.

12. Tia O'Brien, "Frank Quattrone on the Record," *Upside*, July 1, 1998.

13. Lenzner, *Forbes*, May 6, 1996.

14. John Heilemann, "The Sacrificial Lion," *Business 2.0*, June 1, 2003.

11. The Dream Team

1. Perkins and Perkins, p. 114.

2. David Einstein, "Deutsche Bank Lures Morgan's Quattrone," *San Francisco Chronicle*, April 5, 1996.

3. Andrew P. Madden, "The German Occupation," *Red Herring*, May 1, 1996.

4. Perkins and Perkins, p. 114.

12. Amazon

1. Peter Sinton, "Investment Banker Gets the Best," *San Francisco Chronicle*, October 9, 1996.

2. Scott McNealy, letter to Judge Richard Owen, USA/FQ, urging leniency after verdict, n.d.

3. "Assembling a Juggernaut from Scratch," *Investment Dealers' Digest*, November 25, 1996.

4. Bill Gurley letter to Judge Richard Owen, Summer 2004, USA/FQ, urging leniency, n.d.

5. Linda Himelstein and Leah Nathan Spiro, "DMG's Brash Big-Game Hunt," *BusinessWeek*, April 14, 1997.

6. Peter Sinton, "Investment Banker Gets the Best," *San Francisco Chronicle*, October 9, 1996.

7. Sara Calian and Anita Raghavan, "Craven Set to Give Up Grenfell Job," *The Wall Street Journal*, March 26, 1997.

8. Leonard Riggio, author interview, January 20, 2006.

9. Lowenstein2.

10. Bill Gurley, author interview, September 17, 1999.

11. Kessler.

12. Lise Buyer, author interview, March 28, 2009.

13. Frank Quattrone letter to Anita Raghavan, April 23, 1997.

13. The Senator

1. Mike Grunwald e-mail to Frank Quattrone and Bill Brady, March 21, 2000, USA/FQ, government exhibit 2051.

2. Michael R. Sesit and Anita Raghavan, "Kulturshock: Deutsche Bank Hits Many Costly Snags in Its America Foray," *The Wall Street Journal*, May 4, 1998.

3. Ibid.

4. Anita Raghavan, "Credit Suisse Hires Frank Quattrone," *The Wall Street Journal*, July 1, 1998.

5. Sesit and Raghavan, *The Wall Street Journal*, May 4, 1998.

6. Tia O'Brien, "Frank Quattrone on the Record," *Upside*, July 1, 1998.

7. Erick Schonfeld, "The Man Who Rains Money on Silicon Valley," *Fortune*, June 8, 1998.

8. O'Brien, *Upside*, July 1, 1998.

14. Credit Suisse First Boston
1. Christopher Gray, "Ghost Buildings of 1929," *New York Times*, April 26, 2009.

2. Frank Quattrone, National Association of Securities Dealers (NASD) interview, October 3, 2002, produced in FS/CSS.

3. Tia O'Brien, "Frank Quattrone on the Record," *Upside*, July 1, 1998.

4. Hal Lux, "Valley of the Dollars," *Institutional Investor*, June 1, 1998.

5. Contract between Quattrone and Credit Suisse First Boston, June 30, 1998, produced in FS/CSS.

6. O'Brien, *Upside*, July 1, 1998.

7. William Lewis, "Quattrone Cites Strategy Change for CSFB Move," *Financial Times*, July 15, 1998.

8. Erick Shonfeld, "Quattrone & Co. Abandon Deutsche Bank," *Fortune*, August 3, 1998.

9. Anita Raghavan, "First Boston Takes a Corps of Bankers Off Deutsche Bank," *The Wall Street Journal*, July 15, 1998.

10. Technology PCS Group Term Sheet, USA/FQ, government exhibit 3502-D.

11. Ibid., and Quattrone direct examination, April 27, 2004, USA/FQ.

15. The Mule in the Lobby
1. Gary Rivlin, "George Boutros Likes It Rough," *The Standard*, December 25, 2000.

2. Erick Schonfeld, "Powerfest: When Tech Stars and Moneymen Meet," *Fortune*, January 11, 1999.

3. Phil Serafino, "Sessions Give Big Investors First Crack at News," *Austin American-Statesman*, December 19, 1998.

16. The Flaming Ferraris
1. Mary Meeker, *The Technology IPO Yearbook*, Morgan Stanley, October 3, 2003.

2. Frank Quattrone/Credit Suisse First Boston (CSFB) technology group 1999 year-end press release, January 21, 2000; CSFB technology group brochure, 2000.

3. Scott Ryles, author interview, November 23, 2004.

4. David Brodsky testimony, May 5, 2005, RSB/CSFB.

5. Neil Bennett, "Hotshot Traders Split Bonus Worth Up to $13m," *The Sunday Telegraph*, December 21, 1998.

6. Arthur G. Angulo, Federal Reserve Bank of New York, letter to Lukas Muhlemann and Allen Wheat, February 9, 1999.

7. Miki Tanikawa, "Japanese Court Convicts a Bank," *The New York Times*, March 9, 2001.

17. The Friends of Frank

1. Frank Quattrone/Credit Suisse First Boston technology group, 1999 year-end news release, January 21, 2000.

2. Quattrone/CSFB technology group year-end brochure, 1999.

3. Mike Grunwald e-mail to Quattrone and Bill Brady, March 21, 2000, USA/FQ, government exhibit 2051.

4. Michael Siconolfi, "The Spin Desk," *The Wall Street Journal*, November 12, 1997.

5. Quattrone, redirect testimony, April 28, 2004, USA/FQ.

6. Quattrone, National Association of Securities Dealers (NASD) interview, October 3, 2002, produced in FS/CSS.

7. John Schmidt, NASD interview, September 18, 2002, produced in FS/CSS.

8. Grunwald e-mail to Quattrone and Brady, March 21, 2000, USA/FQ, government exhibit 2051.

9. NASD/FQ, March 6, 2003.

10. SEC/CSFB2, April 28, 2003.

11. Quattrone/CSFB technology group year-end brochure, 2000.

12. Scott Herhold, "IPO List Helped Execs' Trusts," *San Jose Mercury News*, March 7, 2003.

13. E-mails between Schmidt and Quattrone, June 15, 1999, USA/FQ, government exhibit 5001.

14. La Nita Burkhead e-mail to Schmidt and Quattrone, June 29, 1999, USA/FQ, government exhibit 5011.

15. Quattrone, NASD interview, October 3, 2002, produced in FS/CSS.

16. Schmidt, NASD interview, September 18, 2002, produced in FS/CSS.

17. Randall Smith and Susan Pulliam, "Buddy System—How a Technology Banking Star Doled Out Hot IPOs," *The Wall Street Journal*, September 23, 2002.

18. E-mail string of September 14 and 15, 1999, among Jill Ford, Anthony Kontoleon, Andy Fisher, Cameron Lester, Brady, and Quattrone, USA/FQ, government exhibit 3070.

19. Quattrone e-mails to and from Donna Dubinsky, February 29, 2000, USA/FQ, government exhibit 4010.

20. Linda-Louse Lund e-mail to Fisher, September 23, 1999, USA/FQ, government exhibit 2010R.

21. Chris O'Brien and Deborah Lohse, "How Quattrone Changed the Valley," *San Jose Mercury News*, March 9, 2003.

22. Susan Pulliam and Randall Smith, "Silicon Touch: For Frank Quattrone, With a Fief at CSFB, Tech Was a Gold Mine," *The Wall Street Journal*, May 3, 2001.

23. Grunwald e-mail to Quattrone and Brady, March 21, 2000, USA/FQ, government exhibit 2051.

18. Monarch of the Valley

1. Jeff Dachis, author interview, October 25, 2004.
2. Greg Ip, Susan Pulliam, Scott Thurm, and Ruth Simon, "The Color Green," *The Wall Street Journal*, July 14, 2000.
3. Ibid.
4. Frank Quattrone e-mail to Credit Suisse First Boston (CSFB) technology group, March 5, 1999.
5. William Hall, "Quattrone Warns Over Internet," *Financial Times*, April 15, 1999.
6. CSFB press release, "Credit Suisse First Boston Announces Market Share Dominance in Technology Banking," August 30, 1999.
7. Michael Malone, author interview, March 7, 2005.
8. John Schmidt, National Association of Securities Dealers (NASD) interview, January 17, 2002, produced in FS/CSS.

19. Leaning on the Analysts

1. Charles Gasparino, "Analysts' Contracts Link Pay to Deal Work," *The Wall Street Journal*, May 6, 2002.
2. Erach Desai testimony to Massachusetts securities regulators, MASD, September 5, 2002.
3. Desai e-mail to Elliott Rogers, "Unwritten Rules for Tech Research," May 30, 2001, MASD, exhibit.
4. Desai testimony.
5. Ibid.
6. Rogers, National Association of Securities Dealers (NASD) interview, September 10, 2002, produced in FS/CSS.
7. MASD, exhibit 12.
8. Christian Berthelson, "Criminal Probe for CSFB," *San Francisco Chronicle*, September 20, 2002.
9. Quattrone e-mails, June 15, 1999, produced in FS/CSS, exhibit 53.
10. Frank Quattrone, NASD interview, October 1, 2002, produced in FS/CSS.
11. Reingold with Reingold.
12. SEC/CSFB2, April 28, 2003.
13. Desai testimony.
14. Desai e-mail to Rogers, May 30, 2001.
15. SEC/CSFB2, April 28, 2003; MASD, exhibit 5.
16. Quattrone response to possible NASD charges, February 13, 2003, produced in FS/CSS.
17. Desai testimony.

18. SEC/CSFB2.

19. Desai testimony.

20. Bhavin Shah e-mail to Rogers and Tim Mahon, October 11, 2000; Mahon reply, October 21, 2002, MASD, exhibit 11.

21. Randall Smith, "E-mails Link CSFB Research with Banking," *The Wall Street Journal*, November 27, 2002.

20. Denver

1. Jim Kirksey, "Wife of Former Cook Chain Co-owner Dies," *Denver Post*, August 14, 1996.

2. Bill Husted, "Denver's Record as a Great Party Town Documented," *Denver Post*, February 11, 1999; other Lustig social events in articles by Joanne Davidson.

3. Ralph Ferrara, PowerPoint presentation to Securities and Exchange Commission and U.S. Department of Justice staff, February 23, 2001.

4. Ibid.

5. Ibid.

6. Ibid.

7. National Association of Securities Dealers (NASD) press release, March 22, 2005.

8. Ferrara PowerPoint presentation.

9. John Schmidt, NASD interview, January 17, 2002, produced in FS/CSS.

10. Michael Grunwald, NASD interview, December 7, 2001, produced in FS/CSS.

11. Scott Bushley, NASD interview, December 11, 2001, produced in FS/CSS.

12. Scott Brown, NASD interview, March 12, 2001, produced in FS/CSS.

13. Scott Bushley, SEC interview, October 30, 2001, produced in FS/CSS.

14. Brown, NASD interview.

15. Ibid.; Susan Pulliam and Randall Smith, "Small Investment Fund That Got Big Chunks of IPOs Is Investigated," *The Wall Street Journal*, May 11, 2001; Pulliam and Smith, "Sharing the Wealth: At CSFB, Lush Profit Earned on IPOs Found Its Way Back to Firm," *The Wall Street Journal*, November 30, 2001; Ronnie Barnes, SEC interview, September 5, 2001, and Richard Calta, SEC interview, August 30, 2001, produced in FS/CSS.

16. Paul Caan, NASD interview, September 7, 2001, produced in FS/CSS.

21. Mike Grunwald

1. Michael Grunwald, interview with Susan Pulliam and Randall Smith, September 6, 2002.

2. Anthony Ehinger letter to Michael Grunwald, October 20, 1999, attachment to Grunwald's April 2, 2002, demand for arbitration against Credit Suisse First Boston (CSFB), MSG/CSFB.

3. SEC/CSFB1, NASD/CSFB, January 22, 2002.

4. Grunwald interview with Pulliam and Smith.

5. Grunwald arbitration demand against CSFB, April 3, 2002, MSG/CSFB.

6. Paul Caan, National Association of Securities Dealers (NASD) interview, September 7, 2001, produced in FS/CSS.

7. Steve Keller e-mail to Ted Hatfield, September 22, 1999, MSG/CSFB, exhibit 3.

8. Joseph Girimonti e-mail to Hatfield, October 13, 1999, MSG/CSFB, exhibit 4.

9. Hatfield e-mail reply to Girimonti, October 13, 1999, MSG/CSFB, exhibit 4.

10. John Schmidt, NASD interview, January 17, 2002, produced in FS/CSS.

11. Grunwald interview with Pulliam and Smith.

12. David Brodsky memo to Lukas Muehlemann and Phil Ryan, April 8, 2001. Exhibit A to David Brodsky, declaration of April 14, 2005, in RSB/CSFB.

13. Ray Dorado e-mail, MSG/CSFB.

14. Grunwald e-mail to Frank Quattrone, Bill Brady, and Schmidt, November 22, 1999, government exhibit 5006.

15. Ian Mount, "The Corporate Mafia," *Maxim*, May 2003.

16. Grunwald e-mail to Quattrone, March 21, 2000, with attachment giving names of 210 Friends of Frank account holders, USA/FQ, government exhibit 2051.

22. The Hottest IPO Ever

1. Mark Veverka, "It's Mork, but Alas No Mindy, at Techie Conference," *Barron's*, December 6, 1999.

2. Don Katz e-mail to author.

3. Adam Lashinksy, "A Year in Review," TheStreet.com, November 28, 2000.

4. Susanne Craig, "Wall Street Stock Research at a Crossroads," *The Wall Street Journal*, November 8, 2002.

5. Mike Grunwald e-mail to Ted Hatfield, Ernesto Cruz, and Andy Fisher, December 5, 1999, USA/FQ, government exhibit 1020.

6. Grunwald e-mail and Frank Quattrone reply, December 7, 2000, USA/FQ, government exhibit 1020.

7. Linda Himelstein with Steve Hamm and Peter Burrows, "Inside Frank Quattrone's Money Machine," *BusinessWeek*, October 13, 2003.

8. Susan Pulliam and Randall Smith, "Sharing the Wealth," *The Wall Street Journal*, November 30, 2001.

9. Ibid.

10. NASD/CSFB; VA Linux institutional allocation list, USA/FQ, defense exhibit 706.

11. SEC/CSFB1, January 22, 2002, paragraphs 22 and 24.

12. Ibid., paragraph 54.

13. NASD letter of acceptance, waiver and consent No. CAF030026, Credit Suisse First Boston, respondent, April 21, 2003.

14. Scott Brown, NASD interview, March 12, 2001, produced in FS/CSS.

15. VA Linux institutional allocation list, USA/FQ, defense exhibit 706.

16. Jay Hoag, author interview, January 2001.

17. Grunwald e-mail to Quattrone and five other bankers, December 16, 1999, USA/FQ, government exhibit 5007.

18. Pulliam and Smith, *The Wall Street Journal*, November 30, 2001.

19. David Brodsky testimony, May 5, 2005, RSB/CSFB; memo from Dierdre von Dornum of Wilmer, Cutler & Pickering, October 24, 2001, to CSFB/IPO allocations file, re: Interview of David M. Brodsky, also for RSB/CSFB.

20. NASD announcement of disciplinary action against Tony Ehinger and George Coleman, August 15, 2002.

23. Grunwald's Blunder

1. Credit Suisse First Boston (CSFB) press release, January 31, 2000.

2. CSFB summary of 1999 total compensation for Frank P. Quattrone, USA/FQ, government exhibit 71B.

3. Mike Grunwald e-mail to Quattrone, March 21, 2000, USA/FQ, government exhibit 2051.

4. FS/CSS, proposed sixth amended complaint, July 14, 2008.

5. Frank Scognamillo, author interview, August 16, 2008.

6. FS/CSS, proposed sixth amended complaint, July 14, 2008.

7. Luc Hatlestad, "Diary of an Internet IPO," *Red Herring*, July 1, 1999.

8. Scott Bushley, Securities and Exchange Commission (SEC) interview, October 30, 2001.

9. SEC/CSFB1, January 22, 2002; David Brodsky memo to Lukas Muehlemann and Phil Ryan, April 8, 2001, produced in RSB/CSFB.

10. John Schmidt, National Association of Securities Dealers (NASD) interview, January 17, 2002, produced in FS/CSS.

11. Bushley, NASD interview, December 11, 2001; Grunwald, NASD interview, December 7, 2001, produced in FS/CSS.

12. Grunwald interview with Susan Pulliam and Randall Smith, September 6, 2002.

13. Brodsky memo to Muehlemann and Ryan, April 8, 2001, produced in RSB/CSFB.

14. Grunwald, NASD interview, produced in FS/CSS.

15. Schmidt, NASD interview, produced in FS/CSS.

16. Bushley, SEC interview, produced in FS/CSS.

17. Grunwald, NASD interview, produced in FS/CSS.

18. SEC/CSFB1, January 22, 2002; Bushley, NASD interview, produced in FS/CSS.

19. SEC/CSFB1.

20. Bushley, NASD interview, produced in FS/CSS.

21. Bushley, SEC interview, produced in FS/CSS.

22. Ibid.

23. Ibid.

24. Brodsky memo to Muehlemann and Ryan, April 8, 2001, produced in RSB/CSFB.

24. JohnDoe526

1. Paul Caan, National Association of Securities Dealers (NASD) interview, September 7, 2001, produced in FS/CSS.

2. Credit Suisse First Boston, plaintiff, complaint against JohnDoe526@Hotmail .com, U.S. District Court, Southern District of New York, February 18, 2000.

3. Caan, NASD interview, produced in FS/CSS.

4. Ibid.

25. A Secret Weapon

1. Sandra Ward, "Still High on Tech," an interview with Larry Bowman, *Barron's*, April 17, 2000.

2. E-mails dated February 11 to 16, 2000, about Bowman IPO allocations, USA/FQ, government exhibits 3000, 3010, 3020, 3030, 3040, 3050, 3060.

3. Mike Grunwald e-mail to Quattrone, Bill Brady, and George Boutros, February 25, 2000, and Quattrone reply, USA/FQ.

4. Quattrone e-mails to and from Donna Dubinsky, February 29, 2000, USA/FQ, government exhibit 4010.

5. Quattrone cross-examination, April 28, 2004, USA/FQ.

26. "A Concerned Citizen"

1. Selectica Inc. post-transaction summary, April 12, 2000, USA/FQ, government exhibit 802.

2. Ibid.

3. SEC/CSFB1, January 22, 2002.

4. Jack Willoughby, "Burning Up," *Barron's*, March 20, 2000.

5. Price-Quattrone e-mails produced by Quattrone in response to October 18, 2000, SEC subpoena for Selectica documents, USA/FQ, government exhibit 800.

6. Mike Grunwald e-mail to Quattrone, March 21, 2000, USA/FQ, government exhibit 2051.

7. Audit of technology group by Credit Suisse Group, April 14, 2000, USA/FQ, defense exhibit.

8. Michael Clark, author interview; author visited Credit Suisse First Boston (CSFB) trading room from 3:15 P.M. to 4:15 P.M. on April 14, 2000.

9. Schmidt-Quattrone e-mail exchange May 1, 2000, USA/FQ, government exhibit 1091.

27. A Last Hurrah for Hot IPOs

1. Joseph Ozag Jr., National Association of Securities Dealers (NASD) compliance examiner, letter to Credit Suisse First Boston (CSFB) compliance director, Michael Radest, May 17, 2000, USA/FQ, government exhibit 11.

2. E-mails between Grace Shentwu and Frank Quattrone, June 2, 2000, USA/FQ, government exhibit 101.

3. Rose Corbett e-mail to Quattrone, June 5, 2000, USA/FQ, government exhibit 102.

4. Shentwu e-mail to Quattrone and other technology group staffers, USA/FQ, June 7, 2000, government exhibit 103.

5. E-mails between Edward Loh and Shentwu, June 8, 2000, government exhibit 104.

6. Randall Smith and Charles Gasparino, "Tech Specialist at First Boston Gets Extension on Contract," *The Wall Street Journal*, June 26, 2000.

7. Quattrone e-mail to technology group members, March 14, 2000, produced in FS/CSS.

8. Ann Griffith e-mail to top CSFB executives about Securities and Exchange Commission (SEC) underwriting exam, July 10, 2000, USA/FQ, government exhibit 201.

9. E-mail exchange between Ted Hatfield and Quattrone, July 19 and 20, 2000, USA/FQ, government exhibit 1070.

10. E-mails between Quattrone and Michael Dell, July 19, 2000, government exhibit 1060; Quattrone cross-examination at first trial, October 10, 2003, USA/FQ.

11. E-mails between Quattrone and Dell, July 19, 2000, USA/FQ, government exhibit 1060.

12. Ibid.

13. E-mails between Quattrone and Andy Fisher, July 20, 2000, USA/FQ, defense exhibit 251.

14. E-mail from Glenn Fuhrman to Quattrone, July 24, 2000, USA/FQ, government exhibit 1061.

15. Quattrone e-mail reply to Fuhrman, July 24, 2000, USA/FQ, defense exhibit 250.

16. E-mail from Hatfield to Quattrone and Fisher, July 25, 2000, USA/FQ, government exhibit 1080.

17. E-mail from Fisher to Quattrone, July 26, 2000, USA/FQ, government exhibit 1081.

18. E-mail from Christie Hannula to Quattrone and others, July 26, 2000, USA/FQ, government exhibit 1082.

19. E-mail from Quattrone to Dell, July 26, 2000, USA/FQ, government exhibit 1060; e-mail from Quattrone to Fuhrman July 26, 2000, USA/FQ, government exhibit 1061.

20. E-mail from Quattrone to Tom Meredith and Alex Smith, July 26, 2000, USA/FQ, government exhibit 1062.

21. E-mail from Quattrone to John Schmidt and Michael Grunwald, July 26, 2000, USA/FQ, government exhibit 1083.

22. Adam Lashinsky, "When the King of Silicon Valley Investment Banking Speaks . . ." TheStreet.com, August 4, 2000.

23. Mary Meeker, *The Technology IPO Yearbook*, Morgan Stanley, October 3, 2003.

28. The Gumshoes Go to Work

1. David Brodsky e-mail to Brady Dougan and others, August 1, 2000, USA/FQ, government exhibit 300.

2. Brodsky e-mail to Dougan and others, August 4, 2000, USA/FQ, government exhibit 301.

3. National Association of Securities Dealers (NASD) hearing panel decision, March 3, 2003, INVD.

4. Joseph Ozag letter to Robert Frenchman, September 11, 2000, USA/FQ, government exhibit 13.

5. David Hermer e-mail to Credit Suisse First Boston (CSFB) sales force, August 3, 2000, USA/FQ, government exhibit 2030R.

6. Frank Quattrone, author interview for *The Wall Street Journal*, August 30, 2000.

7. E-mails about Jim Balsillie allocation of AvantGo, USA/FQ, government exhibit 5009.

29. Culture Clash

1. Fred Lane, author interview, July 13, 2004.

2. Randall Smith and Gregory Zuckerman, "Star Banker Quits CSFB, Joins UBS," *The Wall Street Journal*, November 22, 2000.

3. Gregory Zuckerman, "CSFB Doles Out Hefty Pay Packages to Retain Bankers," *The Wall Street Journal*, March 19, 2001.

4. Jake Peters e-mail to Frank Quattrone and others, October 20, 2000, exhibit to Steven Peikin/David Anders letter to Judge Richard Owen, USA/FQ, August 17, 2004.

5. Quattrone e-mail to Balsillie, November 2, 2000, exhibit to Peikin/Anders letter to Owen, USA/FQ, August 17, 2004.

6. E-mails between Quattrone and Jim Balsillie, November 16 and 17, 2000, exhibit to Peikin/Anders letter to Owen.

30. The Prosecutors

1. Robert Khuzami testimony, April 19, 2004, USA/FQ.

2. Michael D. Wasserman, Securities and Exchange Commission (SEC) document request to Credit Suisse First Boston (CSFB), September 20, 2000, USA/FQ, government exhibit 22.

3. Michael Radest e-mail to Allen Wheat and others, September 20, 2000, USA/FQ, government exhibit 400.

4. Frank Quattrone e-mail to David Brodsky, September 20, 2000, USA/FQ, government exhibit 401.

5. Brodsky e-mail to Quattrone, September 20, 2000, USA/FQ, government exhibit 402.

6. Ibid.

7. Caren Pennington testimony, October 3, 2003, USA/FQ.

8. Dominick Commesso, National Association of Securities Dealers (NASD) interview, November 1, 2000, produced in FS/CSS.

9. Joseph Girimonti, NASD interview, November 7, 2000, produced in FS/CSS.

10. Ladd McQuade, NASD interview, March 8, 2001, produced in FS/CSS.

11. Susan Pulliam and Randall Smith, "Sharing the Wealth: At CSFB, Lush Profit Earned on IPOs Found Its Way Back to Firm," *The Wall Street Journal*, November 30, 2001.

12. SEC/CSFB1, January 22, 2002.

13. Scott Bushley, NASD interview, October 11, 2001, produced in FS/CSS.

14. E-mail from Janine Schampier to Quattrone and Andy Fisher, October 18, 2000, USA/FQ, government exhibit 504.

15. E-mails between Grace Shentwu and Quattrone, October 20, 2000, USA/FQ, government exhibits 505, 506.

16. Ibid., USA/FQ, government exhibit 508.

17. E-mail from Schampier to Quattrone, Bill Brady, and others, October 25, 2000, USA/FQ, government exhibit 510.

18. E-mail from Quattrone to La Nita Burkhead, October 25, 2000, USA/FQ, government exhibit 511.

19. E-mail from Burkhead to Schampier, October 30, 2000, USA/FQ, government exhibit 800.

20. E-mail from Lisa Czaja to Rose Corbett, October 2, 2000, USA/FQ, defense exhibit 54.

21. Brodsky testimony, October 3, 2003, USA/FQ.

22. Grand jury subpoena to CSFB, November 21, 2000, USA/FQ, government exhibit 31A.

23. Subpoenas to George Coleman, Dominick Commesso, Ernesto Cruz, John Coen, Jill Ford, Tony Ehinger, David Hermer, and Steve Keller, USA/FQ, government exhibits 31B through 31I.

24. Robert Khuzami and Kevin McCarthy testimonies, October 1, October 2, 2002, USA/FQ.

25. Brodsky direct examination, October 3, 2003, USA/FQ.

26. Brodsky cross-examination, October 7, 2003, USA/FQ.

31. "Time to Clean Up Those Files"

1. Mark Veverka, author interview, August 6, 2004.

2. David Brodsky testimony, October 3, 2003, USA/FQ.

3. Frank Quattrone testimony, October 9, 2003, USA/FQ.

4. Brodsky e-mail to Quattrone, December 3, 2000, USA/FQ, government exhibit 603.

5. Quattrone e-mail to Brodsky, December 3, 2000, USA/FQ, government exhibit 604.

6. Quattrone testimony, April 27, 2004, USA/FQ.

7. Brodsky e-mail to Quattrone, December 3, 2000, USA/FQ, government exhibit 605.

8. Quattrone e-mail to Brodsky, December 3, 2000, USA/FQ, government exhibit 606.

9. Quattrone e-mail to Brodsky, December 3, 2000, USA/FQ, government exhibit 607.

10. Brodsky testimony, October 3, 2003, USA/FQ.

11. Brodsky e-mail to Quattrone, December 3, 2000, USA/FQ, government exhibit 608.

12. Brodsky e-mail to Quattrone, December 3, 2000, USA/FQ, government exhibit 609.

13. Quattrone e-mail to Brodsky, December 3, 2000, USA/FQ, government exhibit 610.

14. Richard Char e-mail to John Hodge and others, December 4, 2000, USA/FQ, government exhibit 613.

15. Char direct examination. October 8, 2003, USA/FQ.

16. Char e-mail to Hodge and others, December 4, 2000, USA/FQ, government exhibit 613.

17. Quattrone direct examination, October 9, 2003, USA/FQ.

18. Joe Orlando e-mails, August 10, 2000, and November 16, 2000, USA/FQ, defense exhibits 39 and 98.

19. Char e-mail, December 4, 2000, to CSFB technology investment banking division, USA/FQ, government exhibit 615C.

20. Quattrone direct examination, October 9, 2003, USA/FQ.

21. Recipients of e-mails addressed to ##csfb-tech-ibd, USA/FQ, government exhibit 53.

22. Quattrone draft e-mail, December 4, 2000, USA/FQ, government exhibit 615B.

23. Quattrone testimony, April 27, 2004, USA/FQ, p. 1856.

24. Ibid., p. 1859.

25. Ibid., p. 1863.

26. Brodsky e-mail to Allen Wheat and others, December 5, 2000, USA/FQ, government exhibit 619.

27. Brodsky e-mail to Wheat and others, December 5, 2000, USA/FQ, government exhibit 620.

28. Brodsky direct examination, October 3, 2000, USA/FQ.

29. Quattrone direct examination, October 9, 2003, USA/FQ.

30. Brodsky and Quattrone testimony, October 3 and 9, 2003, USA/FQ.

31. Quattrone direct examination, October 9, 2003, USA/FQ.

32. Quattrone e-mail to Brodsky, December 5, 2000, USA/FQ, government exhibit 622R.

33. John Bateman e-mail to Lisa Czaja, December 4, 2000; Czaja e-mail to Brodsky, December 5, 2000, USA/FQ, government exhibit 617.

34. Kevin McCarthy direct examination, October 2, 2003, USA/FQ.

35. Brodsky direct examination, October 7, 2000, USA/FQ.

36. Quattrone direct testimony, April 27, 2004, p. 1879.

37. USA/FQ, defense exhibit 190.

38. Quattrone direct testimony, October 9, 2003, USA/FQ.

39. Char e-mail to Quattrone, December 5, 2000, USA/FQ, government exhibit 626.

40. Quattrone direct examination, October 10, 2003, USA/FQ.

41. Adrian Dollard testimony, October 9, 2003, USA/FQ.

42. Char e-mail to Dollard and Francisco Paret, December 6, 2000, USA/FQ, government exhibit 4019.

43. Linda Jackson direct examination, October 3, 2003, USA/FQ.

44. E-mails from Michael Ounjian, December 5 and 6, USA/FQ, government exhibits 627, 628, and 629.

45. E-mail from Dollard to CSFB technology group banking division members, December 6, 2000, USA/FQ, government exhibit 645.

46. Brodsky e-mail to Czaja and Bruce Albert, December 6, 2000, USA/FQ, government exhibit 648.

47. Randall Smith and Susan Pulliam, "U.S. Probes Inflated Commissions for Hot IPOs," *The Wall Street Journal*, December 7, 2000.

48. Quattrone redirect testimony, October 14, 2003, USA/FQ.

49. Albert e-mail to Brodsky and others, December 7, 2000, USA/FQ, government exhibit 650.

50. Brodsky e-mail to Quattrone, December 7, 2000, USA/FQ, government exhibit 652.

51. McCarthy and Albert e-mail to CSFB technology group members, December 7, 2000, USA/FQ, government exhibit 654.

52. Quattrone and Brodsky testimony, October 7 and 10, 2003, USA/FQ.

53. Brodsky e-mail to Quattrone, December 7, 2000, USA/FQ, government exhibit 659.

54. Brodsky direct examination, October 7, 2003, USA/FQ.

55. Brodsky e-mail to McLaughlin, December 7, 2000, USA/FQ, defense exhibit 168.

32. The Denver Traders Talk

1. Credit Suisse Group audit of Credit Suisse First Boston (CSFB) San Francisco branch office, March 5, 2001, USA/FQ, government exhibit 5000.

2. SEC/CSFB2, April 28, 2003.

3. Chris Nolan, "Frank's Friends Favored," *The New York Post*, January 11, 2001.

4. E-mails between Frank Quattrone and David Brodsky, January 11, 2001, obtained by author.

5. Mike Grunwald e-mail to Quattrone and Bill Brady, March 21, 2000, USA/ FQ, government exhibit 2051.

6. Kenneth Gilpin, "Newspaper Settles with Reporter in Stock-Trading Dispute," *The New York Times*, May 14, 2001.

7. Quattrone draft letter to newspaper editors, January 11, 2001, obtained by author.

8. Ralph Ferrara PowerPoint presentation to regulators, February 23, 2001, entitled "Confidential Material Pursuant to February 21, 2001 Common Interest Agreement," obtained by author.

33. Damage Control

1. Mike Grunwald interview with Susan Pulliam and Randall Smith, September 6, 2002.

2. David Brodsky memo to Lukas Muehlemann and Phil Ryan, April 8, 2001, produced in RSB/CSFB.

3. Scott Bushley, National Association of Securities Dealers (NASD) interview, December 11, 2001, FS/CSS.

4. Susan Pulliam and Randall Smith, "CSFB Fines Employees In IPO Case," *The Wall Street Journal*, February 20, 2002.

5. Ibid.; memo from Dierdre von Dornum of Wilmer, Cutler & Pickering, to CSFB/IPO allocation file, re: Interview of David M. Brodsky, October 24, 2001, produced in RSB/CSFB.

6. Brodsky memo to Muehlemann and Ryan, produced in RSB/CSFB.

7. Randall Smith and Susan Pulliam, "IPO 'Rogue' Battles to Clear His Name," *The Wall Street Journal*, September 17, 2002.

8. Bushley, NASD interview, FS/CSS.

9. Charles Ward statement released by Credit Suisse First Boston, May 1, 2001.

34. The Unwritten Rules of Research

1. Charles Gasparino, "All Star Analyst Faces Arbitration," *The Wall Street Journal*, March 2, 2001; Charles Gasparino, "Merrill Is Paying in Case of Analyst's Call," *The Wall Street Journal*, July 20, 2001.

2. SEC/CSFB2, April 28, 2003.

3. Brad Henske, author interview, January 23, 2006.

4. Erach Desai testimony to Massachusetts securities regulators, September 5, 2002, MASD.

5. E-mails between Chris Legg and Frank Quattrone, March 1, 2001, exhibit H to Steve Peikin letter to Judge Richard Owen, August 17, 2004, USA/FQ.

6. E-mails between Legg and Quattrone, March 8, 2001, MASD, exhibit 6.

7. Quattrone e-mail to Allen Wheat, May 12, 2001.

8. Quattrone e-mail to Brady Dougan and others, May 14, 2001.

9. E-mails between Quattrone and Elliott Rogers and other research staff, May 14, 2001.

10. E-mails between Jack Kirnan and Quattrone, May 22, 2001.

11. Desai testimony, MASD.

12. Henske, author interview, January 23, 2006.

13. Desai e-mail to Rogers, May 30, 2001, MASD, exhibit 7.

14. SEC/CSFB2, April 28, 2003.

15. Desai testimony, MASD.

16. Quattrone e-mail to Rogers, May 30, 2001.

17. Desai testimony, MASD.

18. SEC/CSFB2, April 28, 2003; Quattrone lawyers' Wells response to notice of possible charges, February 13, 2003.

35. A Vote of Confidence

1. Susan Pulliam and Randall Smith, "CSFB's Defense: We Didn't Break IPO Rules," *The Wall Street Journal*, June 12, 2001.

2. Charles Pretzlik, "CSFB Set to Defend Itself Over Broking Ban in India," *Financial Times*, April 30, 2001.

3. Charles Gasparino, Randall Smith, Susan Pulliam, and Gregory Zuckerman, "CSFB's Chief Seen Reining in Quattrone Team," *The Wall Street Journal*, July 13, 2001; Charles Gasparino and Gregory Zuckerman, "CSFB Seeks to Trim Pay of Some Stars," *The Wall Street Journal*, July 27, 2001.

4. Susan Pulliam and Randall Smith, "Small Investment Fund That Got Big Chunks of IPOs Is Investigated," *The Wall Street Journal*, May 11, 2001; Susan Pulliam and Randall Smith, "Sharing the Wealth: At CSFB, Lush Profit Earned on IPOs Found Its Way Back to Firm," *The Wall Street Journal*, November 30, 2001.

5. "NASD Fines Worldco," National Association of Securities Dealers (NASD) announcement, USA/FQ, January 9, 2004.

6. Securities and Exchange Commission (SEC) interviews produced in FS/CSS: Anthony Bruan, August 29, 2001; Richard Calta, August 30, 2001; Ronald Barnes, September 5, 2001.

7. Paul Caan, NASD interview, September 7, 2001, produced in FS/CSS.

8. Davis Polk & Wardwell, attorneys for CSFB, undated memorandum of law submitted to U.S. attorney for Southern District of New York, and of counsel, Wilmer Cutler & Pickering, obtained by author.

9. Randall Smith and Marcus Walker, "CSFB Will Report a Loss, As Wall Street Profits Fall," *The Wall Street Journal*, October 10, 2001.

10. Erach Desai testimony to Massachusetts securities regulators, September 5, 2002, MASD.

11. Patricia Sellers, "The Trials of John Mack," *Fortune*, September 1, 2003.

12. Charles Gasparino and Randall Smith, "Wall Street Superstars Find Super Pay Isn't 'Guaranteed,'" *The Wall Street Journal*, November 13, 2001.

13. Jenny Anderson, "Hindsight Highlights Mack's Wrong Move," *The New York Post*, April 24, 2003.

14. Vitria chief financial officer Paul Auvil, SEC interview, November 1, 2001, produced in FS/CSS.

15. Susan Pulliam, Randall Smith, Anita Raghavan, and Gregory Zuckerman, "Coming to Terms: CSFB Agrees to Pay $100 million to Settle Twin IPO Investigations," *The Wall Street Journal*, December 11, 2001.

16. SEC interviews of George Coleman, January 25, 2002; Anthony Ehinger, January 30, 2002.

17. SEC press release, January 22, 2002.

18. NASD/CSFB, January 22, 2002.

19. Susan Pulliam and Randall Smith, "CSFB Fines Employees in IPO Case," *The Wall Street Journal*, February 20, 2002.

36. Eliot Spitzer

1. Eric Dinallo affidavit, April 8, 2002, NYSC.

2. Ibid.

3. Charles Gasparino, "Merrill Lynch Analysts Told to Change Ways," *The Wall Street Journal*, April 9, 2002.

4. Ibid.

5. Charles Gasparino, "SEC Joins Pack, Opens Inquiry Into Analysts," *The Wall Street Journal*, April 26, 2002.

6. *Dot.Con, Frontline* documentary series, Public Broadcasting System, broadcast January 24, 2002.

7. Erach Desai testimony to Massachusetts Securities regulators, September 5, 2002, MASD.

8. Ibid.

37. Spinning

1. Susanne Craig and Charles Gasparino, "Salomon Used IPOs as Lure, Broker Says," *The Wall Street Journal*, July 18, 2002.

2. MSG/CSFB.

3, Randall Smith and Susan Pulliam, "CSFB, Banker Named in Suit by Ex-Executive," *The Wall Street Journal*, July 12, 2002.

4. Randall Smith, "Two CSFB Executives Are Fined, Suspended," *The Wall Street Journal*, August 16, 2002.

5. Mike Grunwald, National Association of Securities Dealers (NASD) interview, September 17, 2002, produced in FS/CSS.

6. John Schmidt, NASD interview, September 18, 2002, produced in FS/CSS.

7, Randall Smith and Susan Pulliam, "How a Star Banker Pressed for IPOs," *The Wall Street Journal*, September 5, 2002; Randall Smith and Susan Pulliam, "IPO 'Rogue' Battles to Clear His Name,' *The Wall Street Journal*, September 17, 2002.

8. Randall Smith and Susan Pulliam, "Buddy System: How a Technology-Banking Star Doled Out Shares of Hot IPOs," *The Wall Street Journal*, September 23, 2002.

9. Randall Smith, "Wall Street Has E-Mail Problems," *The Wall Street Journal*, August 2, 2002.

10. Frank Quattrone, NASD interview, October 1, 2002, produced in FS/CSS.

11. Adrian Dollard testimony, April 23, 2004, USA/FQ.

12. Dollard and Quattrone testimonies, October 9, October 10, 2003, USA/FQ.

13. Quattrone, NASD interview, October 3, 2002, produced in FS/CSS.

14. Randall Smith, "CSFB Faces Civil Charges in Massachusetts," *The Wall Street Journal*, October 21, 2002.

15. MASD.

16. Jessica Sommar, "Settlement Scuffle: CSFB Battles Regulators over Big Fines," *The New York Post*, December 1, 2002.

17. Randall Smith, "E-Mails Link CSFB Research With Banking," *The Wall Stret Journal*, November 27, 2002.

18. Charles Gasparino, "Paperless Trail: How a String of E-Mail Came to Haunt CSFB and Star Banker," *The Wall Street Journal*, February 28, 2003.

19. Joint regulatory press release announcing charges against ten securities firms, April 28, 2003. The regulatory agencies were the Securities and Exchange Commission, the National Association of Securities Dealers, the New York Attorney General, the New York Stock Exchange, and the North American Securities Administrators Association.

20. Joint regulatory press release announcing charges against Jack Grubman and Henry Blodget, April 28, 2003. The regulatory agencies included the Securities and Exchange Commission, the National Association of Securities Dealers, the New York Attorney General, and the New York Stock Exchange.

21. NASD press release, "NASD Regulation Charges Dean Witter Reynolds Inc. With Securities Fraud and Other Violations [in] Marketing . . . of Term Trusts," November 20, 2000.

38. Obstruction

1. Gary Lynch testimony, October 8, 2003, USA/FQ.

2. Randall Smith, Susan Pulliam, and Charles Gasparino, "CSFB E-Mail Urged Deletion of IPO Documents," *The Wall Street Journal*, January 30, 2003.

3. Lynch testimony.

4. Frank Quattrone testimony, October 10, 2003, USA/FQ.

5. Quattrone e-mail to Jeanmarie McFadden, January 30, 2003.

6. Charles Gasparino, "Paperless Trail: How a String of E-Mail Came to Haunt CSFB and Star Banker," *The Wall Street Journal*, February 28, 2003.

7. Ibid.

8. Adrian Dollard testimony, April 23, 2004, USA/FQ.

9. David Brodsky cross-examination, October 7, 2003, USA/FQ.

10. Quattrone response to notice of possible charges by National Association of Securities Dealers, February 13, 2003, produced in FS/CSS.

11. NASD press release, "NASD Charges Frank Quattrone," March 6, 2003 (NASD/FQ).

12. Paul Braverman, "Hard to Beat," *American Lawyer*, January 2005.

13. Deborah Lohse, "Bay Area Executives Won Access to Offers," *San Jose Mercury News*, March 7, 2003.

14. Randall Smith and Kara Scannell, "Quattrone Case Won't Be a Layup," *The Wall Street Journal*, May 1, 2003.

15. Abigail Rayner, "Judge That Defendants Dread Has No Regrets," *The Times*, September 18, 2004.

16. SEC/CSFB2.

39. The Courthouse Steps

1. Dan Gillmor, column, *San Jose Mercury News*, May 7, 2003.

2. T. J. Rodgers, interview, *Kudlow & Cramer*, CNBC, May 7, 2004.

3. John Heilemann, "The Sacrificial Lion," *Business 2.0*, June 1, 2003.

4. "Ex-Banker: I'm Innocent," Reuters News Service, *Newsday*, May 28, 2003.

40. Quattrone Takes the Stand

1. Randall Smith and Kara Scannell, "Inside Quattrone Jury Room," *The Wall Street Journal*, October 27, 2003.

41. Juror Number 1

1. Author interviews of jurors Jonathan Miller and Denis Crosley after the trial.

2. Terry Krivan, vice president of development, The Tech Museum of Innovation, letter to Judge Richard Owen, Summer 2004, USA/FQ.

44. The Verdict

1, This chapter is largely based on author interviews with Jonathan Miller, Denis Crosley, Sheldon Silver, and three other jurors who asked not to be identified.

2. Chris Huntington, *New York Stock Exchange Update*, CNNfn, May 3, 2004; Walter Hamilton and Thomas S. Mulligan, "Star Silicon Valley Banker Convicted of Obstruction," *Los Angeles Times*, May 4, 2004.

3. Huntington, *New York Stock Exchange Update*, May 3, 2004; Andrew Ross Sorkin, "Wall Street Banker Is Found Guilty of Obstruction," *The New York Times*, May 4, 2004.

4. Colleen DeBaise, "Jury Has Verdict in Frank Quattrone Retrial," Dow Jones Newswires, May 3, 2004.

5. Deborah Lohse, "Retrial Jury Finds Former California Financier Guilty," *San Jose Mercury News*, May 4, 2004; Sorkin, "Wall Street Banker Is Found Guilty," May 4, 2004.

6. Sorkin, "Wall Street Banker Is Found Guilty," May 4, 2004.

7. *Kudlow & Cramer*, CNBC, May 3, 2004.

45. Reversal

1. *Kudlow & Cramer*, CNBC, September 14, 2004.

2. Carolyn Said, "News Analysis: Banker Becomes Symbol of Dot-com Era's Excess," *San Francisco Chronicle*, May 4, 2004.

3. Editorial, "Into Quattrone's Life, Some Jail Time Must Fall," *San Jose Mercury News*, September 9, 2004.

4. Joseph Graham, "The Scapegoating of Alum Frank Quattrone," *The Wharton Journal*, September 20, 2004.

5. Carleen Hawn, "The Fall and Rise of Frank Quattrone," *San Francisco*, May 2006.

6. Denise Quattrone, letter to Judge Richard Owen urging leniency, July 5, 2004, USA/FQ.

7. Floyd Norris, "Empty Rooms. Look Familiar?" *The New York Times*, March 12, 2006.

8. Randall Smith, "NASD Charges [Invemed] Broke Rules on IPOs," *The Wall Street Journal*, April 18, 2003.

9. Randall Smith, "Tough Battle Over IPO Abuse Falls Short at the End," *The Wall Street Journal*, March 4, 2006.

10. Larry Neumeister, "1990s Banker Has Ample Reason to Smile After End of Criminal Case," Associated Press, August 22, 2006.

46. Epilogue

1. Erik Portanger, "U.K.'s Standard Chartered Settles Prolonged Pricewaterhouse Case," *The Wall Street Journal*, November 8, 1999.

2. Excerpt from George Boutros deposition, February 8, 2008, prepared by Frank Scognamillo attorney Ken Mann, FS/CSS.

3. Scognamillo, author interview, August 16, 2008.

4. Stephen D. Hibbard, lawyer for George Boutros, letter to author, August 3, 2009.

5. Lise Buyer, e-mail to author, May 10, 2009.

6. Jay Ritter e-mail to author, July 24, 2008; author interview, August 25, 2008.

7. Ken Hausman letter to Jay Ritter, March 24, 2008.

8. Ritter, author interview, August 25, 2008.

INDEX